T0230232

Lecture Notes in Computer Science   1174

Edited by G. Goos, J. Hartmanis and J. van Leeuwen

Advisory Board: W. Brauer   D. Gries   J. Stoer

Springer

Berlin
Heidelberg
New York
Barcelona
Budapest
Hong Kong
London
Milan
Paris
Santa Clara
Singapore
Tokyo

Ross Anderson (Ed.)

Information Hiding

First International Workshop
Cambridge, U.K., May 30 - June 1, 1996
Proceedings

Springer

Series Editors

Gerhard Goos, Karlsruhe University, Germany

Juris Hartmanis, Cornell University, NY, USA

Jan van Leeuwen, Utrecht University, The Netherlands

Volume Editor

Ross Anderson
Cambridge University, Computer Laboratory
Pembroke Street, Cambridge CB2 3QG, UK
E-mail: rja14@cl.cam.ac.uk

Cataloging-in-Publication data applied for

Die Deutsche Bibliothek - CIP-Einheitsaufnahme

Information hiding : first international workshop, Cambridge,
UK, May 30 - June 1, 1996 ; proceedings / Ross Anderson (ed.).
- Berlin ; Heidelberg ; New York ; Barcelona ; Budapest ;
Hong Kong ; London ; Milan ; Paris ; Santa Clara ; Singapore ;
Tokyo : Springer, 1996
  (Lecture notes in computer science ; Vol. 1174)
  ISBN 3-540-61996-8
NE: Anderson, Ross [Hrsg.]; GT

CR Subject Classification (1991): E.3, K.6.5, D.4.6, E.4, C.2, J.1, K.4.1,
K.5.1, H.4.3

ISSN 0302-9743
ISBN 3-540-61996-8 Springer-Verlag Berlin Heidelberg New York

© Springer-Verlag Berlin Heidelberg 1996
Printed in Germany

Typesetting: Camera-ready by author
SPIN 10549111   06/3142 – 5 4 3 2 1 0   Printed on acid-free paper

Foreword

Sometime in early 1995, I realised that there were at least five different research communities doing work on hiding information, and that they were mostly unaware of each others' existence.

Firstly, recent moves towards the digital distribution of films, music and other intellectual property have raised the question of how the ownership of digital objects can be established. One candidate technology is watermarking — embedding hidden copyright notices in digital objects to prove ownership in the event of a dispute. Doing this in ways that do not perceptibly degrade pictures or music, and yet are still hard for a pirate to remove, is an interesting technological challenge.

Secondly, a number of teams have been working on anonymous communications, digital cash, online elections and making mobile communications hard for third parties to trace. The big question here is whether the existing privacy properties of everyday transactions can be preserved in the electronic age, or whether technological progress will inevitably lead to a surveillance society.

Thirdly, computer security researchers and system builders have worried for over twenty years about covert channels — channels which arise when users of a shared resource (such as a computer operating system) can signal to each other by modulating the system's performance (e.g., by selective resource exhaustion). The concern is that a virus might use such a channel to leak information from a highly protected to a less protected part of the system. The related problem of subliminal channels in digital signature schemes, which was brought to the attention of the crypto community by Gus Simmons, has also inspired some interesting research.

Fourthly, there is steganography, in which people try to conceal the existence of messages, often in other messages. An example is when a prisoner of war spells out a message in Morse Code in the dots and dashes on the letters i, j, t and f in a letter home. This field has attracted renewed interest recently, as a result of various governments' recent attempts to ban or control the use of cryptography; programs have appeared on the Internet that let a user embed an encrypted file in a digital picture.

Finally, a number of essentially physical means of unobtrusive communication have been developed over the past fifty years or so, mainly at the instigation of the military. These include spread-spectrum and meteor scatter radio, and the use of highly directional media such as lasers.

These areas of study are closely linked, and it struck me that a workshop on the whole topic of information hiding could be timely and effective.

A suitable opportunity was given by a research programme in Computer Security, Cryptology and Coding Theory, which I was organising for the following year at the Isaac Newton Institute in Cambridge. So a programme committee was put together, consisting of myself, Robert Desourdis, Steve Low, Ira

Moskowitz, Andreas Pfitzmann, Gus Simmons and Michael Waidner — who between us covered all the above research groups; and in August 1995 we issued a call for papers.

The response far exceeded our expectations. At the workshop, which was held at the Isaac Newton Institute from the 30th May to the 1st June 1996, we heard of the latest research in a very wide range of applications, and managed to spend a significant amount of time in discussion, both formal and informal. This culminated in a closing plenary session, where we tackled the problem that everyone was using different terminology. After a long discussion and a number of votes, we arrived at some agreed terms and definitions, which are presented in the last paper in this volume.

The rest of the book consists of twenty refereed papers followed by three rump session papers. These must speak for themselves. However, we believe that this workshop will come to be seen as one of those landmark events that mark the birth of a new scientific discipline.

We would like to thank the staff at the Isaac Newton Institute, and in particular the Institute's conference secretary Mike Sekulla, for taking good care of the administrative arrangements. We are also grateful to the British government for funding the Newton programme through its Engineering and Physical Sciences Research Council; to both Trinity College and St John's College, Cambridge, for additional financial support; and to NM Rothschild for funding a visiting chair for Gus Simmons.

We plan to hold the second workshop in this series in Portland, Oregon, in April 1998.

Ross Anderson
Cambridge, September 1996

CONTENTS

The History of Steganography

David Kahn

120 Wooleys Lane
Great Neck, New York 11023

This is an extremely interesting and a very important conference — the first of its kind. I salute the people who had the idea of doing it. It may go down as a landmark conference in the history of cryptology.

I am going to talk to you today about the history of steganography. Steganography deals with the hiding of messages so that potential monitors do not even know that a message is being sent. It is different from cryptography where they know that a secret message is being sent. The latter might consist of a message like ZQVBL, while the former might use secret ink. .

The origin of steganography, it seems to me, is biological or physiological. Examples of what we call steganography today abound in the animal kingdom. When dogs attempt to do something secret and are caught, they sometimes look a little ashamed. Among chimpanzees or wolves, when beta males want to mate with the females of alpha males they will try to do it in a surreptitious way. So secret and suppressed methods of communication and of action exist among animals.

In the human world, children pass notes in school so that the teacher won't catch them. In criminal human behaviour, plotters attempt to do things in a secret way and not in an overt way.

Steganography conceals the very existence of the secret message. It's therefore broader than cryptography, but there's no theory yet, as far as I know, of steganography.

The root metaphor — as some philosophers would say — of steganography is a hiding place. Messages can be communicated not only through space but also through time. For example, turtles will bury eggs — that's kind of a secret message through time. People will bury treasure.

The term *steganography* itself means "covered writing" — it comes from the Greek $\sigma\tau\epsilon\gamma\alpha\nu\omega$. Cryptography means "secret writing". Steganography seems to me connected to a great extent with protection. Still protection is only an accompanying characteristic not necessarily a defining one.

Perhaps because of steganography's biological roots, we can go far back in history and find examples in which steganography has been used. Herodotus, the father of history, gives several cases. A man named Harpagus killed a hare and hid a message inside its body. He sent it with a messenger who pretended to be a hunter.

One Histaieus wished to inform his friends that it was time to begin a revolt against the Medes and the Persians. He shaved the head of one of his trusted slaves, tattooed the message on the head, waited till his hair grew back, and sent him along. It worked: the message got to his correspondents in Persia, the revolt succeeded. Things worked more slowly in the days before faxes and email!

Herodotus also tells of a man named Demeratus who wanted to report from the Persian court back to his friends in Greece that Xerxes the Great was about to invade Greece. He concealed his message under writing tablets. These were usually two pieces of wood, hinged as a book, with each face covered with wax. One wrote on the wax; the recipient melted the wax and reused the tablet. Demeratus' technique was to remove the wax, write the message on the wood itself, and re-cover it with wax. He then sent the apparently blank tablets to Greece.

At first nobody could figure out what they meant. Then a women named Gorgo guessed that maybe the wax was concealing something. She removed it and became the first woman cryptanalyst. Unfortunately her ingenuity had fatal consequences for her husband Leonidas, the King of Sparta; he died with the band of Greeks holding off the Persians at Thermopylae.

Aeneas the Tactician, who wrote on military matters including secret communication, invented the astrogal. He a ball or a cube of material, maybe wood, and drilled holes in it. Each hole represented a particular letter. He passed thread through these holes to spell out the message. The recipient had to unravel it carefully, noting the successive holes through which the thread passed, then reverse the sequence to read the secret message. The hope was that if it were intercepted, it might be regarded as a toy or game.

Another idea he proposed was putting almost invisible pin pricks above the letters of an innocuous message. This device was used all the way through the Renaissance, and even in World War 1 the Germans pricked letters in magazines. In other cases, they dotted letters with invisible ink which then had to be heated to show the plaintext letters.

Harpagus' hare technique was refined — or brutalized — in the Renaissance. Giovanni Batista Porta, one of the great cryptologists of his time, proposed feeding a message to a dog and then killing the dog when you wanted to get this message. Would the RSCPA permit that today?

An important technique was the use of sympathetic inks. They are very old, appearing in the classical literature. Ovid in his "Art of Love" suggests using milk to write invisibly. To develop it, the recipients sprinkles soot or carbon black on the paper and it will stick to the milk residue. Most of the early inks were simply organic fluids which upon being heated very gently with a candle would char and reveal the secret message.

Later, chemically affected sympathetic inks were developed. These were chemicals that could be treated with other chemicals causing a reaction that would make the result visible. Some of these were known very early on in classical times; Pliny mentions some of them. One is gallotanic acid made from gall nuts which will become visible if copper sulphate is painted over it.

In World Wars 1 and 2, chemicals were developed that reacted only with very specific developers. Censors tried to discover these secret inks by taking four or five brushes that were wired together, dipping them in several general reagents, and 'striping' a letter suspected of secret inks with them. This would bring out some of the simpler inks. The more sophisticated ones used by the Abwehr or the SD were a little more difficult to find. A secret ink more specific than most was based on a compound very widely used in laxatives — phenolphthaline. So you could use certain types of laxative as secret ink.

Photography permitted great reduction in images, so a page could be made very small. In the Franco-Prussian war, when Paris was under siege, people wanted to get messages out. They took photographs of their letters, reducing them to images about an inch by half an inch on the film, wrapped the film around the legs of pigeons and freed them to fly out of Paris. Examples are in the postal museum in Paris.

With the development of better lenses and of film that could be developed down to molecular resolution, photographers were able to reduce the size down to the size of a printed period. These microdots were used by the Germans in World War 2. Tiny images on strips of film hidden under envelope flaps transmitted technical publications from Mexico that were embargoes by censors.

Spread spectrum communications spread a transmission over a wide band of frequencies. Brief successive portions of the message are sent over a pre-arranged sequence of frequencies. The recipient must of course know this sequence. But the portion sent on a particular frequency is so short that a monitor will usually not notice it.

Anyhow, all of these techniques constitute technological steganography. A whole other branch of steganography, linguistic stenography, consists of linguistic or language forms of hidden writing. These are the semagram, and the open code.

A semagram is a secret communication that is not in written form. For example, during World War 2, censors intercepted a shipment of watches. Fearing that the position of the hands of the watches could be spelling out a secret message, they changed the position of the hands.

Another system used long blades of grass in a picture as dashes in Morse code, with short blades for dots. People have also used musical notes for letters — but it doesn't look anything at all like music and it doesn't sound like music. In *A Tale of Two Cities*, Madame Defarge, knitting at the foot of the guillotine, is looping the names of those to be put to death into her lengths of cloth. Dickens calls them her shrouds.

Open codes use illusions or code words. In World War 1, for example, German spies used fake orders for cigars to represent various types of British warships — cruisers and destroyers. Thus 5,000 cigars needed in Portsmouth meant that five cruisers were in Portsmouth.

A woman named Valerie Dickinson used dolls as codewords for American vessels in New York to transmit information to the Japanese during World War 2. Small dolls would represent destroyers, larger dolls might stand for aircraft carriers or battleships.

In null ciphers, the first letter of each word spells out a message. But messages are very hard to construct and always sound strange. The strangeness can be reduced if the constructor has enough space and time. Possibly the most famous case of a null cipher specified, in concealed form, the authorship of a book usually regard as the most beautiful ever printed — the 'Hypnerotomachia Poliphili' of 1499. A secret message was spelt out as the first letter of each chapter; this provided plenty of room for covertext to submerge it. The message was "Father Colona passionately loves Polia". It was not good for a Catholic priest to be admitting this kind of thing, hence the need for secrecy. But the cipher was discovered after a few years, and although the book carries no author's name on the title page, Colonna's role has since then never been doubted.

Likewise the work of the Englishman Thomas Usk, who concealed his authorship in the same way. But when selected letters of successive words spell out a message, the text always sounds funny and raises suspicion.

There are geometrical open codes, of which the oldest form is the Cardan Grille. In a sheet of cardboard, word-length holes are cut at random. A copy is made and sent to the recipient. The encipherer places his grille on a sheet of paper and writes the secret message in the holes. He removes the grills, and fills in empty spaces between these words with other words and mails the letter. The recipient places his grille on it and reads the secret message. But constructing a sensible sounding cover message is, as with null ciphers, difficult. Grille messages always sound funny, so often they are detected as well.

This is the history of steganography. Now, as we are hearing today, information is hidden in music and in images to protect property rights. I was once told that 'Muzak', which produces elevator music, hides in its music some kind of a signature indicating that it's a Muzak arrangement, so that if anybody copies that music, Muzak can identify it in court.

What are the ways in which steganography works? Is it simply by escaping observation, by making things small or hard to see, or is it by swamping would-be detectors with extraneous information so they will overlook the hidden information?

Perhaps this conference will talk about it a little more and will begin to construct a theory of steganography. As with cryptology, the field is growing; there is plenty to do.

Thanks very much.

David Wheeler: Would you say that camouflage is a form of steganography? In the animal kingdom information is hidden so that no-one can read it, rather than someone.

David Kahn: I would, yes. Wouldn't you think so? It's an interesting question. But what about your own forces. Should they know?

David Wheeler: I did say the animal kingdom.

Whitfield Diffie: If we're going to be crediting women in particular, there's another one. Hedy Lamarr holds the patent of the first spread spectrum system. It's a frequency hopper for a remotely controlled surface running torpedo.

Question: You mentioned various examples of German steganography. Were there any different techniques used by the Allies, or could the reasons that the German examples are known be because the Allied techniques were kept classified afterwards?

David Kahn: I don't know for sure and they are being kept classified. But I would say we had many fewer spies or attempted spies in Germany than the Germans had in the Allied areas as far as I know. There were resistance fighters, but there hasn't come to light a great deal of information about Allied espionage. Immediately before D Day, we sent over such messages as "The elephants are eating the strawberries" which meant to a particular resistance group, "Now's the time to begin blowing up bridges". But as for technological things like invisible inks — there must have been some, but I've never seen any information about them at all.

Thanks very much.

Computer Based Steganography:
How It Works and Why Therefore Any Restrictions on Cryptography Are Nonsense, at Best[*][+]

Elke Franz[1], Anja Jerichow[1], Steffen Möller[2], Andreas Pfitzmann[1], Ingo Stierand[2]

[1]University of Dresden, Institute of Theoretical Computer Science, D–01062 Dresden
Germany, {efl, jerichow, pfitza}@inf.tu-dresden.de

[2]University of Hildesheim, Institute of Computer Science, PF 101 363,
D-31113 Hildesheim, Germany, {moeller, stierand}@informatik.uni-hildesheim.de

Abstract: In the future, messages, e.g. speech, text or pictures, will be transmitted digitally since this is cheaper, more perfect and more flexible. It is possible to hide messages, which are of necessity much shorter, nearly unrecognizable for outsiders in such digitized messages. In this article we describe how computer based steganography works and give a summary on the results of our implementation.

Keywords: encoding, encryption, digitization, hissing noise, background noises, listening tests, cryptography, ISDN, method with threshold values, sonogram, steganography, hidden transmission

1   Introduction

It is a fact that at all times people want to hide certain things of their private life or of business interests. Presumably it was one of the first inventions by people to do something against the fact that strangers get to know any secret.

There are two basic ideas how to keep something as a secret. An object can be hidden at a secret place. One can hope that nobody will find this object except people who are familiar with the secret. Another possibility is to put the object somewhere in such a way that only certain people are able to use or to see it. One example of the latter is a safe. Only people who know the correct combination to open the safe can access the object. In this case it does not matter how many people know the content of the safe.

But not only objects or things should be hidden. Often messages are supposed to be readable only by the intended recipient. The idea how to do so was already used in antiquity: a message will be encrypted. So only the person who can decrypt it is able to read the contents of the message.

Things are different now. When in former times a herald had to be on his way for many days to deliver a message, nowadays computers take on the communication for us. Digital communication networks are used all over the world. By introducing computers for communication, cryptography can also be realized. A computer can work with algorithms to encrypt a single page of text which would take a person many years. Thus encrypting and transmitting data is very fast and user-friendly in the computer age.

---

[*]   Most of the text was originally published by Steffen Möller, Andreas Pfitzmann and Ingo Stierand in German in the Journal "DuD, Datenschutz und Datensicherung" 18/6 (1994) 318-326.

[+]   We thank the German Science Foundation (DFG) and the Gottlieb-Daimler - and Karl-Benz Foundation, Ladenburg (Germany) for their financial support.

1.1 Cryptography under Supervision

Since the technological progress has made the use of encryption potentially cheap and easy, there has been a discussion about restricting the use of cryptography. In some countries different restrictions on the use of cryptography are already laid down by law. The official argument is that without effective restrictions on cryptography, the fight against international criminality would be considerably obstructed.

It is proposed that the registration of cryptographic systems should be a duty, whether they are products of hardware or software. Moreover, some people would like that for supervision, everybody who wants to encrypt his data, should receive the secret key from a nationalized allocation office. This was motivated by governmental efforts in order to decode secret messages which were intercepted. Definitely, such restrictions would succeed in a serious degrading of cryptography, one of the most important and efficient protection methods available in computer science.

"I want to have the right to protect my data against unwanted access. But the interest of the investigation offices to catch a criminal person should go forward." Certainly, it is legitimate to argue like that. But probably it is not clear to everybody that the restriction of cryptography can as little protect against the transmission of secret data (e.g. data about illegal drug transports) as the ban on disguising can protect against bank robbery. Even if we assume that criminals would adhere to these restrictions there are still methods to overcome them. Steganography is one simply to use method. Investigators are not able to establish the mere existence of a hidden message, not to mention its content. Computer based steganography cannot be prevented as long as the estate of programmable computers is widespread. It supplies enough "hidden" bandwidth for planning and coordination of crimes. Hence, any effort to restrict encryption is ineffective with respect to criminal prosecution. Moreover, such a law would make it even more difficult to observe their activities. Cryptography by law would be a great restriction of the personal rights of everybody.

Trustworthy encryption is essential for the citizens if they want to protect their right of informational self-determination. Trust in a protective measure requires its free knowledge, organization and usage. Therefore, we strongly advise against any efforts to restrict the use of cryptography.

With this article we make a contribution for a broad disapproval of a law of regulating cryptography. In a few years investigation offices would also have to recognize that a restriction of cryptography would not be a good solution. We proved that it is possible to hide the transmission of data which we want to keep secret!

1.2 Hiding Messages to Overcome Restrictions on Cryptography

1.2.1 In General

Though the encoding of data can be monitored, one may send a letter or a painting which appears absolutely inconspicuous to an observer. E.g. one could send a letter to his brother containing a painting from his three years old daughter – the painting of an apple tree. A normal observer like a police man would see the picture – the painting of the apple tree. The covering letter will tell him that the proud father has sent the painting of his daughter. But the brother would count the number of apples on the picture and know: "Our meeting will be at 3 pm."

If a letter is sent which apparently can be read by everybody, then nobody would become suspicious and start looking for secret messages. Also if somebody suspects a criminal act, e.g. if it is known that the sender of the letter does not have a daughter, both parties can still find an explanation about sending this picture. Anyway, how could one definitely prove the transmission of a secret information?

1.2.2 Digitized Speech

In this article we do not want to count apples. Our "painting" is a usual telephone talk. It could be very short like between two foreign parties: "... Sorry, I must have dialed the wrong number ... doesn't matter ..." or anything unsuspicious. We tested if it was possible to transmit secret data in addition to the speech information when making a phone call – without giving the opportunity of observation.

To analyze the telephone has two reasons: First, the telephone is the most widespread telecommunication tool (e.g. nearly every household owns a telephone). Second, the new ISDN (Integrated Services Digital Network, see also Section 2) offers the basic requirement for our manipulations: The transmission of telephone talks is **digital**. With the fast growing internet it is no longer necessary - by now there are more internet accounts than ISDN phones. The internet adds the possibility to stay anonymous to the possibility of hidden data transmission.

1.3   Using Methods for Detecting Steganography to Improve Steganography

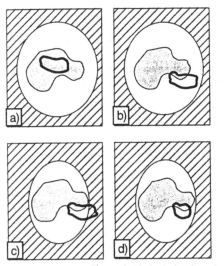

a) perfectly secure stegosystem: It modifies only inside the nondeterminism. It is impossible to find a stegoanalytical method for detecting, because each method must accept the existing nondeterminism (see also §4.3.2).
b) pragmatically secure stegosystem: It also modifies samples which would be determined. The modifications, however, are unrecognizable again if the stegoanalytical method is not good enough.
c) insecure stegosystem: The stegoanalytical method for detecting hidden data was improved. Now secret messages are found.
d) improved stegosystem: By using the stegoanalytical method of c), the stegosystem has been improved. The modifications are again in the sector in which they are not recognized.

⊂⊃ nondeterminism, i.e. the area in which bits are not determined because of background noises and also quantization errors
⬭ stegosystem
⊂⊃ area in which modifications cannot be recognized by the stegoanalytical method
⊘ area in which modifications are recognized by the stegoanalytical method

Figure 1: Methods for detecting and improving steganography

In the long run, it is not possible to prove steganography to court. Even if there would be a way to prove it once, in any case it is not possible in the long run:

For hiding data, we use a stegosystem. Let us suppose that a stegoanalytical method is found which allows to detect hidden data. But the detection is not enough. If somebody is blamed for using steganography, this use must be proved by explaining the stegoanalytical method. Now this stegoanalytical method can be used to improve the stegosystem: It serves as a method of testing. When our secret data could be detected by this method, the stegosystem is not allowed to modify anything. That means we now hide our data in such a way that the stegoanalytical method cannot find them. A new stegoanalytical method would be necessary to see our data, and if one has been developed we can use it again as a method of testing. That way, we successively improve the security of our stegosystem, cf. Figure 1. The price we have to pay is that the capacity of the stegochannel decreases.

2   ISDN – Integrated Services Digital Network

2.1   ISDN in General

Twin wires, already used in the plain old telephone network, form the physical channel of ISDN. By sophisticated signal processing, two 64 kbit/s-channels for data and one control channel of 16 kbit/s are available per direction. It is also possible to use as many as 30 data channels in this network, but for this four wires are necessary. A special connection device, the so-called NT-socket, is needed to be able to link up the various devices, e.g. the telephone, with the net.

For our application it is very important that in the ISDN data is transmitted digitally and without any changes.

2.2   Important for us: Digitization of Speech

Sound waves, like speech or music, can be transformed into analogous voltages by a microphone. An oscilloscope shows this voltages as overlaid sine curves. But it is not easy to see that there are really only sine curves, because there is a jumble of lines on the screen.

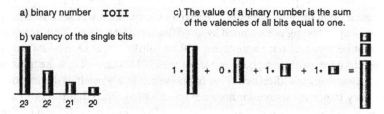

Figure 2: Transforming binary numbers into analogous values and conversely

These voltages can be digitized by a so-called analog/digital-converter. For that the A/D-converter measures the current amplitude (i.e. the value of the voltage) in short periods of time and transforms it into a binary number (Figure 2).

This "sampling" takes place several times per second, and thus nearly the original signal can be reconstructed from the established data (Figure 3).

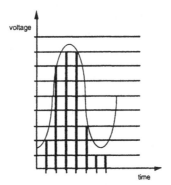

Figure 3: Encoding of noises as a succession of binary numbers

3   Hiding of Messages in Digitized Speech

Our goal is to transmit data simultaneously and unobservably in addition to the speech during a call. Therefore we want to "hide" data in the speech. We are allowed to do so since in every quantization there is some noise. Especially in phone calls additional noise is produced by cheap microphones and from the background. It is due to the noise that we can insert our data undetectably into the speech. Then they have themselves transmitted unnoticed like a fare dodger and being drowned out by the other noises.

If we speak about hiding we do not mean insertion of data into the speech but replacement of hissing noise. We replace the hissing noise "in the line" by our own one.

3.1   Our Idea of Hissing Noise

In this article we do not want to formalize the basic idea of noise but try to find out how background noises can be used in a pragmatic way.

The stegosystem must pick the hissing noise to pieces to decode the message. But for this it is necessary that the hissing noise is received exactly like it was sent. In analogous lines there is always a hissing noise caused by amplification of the signal. That is the reason why we cannot be sure that our requirement will be fulfilled. Our secret data would be falsified. Therefore we use the telephone service of the ISDN. There all data are transmitted digitally and without any modifications. Thus our noise can safely reach its destination.

Another very important source for noises is quantization. Each digitization is tainted with an error caused by the resolution of the A/D- and D/A-converters. These quantization errors are also important for the (im)possibility to detect our manipulations. We will later discuss this point.

3.2   Basic Ideas about Hiding Messages in Digitized Speech

It is very important to bear the fact in mind how sensitive ears and measuring instruments can be. If we really want to stay undetected, we must basically think about the points we have to respect by our "manipulations".

We want to change the speech as unobtrusive as possible. Surely, there are various approaches. Here we describe a first simple approach. If we set definite samples to an even or an odd value the recipient will get information of one bit with each of these values. But the recipient must know which values have been changed. There is no difference between the modified values and the others around them, because the hissing noise described above superimposes the speech.

Section 3.3 describes a method to apply this approach by modifying only the least significant bits.

It is wise to select the places for modification randomly and to insert a random bit stream. The latter would be automatically done by transmitting only compressed or encrypted data. These facts would complicate the proof of a hidden transmission. Besides this, the following is clear: The less bits we modify, the less modifications can be detected.

In addition to that, any number of conditions can be found which decide whether it is allowed to modify the value of the amplitude or not. We will also describe a modification which depends on the amplitude. This is an example for such conditions.

What happens if a 'censor' adds noise to the audio signal? If the artificial noise is small it should be sufficient to use error correcting codes. If the least significant bit becomes unusable due to "white noise" added by the government, it is still possible to use a slightly more significant bit. Therefore one has to adapt the bits prior and posterior to the modified position. But this is beyond our experiment. If that is also no longer possible one would start to use usual steganographic techniques like coding something in a melody that is played with a flute or on a keyboard - what can be automatically deciphered with a computer. As long as any information can pass from one end at a phone line to the other, it is possible to hide data during the connection. As a consequence noise would have to be added until the phone is no longer usable for normal speech, too. The moment the state adds "noise" to digital phone calls might be the moment one should consider to leave the country.

3.3 The Process

The principle of our simulation can be seen in Figure 4. The lowest bit of any byte of a file with digitized speech (original byte stream) can be set to the value of a bit stream of a second file (bit stream to be hidden). This second file represents the information which should be transmitted unnoticed. The distance between two encoded bits of the secret message is controlled by a random value, the maximum of which is a parameter for our process. The maximum is adjustable between 1 and 255. The distance is defined as the number of bytes between the two bytes which should be modified. The random values to control the distances are equally distributed between 0 and the maximum, they are a secret between the sender and the recipient. They correspond to a secret key in a symmetric cryptosystem and allow our stegosystem to be published in any detail and to be shared by anybody. The secrecy of the encoded message depends only on the secrecy of this key – this is Kerckhoff's principle applied to steganography. There are two ways of generating the random values. They could be established from a file with random numbers which the recipient must also have.

The more elegant way to produce these random numbers is the usage of a pseudo-random-generator. The latter has the advantage that only a "starting value" would have to be transmitted between sender and recipient. Such a starting value can be seen as a password which has to be fed in before using the real information.

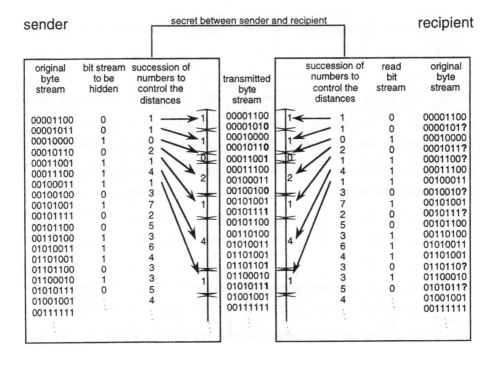

between the modified samples.

If you want to concentrate on a supposed sound, you will automatically lower your voice to better concentrate on it. You possibly ask bystanders to be quiet for a moment.

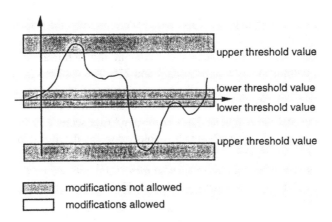

Figure 5: Only values which are greater than the threshold values will be modified a little bit.

So we came to the conclusion that it would be wise to transmit our data only when people were speaking. For this we implemented a method, in which a sample will only be modified when the current volume is greater or less than a threshold value, cf. Figure 5.

Even if the quantization is linear, this modification keeps the relative error small. This method does not exclude any of the others. They can be used in combination.

If the modification depends on the amplitude, it must be questioned if the recipient can safely decide whether the respective bit was set or not. Is it possible that the modified value changes the fulfillment of the conditions for modification and therefore the recipient must assume that this bit was not set? In order to prevent this situation we adhere to the following rule. If we want to set the lowest bit we must check whether the bits before fulfill our condition, i.e. our threshold values do not include the lowest bit. Generally, our threshold values should not include the bits we possibly want to change. Thus the recipient tests the bits which are not modified and finds the same conditions as the sender.

4   Fixing the Quality

We have implemented a small program for Apple Macintosh, called DigiStilz, to simulate such a covert transmission and to gain experience for the possibility to hear such a transmission.

4.1   Fundamental Questions about Measuring the Quality

To determine the quality of a machine, at first it is necessary to know its purpose and second how the fulfillment of this purpose can be measured. The purpose can be defined easily: We have a machine which should transmit additional data unnoticed by others. Measuring will be more difficult. How can it be measured whether transmitted speech was noticeably falsified?

4.2   Methods of Testing and Measuring

4.2.1   Listening Tests

The sense of hearing cannot be designated as objective, but our ears were the simplest and surely not the worst aid for testing our modifications. By listening tests we wanted to find out whether it was possible to hear our data. In case of hearing any change between original and modified version, we concluded that the modification selected was not suitable. An important criterion of quality was the "empty test". For this we used a sound file where "total silence" was recorded. Everything possible to hear must be caused by our modifications. We have also recorded talks in different natural environments. We wanted to test the influences of background noises on the sensitivity for our interferences.

For evaluation of the modified recordings you should remember that we always compared with the original to judge the hiding. An eavesdropper does not have this possibility. That is why we can assume that our results are on the safe side.

4.2.2   Sonogram

The shares of frequency in our modified sound files were analyzed by the program "SoundEdit": A sonogram filters out several shares of frequency and shows the intensity of the shares in relation to time. If a single frequency, e.g. 1000 Hz, is measured by the sonogram, a clear line will be seen at the 1000 Hz mark. Thus we could find out whether and how strong our manipulations changed the characteristic of our noises. This was a good measuring tool.

During transmitting ASCII-text with the constant distance 0 you could see a constant line in the sonogram for the also audible "data noise". It is interesting that this line was not yet recognizable by a variable distance of one at maximum. As expected, the sonogram always yields most minimal differences. But not any recognizable characteristics are provided which would be typical of hidden sounds. In the evaluation we will not further deal with the sonogram.

4.2.3   Distributions

Of course, only real existing things can be measured. Thus, the number of bits modified on average by the respective method should be used as a standard for quality. Therefore we assumed the following: If we set a bit we really change one. Let us suppose that we use the method with random distances. There is a file which controls the distances between the bits to be modified. If the bits of the file are equally distributed, then we can assume that the distance is also equally distributed. By a maximum distance of d_{max}, we receive on average a distance of $d_{max}/2$. E.g. we have selected a maximum distance of 4 bits. On average we then modify with a distance of 2, by a maximum distance of 32 bit with a distance of 16, etc. It can be seen that very small probabilities of modifications are achievable by expanding the maximum distance.

However, you cannot say for sure whether our modifications are detectable or not. If the bits of a text are not equally distributed and random, the text will be more observable. To draw conclusions from that would mean to ignore the features of the original data, i.e. the data, in which our secret data shall be encoded. Making specific statements which are based on distributions requires knowledge of the distribution of the digitized noises. Noise is usually equally distributed. Nevertheless, we are forced to allow correlations between the bits of the original data. But we still believe that the unobservability of inserting our data will be further maintained. The reasons will be explained in the following section.

Such assumptions are meaningful for the hiding algorithm. Surely, also other and possibly more skillful methods for hiding data can be used. E.g. several values of a sample could be changed. In order to prevent the noticeability of this change the environment will be adapted by modifying additional bits. That way, these vast modifications may be no more recognizable than single-bit modifications.

4.3   Results of the Methods

It is very difficult to make absolute statements about the quality. Especially it is difficult to speculate which measuring methods will be used or invented to discover steganographic modifications. However, in the next sections we will represent the results of applying our methods and critically analyze them.

4.3.1 Sonogram

Comparing the original and the modified sound file has shown which frequencies have changed their intensities and how strongly. But again, it is difficult to make absolute statements. When are these modifications audible? The answer of this question strongly depends on the respective listener.

4.3.2 Statistical Approach

A reasonable statistical approach would allow us to make precise statements about the quality of our modifications of noises. For this it must be questioned before how the original data are distributed.

Do chronological correlations between different samples exist, or even correlations between the separate bits of a single sample?

To answer these questions would mean to specify and to check all imaginable influences. You must consider that there are no simple, yet accurate models for all conceivable sounds. The possibilities for influences are nearly endless.

It is safe to say that the succession of numbers which comes into being during the digitization is not completely determined a priori. So there must be randomness in the distributions of the bits. That means again that it must be possible to modify randomly. Therefore we can assume that our modifications will not be detected if we will make them rarely enough and without destroying existing correlations.

A simple example for the existing nondeterminism are errors caused by quantization. In order to make this clear we want to give an example:

The signal, which should be digitized, amounts to 4,9 mV at a special moment. The linear 8 bit A/D-converter can digitize voltages in steps of 2 mV. (This is equivalent to a possible maximum voltage of about 0,5 V.) The result is 2, or 10 as a binary number.

If we change this value to 11 (binary), or 3 (decimal), a voltage of 6 mV will be produced by reconversion instead of 4 mV. However, the error will be only 0,2 mV greater than the error by reconverting the original established value of 2.

But what will happen, if new statistical methods will be developed which are able to track down our modifications? We can argue with the nondeterminism again (Figure 1). Each stegoanalytical method must work with this nondeterminism. That means it must include gaps. Thus each such stegoanalytical method must accept constellations of bits which cannot be identified as modified. On condition that this stegoanalytical method will be known, these gaps can be used in our algorithms to change these bits anyway.

Probably, we will never gain final certainty that our steganographic changes are undetectable. But using surely existing nondeterminism (which has to exist despite of possibly existing correlations) we may assume that after all our stegosystem can resist even great stegoanalytical expenditure.

4.3.3 About the Tests

At the beginning we recorded a number of "sounds" with our program for the listening tests. For that purpose we used a PowerBook to be able to record talks in various environments. In all, we so recorded 12 "sounds": in big and in small rooms, with much or less background noise, in a telephone box, at the street and in the countryside. We wanted to simulate various standard situations which can occur during a telephone call. For all tests apart from the last we used the same text as secret message protected by steganography. Thus we have not to expect falsifications of the results caused by different texts.

We started several series of tests:

1. In the first place we confined ourselves to the method with constant distances. We expanded the distances in each sound till it was not yet possible to hear any difference between the original and the sound with the inserted data. From this we obtained an overview about the influence of the environment. So we could see how the background noises themselves influence the quality of the methods. This phase serves as a basis for the following series of tests.
2. Here we used the method with the random distances. For this we started with the distance of which differences were not yet audible by constant distances. Then it was reduced till the steganographically modified sound began to noise. This series of tests should answer the question how much better the usage of random distances is in comparison to constant distances.
3. In the 3rd series of tests we inserted the text with constant distance 0 into a sound. For this we used various threshold values, see §4.3.3.3.
4. In this experiment we looked for an optimal method (on a very heuristic way). We modified the methods and parameters till especially good results were achieved. Good means that so much data as possible could have been hidden unnoticed.
5. Here we checked the influences of the distribution of the bits in the data to transmit on the quality of our modification. Like in the first series of tests, we expanded the constant distances till the modifications were not audible. However, we used only one "sound".

Of course, this is only a small selection of experiments, which are possible or meaningful. But we had to decide for some things, because growing of possibilities causes growing of the number of tests. All in all, we made over 200 listening tests.

In the following paragraphs we will describe the results and draw conclusions from them. The table gives an overview about the results.

4.3.3.1 Series of Tests 1

This test should give information on the influence of the environment noises. It was clear that the environment is surely important, but we were astonished how influential this factor is. Thus we could insert into the sound which was recorded directly at the street, 2750 bits per second (each 8th bit). In a quiet environment, it was only possible to insert about 170 bits per second (each 128th bit). This shows us that it will be useful to reflect on this topic in the future.

Description of the Sounds

(1) big room with only little background noises
(2) ,countryside' with much background noises
(3) ,countryside' with less background noises
(4) telephone box in a quiet area
(5) telephone box, very quiet
(6) telephone box, situated on a busy road
(7) very busy road (directly by the pavement)
(8) rather small, quiet room

Table for the 1st and the 2nd Series of Tests:

distance	sound 1		sound 2		sound 3		sound 4	
	constant	random	constant	random	constant	random	constant	random
0	++++	–	++++	–	++++	–	–	–
1	++++	–	++++	–	++++	–	++++	–
3	++++	++++	+++	–	+++	+++	++++	–
7	+++	+++	+	+++	++	++	++++	–
15	+++	+++	0	++	+	+	+	–
31	+++	++	–	0	0	0	+	+
63	+	0	–	–	–	–	0	0
127	0	–	–	–	–	–	–	–

distance	sound 5		sound 6		sound 7		sound 8	
	constant	random	constant	random	constant	random	constant	random
0	++++	–	++++	–	+++	–	++++	–
1	++++	–	++++	–	++	+++	+++	–
3	+++	–	+++	–	+	++	++	–
7	++	–	+++	–	0	+	+	++
15	+	+	++	–	–	0	0	0
31	+	+	+	+	–	–	–	–
63	0	0	0	0	–	–	–	–
127	–	–	–	–	–	–	–	–

++++ = well audible	++ = hardly audible	0 = not audible
+++ = audible	+ = at the border of audibility	– = not tested

Comparison of the 1st and the 2nd Series of Tests

1st series of tests: constant distances, no threshold values

2nd series of tests: random distances (the maximum distance is declared, thus nearly twice as much bits than by constant distances can be inserted on average), no threshold values

4.3.3.2 Series of Tests 2

We intentionally strived for a comparison of the two methods. It can clearly be seen that the method with random distances is substantially better than the method with constant distances. We could hide about twice as much of data by random distances in most of the sounds.

4.3.3.3 Series of Tests 3

We supposed that it would be wise to transmit hidden data only when the basic noise is loud. Our supposition was confirmed by this series of tests. We could affect the hiding by usage of an upper and a lower threshold value, which are adjustable between 0 and 128. A modification was only allowed when the amplitude was between these threshold values.

The relative errors of the modification are big by using an upper threshold value of 5 (and a lower one of 0), and this was really audible. On the other hand, modifications were not audible by a lower threshold value of 80 (and an upper one of 128).

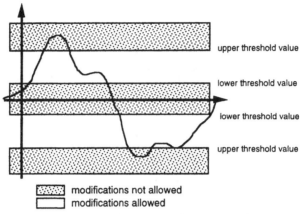

Figure 6: Ban on modifications depending on threshold values

4.3.3.4 Series of Tests 4

We selected the sound with the "worst" features as a reference, i.e. the sound which requires the greatest distances. We started with the random distance, on which the modifications began to be audible. Then we raised the distance till it was not yet possible to hear our modifications. The same was done with various smaller distances. In order to compare we established the quantity of data which could be inserted into the sound by different random distances. By random distance with a maximum of 1 and a lower threshold value of 60 more data could secretly be transmitted on average than by all other methods, on which there were no noise caused by modification.

Table for the 3rd Series of Tests:	Table for the 4th Series of Tests:
sound (1), constant distance 0, variable threshold values (adjustable between 0 and 128)	sound (1), random distances, variable threshold values

distance	threshold value		sound 1	distance	threshold value		sound 1
	lower	upper		(random)	lower	upper	
0	0	1	+++	15	30	128	+++
0	0	5	+++	15	40	128	0
0	0	10	+++	7	40	128	+
0	120	128	0	3	40	128	+++
0	100	128	0	3	50	128	0
0	80	128	0	1	50	128	+
0	70	128	+	1	60	128	0
0	60	128	++	0	80	128	0
0	50	128	++				
0	40	128	+++				

++++	= well audible	++++	= well audible
+++	= audible	+++	= audible
++	= hardly audible	++	= hardly audible
+	= at the border of audibility	+	= at the border of audibility
0	= not audible	0	= not audible
--	= not tested	--	= not tested

This result has to be expected in so far as the quantity of data which can be transmitted is mostly determined by the distances. This method was developed on the sound with the worst features. As we expected, it could also be used for all other sounds.

4.3.3.5 Series of Tests 5

In the tests described above we used for secret transmission a text which consists of a random and equally distributed succession of letters, numbers and some standard special characters.

Table for 5th Series of Tests: sound (5), constant distance, several different texts

distance (constant)	sound 5				
	text with zeros	text with zeros and ones	ASCII text	equally distributed text	
3	+++	--	--	--	++++ = well audible
7	+++	--	--	--	+++ = audible
15	++	++	++	++	++ = hardly audible
31	+	+	+	+	+ = at the border of audibility
63	0	+ / 0	0	0	0 = not audible
					-- = not tested

In the last experiment we inserted a text with only zeros, an ASCII-text, a text with alternating zeros and ones and a text which consists of an equally distributed stream of zeros and ones. To our surprise the results did not show great differences. So it might be assumed that the distribution of the text is not so important. It may be that the values of the bits do not make any difference by greater distances.

4.3.3.6 Remarks

Our expectations were not in any case confirmed by our series of tests. Something was quite unexpected. Thus hissing noises which were caused by too low or too high threshold values are more similar to distortions than to noise. However, we tried to be as objective as possible. We mostly did "blind tests". For that, one had to guess which the original and which the stego-modified version is. Besides, we used headphones in order to achieve a good quality for playback. A lot of tests were repeated on the next day to reduce mistakes.

5   Outlooks

5.1   Can the Method be Used in Reality?

Our system would not be a relevant contribution to the existing discussion if there were no possibility for a real time application. Therefore we wanted to find out which possibilities are available to implement this system into the ISDN. The Macintosh Toolbox supports processing of bit streams very well. We could achieve a throughput of data of more than the required 8000 bytes per second by its help. To be less audible means less to modify. Thus the program can work faster by raised demands, even though that sounds paradoxical.

As mentioned in Section 3.3, a linear quantization was used for the simulation. The relative error was kept small by modifying only great amplitudes.

If logarithmic quantization is used the relative error is equal for all amplitude values. Therefore another approach is needed. One possible way is to modify when the amplitude changes. But this is beyond the scope of this paper.

Further work has also to be done e.g. in the area of statistical analyses.

5.2   Conclusion

Steganography is the science of hiding data. We gave a clear example how to hide data in telephone calls by using the ISDN. We do not show a solution working in real time, but we hope that it is clear that this would not be a serious problem. We think it would take a software house only a few months to realize such an application by using suitable hardware. Using such a secret-communication-by-stego-in-ISDN-application prevents any observation of communication in networks.

But there are also other possibilities for hiding data. There are the numerous programs for hiding data in pictures, cf. e.g. `http://www.site.gmu.edu/~njohnso5/stegdoc/stegdoc.html`. Peter Wayner introduced a method to construct a text from data. There is not any meaning in this text, but you will see this only at a closer look. However, all secret information is included.

In addition to hide the data by steganography, the messages which should be kept secret can be encoded by cryptography first. Even if the hidden data should be detected, they cannot be understood by persons who do not know the cryptographic key. Thus it is even more difficult to prove the existence of a secret hidden message. So we can see that it is not possible to succeed in getting a ban on steganography done in a state founded on the rule of law.

A law restricting the use of cryptography will cause criminals to use steganographical measures. Therefore it is dangerous and must not become effective.

Literature

Steffen Möller, Andreas Pfitzmann, Ingo Stierand: Rechnergestützte Steganographie: Wie sie funktioniert und warum folglich jede Reglementierung von Verschlüsselung unsinnig ist; Datenschutz und Datensicherung DuD 18/6 (1994) 318-326.

Peter Bocker: ISDN – The Integrated Services Digital Network; Concepts, Methods, Systems; In collaboration with G. Arndt, V. Frantzen, O. Fundneider, L. Hagenhaus, H. J. Rothamel, L. Schweizer; Springer-Verlag, Heidelberg 1988

Peter Wayner: Mimic Functions; Cryptologia XVI/3 1993, pp. 193-213

Newsgroup: sci.crypt.research

Romana Machado: Stego; http://www.fqa.com/romana/romanasoft/stego.html

Further information on steganography at www–serveers of the internet such as
    http://www.iquest.net/~mrmil/stego.html   and
    http://www.cs.hut.fi/ssh/crypto/software.html#stego

Hiding Data in the OSI Network Model

Theodore G. Handel and Maxwell T. Sandford II

Weapon Design Technology Group
Los Alamos National Laboratory
Los Alamos, NM 87545
email: {thandel, mts}@lanl.gov

Abstract. Rather than searching for the holy grail of steganography, this paper presents the basis for development of a tool kit for creating and exploiting hidden channels within the standard design of network communications protocols. The Alice and Bob analogy, derived from cryptology, is used to present network protocols in a way that more clearly defines the problem. Descriptions of typical hidden channel design for each layer of the Open Systems Interconnect (OSI) network model are given. Methods of hiding and detection probabilities are summarized. Denying Bob and Alice the ability to communicate electronically may be the only absolute solution.

1 Introduction and Background

Rather than joining the quest for the holy grail of steganography, this paper focuses on the implementation of hidden writing techniques and covert channels within the OSI network model.

Our objective is to demonstrate the covert channels that exist throughout the network protocol architecture. It is important that network designers and security managers understand that their network systems may be effectively subverted in a wide variety of locations within the network. Inherent vulnerabilities included with network functionality cannot be ignored. The OSI model is the standard network model against which nearly all current network models are compared. However, the OSI model does not exist *per se* in functional systems. The most useful purpose of this model is to break complex networks into manageable pieces that can be easily understood.

We use the Bob and Alice analogy to describe the function of the OSI network protocol in a way that does not encumber the reader with the details of specific equipment. The examples given are not necessarily exceptional steganographic techniques, but are used to illustrate the principles of how data may be concealed within the OSI layers.

2 The Alice and Bob Protocol Analogy

This analogy is used to describe the details of any protocol in a palatable way (Schneier[1]). It describes the concept of the protocol without getting into numerous specific technical details.

2.1 The Plot

Bob and Alice are incarcerated in prison. They want to communicate overtly (which is permitted by Walter, the warden) and covertly (which is absolutely not permitted). Furthermore, if Walter discovers that Alice and Bob are using cryptography or communicating covertly, he will permanently disallow all subsequent communication between them. Alice and Bob can communicate using networked computers. Walter manages the network, and can monitor their message traffic. Bob and Alice wish to devise ways to communicate secretly. It is up to Walter to foil Alice and Bob's attempts at secret communication, and to devise a way to alter the contents of the secret communication.

We will attempt to answer these questions:

1.) Does technological improvement of the information system benefit Alice and Bob?

2.) Does the technological improvement of the information system benefit Walter?

3.) Does placing additional Walters or Eves in the system assure detection of hidden messages?

3 Potential impact of data hiding on information security

3.1 A tool kit of potential techniques

Functionality is present that can exploited in every layer of the OSI Model. One or more of these techniques to be discussed may be selected. Security

---

1 Applied Cryptography Chapter 2. See references

personnel should be aware that there is a broad spectrum of exploitation opportunities that should not be overlooked.

Not all techniques work in all systems. Therefore, several techniques should exist to cover a range of possibilities. Multiple techniques will assure that if one is discovered, others may remain secure. A litmus test exists for finding the system resources qualifying for exploitation, for covert communication, and for hiding data.

For covert channels, system elements that arbitrate resources are likely candidates. The quality of the covert channel can be expressed in terms of delectability (arbitration must be measurable by the recipient), indistinguishability (false arbitration versus real arbitration) and bandwidth (arbitrations per second).

For hiding data, the system elements having uncertainty, redundancy, or degeneracy are likely candidates as containers. The quality of the container can be expressed in terms of concealment (hidden data cannot be recognized as an uncorrelated component of cover data), indistinguishability (hidden data cannot be separated from the cover information), and bandwidth (ratio of hidden data to cover data).

We develop the toolkit from the basic source code for each layer of the OSI model. The modified source code is compiled and the new executable modules replace the existing modules. In some cases it is not necessary to replace existing modules, but merely to create an application that can access the internal network caches or tables already existing in the target system. A protocol analyzer, a C language compiler, an assembler, a general knowledge of network architecture, and some degree of programming skill fill out the remaining requirements. Note that protocol analyzers, complete with source code, now exist as software packages[2] that can be installed on a workstation utilizing existing network hardware. As it can be seen, the capital investment for such a venture is trivial, and well within the means of individuals so motivated. Hardware modification is not necessary. Except for the physical layer, hardware can be completely avoided.

3.2 Detection and countermeasures

Designers must realize that covert channels and data hiding locations exist, can be exploited, and are *inherent* components of the information system. It must be understood clearly that there is unknown functionality in modern information system components. Security can deal effectively with known vulnerabilities, but not with unknown functionality. The effectiveness of security is limited by cost-performance tradeoffs, and penalties for additional overhead of logging and analysis. Unknown functionality exists for a number of reasons. Design errors, project deadlines, production shortcuts, after-market

---

2 The "Snooper", from General Software, Redmond, WA. ($350 US)

modifications, upgrades, system integration oversights and the like, all contribute to creating a rich exploitation environment. Critical tasks once assigned to humans are now given to information systems without the inherent oversight capability to detect anomalous behavior that can be detected by humans.

4 Overview of the OSI Model

4.1 Background

The Open Systems Interconnection (OSI) model was designed to be just that; an open system. The design features are not proprietary, meaning that complete details of the system are available and can be used freely. The OSI model is documented fully and provides hooks that can be used to develop programs, or to "enhance" the system. Source code for the various layers is available from a number of locations or vendors, and freely across the Internet. The OSI model is derived from a model set forth by the International Standards Organization, ISO[3].

4.2 Why is the OSI Model is used?

The OSI model represents an idealized network. The model uses layers to organize the network into well defined, documented, functional modules. In the layered network, each layer provides specific functionality or services to the adjacent layer. In reality, the actual design of the network may differ from the idealized model, and from other networks designed using the same model.

4.3 Characteristics of each layer

The OSI model contains seven functional layers (figure 1). The OSI model is used because it gives logical structure to the network function. Each layer provides a communication service to the layer above it. The implementation details of each layer is hidden, by design, from the other layers. The objective of the OSI network model is to make the operation of the information system independent from the operation of the network. Some network designs do not clearly define all of the OSI layers. Such designs may integrate the functionality of two or more layers, or ignore some layers completely. Regardless of the network design, specific functionality of the network can be

---

3 Complete reference material on TCP/IP is available on-line. See References.

correlated to the OSI model. The network model for Windows NT is shown in figure 2.

We will discuss each layer of the OSI model beginning with the physical layer, and present one or more examples of hidden communication possibilities for each layer. Let us again stress that these are only examples. Many more proprietary examples are known to exist, and we hope that your imagination will be further stimulated to produce an even larger set of examples that can be included in the toolkit.

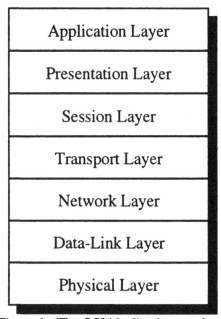

Figure 1: The OSI idealized network model

The modularized design of the OSI model makes discovery and exploitation of hidden communication channels an easier task than would be possible by attempting to analyze or exploit the network design as a whole. For example, hidden data may pass from one layer to an adjacent layer, but not to layers much higher or lower in the stack.

Although the physical communication between hosts occurs only at the lowest, physical layer, virtual connections exist at each layer between hosts. This gives the appearance of connection between corresponding layers between hosts. When properly implemented, the virtual connections allow hidden communications to exist between hosts.

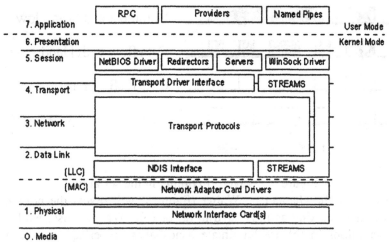

Figure 2: Typical Network Model (Windows NT)

5 Data Hiding in the Physical Layer

5.1 Function of the physical layer

The physical layer transmits data through the network's communications channels. The physical layer contains all the hardware necessary to accomplish this task. Network interface cards are the major component of this hardware. Depending on the network, several variants of hardware can exist. The communications method, including control signals and timing are included in the physical layer.

5.2 Serial Communications Port Manipulation

There is a difference between channel capacity and throughput. The baud rate of the serial communications port can be adjusted over a wide range, and its setting generally defines the channel capacity. The throughput is adjusted by a handshaking mechanism that controls data flow. This mechanism is necessary in the event that data cannot be processed as quickly as it is received.

Throughput can be biased using the Clear to Send/Ready to Send (CTS/RTS) signals, and can be adjusted independently from the data rate. It should be noted that even though Alice and Bob may not "own" the serial data being transmitted, they may exercise some latitude of control over the throughput by manipulating the control lines.

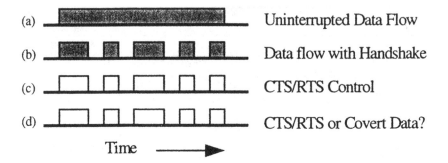

Figure 3: Waveform timing in the serial link.

Analysis of the channel by Walter (figure 3) will reveal the normal data flow with handshaking as illustrated in (a) or (b). Walter must decide if the signal variations in (b) are legitimate handshakes or perhaps a hidden data stream at a lower data rate. On 9600 BPS channels it is quite feasible to toggle the CTS/RTS at 300 BPS thus establishing a second communication channel for sending hidden messages. Interestingly, the CTS/RTS data (c and d) does not need to be ASCII, and thus can be any signaling technique that one would care to devise (including Morse Code). Careful design of control software and use of encryption on the hidden channel (d) make discovery and identification of this hidden channel difficult.

This method is of limited use because it exploits point-to-point connections that are not universal to networks. The greatest utility would be applications where network connections are made over dial-up circuits or dedicated links.

5.3 CSMA/CD Manipulation

The collision detection system in the Ethernet physical layer can also be modified to transmit hidden data. On packet collision, a jamming signal is issued and both parties "back off" a random amount of time and retry transmission. Collision control and random number generation are controlled by software operating in conjunction with the hardware.

This control mechanism can be adjusted (figure 4) so that any packets generated by Carol (another user) will be jammed by Alice. By setting Alice's delay to either zero or maximum, packets retried by Alice will either lead or lag packets regenerated by Carol, thus creating a bit-per-packet hidden channel.

Bob recovers the hidden data by detecting the collision and analyzing the order of arrival of packets from Alice and Carol over the network. In this example, Carol serves merely as a pivot point for data transmitted by Alice. Note that if Carol randomly selects to re-transmit at zero or maximum time, and Alice selects the same delay time, collisions will result until Carol delays a different amount than zero or maximum, thus maintaining the correct sequence. Alice and Bob need not pick on Carol, but may use the next available packet. Bob knows that if he senses a collision and Alice is involved, the next packet he receives will have hidden data for him.

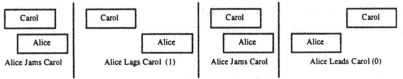

Figure 4: CSMA Collision manipulation

Walter must determine if Alice is deliberately jamming Carol's packets in an effort to transmit hidden data to Bob. Note that this technique does not require a recipient. Alice need not establish a connection with Bob. Bob must be able to monitor packets from both Alice and Carol in order to recover the hidden message. Likewise, Alice need only to be able to monitor packets from Carol and Bob in order to recover the hidden message.

6 Hiding in the Data Link Layer

6.1 Function of the Data Link layer

The data link layer shapes the network data structure. Frames are created containing data to be transmitted over the physical circuits.. Frame headers contain to/from information. Trailers contain error control information (usually a cyclic redundancy check -- CRC). The primary function of the data link layer is to prevent data corruption within the physical layer. Implementation of the data link layer is usually little more than a buffer for storing data received from the network layer and forwarding it to the physical layer.

6.2 Data Frame Manipulation

Unused (slack) portions of the frame can be used to store covert data. A similar technique has been used successfully to store information in the slack space of allocated clusters in magnetic media. This technique is used to hide an auditing system that does not occupy any "real" disk space.

Hidden data is stored in the buffer, beginning at the end of the buffer and working toward the valid data. When the packet is transmitted, the entire buffer is exported, including the covert data. Some minor software modifications may be required. It is necessary to reduce the maximum number of legitimate bytes by two in order to provide at least one byte of hidden storage per packet. The second byte of the two is used as a data separator.

The process is reversed for data received from the physical layer. Data up to the delimiter is sent to the network layer. Data from the delimiter to the end of the frame buffer is sent to the covert process.

7 Hiding Data in the Network Layer

7.1 Function of the Network Layer

The network layer is the internal delivery system. Routing information and error control are added to the data as headers and trailers that define the source and destination for the packet, as well as error control for the data. Most of the variations in hardware and network topology become invisible at the network layer. This layer assures correct delivery and receipt of packets. The network layer may fragment packets at the source and reassemble them at the destination or at an intermediate location (such as a router).

7.2 Hiding data in the Internet Packet

Within the IP packet header there is an 8 bit type-of-service byte (figure 5), of which the two least significant bits are not used in current implementation. The bits can be used to store additional information.

Another subtle implementation of the IP packet can be made. Packets can be optionally time stamped. Thus, by using a coding sequence within the time stamp, additional data may be stored. Packets sent on even time increments represent a logical zero. Packets sent on odd increments represent a logical one. Time stamping is normally used for diagnostic testing and accounting purposes.

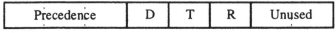

| Precedence | D | T | R | Unused |

Figure 5: IP Type of Service Field

Destruction of hidden will occur if intermediate handling devices (such as routers) are modified to strip out data from these locations.

7.3 Alternative Method

A more subtle method of data hiding exists. The Internet control message protocol (ICMP) works with IP to provide error control. The source-quench command adjusts the sending device data rate when the destination or intermediate node cannot keep up with the data rate. Flow control in this layer is similar to the CTS/RTS implementation in hardware, where the hidden data is in the flow control and the cover data is irrelevant. Note that the hidden channel flow is reversed. Hidden data flow is toward the source, not toward the destination.

8 Hiding Data in the Transport Layer

8.1 Function of the Transport Layer

The transport layer is responsible for delivering data from the network to the correct process within the host computer. The transport layer must interact with multiple programs running on the host, and has system level access to processes. Transmission Control Protocol (TCP) is the Internet implementation of this layer. The transport layer can receive data strings of unlimited length from the upper processes and provides duplex acknowledged, connection oriented, flow controlled transport to remote network stations.

8.2 TCP Packet Manipulation

There are unused data bits in the TCP header (figure 6) similar to those found in the IP header. Six bits are available between the data offset byte and the urgent pointer. These bits are not used in the current implementation. These six bits, combined with the two bits in the IP header provide one byte of hidden data per packet transmitted.

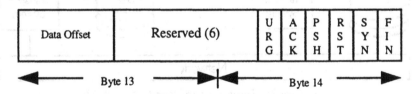

Figure 6: Reserved bytes in TCP Packet Header

Walter can discover the use of this reserved space if he has packet monitoring in place to detect the usage of reserved areas. Some routers may strip out this information, depending on how the router software is implemented. However, this data is hidden from normal analysis.

9 Hiding Data in the Session Layer

9.1 Function of the Session Layer

The session layer is the user's access point to the network. The session layer establishes connections between processes on different hosts, thus the name "session." The session layer is used by Windows® (NETBEUI) network. Users retain full control over their workstation, but accessing the network requires user ID and password. Once on the network, users may have access to restricted resources of other users on the network. including servers that may require further authentication. Functionality at the session layer is achieved through the use of a redirector. The redirector determines if the requested function call can be processed by the local operating system, or processed on the remote system using remote procedure calls (RPC).

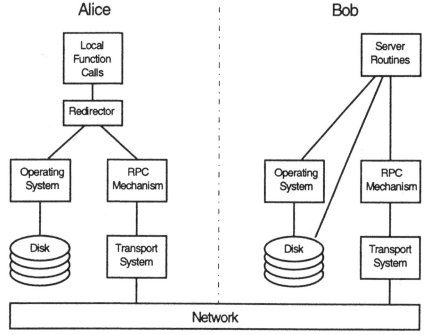

Figure 7: Redirector in Peer-to-Peer LAN.

9.2 Covert Channel Using Session Level Redirectors

The most common use of a redirector (figure 2) is to "mount" remote disks on a local machine. If a user can read a remote disk, then a covert channel can be established. For example, Bob may place two files on his disk that Alice can read remotely. Bob can monitor his local disk activity. Whenever Alice reads the first file, Bob records a logical zero, and whenever she reads the second file, Bob records a logical one. The file contents are irrelevant. Thus, Walter's suspicions are not raised. Figure 7 shows half of the affected hardware; the client portion of Alice, and the server portion of Bob.

A subtle variant of this scheme was demonstrated at Los Alamos in 1982 using a Wang word processor. A Silent 700™ terminal was connected to the seek driver of the Wang's hard disk. Data was successfully transmitted over the covert channel to the Silent 700 at 300 BPS. The technique is similar to the seek timing techniques used to make the older disk drives "walk" across the floor.

10 Hiding Data in the Presentation Layer

10.1 Function of the Presentation Layer

The presentation layer handles the network's interface to devices, such as printers, video displays, and the file system. The presentation layer is what begins to make differences in operating systems transparent. The Windows® API is implemented at this layer. The presentation layer is the proper location for encryption and compression processes, etc.

10.2 Data Embedding

The multimedia components of the presentation layer can act as hidden data transport mechanisms. The statistical properties of audio and video information contain stochastic noise that can be characterized and modified. The stochastic noise can be replaced with pseudo-random noise containing hidden data. Multimedia files are traditionally large data sets, making them attractive hosts for storing hidden data. An example of a data embedding method is given by Sandford, Handel, and Bradley (1995)[4].

Other hiding locations exist. The messaging system in Windows® permits passing data between processes through user-defined messages. Much of the presentation layer facilitates transporting data in the system. Data can be hidden within the fields of system messages that are passed to all active processes.

---

4 Sandford, et. al., The Data Embedding Method, see references.

11 Hiding Data in the Application Layer

11.1 Function of the Application Layer

The application layer is nearest the user. Users create applications utilizing system resources, including the network. Functional examples include browsers (Mosaic), terminal emulators (telnet), file transfer programs (ftp), e-mail, word processing, and distributed databases.

11.2 Language Manipulation

Many of the classical steganographic approaches can be used at the application level. What was originally done with pencil and paper can be done here. For example, a covert messaging system can be devised (figure 8) using word substitution. Alice selects words for the cover message from two dictionaries that contain words having synonymous equivalents. Words selected from dictionary A will define one hidden message state, while words from dictionary B will define the other hidden message state. Words not found in either dictionary have no covert message content.

When Bob receives the message, he filters the cover message through a decoding macro that searches the two dictionaries using a technique similar to a spelling checker. The decoded output is then checked for errors, and the resulting index is used to lookup the corresponding message.

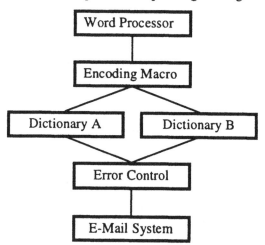

Figure 8: Language substitution steganography.

Assuming that Walter suspects this technique and alters any word in the message, an error detection and correction scheme is implemented to find and correct the word that was changed. Several algorithms are available[5] to detect and correct impulsive (single bit) errors. Walter would need access to a significant amount of information in order to decode the hidden message, including both dictionaries and the abbreviated message table.

Creating a message with n substitutions would yield a reduced message set of 2^n combinations of possible messages. This technique would be most suitable for a table lookup message system. Being generous with error detection, one could set n=20, allowing 2^{20} possible messages, a message table that is well over one million.

Several examples of language steganography exist. The most common example would be to give secondary meaning to the first letter of every word in a sentence. The process requires certain skills in language arts that do not lend themselves readily to automation. The important thing to remember is that Alice and Bob now have access to highly sophisticated information systems. Word processors are now fully programmable, even allowing system API calls. Stenographic techniques once thought to be too complicated to attempt can now be integrated directly into word processing applications on networked platforms.

12 Summary

The OSI model reveals that a variety of locations exist for hiding data. The most common implementation of the OSI model is TCP/IP, a widely accepted and commonly used protocol for large networks. At least one credible example can be given for each layer of the protocol. The examples for each layer, differ in complexity and difficulty of implementation. Alice and Bob can freely select methods for communicating. Walter must monitor and analyze activity on all layers of the protocol stack. Discovery of one hiding place does not necessarily compromise other hiding places. Careful use of error correction and detection in the hidden channel alerts Alice and Bob to the possibility that Walter discovered the channel, and altered the message.

13 Conclusions

Modern information systems provide a very rich environment for hiding data. The flexibility intentionally designed into network communications using the layered model makes identifying and exploiting covert channels easier than for stand-alone systems.

Alice and Bob can communicate covertly, as long as they can communicate overtly. The greater the access Alice and Bob have to system resources, the

---

5 Digital Communications by Satellite, chapters. 11-15, (see references)

more opportunities exist to send hidden messages. In some circumstances, other network users such as Carol may be unwitting participants.

Walter's problem is complicated because he must design several measurements to analyze message content for hidden data. Transaction logging is meaningful for only as long as someone is willing to analyze and interpret the logs. Some automation is possible, but existing automated systems are based on heuristic detection of anomalous events. Hidden communication is possible because the transactions are ordinary, and raise no alarm for such detectors.

The vulnerability of an information system is more a function of Alice and Bob's skill to discover and implement unknown or ignored functionality within the system architecture. The security of the information system is more a function of the skills Walter can apply to detect subtle anomalies in communication between Alice and Bob.

Redesigning the system to foil Alice and Bob can and will, in many cases, create other opportunities for exploitation.

References

Schneier, Bruce. *Applied Cryptography* Second Ed., J Wiley & Sons, 1996

Jamsa, et al. *Internet Programming,* Jamsa Press, 1995

Novell, Inc. *Networking Technologies,* Novell Press, 1992

Connally, D.R., et. al. *Windows 3.1 Connectivity Secrets,* IDG Books, 1994

Bhargava, V.K. et. al. *Digital Communications by Satellite,* J Wiley & Sons, 1981

Sandford, M.T., Handel, T.G., and Bradley, J.N., *The Data Embedding Method,* proc. SPIE Photonics East, 22-24 Oct., 1995. Available electronically in PostScript format from:
    http://info-server.lanl.gov:52271/usr/u078743/embed1.htm

ftp://nic.ddn.mil/rfc *Complete Internet Specification Archive*
        rfc-index.txt - Index of documents (234 Kb)
        rfc1780.txt - Official Internet Protocol (84 Kb)

Additional Reading

Tomassini, Marco. 1991, _"Programming with Sockets."_ The C Users Journal Volume 9 (September 1991): 39-56.

Baker, M. Steven. 1992. _"Network Delivers." Windows Tech Journal"_, Volume 1 (August 1992): 22-29.

Volkman, Victor R. 1992. _"Plug into TCP/IP with Windows Sockets."_ Windows/DOS Developer's Journal Volume 3 (December 1992): 6-17.

Calbaum, Mike; Porcarro, Frank; Ruegsegger, Mark; Backman, Bruce. 1993. _"Untangling the Windows Sockets API."_ Dr. Dobb's Journal Volume 18 (February 1993): 66-71.

Jablon, David P. 1994. _"Windows Sockets."_ UNIX Review Volume 12 (October 1994): 37-44.

Stretching the Limits of Steganography

Ross Anderson

Cambridge University Computer Laboratory
Pembroke Street, Cambridge CB2 3QG, UK
Email rja14@cl.cam.ac.uk

Abstract. We present a number of insights into information hiding. It was widely believed that public key steganography was impossible; we show how to do it. We then look at a number of possible approaches to the theoretical security of hidden communications. This turns out to hinge on the inefficiency of practical compression algorithms, and one of the most important parameters is whether the opponent is active or passive (i.e., whether the censor can add noise, or will merely allow or disallow a whole messages). However, there are covertexts whose compression characteristics are such that even an active opponent cannot always eliminate hidden channels completely.

1 Introduction

Steganography is about concealing the existence of messages, and it goes back to ancient times. Kahn tells of a classical Chinese practice of embedding a code ideogram at a prearranged place in a dispatch; of the warning the Greeks received of Xerxes' intentions from a message underneath the wax of a writing tablet; and a trick of dotting successive letters in a covertext with secret ink, due to Aeneas the Tactician [8].

The opponent may be passive, and merely observe the covertext, but he may also be active. In the US post office during the second world war, postal censors deleted lovers' X's, shifted watch hands, and replaced items such as loose stamps and blank paper. They also rephrased telegrams; in one case, a censor changed 'father is dead' to 'father is deceased', which elicited the reply 'is father dead or deceased?'

The study of this subject in the open scientific literature may be traced to Simmons, who in 1983 formulated it as the prisoners' problem [16]: Alice and Bob are in jail, and wish to hatch an escape plan. All their communications pass through the warden, Willy. If Willy sees any encrypted messages, he will frustrate their plan by putting them into solitary confinement. So they must find some way of hiding their ciphertext in an innocuous looking covertext. As in the related field of cryptography, we assume that the mechanism in use is known to the warden, and so the security must rely solely on a secret key.

There are many real life applications of steganography. Apparently, during the 1980's, British Prime Minister Margaret Thatcher became so irritated at press leaks of cabinet documents that she had the word processors programmed to encode their identity in the word spacing of documents, so that disloyal ministers could be traced. Similar techniques are now undergoing trials in an electronic publishing project, with a view to hiding copyright messages and serial numbers in documents [10].

Simmons' real application was more exotic — the verification of nuclear arms control treaties. The US and the USSR wanted to place sensors in each others' nuclear facilities that would transmit certain information (such as the number of missiles) but not reveal other kinds of information (such as their location). This forced a careful study of the ways in which one country's equipment might smuggle out the forbidden information past the other country's monitoring facilities [17, 19].

Steganography must not be confused with cryptography, where we transform the message so as to make its meaning obscure to a person who intercepts it. Such protection is often not enough: the detection of enciphered message traffic between a soldier and a hostile government, or between a known drug-smuggler and someone not yet under suspicion, has obvious implications.

However, we still have no comprehensive theory of steganography, in the way that Shannon gave us a theory of encryption [15] and Simmons of authentication [18]. In this article, we will try to move a few small steps towards such a theory.

2   The State of the Art

A number of computer programs are available that will embed a ciphertext file in an image. The better systems assume that both sender and receiver share a key and use a conventional cryptographic keystream generator [13] to expand this into a long pseudo-random keystream. The keystream is then used to select pixels in which the bits of the ciphertext are embedded.

Of course, not every pixel may be suitable for encoding ciphertext: changes to pixels in large fields of monochrome colour, or that lie on sharply defined boundaries, might be visible. So some systems have an algorithm that determines whether a candidate pixel can be used by checking that the variance in luminosity of the eight surrounding pixels is neither very high (as on a boundary) nor very low (as in a monochrome field). A bit can be embedded in a pixel that passes this test by some rule such as setting its low order bit to the parity of the surrounding pixels (though in practice one might use something slightly more complicated to avoid leaving telltale statistics).

Of course, the more bits per pixel, the less correlated the low order bits will be with neighbouring bits and with higher order bits in the same pixel. Some quantitative measurements of the correlations between pixels on different bit planes in digital video may be found in [20]. In effect, the bits that Alice can use to embed covert data are redundant in that Willy will be unaware that they have been altered. It follows that they might be removed by an efficient compression scheme, if one exists for the image or other covertext in use.

So when the image is to be subjected to compression (whether before or after the insertion of covert material), things become more complicated, and we have to tailor the embedding method. For example, with .gif files one can swap colours for similar colours that are adjacent in the current palette [7], while if we want to embed a message in a file that may be subjected to JPEG compression and filtering, we can embed it in multiple locations [9] or in the frequency domain by altering components of the image's discrete cosine transform [3] [23]. Further papers on the topic may be found in this volume.

So the general model is that Alice embeds information by tweaking some bits of some transform of the covertext. The transform enables her to get at one or more bits which are redundant in the sense that tweaking them cannot be detected easily or at all. To a first approximation, we will expect that such transforms will be similar to those used for compression, and that there are many low-bandwidth stego channels arising from redundancy whose elimination, by compression or otherwise, is uneconomic for normal users of the cover system. We will not expect to find many high bandwidth channels, as these would normally correspond to redundancy that could economically be removed.

3   Public Key Steganography

So far, we have merely stated the general intuition of people who have thought about these topics. They generally assume that steganography, in the presence of a capable motivated opponent who is aware of the general methods that might be used, requires the pre-existence of a shared secret so that the two communicating parties can decide on which bits to tweak. So there has been a general assumption that public-key steganography is impossible.

However, this is not the case. We will now show how a hidden message can be sent to a recipient with whom the sender has no shared secret, but for whom an authentic public key is available.

Given a covertext in which any ciphertext at all can be embedded, then there will usually be a certain rate at which its bits can be tweaked without the warden noticing (we will discuss this more fully below). So suppose that Alice can modify at least one out of every hundred bits of the covertext. This means that Willy cannot distinguish the parity of each successive block of a hundred bits from random noise, and it follows that she can encode an arbitrary pseudorandom string in these parities.

This pseudorandom material will lie in plain sight; anyone will be able to read it. So Willy cannot simply check a covertext by seeing whether a pseudorandom string can be found in it. Indeed, a suitable parity check function will extract pseudorandom-looking data from any message in which covert information can be inserted at all.

Now suppose that Alice and Bob did not have the opportunity to agree a secret key before they were imprisoned, but that Bob has a public key that is known to Alice. She can take her covert message, encrypt it under his public key, and embed it as the parity of successive blocks. Each possible recipient will then simply try to decrypt every message he sees, and Bob alone will be successful. In practice, the value encrypted under a public key could be a control block consisting of a session key plus some padding, and the session key would drive a conventional steganographic scheme as described elsewhere in this volume.

Normal public key cryptography means that users can communicate confidentially in the absence of previously shared secrets; our construction of public key steganography shows that they can also communicate covertly (if this is at all possible for people with previously shared secrets). Public key stego scales less well than public key crypto, as every recipient has to try to decrypt every message. However, this appears to be an intrinsic property of anonymous communications.

4 Theoretical Limits

Can we get a scheme that gives unconditional covertness, in the sense that the one-time pad provides unconditional secrecy?

Suppose that Alice uses an uncompressed digital video signal as the covertext, and encodes ciphertext at a very low rate. For example, the kth bit of ciphertext might become the least significant bit of one of the pixels of the kth frame of video, with the choice of pixel being specified by the kth word of a shared one time pad. Then we intuitively expect that attacks will be impossible: the ciphertext will be completely swamped in the covertext's intrinsic noise. Is there any way this intuitively obvious fact could be rigorously proved?

This leads us to ask what a proof of perfect covertness would look like. A working definition of of a secure stegosystem might be one for which Willy cannot differentiate between raw covertext and the stegotext containing embedded information, unless he has knowledge of the key. As in the case of cryptography, we might take Willy to be a probabilistic polynomial Turing machine in the case where we require computational security, and assume that he can examine all possible keys in the case where we require unconditional security.

In the latter case, he will see the actual message, so the system must generate enough plausible messages from any given stegotext, and the number of such messages must not vary in any usable way between the stegotext and a wholly innocent covertext.

This much is straightforward, but what makes the case of steganography more difficult than secrecy or authenticity is that we are dependent on the model of the source. There are a number of ways in which we can tackle this dependence, and we will present three of them. It is an open question whether any of them will yield useful results in any given application.

4.1   Selection channel

Our first idea is inspired by the correction channel that Shannon uses to prove his second coding theorem. This is the channel which someone who can see both the transmitted and received signals uses to tell the receiver which bits to tweak, and produces various noise and error correction bounds [14].

In a similar way, when Alice and Bob use a shared one-time pad to decide which covertext bit will contain the next ciphertext bit, we can think of the pad as a selection channel. If Willie is computationally unbounded, he can try all possible pads (including the right one), so the number of them which yield a plausible ciphertext must be large enough that he cannot reasonably accuse Alice of sending stegotext rather than an innocent message.

It may be useful at this point to recall the book cipher. The sender and receiver share a book and encipher a message as a series of pointers to words. So the cipher group '78216' might mean page 78, paragraph 2 and the 16th word. Book codes can be secure provided that the attacker does not know which book is in use, and care is taken not to reuse a word (or a word close enough to it) [8]. The book cipher is just a selection channel. The model of computation may be different, in that with a book cipher we start off with the book and then generate the ciphertext, whereas in a stegosystem, we start off with the text to be embedded and then create the stegotext; but they are clearly related.

A repetitive book will have a lower capacity, as we will be able to use a smaller percentage of its words before inference attacks from the context become possible. Similarly, if the covertext to be used in a stegosystem has unusual statistics (such as an unequal number of zeros and ones) then its stego capacity will be lower, as only a small proportion of candidate ciphertexts would look random enough.

We mentioned systems that generate a number of candidate locations for a ciphertext bit and then filter out the locations where actually embedding a bit would have a significant effect on the statistics thought to be relevant (in the case of hiding in an image, this could mean avoiding places where the local variance in luminosity is either very low or very high).

Our information theoretic approach suggests a better way. We will use our keystream generator to select not one pixel but a set of them, and embed the ciphertext bit as their parity. This way, the information can be hidden by changing whichever of the pixels can be changed least obtrusively.

From the information theoretic point of view, if the covertext is '1' with probability 0.6, and we encode in bit pairs, then the probability that a bit pair will have parity 1 is 0.52; if we move to triples, the parity is 1 with probability 0.504, and so on. As the improvement is geometric, we can with little difficulty get the discrepancy as low as we like and thus — provided that our selection channel is broad enough — we can hide information quite efficiently.

Indeed, there is a tradeoff: the more bits in the selection channel, the more bits we can hide in the covertext. In practice our selection channel will be a cryptographic pseudorandom number generator, and we can draw from it as many bits as we like.

But clearly there is an ultimate limit to the amount of information that can be hidden.

For example, suppose that there is an allowed set of cover texts M (we might be using the cover of a news agency; we have to report a reasonably truthful version of events, and transmit photographs — perhaps slightly doctored — of events that actually took place). Suppose also that there is an allowed set of encodings E. Then the covert capacity will be at most $H(E) - H(M)$. Can we tighten this upper bound or — better still — get any kind of lower bound?

4.2 Equivalence classes

We can consider equivalence classes of messages. Suppose Alice uses a keyed cryptographic hash function to derive one bit from each sentence of a letter. As she prepares her stegotext letter to Bob, she has a routine which checks this bit and beeps if it is wrong. This will go off about every other sentence, which she can then rewrite.

Of course, if she uses standard changes such as [is able ↔ can], then clearly she must not alter their statistics to the point that Willy can detect the change. It is even an open question whether a computer can alter a natural language text in a way that is undetectable to a human [21] — that is, embed a ciphertext using the technique described above — and the problem is commended to the research community as a weak form of the Turing test.

The converse is that writing a program to scan for human inserted steganography might be rather hard. This is an area in which competitive research might prove interesting!

Equivalence classes can also arise naturally. For example, when making a map from a larger scale map, many arbitrary decisions have to be taken about which features to incorporate, especially with features such as coastlines that are to some extent fractal [12]. Also, when software is written, it contains 'birthmarks' such as the order in which registers are pushed and popped, and these were used by IBM in litigation against software pirates who had copied their PC-AT ROM [6].

Equivalence classes of messages are tied up with compression. If covertext C_1 means the same as covertext C_2, then a compression algorithm need only select one representative from this equivalence class. However, if $C_1 \neq C_2$, then this choice throws away information, and so the compression is lossy.

Information theorists assume that any signal can in theory be completely compressed. But if this could ever be done in practice, then the steganography problem would become trivial: Alice can just 'uncompress' her ciphertext getting a comprehensible message, and Willy would have to pass the result. So Willy can only do his job at all because perfect compression is unfeasible. So regardless of whether we talk in terms of compression or of equivalence classes, Willy's performance of his job depends on his having a model of the source, and the danger to Alice and Bob is that his model might be better than theirs.

4.3   Conditional entropy

If Alice does not trust her ability to spot which bits of the covertext (or some transform of it) will appear noise-like to Willy, she might try to use conditional entropy. If the ciphertext is random, its mutual information with the covertext will be zero, and entropy will be additive — the entropy of the loaded covertext will be exactly equal to the entropy of the pure covertext plus that of the ciphertext.

Thus the maximum amount of ciphertext that she can hide from Willy depends on the uncertainty of the covertext entropy. Confidence levels can be computed in the obvious way: if the ciphertext rate is R_1, then the warden must not be able to detect with probability P a change of R_1 in the covertext rate R_2.

Thanks to the Central Limit Theorem, the more covertext we give the warden, the better he will be able to estimate its statistics, and so the smaller the rate at which Alice will be able to tweak bits safely. The rate might even tend to zero, as was noted in the context of covert channels in operating systems [11]. However, as a matter of empirical fact, there do exist channels in which ciphertext can be inserted at a positive rate [4], so measuring entropy may be useful in a number of applications.

However, it still does not give us a way to prove the unconditional covertness of a system. The reason for this is that once Alice assumes that Willy is smarter than she is, she has no way of estimating the variance in his estimates of the entropy of her covertext. A purist might conclude that the only circumstance in which she can be certain that Willy cannot detect her messages is when she uses a subliminal channel in the sense of Simmons; that is, a channel in which she chooses some random bits (as in an ElGamal digital signature) and these bits can be recovered by the message recipient [1].

5   Active and Passive Wardens

The applications discussed above include both passive wardens, who monitor traffic and signal to some process outside the system if unauthorised message traffic is detected, and active wardens who try to remove all possible covert messages from covertexts that pass through their hands. A good example of the latter was the world war two postal censor described in the introduction, and a highly topical example is given by software piracy.

Software birthmarks, as mentioned above, have been used to prove the authorship of code so that pirates could be prosecuted. They were serviceable with hand assembled system software, but might be harder to find now that most code is produced by a compiler. A possible remedy is to embed copyright information by mangling the object code in some way. The automatic, random replacement of code fragments with equivalent ones is used by Intel to customise security code [2]. This may be adequate in that application, where the goal is to prevent a single patch defeating all instances of a protective mechanism; but copyright marking is harder. One could imagine a contest between software authors and pirates to see who can mangle code most thoroughly without affecting its performance too much. If the author has the better mangler, then some of the information he adds will be left untouched by the pirate.

In fact, the World Intellectual Property Organisation has proposed a system of numbering for all digital works, including books, sound and video recordings, and computer programs; it claims that the boundaries between these are breaking down. Software publishers are sceptical; they claim to have had no difficulty yet in establishing ownership [5]. But whatever the legal value of copyright marking, the software pirate is a good example of an active warden.

In such a case, the simple public key scheme described in section two above will not work. Even in the shared-key model, there are cases where an active warden can completely block the stego channel. For example, if (a) his model of the communication at least as good as the prisoners' (b) the covertext information separates cleanly from the covert information, then he can replace the latter with noise. This is the case of a software pirate who has a better code mangler than the software author.

6 Limits on Active Wardens

However, there are many other cases where the stego channel is highly bound up with the covertext. For example, Jagpal [7] measured the noise that can be added to a .gif file before the image quality is degraded, while Möller and others have done the same for digitised speech [4].

The point here is that if Alice can add an extra X% of noise without affecting the picture, then so can Willy; but she can stop him finding out which X% carries the covert message by using a keystream to select which bits of covertext to tweak. In this case, all Willy will be able to do is to cut the bandwidth of the channel — a scenario that Trostle and others have explored in the context of covert channels in operating systems [22].

This bandwidth limitation will also be effective against systems that embed each ciphertext bit as a parity check of a number of covertext bits. When the warden is active, the more covertext bits we use in each parity check, the more easily he will be able to inject noise into our covertext.

It is an open question whether public key steganography can be made to work against an active warden who can add only a limited amount of noise. It may also be of interest to consider whether one can implement other cryptographic primitives, such as the wiretap channel and bit commitment [13]. If it turns out that the kind of public key steganography that we have described here cannot be made to work, then key exchange well might be possible by combining techniques like these.

7 Conclusions

We have stretched the limits of steganography somewhat. Firstly, we have shown how to do public key steganography. Secondly, we have discussed a number of possible approaches to a theory of the subject, which suggest various practical techniques for improving the covertness of existing steganographic schemes. Thirdly, we have highlighted one of the most important topics, namely whether the warden is active or passive, and shown how this interacts with both the public key and theoretical approaches to the subject.

Acknowledgements: Some of the ideas presented here were clarified by discussion with David Wheeler, John Daugman, Roger Needham, Gus Simmons, Markus Kuhn, John Kelsey, Ian Jackson, Mike Roe, Mark Lomas, Stewart Lee. Peter Wayner and Matt Blaze. I am also grateful to the Isaac Newton Institute for hospitality while this paper was being written.

References

1. "The Newton Channel", RJ Anderson, S Vaudenay, B Preneel, K Nyberg, *this volume*
2. "Tamper Resistant Software: An Implementation", D Aucsmith, *this volume*
3. "Watermarking Digital Images for Copyright Protection", FM Boland, JJK Ó Ruanaidh, C Dautzenberg, *Proceedings, IEE International Conference on Image Processing and its Applications, Edinburgh 1995*
4. "Computer Based Steganography", E Franz, A Jerichow, S Moeller, A Pfitzmann, I Stierand, *this volume*
5. "A voluntary international numbering system — the latest WIPO proposals", R Hart, *Computer Law and Security Report* v 11 no 3 (May-June 95) pp 127–129
6. Talk on software birthmarks, counsel for IBM Corporation, BCS Technology of Software Protection Special Interest Group, London 1985
7. *'Steganography in Digital Images'*, G Jagpal, Thesis, Cambridge University Computer Laboratory, May 1995
8. *'The Codebreakers'*, D Kahn, Macmillan 1967
9. "Towards Robust and Hidden Image Copyright Labeling", E Koch, J Zhao, *Proceedings of 1995 IEEE Workshop on Nonlinear Signal and Image Processing* (Neos Marmaras, Halkidiki, Greece, June 20–22, 1995)
10. "Electronic Document Distribution", NF Maxemchuk, *AT & T Technical Journal* v 73 no 5 (Sep/Oct 94) pp 73–80
11. "Covert Channels — Here to Stay?", IS Moskowitz, MH Kang, *Compass 94* pp 235–243
12. RM Needham, *private conversation*, December 1995

13. *'Applied Cryptography — Protocols, Algorithms and Source Code in C'* B Schneier (second edition), Wiley 1995
14. "A Mathematical Theory of Communication", CE Shannon, in *Bell Systems Technical Journal* v 27 (1948) pp 379–423, 623–656
15. "Communication theory of secrecy systems", CE Shannon, in *Bell Systems Technical Journal* v 28 (1949) pp 656–715
16. "The Prisoners' Problem and the Subliminal Channel", GJ Simmons, in *Proceedings of CRYPTO '83*, Plenum Press (1984) pp 51–67
17. "How to Insure that Data Acquired to Verify Treaty Compliance are Trustworthy", GJ Simmons, *Proceedings of the IEEE* v 76 (1984) p 5
18. "A survey of information authentication", GJ Simmons, in *Contemporary Cryptology — the Science of information Integrity*, IEEE Press 1992, pp 379–419
19. "The History of Subliminal Channels", GJ Simmons, *this volume*
20. *'High Quality De-interlacing of Television Images'*, N van Someren, PhD Thesis, University of Cambridge, September 1994
21. K Spärck Jones, *private communication*, August 1995
22. "Modelling a Fuzzy Time System", JT Trostle, *Proc. IEEE Symposium in Security and Privacy 93* pp 82 - 89
23. "Embedding Robust Labels Into Images For Copyright Protection", J Zhao, E Koch, *Proc. Int. Congr. on IPR for Specialized Information, Knowledge and New Technologies* (Vienna, Austria, August 21-25, 1995)

Trials of Traced Traitors

Birgit Pfitzmann[*]

Universität Hildesheim, Institut für Informatik
D-31141 Hildesheim, Germany
pfitzb@informatik.uni-hildesheim.de

Abstract. Traitor tracing schemes as introduced by Chor, Fiat, and Naor at Crypto '94 are intended for tracing people who abuse a broadcast encryption scheme by allowing additional, illegitimate users to decrypt the data. The schemes should also provide legal evidence for such treachery.

We discuss and improve the quality of such evidence, i.e., the security of trials that would be held about supposedly traced traitors. In particular, previous traitor tracing schemes are symmetric in the sense that legitimate users of the broadcast information share all their secrets with the information provider. Thus they cannot offer non-repudiation. We define asymmetric traitor tracing schemes, where the provider, confronted with treachery, obtains information that he could not have produced on his own, and that is therefore much better evidence. Examples of concrete constructions are given.

We also discuss the general model of traitor tracing and propose improvements to the symmetric schemes.

1 Introduction

Traitor tracing schemes were introduced in [ChFN_94]. Their goal is copyright protection for broadcast information, based on broadcast encryption.

1.1 Broadcast Encryption

Broadcast encryption is intended for applications where an *information provider* broadcasts a lot of information in encrypted form, and only several legitimate *users* are supposed to be able to decrypt it. The typical example is Pay-TV, if the information is actually transmitted over a broadcast channel. Broadcast encryption schemes have at least been considered in [Blom_80, Berk_91, FiNa_94, BlCr_95].

The broadcast encryption schemes in [ChFN_94] have three phases:

- *Provider initialization*, where the information provider generates some information that he will need with all users. We call it the *initial record*.

- *User initialization*, where an individual user registers with this information provider. The information that the user stores after this phase is called this user's *personal key*. The information provider may update his initial record after each user initialization.

- *Session sending*. Now data are transmitted, divided into smaller parts called sessions. Each session is encrypted with a different *session key*, and some additional information

---

[*] Future address Universität Dortmund, Informatik VI, D-44221 Dortmund 50, Germany

is broadcast that allows all the legitimate users to decrypt the session key with their personal keys, and thus to decrypt the real data.

Other broadcast encryption schemes have an additional *purchase phase* between user initialization and session sending, where one or more users decide that they actually want to decrypt some information, e.g., to watch the coming movie, and the information provider enables precisely these users to decrypt the coming information [FiNa_94]. In contrast, in [ChFN_94] all initialized users are legitimate users of all the information.

Note that the model of broadcast encryption does not allow interaction between users, neither in initialization nor later. This is realistic for applications like Pay-TV, and it is one of the features that distinguish broadcast encryption from conference key distribution (see, e.g., [BDHK_93]).

1.2 Tracing Traitors

The additional goal in [ChFN_94] that extends broadcast encryption to traitor tracing is that legitimate users should not be able to make the data accessible to outsiders without being traced and finally convicted. Users who redistribute data are called *traitors*, outsiders who use this information are called *pirates*, and the pirates' devices are called *pirate decoders*.

The goal of a traitor tracing scheme for broadcast encryption is quite similar to what is often called fingerprinting with other types of data (see, e.g., [Wagn_83, BIMP_86, Caro_95, BoSh_95, ZhKo_95] and these proceedings), except that it is not the broadcast data themselves that are fingerprinted, but, at least in principle, a virtual cryptographic key that is used to encrypt the broadcast data. Before explaining this, however, we discuss the goals of traitor tracing more precisely from the point of view of the application.

Cleartext Redistribution Not Addressed — What Exactly Does This Mean?
Traitor tracing schemes do not address treachery where the traitors retransmit the broadband cleartext they obtain to outsiders. This is in contrast to normal fingerprinting, which does address the situation where traitors redistribute the pictures, texts, or programs they obtain. The explanation for this restriction is that operating a pirate TV-broadcast station is deemed too expensive and too risky. More precisely, the information provider will have to perform risk management in his choice between fingerprinting of the actual data and traitor tracing: Fingerprinting is more secure, but does not allow the use of a cheaper broadcast distribution medium. Broadcast encryption with traitor tracing would therefore typically be chosen if the value of the information itself is not very high compared with the price of its distribution.

The formalization of the restriction that traitor tracing does not address cleartext redistribution in Definitions 1 and 2 in [ChFN_94] is that the traitors only redistribute information obtained during user initialization. This is a much stronger restriction; it permits that traitors cannot be traced if they redistribute a tiny amount of data obtained after user initialization. Such a definition may fit applications where timeliness is crucial and the traitors may not be able to redistribute even a tiny amount of data fast enough. For other applications, where pirates can buffer the received encrypted data until the traitors can send them the necessary information, the definition should be extended to include workfactors as parameters. A particularly important one is the ratio between the additional bandwidth the information provider needs on the broadcast channel and the bandwidth the traitors need to remain untraceable. Such parameters can immediately be used in the information provider's risk management.

With the concrete schemes proposed so far (see Section 2.1), the traitors have to redistribute one session key per session to remain untraceable. For the example session length of one minute and a normal encryption system, they would certainly not need a pirate TV-broadcast station, but of course quite some organization. More generally, the ratio between the additional bandwidth the information provider needs on the broadcast channel and the bandwidth the traitors need to distribute the session keys is still quite large and may prevent the use of the schemes, e.g., for encrypted CD ROMs.

No Tamper Resistance Needed. It is not assumed in traitor tracing that the personal keys are in tamper-resistant boxes, which would prevent the traitors from redistribution a priori. One of the reasons is that good tamper-resistant boxes are deemed too expensive. Thus it is assumed that the traitors have found access to their own personal keys and can redistribute them. The goal is to *trace* them if they do so, both for punishment after the fact and for deterring them from redistribution in the first place.

What Input is Needed for Tracing? Of course, tracing is impossible if the redistribution remains entirely secret. In other words, it has to be assumed for tracing that the information provider has found some redistributed information or a pirate decoder. This is quite a reasonable assumption for large-scale redistribution, which is most feared by information providers.

In most cases in practice, the information found will be a decryption key that has some close relation to the personal keys it was derived from. It is therefore both realistic and helpful for understanding to start with such an assumption when describing a tracing algorithm. However, it is also worthwhile considering the more general case, because such an assumption means three things: that the pirate decoder is not too tamper-resistant, that its contents are not too scrambled, and that the encryption scheme does not allow traitors to construct pirate decoders that contain information of a different form and still decrypt successfully.

It was already mentioned in [ChFN_94] that the information provider only needs to use the pirate decoder as a black box, i.e., without opening it, but details were omitted. (The actual procedure sketched below is the same as the authors had in mind.) Thus we mention a few such details, in particular because the question becomes more interesting in the asymmetric case, where the information provider knows less about the users' keys, and thus the information he obtains by experimenting with a black-box pirate decoder will not always be keys.

We assume that the pirate decoder analyzed as a black box does not defy analysis by access control, e.g., by requiring a password before operating. Having found a pirate decoder, but not being able to operate it at all, counts as not having found it. In reality, this means that a pirate cooperates with the information provider against a traitor, willingly or not.

Nevertheless, if the pirate decoder is given in hardware, we do not yet see a procedure that works if the pirate decoder shuts down if it is given inputs that it can identify as incorrectly constructed. As a countermeasure, the information provider might intersperse incorrect data into the normal broadcast data to shut down such pirate decoders while the pirates use them. However, this measure has to be applied with caution, because from the point of view of the honest users this could also be the result of an attack on the broadcast channel.

If the pirate decoder is given in software, the information provider has the additional possibility to reset it to its initial state, and this will also be possible with many hardware pirate decoders. This is the model used below. Furthermore, we will assume for simplicity that the pirate decoder always outputs the correct cleartext if it gets correct data, i.e., it does not take measures that might fool an analyzer, but would also disturb the pirate.

Another Approach. An alternative to traitor tracing is presented in [DwLN_96], so-called signets. In these schemes, the information provider does not trace a traitor at all; he need not even find a pirate decoder. Instead, a traitor has to either divulge some private information to the pirates or distribute a fairly large amount of data. However, the same private information must be divulged to the information provider, which makes the model underlying this cryptographically very interesting scheme somewhat doubtful. (The main proposal is to use credit card numbers. This does indeed fit the widespread understanding of credit card numbers as secrets, although they are divulged to hundreds of merchants and on the telephone, but I would prefer to have this understanding changed than utilized further.) One can, however, try to combine those techniques with the following asymmetric ideas, so that the private information can also remain private from the information provider.

1.3 Asymmetric Traitor Tracing

The main purpose of this paper is to introduce *asymmetric traitor tracing*. This is similar to asymmetric fingerprinting, recently introduced in [PfSc_96]. The basic observation is that previous traitor tracing schemes are symmetric in the sense that legitimate users share all their secrets with the information provider. Thus when seemingly redistributed information is found, it could just as well have been produced by the information provider himself, or by dishonest personnel or someone with illegal access to the information provider's equipment, as by a traitor. The result of tracing is therefore no real evidence that could unambiguously convince a third party, just as symmetric message authentication codes do not provide non-repudiation, in contrast to asymmetric digital signature schemes.

The asymmetric traitor tracing schemes introduced here avoid this problem: The information provider, confronted with treachery, obtains information that he could not have produced on his own, and that is therefore real evidence of the treachery.

1.4 Fully Frameproof Symmetric Schemes

Our main contribution to symmetric traitor tracing is to introduce and construct fully frameproof schemes.

In [ChFN_94], there is only one parameter k for collusion sizes, i.e., the maximum number of traitors against which the schemes are secure. More than k traitors can not only redistribute information without being traced, but also *frame* an honest user, i.e., make this user seem a traitor. This seems quite unacceptable, at least if third parties sometimes do believe an accusation by the information provider even though the scheme is only symmetric. At least, framing is far worse than undetected redistribution, which underlies the normal risk management by the information provider. Moreover, the maximum collusion size is quite small in practice because of the performance of the existing constructions; $k = 32$ is mentioned as a realistic example in [ChFN_94]. Thus the traitors might, e.g., be a school class. The definition would even allow them to selectively frame their teacher. (The constructions do not.) One may argue that the class could also claim to have watched their teacher shoplifting, but in that case it is at least clear who is making the accusation, and they can be questioned, whereas in the traitor tracing schemes, they remain anonymous.

Thus we propose that there should be a separate, much larger parameter k_{frame} for the size of collusions that cannot frame. We call a scheme *fully frameproof* if no collusion of traitors can frame another user, i.e., if $k_{frame} = N$, where N is the number of users. Of course, even fully frameproof symmetric schemes do not prevent the information provider from framing a user. They can be seen as an intermediate step between previous symmetric schemes, where small collusions of users can frame someone, and asymmetric schemes, where even arbitrary collusions including the information provider cannot frame anyone.

2 The Chor-Fiat-Naor Schemes

We first sketch the constructions from [ChFN_94], which are the basis of all our constructions.

2.1 Use of Session Keys

Two items are central to all these schemes:

- Each session is encrypted with an ordinary symmetric encryption scheme under a new, randomly generated *session key*. We assume that a symmetric encryption scheme has been fixed.

- Before each session, a so-called *enabling block* is sent. This may happen on a separate signaling channel so that the broadcast transmission is not interrupted. The enabling block contains an encryption of the next session key. This encryption is done in a complicated way that allows traitors to be traced.

Before going into details of this encryption, we can already substantiate two claims made in Section 1.2.

First, we can see that traitors who redistribute session keys instead of their personal keys cannot be traced, because the session key is the same for all.

Secondly, we can see how such traitor tracing schemes can be partitioned into fingerprinting of a key and normal encryption. Fingerprinting normal information, in particular texts and images, means that each user obtains a slightly different copy, where "slightly different" usually primarily means that the difference is not perceptible by humans. The intrinsic meaning is some semantic equivalence or at least similarity of copy and original. With decryption keys, the natural semantic equivalence is the ability to decrypt the same information. Thus we can see the following as fingerprinting a virtual master key that decrypts all the session keys, where the decryption function is also modified by fingerprinting.

2.2 Overview of Key Fingerprinting

We restrict ourselves to the so-called one-level schemes from [ChFN_94]. They have the following common elements, illustrated in Figure 1:

- During provider initialization, the information provider generates l sets of b keys each, where l and b are parameters to be determined later for each individual scheme. (Two necessary conditions are $l > k$ and $b^l > N$; recall that k is the maximum number of traitors and N the number of users.) These keys also belong to the given symmetric encryption scheme. We call each such set a *bucket*. The keys in the i-th bucket are denoted $key_{i,1}, \ldots, key_{i,b}$.

- During user initialization, each user gets one key from each bucket. (The trick is which ones.) We call the indices of these keys the user's *codeword*, i.e., a codeword $(c_1, \ldots, c_l) \in \{1, \ldots, b\}^l$ means that this user has the keys $key_{1,c_1}, \ldots, key_{l,c_l}$.

- Each session key s is the exor (the bitwise exclusive or), of l random values $s_1, \ldots, s_l$. We call them the *shares* of the session key. For all i, the enabling block contains the encryptions of s_i under each key from the i-th bucket. As each user has one key from the i-th bucket, she can decrypt one of these b encryptions of the i-th share, and finally reconstruct the session key.

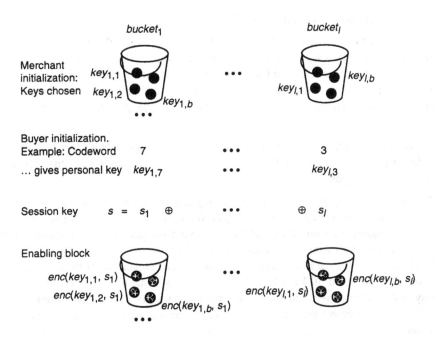

Figure 1   One-level traitor tracing scheme

- The simplified assumption for tracing is that the information provider has opened a pirate decoder and found one key from each bucket. He may find more, of course; then he selects, say, the lexicographically first one.

  If the pirate decoder is only given as a black box with resetting, a procedure of the following type is used to identify the index of one key in bucket i: For $j = 1, \ldots, b - 1$, the information provider makes many trials where the first j shares for this bucket are random and the others correct. For each trial, the decoder is reset to its initial state. If the observed probability of correct decryption for j is smaller than that for $j - 1$ by a certain threshold, the information provider concludes that $key_{i,j}$ is present.

- The idea for tracing is as follows: If up to k traitors had to provide l keys for a pirate decoder, at least one of them must have provided at least l/k keys. The information provider simply looks from which user the largest number of keys is present in the pirate decoder, and calls her a traitor.

For the particular method used to select the users' codewords, it has to be proved that up to k traitors will not succeed in having an honest user traced in this way, except with negligible probability.

In the terminology of information hiding agreed upon at this workshop (even though it is at its limits in this application), the stegomessages are the personal keys; the embedded messages are the identities or immediately the codewords of the users; there is no real covermessage (the totality of the keys in all buckets comes quite close); and the stegokey consists of all the secret choices the information provider makes and stores.

2.3 Codes, Constructive and Non-Secret Schemes

Because of the way the codewords are chosen, the schemes in [ChFN_94] are mostly non-constructive, i.e., existence is proved, but no explicit construction is given. Furthermore, the more efficient schemes are called secret schemes. This sounds bad, but actually, we can get rid of both these undesirable properties without any real change to the schemes. For instance, we can present the "Secret One-Level Scheme" from [ChFN_94, Section 3.3] as follows:

- For each new user, the information provider randomly and independently chooses a codeword from $\{1, ..., b\}^l$ and stores it in a table under this user's identity. The user obtains the corresponding keys.

In [ChFN_94], there is an additional secret mapping from real user identities to other numbers, for which we do not see the need. (A proof of this modified scheme is implicit in Section 3.) Furthermore, Chor, Fiat, and Naor see two disadvantages of such schemes with random codewords over their other, so-called "open" schemes.

The first one is that the honest users' codewords must remain secret from the traitors. However, the full set of all keys from all buckets must remain secret from the traitors anyway, just as almost any cryptographic scheme needs secrets. The scheme would only be "secret" in the undesirable sense if the codewords of the *traitors* had to remain secret from the traitors.

The second disadvantage Chor, Fiat, and Naor see is that there is an error probability, i.e., if the traitors select a codeword among those for which they know the keys, there is sometimes a small chance that this is an honest user's codeword. For this reason, they prefer non-constructive schemes, i.e., schemes of which they only prove existence, where small sets of traitors do not possess a set of keys that would lead to an honest user being traced. However, even in those schemes, the traitors can guess keys they do not possess with a small probability. Thus, it suffices to make the probability of guessing the right codeword equally small as that of guessing the right keys.

In our case, let $X_i = 1$ denote that the traitors guessed the i-th symbol of the honest user's codeword correctly. Thus $p = 1/b$. We want to bound the probability that $S \geq l/k$. If $b \geq 3k$, then

$$Pr(S \geq l/k) = Pr(E \geq 1/k) \leq Pr(E \geq 3/b) < 2^{-l/b}.$$

This is exponentially small, say $\leq 2^{-\sigma}$, if $l \geq \sigma b$, i.e., for instance for

$$b = 3k, l = 3\sigma k. \qquad \Box$$

For security against active attacks in situations where broadcast is not guaranteed to be reliable, one should at least change the personal key of a user if this user has noticed a wrong enabling block three times.

4 Asymmetric Schemes

First we introduce some notation that is needed for asymmetric traitor tracing.

- We distinguish a *tracing* algorithm and a *trial* protocol.

- Tracing is done by the information provider on his own. For the input to tracing, there is again a choice: Either one simply assumes that a pirate decoder has been opened and information of a certain type has been found inside, or one considers the more general scenario where the pirate decoder is a black box that can be used and reset. The result of tracing is either *failed* or the identity of a user and a string *proof*.

- In the trial protocol, the information provider tries to convince an arbitrary third party, called a *judge*, of the traced user being a traitor. For this, the information provider uses the string *proof* from tracing. Furthermore, the judge needs some input reliably linked to the accused user. We call it the *public key* of this user.

    In some schemes, the accused user has to take part in the trial, others do not need this (in the technical sense). We call such trials 2- and 3-party trials, respectively.

- There is a *key distribution* phase, before or during user initialization, where the user has to distribute a public key reliably (at least so that any future judges will use the correct key, and the same one as the information provider). In all our examples, this will be the key of a digital signature scheme, and it can be used for many other purposes besides the traitor tracing scheme.

- User initialization is now a real protocol where the user also sends at least one message to the information provider.

Now we present several example constructions of asymmetric traitor tracing schemes. More precise definitions could be made similar to [PfSc_96].

4.1 A Simple Scheme with Linear-Size Enabling Blocks

The following simple scheme shows that the idea of asymmetric traitor tracing works for any parameters, i.e., any number of users, any collusion-size, and an arbitrarily small error probability. It is also computationally efficient. Nevertheless, it may not fully count as a broadcast encryption scheme, because the size of the enabling block is linear in N, the number of legitimate users of this session. We call this a *linear-size* scheme, and a scheme where the enabling block is polylogarithmic in N a *log-size* scheme.

3   Making Symmetric Schemes Fully Frameproof

In this section, we modify the scheme described in the previous section so that it becomes fully frameproof, as introduced in Section 1.4.

We replace the decision rule in tracing by the following rule:

- Each user from whom at least l/k keys are found in the pirate decoder is called a traitor. If there is no such user, the output of tracing is *failed*.

Thus the new output *failed* denotes the fact that tracing a traitor failed, because there must have been too many traitors. If at least l/k keys from more than one user are present, the information provider can identify any or all of them as traitors.

Lemma 1. *The symmetric traitor tracing scheme described in Section 2 (in particular Section 2.3) with this new decision rule is*

a) *computationally secure for the information provider if there are at most k traitors, and*

b) *fully frameproof with an exponentially small error probability if the parameters l and b are suitably chosen (as long as the broadcast channel is reliable — a precondition that would also be needed with the original secret one-level scheme in [ChFN_94]).*

Proof. The security for the information provider is clear: As before, if up to k traitors have to provide l keys for a pirate decoder, at least one of them must provide at least l/k keys, unless they can find out a key that is not among the personal keys of any of them, which is infeasible if the encryption scheme is secure against known-plaintext attacks.

Now we show that any honest user can only be framed with exponentially small probability. We consider the worst case where all the other users (but not the information provider, because this is a symmetric scheme) collude against her and know all the keys. Recall that the input to the tracing algorithm is one key from each bucket. We can assume without loss of generality that these keys were chosen entirely by the traitors, because the lexicographic selection by the information provider if the pirate decoder contains more keys cannot be worse than a selection by the traitors. Thus, formally the problem is simply: Given the codeword that the traitors have selected, compute the probability that it has at least l/k symbols in common with the honest user's codeword.

The honest user's codeword is chosen randomly and independently, and no information about it becomes known to the traitors. (Here we need the fact that the broadcast channel is reliable, in particular, that honest users only process enabling blocks from the information provider: Otherwise the traitors could send incorrect enabling blocks to the honest user and try to observe at which faults she complains.) The probability that the selected word has l/k symbols in common with a random word can be bounded by using the same version of the Chernoff bound as in [ChFN_94]: Let $X_1, ..., X_l$ be independent binary random variables with $Pr(X_i = 1) = p$. Let S denote their sum and E their average, i.e., $S = X_1 + ... + X_l$ and $E = S/l$. Then, for all $\beta \geq 1$,

$$Pr(E \geq \beta p) < (e^{\beta-1}/\beta^\beta)^{pl}.$$

For $\beta = 3$, this implies

$$Pr(E \geq 3p) < 2^{-pl}.$$

Anyway, this scheme could be the method of choice for applications with a small number of users per session, or even a medium number if the information provider fears a large number of traitors, because the efficiency of this scheme does not depend on k. Furthermore, it is natural in applications where individual users ask for permission to decrypt certain data at different times, so that broadcasting enabling blocks is not so suitable anyway.

The scheme works as follows:

- No provider initialization is needed.

- User initialization. The user generates a key pair of an asymmetric encryption scheme, gives the encryption key to the information provider, and signs that the decryption key corresponding to this encryption key will be used exclusively in the traitor tracing scheme. (Recall that many users will already have a key for signing, and the others carry out the key distribution phase as a preamble to user initialization.) The information provider verifies this signature with the public key of this user.

- Session sending. The enabling block contains the session key, encrypted under each encryption key of a legitimate user of this session. This can be seen as a variant of the previous schemes with only one bucket.

- Tracing. The simpler assumption is that a pirate decoder has been opened and the secret decryption key of a traitor has been found inside. The information provider finds out to which encryption key it belongs; if there is no simple predicate to decide this, he can use the ability to decrypt encrypted random messages. If the pirate decoder is a black box with resetting, he uses the same procedure as in Section 2.2 for the one bucket to find out the index j of a key that must be present.

- Trial. The information provider first shows the judge the accused user's signature about the use of her encryption key, and the judge verifies it. Next, if the information provider has actually found a decryption key, he shows it as a proof, and the judge verifies that the de- and encryption keys belong together in the same way as the information provider did. If the information provider has only found the index of a key, he has to hand the pirate decoder to the judge, who verifies that the observed probability of correct decryption for j is smaller than that for $j - 1$ by a certain threshold (smaller than the information provider's threshold).

Lemma 2. *The asymmetric traitor tracing scheme constructed above is computationally secure.*

Proof sketch. First we consider the case where the information provider actually finds a key. The security for the information provider is clear in this case. The security of honest users, i.e., frameproofness against arbitrary collusions even including the information provider, follows from the security of the encryption scheme: It is infeasible to find out any decryption key that belongs to the encryption key of an honest user, and also to find any other way of decrypting encrypted random messages with a significant probability of success. Note that the honest user in the traitor tracing scheme only uses the decryption key to decrypt session keys, which is within the limits for which an encryption scheme should offer security.

In the black-box case, and with a threshold of at most $1/N$, the information provider will certainly identify an index j. If the size of the thresholds and the number of trials are well adapted, the probability that the observation of the judge is below the smaller threshold should be negligible. The security of the honest users, as in the symmetric case, relies on the fact that it is infeasible to distinguish encryptions of a known share from encryptions of random values from the message space. □

Note that in the black-box case, we have used strong cryptographic properties of the encryption scheme. In particular, it would be insecure with deterministic encryption.

4.2 Schemes with Shorter Enabling Blocks

Now we show an approach to turn a given symmetric scheme whose enabling blocks are shorter than linear in the number of legitimate users into an asymmetric scheme. In this section, we only obtain an instantiation for $k = 1$, like the very first symmetric scheme in [ChFN_94]. In Section 4.3, we present a variation of the construction that allows $k > 1$ at the cost of an error probability that is not exponentially small.

The construction is similar to that of asymmetric fingerprinting in [PfSc_96]. The following assumptions have to be made about the way the users' codewords are chosen in the given symmetric scheme:

1. The input to the tracing algorithm is only the information found in a pirate decoder and the information provider's initial record, i.e., no records from individual user initializations are needed.

2. The identity space is nevertheless large enough to serve as the preimage of a one-way function.

We first show that the scheme for $k = 1$ at the beginning of [ChFN_94, Section 3.1] is of this form: A user's codeword is simply this user's identity. (Note that for $k = 1$, codewords need not be secret, because one traitor alone has no other keys than exactly her own ones to put into a pirate decoder.) The tracing algorithm, upon finding one traitor's personal key, and thus this traitor's codeword, immediately has the identity. The identity space can be made exponentially large, because the scheme is polynomial in the length of the identities.

For the following construction, two cryptographic primitives must be fixed. One is a one-way function f. The other is a protocol for secure 2-party computation. Such a protocol achieves the following goal: Two parties have secret inputs x_1 and x_2, respectively. Both or one of them want to know $g(x_1, x_2)$, where g is a function known to both of them. However, Party 1 should not gain additional information about x_2, nor Party 2 about x_1. A nice example is the millionaires' problem from [Yao_82]: The parties are millionaires, and x_1 and x_2 denote how many millions they own. They want to find out who is richer, but without telling each other x_1 and x_2. Constructions have been given, e.g., in [Yao_86, ChDG_88, GMW_87].

Given the one-way function and the 2-party protocol, the asymmetric traitor tracing scheme is constructed as follows:

• Provider initialization is the same as in the symmetric scheme.

- User initialization works as follows: The user first chooses a random "identity" id_{sym} that remains secret from the information provider. Then the 2-party computation protocol is used for the following secret computation:

  - The user secretly inputs id_{sym} and her secret signing key.

  - The information provider secretly inputs the $l \cdot b$ secret keys from provider initialization and (not necessarily secretly) the user's public test key.

  - The one-way image $f(id_{sym})$ and a signature sig under it (and a suitable explanatory text) with the user's secret key are computed. The signature is internally verified with the test key input by the provider. If it is wrong, e.g., because the user has input an incorrect secret key, the protocol is aborted. Then the codeword and thus the personal key corresponding to id_{sym} are computed.

  - First, $f(id_{sym})$ and sig are output to the information provider, who stores them under the real identity of this user. Secondly, the personal key is output to the user.

- In tracing, the information provider uses the symmetric tracing algorithm (black-box or not) to find out id_{sym}. He applies f to it and compares the result with the stored values $f(id_{sym})$ to find out the real identity of the user who used this id_{sym}.

- In a trial, the information provider uses id_{sym} and sig as a proof. The judge verifies that sig is a signature by the accused user on $f(id_{sym})$ and the explanatory text.

Lemma 3. *Let a secure symmetric traitor tracing scheme fulfilling Conditions 1 and 2, a secure one-way function, and a secure 2-party protocol (in the sense that it can replace a trusted oracle computing the same function) be given. Then the asymmetric traitor tracing scheme constructed above is computationally secure.*

This holds for the same reasons as the security of Construction 1 in [PfSc_96]. We omit a proof sketch, but present a related one in Section 4.3.

As to efficiency, note that the 2-party protocol only has to be carried out once in user initialization and does not affect the transmission of the actual broadcast data. Nevertheless, the scheme is rather theoretical as long as a general 2-party protocol has to be used. One can certainly try to improve the efficiency by exploiting the specific structure of the function computed here; in particular, the selection of the keys is a kind of all-or-nothing disclosure of secrets.

4.3 3-Party Trials for Small Codes

We now consider the case where we cannot fulfil the conditions of Section 4.2 and present schemes that are not fully secure asymmetric schemes, but where an honest user can at least fend off a false accusation with a certain probability, such as $1-2^{-10}$. Such a scheme makes both treachery and false accusations quite risky (under the assumption that false accusations will at least decrease the reputation of the information provider and may even be punished). If the underlying symmetric scheme is fully frameproof, an honest information provider is protected from making false accusations and thus endangering his reputation.

Thus we use the symmetric scheme that was considered in Lemma 1. To be slightly more general, we represent it as follows:

- In provider initialization, the information provider already makes all the random choices that he may need later. This may simply mean generating a sufficiently long string of random bits for later use. The result of provider initialization is still called the initial record, *record* = (*keys*, *code_randomness*), where *keys* is the matrix of all the keys in all the buckets.

- In user initialization, the information provider assigns a number $i \in \{1, ..., N\}$ to the user and computes the user's codeword as *code*(*code_randomness*, *i*), where *code* is a certain globally known, deterministic algorithm.

- The decision rule in tracing remains the same, and we also still presuppose that full frameproofness would be guaranteed even if the traitors could choose their own codewords. (We can omit this last condition by choosing the value *evid* within the 2-party protocol in the construction below.)

In this notation, the scheme where codewords are chosen randomly looks like this: *code_randomness* is a table that assigns a random codeword to each user number $i \in \{1, ..., N\}$, and *code* is the fixed table-lookup function. One can easily see from the proof of Lemma 1 that the last condition holds in this case. In a scheme with a deterministic code, *code_randomness* would be empty, and *code* would be the code in the usual sense.

The idea for constructing an asymmetric scheme from such a symmetric scheme is similar to Section 4.2, but instead of hiding the whole identity computationally, we now hide a few bits information-theoretically. Thus, instead of a one-way function, we use commitments. Commitments are the cryptographic analog of the following protocol: In the *commit* phase, one party puts some bits in a wooden box, locks the box, and sends it to the other party or puts it in a public place. Now the bits are hidden, but they can no longer be changed. In the *reveal* phase, the party hands over the key of the box, so that the recipients can verify what bits the box contains. More technically, the commit phase has two outputs: the commitment, *com*, is an output for both parties, and the committing party additionally obtains a string *reveal_info*, which later enables her to carry out the reveal phase. For several cryptographic realizations, see [BrCC_88]. Among them, we need one where the bits are information-theoretically hidden, whereas the fact that the bits cannot be changed after the commit phase need only hold computationally.

For the asymmetric traitor tracing scheme, the identities of the symmetric scheme are divided into two substrings. The first one will be called the *tracing identity*, the second one the *evidence of treachery*. For instance, $N = 10^9$ was mentioned as realistic in [ChFN_94]. We can use this for 20-bit tracing identities and 10-bit evidence of treachery, which means that about 10^6 users can take part, and that they can fend off false accusations with a probability of about $1 - 10^{-3}$.

As in Section 4.2, each user must have published the public key of a signature scheme, and we need a protocol for secure 2-party computation.

- In user initialization, a user is assigned a tracing identity id_{trace} by the information provider. The user secretly chooses the evidence of treachery, *evid*. Now the 2-party protocol is used:
  - The information provider secretly inputs *record* = (*keys*, *code_randomness*) and (not necessarily secretly) id_{trace} and the public key of this user.
  - The user secretly inputs *evid* and her secret signing key.

- A commitment *com* to *evid* is made, and a signature *sig* on *com* (and a suitable explanatory text) is computed with the user's secret key. The signature is verified with the user's public key. If this fails, the protocol is aborted. Otherwise, the concatenation of id_{trace} and *evid* is called id_{sym}, and the user's codeword *code*(*code_randomness*, id_{sym}) and the corresponding personal key are computed.

- First, the string *reveal_info* needed to open the commitment is output to the user, then *com* and *sig* are output to the information provider, and finally the personal key is output to the user.

- In tracing, the information provider uses the symmetric tracing algorithm (black-box or not) to find a word of indices of keys used. He searches for a codeword, i.e., a value in the range of *code*(*code_randomness*, •), that equals the given word in at least l/k positions. If none is found, the output is *failed*. Otherwise, he splits the corresponding value id_{sym} into id_{trace} and *evid*. He looks up the real identity of the user who was assigned id_{trace} and the corresponding values *com* and *sig*.

- In the trial, the information provider uses the triple (*evid*, *com*, *sig*) as a proof. The judge first verifies that *sig* is a signature on *com* and the appropriate text by the accused user. Intuitively, the information provider's claim is now that *evid* is the content of *com*. To fend off such an accusation, the user has to prove that she can open her commitment in a different way. This can simply be done by showing the real *evid* and *reveal_info*, if the user can never be accused about this commitment again. Otherwise, a zero-knowledge proof has to be used. (This is at least no problem if the reveal phase is non-interactive, which is the case in most realizations.)

Lemma 4. *If the symmetric traitor tracing scheme is fully frameproof and the commitment scheme and the 2-party protocol used are secure (the latter in the sense that it can replace a trusted oracle computing the same function), the asymmetric traitor tracing scheme just constructed is secure, except that the probability that an honest user cannot fend off a wrong accusation is not exponentially small, but of the order $2^{-\sigma}$, where σ is the length of evid.*

Proof sketch. a) First we consider an honest user. Assuming that the 2-party protocol has been replaced by a perfect oracle, the only information about *evid* that becomes known to anybody else is (*com*, *sig*). By the security of the commitment scheme, this means that any accusation has to be based on a random guess at *evid*, which will only be correct with the probability $2^{-\sigma}$. If this guess is wrong, the user can fend off the accusation: The judge in a trial only accepts a value *com* signed by this user with the correct explanatory text, i.e., the information provider has to use the correct commitment, and the user can open it to reveal the correct *evid*. (This is why *reveal_info* had to be output first.)

b) Next we show that even an arbitrary number of traitors cannot trick the information provider into making false accusations, except with exponentially small probability: The traitors have to choose a word to put into the pirate decoder. By the full frameproofness of the symmetric scheme (even if the traitors can choose *evid*, by our preconditions), with very high probability, this word does not have l/k symbols in common with any honest user's word. Thus the information provider will not accuse an honest user.

c) Finally, we show that it is infeasible for at most k traitors to cheat the information provider. As in the symmetric scheme, at least one traitor has to provide at least l/k keys. Thus the word found in tracing has l/k positions in common with the codeword of a traitor.

Furthermore, by Part b) it does not have l/k positions in common with any honest user's codeword (except with negligible probability). Thus the information provider identifies the codeword of a traitor. By the security of the 2-party protocol, the corresponding value id_{sym} = $(id_{trace}, evid)$ was used in user initialization with this traitor, and $evid$ is the content of this traitor's commitment. By the security of the commitment scheme, the traitor cannot prove that she can open the commitment differently, and thus cannot fend off the accusation.　□

5　Summary and Outlook

We have presented improvements to traitor tracing schemes for broadcast encryption, in particular to the possibility of trials based on them.

Primarily, we introduced asymmetric traitor tracing, which allows responsibility for redistributed information to be assigned to one particular person, and we presented example constructions. Only one special case, though, is already efficient enough for practical use. In future work, we will construct more efficient schemes with 2-party trials from the two-level schemes of [ChFN_94] and more general schemes with 3-party trials.

We also presented efficient improvements to symmetric traitor tracing, in particular fully frameproof schemes, where no collusion of users can frame another user as a traitor. Furthermore, we discussed the general restrictions of traitor tracing that must be taken into account when choosing between traitor tracing and fingerprinting of the actual data.

Acknowledgments

I am happy to thank *Matthias Schunter* and *Michael Waidner* for helpful comments on a draft of this paper, and the Isaac Newton Institute in Cambridge for hosting me during a revision.

References

BDHK_93　Carlo Blundo, Alfredo De Santis, Amir Herzberg, Shay Kutten, Ugo Vaccaro, Moti Yung: Perfectly-Secure Key Distribution for Dynamic Conferences; Crypto '92, LNCS 740, Springer-Verlag, Berlin 1993, 471-486.

Berk_91　Shimshon Berkovits: How To Broadcast A Secret; Eurocrypt '91, LNCS 547, Springer-Verlag, Berlin 1991, 535-541.

BlCr_95　Carlo Blundo, Antonella Cresti: Space Requirements for Broadcast Encryption; Eurocrypt '94, LNCS 950, Springer-Verlag, Berlin 1995, 287-298.

BlMP_86　G. R. Blakley, Catherine Meadows, G. B. Purdy: Fingerprinting Long Forgiving Messages; Crypto '85, LNCS 218, Springer-Verlag, Berlin 1986, 180-189.

Blom_80　Rolf Blom: Key Distribution for Broadcast Cryptography; Third International Conference: Security Through Science and Engineering, September 23-26, 1980, Technical University Berlin, 19-23.

BoSh_95　Dan Boneh, James Shaw: Collusion-Secure Fingerprinting for Digital Data; Crypto '95, LNCS 963, Springer-Verlag, Berlin 1995, 452-465.

BrCC_88　Gilles Brassard, David Chaum, Claude Crépeau: Minimum Disclosure Proofs of Knowledge; Journal of Computer and System Sciences 37 (1988) 156-189.

Caro_95　Germano Caronni: Assuring Ownership Rights for Digital Images; Proceedings VIS '95, Vieweg, Wiesbaden 1995, 251-263.

ChDG_88 David Chaum, Ivan B. Damgård, Jeroen van de Graaf: Multiparty computations ensuring privacy of each party's input and correctness of the result; Crypto '87, LNCS 293, Springer-Verlag, Berlin 1988, 87-119.

ChFN_94 Benny Chor, Amos Fiat, Moni Naor: Tracing traitors; Crypto '94, LNCS 839, Springer-Verlag, Berlin 1994, 257-270.

DwLN_96 Cynthia Dwork, Jeffrey Lotspiech, Moni Naor: Digital Signets: Self-Enforcing Protection of Digital Information; to appear at 28th Symposium on Theory of Computing (STOC) 1996; preliminary version received April 1996.

FiNa_94 Amos Fiat, Moni Naor: Broadcast Encryption; Crypto '93, LNCS 773, Springer-Verlag, Berlin 1994, 480-491.

GMW_87 Oded Goldreich, Silvio Micali, Avi Wigderson: How to play any mental game – or – a completeness theorem for protocols with honest majority; 19th Symposium on Theory of Computing (STOC) 1987, ACM, New York 1987, 218-229.

PfSc_96 Birgit Pfitzmann, Matthias Schunter: Asymmetric Fingerprinting; Eurocrypt '96, LNCS 1070, Springer-Verlag, Berlin 1996, 84-95.

Wagn_83 Neal R. Wagner: Fingerprinting; Proceedings 1983 IEEE Symposium on Security and Privacy, April 25-27 1983, Oakland, California, 18-22.

Yao_82 Andrew C. Yao: Protocols for Secure Computations; 23rd Symposium on Foundations of Computer Science (FOCS) 1982, IEEE Computer Society, 1982, 160-164.

Yao_86 Andrew C. Yao: How to Generate and Exchange Secrets; 27th Symposium on Foundations of Computer Science (FOCS) 1986, IEEE Computer Society, 1986, 162-167.

ZhKo_95 Jian Zhao, Eckhard Koch: Embedding Robust Labels Into Images For Copyright Protection; Congress on Intellectual Property Rights for Specialized Information, Knowledge and New Technologies, R. Oldenbourg Verlag, München 1995 (also at http://www.igd.fhg.de/www/igd-a8/pub/EmbedLabel.ps).

Establishing Big Brother Using Covert Channels and Other Covert Techniques

Yvo Desmedt

Department of Electrical Engineering and Computer Science, University of Wisconsin–Milwaukee, WI 53201-0784, U.S.A., e-mail: desmedt@cs.uwm.edu

Abstract. Weiser's vision about computers in the next century is that they will be ubiquitous and in MIT's Media Lab project, called Things That Think, they will be embedded in such objects as shoes, belt buckles, tie clasps, etc. In this paper we explain how covert technology, such as covert channels, covert sensors and covert computing facilitates the set up of Big Brother, for example in a society where computers are ubiquitous. Detecting the absence of covert hardware and covert software is actually undecidable and cryptography alone seems inadequate to protect against the abuse of covert technology, extending the work of Anderson regarding the limitations of cryptography. Also, the use of covert technology to protect copyright can be abused to suppress freedom of expression.

1   Introduction

In September 1995, Fred Guterl reported about MIT's Media Lab project called Things That Think [7] (see also [23]), which is a generalization[1] of ubiquitous computing [24]. The idea is to put sensors and microcomputers in objects, in particular clothes, e.g. in "sneakers, belt buckles, tie clasps, and wristwatches" [7, p. 44]. These chips would communicate among themselves and with sensors. They would for example allow a user to be identified when arriving in the lobby of an hotel, and "the elevator knows which floor to take him to, and the door to his room swings open as if by magic when he approaches" [7, p. 44]. Additionally, [7, p. 44]:

> skiers will get electronic IDs instead of lift tickets. ...sensors around the resort ...will keep track of where visitors are at any given moment and eventually, automatically route telephone calls to the nearest phone ...The devices will communicate with one another through a "body net," a weak electric current sent through the wearer's body, and, via radio, with other computers placed in the "environment"— which means virtually anywhere.

It is clear that the above example is a variant of the Olivetti Cambridge research laboratory employee I.D. card [24], but there are several differences that are

---

[1] It could in fact be viewed as a special case of ubiquitous computing, but Weiser's paper [24] could be viewed as too oriented towards computers with some display capability.

important in our context. The Olivetti Cambridge I.D. is a badge, while MIT's is hidden in clothing as shoes. This implies for example that the Olivetti Cambridge one can easily be removed, while not everybody wants to run around without shoes! Another property of Things That Think which should further be noted is that [23]:

> using batteries or beaming in remote power is frequently unacceptable. We are developing the materials and mechanisms to recover the watts of energy discarded by a person (for example, by walking) and use this to power personal systems.

Our paper has two goals. First to state that the appropriate combination of modern covert (embedded) channels, covert hardware, covert computation, covert sensors, covert computer viruses can be used by Big Brother against society at large. Traditionally the threat of covert (embedding) techniques has focussed on covert communication from man-to-man with computers as potential media (as cover). We will see that machine-to-man communication based on the combination of different covert techniques can pose even larger threats (as a cover). The second goal of our paper is to be a black paper against Things That Think and to a certain extent a black paper against Ubiquitous Computing, by demonstrating that these dramatically facilitate the set up of Big Brother. We will additionally see that cryptographic protection alone is inadequate against such threats. In some sense this adds a new chapter to the work by Anderson who has demonstrated that cryptography is not enough to obtain security [1].

Let us now overview the organization of this paper. Several known and not so well-known technologies that allow one to hide information are overviewed in Section 2. In Section 3 we discuss how Big Brother could use covert technology to achieve covert identification of a fraction of the population and/or how to monitor their behavior. This fraction will increase depending on how popular Things That Think get to be. We also discuss how techniques to copyright digital objects may be used by Big Brother to suppress freedom of expression. We conclude in Section 4.

2 Covert techniques

In this section we overview known and not so well-known covert (embedding) techniques. The classical methods to hide information through covert channels [12], e.g., by timing channels, are only one of many other techniques to hide information. The most classical ones, but now outdated in a digital age, are invisible inks. Traditionally covert channels have been studied within a multilevel computer [8, 16] but covert channels are also possible between computers. For example, computer viruses have been suggested for hiding communication [25], since a "well" designed virus must have covert properties to avoid detection. In general, covert transmission can be between two devices, and techniques ranging from well known electrical engineering principles to advanced mathematics can be used. Of the last approach Simmons' subliminal channel technique [19, 21, 20] is an illustration.

Not only can information be hidden but also the processing of information and this might have worse consequences to society. This can occur on a software or a hardware level. On a hardware level a chip may have been designed purposely to perform differently (on occasion or on demand) than specified in the specifications of the chip (see, e.g., [5]). Although it may seem easy to detect that the hardware is different than the specified one, the problem is actually undecidable [9, p. 281]. On a software level one speaks about covert computation, which is a computation of which the legitimate users/owners of an unmodified computer are unaware (see, e.g. [17, 13, 25]). Clearly it is undecidable as well to detect whether a program is free of covert computation. The effects of covert hardware and covert software are similar, but a covert computation on a hardware level affects moreover non-programmable chips. In both, the covert processing capability could have been planned by the designer of the hardware/software or could have been installed by a third party, using for example a computer virus only targeting the CAD program/operating system used to develop the chip/software [5]. The result of this covert processing can be transmitted to its intended destination encrypted and/or using covert channels.

Covert hardware is not only important in the context of computation, but also in the context of covert sensors. Is the hardware able to perform the role of a sensor when it should not, or is the hardware able to perform a non-specified sensor function which it should not? An illustration of covert sensors is given in Section 3.

3 Covert identification

We discuss three methods in which covert techniques can be used to covertly identify a certain part of the population and/or to monitor their behavior.

First, any technique using covert channels to copyright digital objects may be used to covertly trace the author or distributor of a document, e.g. in some country where there is no free press. To realize this, the program that prints the data could run a covert subroutine (see Section 2) that covertly inserts the login name (or full identification if possible) of the person who prints the data. Clearly, a higher resolution of the printout (nowadays 600 dpi printers are quite common) induces a higher bandwidth of the potential covert channel [11]. A variant scenario to accomplish covert identification relies on the fact that data itself is often a program and that programs can be fingerprinted to protect copyright. Postscript data, latex files, etc., are such illustrations. Moreover such data is often converted from one format to another. The editor, the text-processor, the data converter, the e-mail program, etc. can all be used to covertly fingerprint the data to identify the author of documents which are supposed to be anonymous. (Clearly, encryption techniques should be used to prevent the name of the author to be readable in the clear.)

The next two methods are related to the ideas of Things That Think and ubiquitous computing. As Weiser pointed out [24, p. 94] writing is ubiquitous, *e.g.*, in "books, magazines, newspapers, ..., street signs, billboards, shop signs ...." He predicts that next century computers will be too. In this context, we can indeed envision that in the future books will have a chip embedded in the cover to give the buyer access to a private multimedia environment while maintaining copyright, in a similar way as chipcards do today. To interact with their environment, communication equipment, such as an antenna[2], will be in the cover of the book. Suppose that an agency wants to find out, secretly, who buys books about a topic considered of interest to national security. Covert hardware could be used to reach this goal to a certain extent. The Global Positioning System (GPS) [18] allows pinpointing one's location with an accuracy of a few meters. Since the aforementioned hardware has an antenna built-in, it may be used[3] to obtain the positioning of the book on earth and the covert hardware would compute the location. So the antenna and the covert hardware become a covert sensor. The positioning information may be covertly transmitted when the book is used in its multimedia context. This may enable one to trace the location of the owner. Observe that in countries where one has to register where one lives, this identifies the owner of the book. In several European countries this mandatory registration is enforced in several ways. (The use of GPS to identify oneself purposely was proposed in [3].)

Our next illustration is similar to the last one. Instead of using chips embedded in the cover of a book, we use the Things That Think scenario in which chips are in sneakers, belt buckles, tie clasps, etc. We also use the GPS system in this example and if enough chips are at fixed locations in the "environment" a higher accuracy can be achieved than with normal GPS and the need to rely on GPS can be diminished. It should be noted that a global positioning (with a precision of 2 meters) only requires 6 bytes, as one can easily verify. This means that it only takes roughly 1.5 Gbytes to store the global positioning of the whole U.S. population (approximately 250 million) while an inexpensive 8 mm "videotape" can store (roughly) 5Gbytes. If one is not interested in recording such travel as commuting between home and work, but only to track who travels further away and to where, and who approaches sensitive locations which may be targets for terrorist activities or places where one can buy material to make bombs, etc., then the data can easily[4] be compressed significantly. The things-that-think need communication equipment, as mentioned in Section 1. So they could covertly sensor the positioning of its bearer, as explained in the previous

---

[2] For example, flexible antennas that have the thickness of paper and are used to protect medium priced merchandise against theft in shops, can easily fit in a fraction of the cover of a book.

[3] The design should take into account that antennas do not capture all frequencies equally and that antennas have been designed that are able to capture several frequencies simultaneously.

[4] One could question whether such gigantic amount of data could easily be processed. However, one should know that several laboratories in the world have computers each having several Gbytes of RAM, so that the task is rather easy.

example and covertly transmit it to the computers in the "environment". These send the data to their intended destination and/or could replace the need to rely on GPS. If the things-that-think know the identity of its bearer (as in the examples we overviewed in Section 1), the identification is straightforward, otherwise it might be deduced when correlating the data with other databases.

Even if one travels to remote locations that do not have an abundance of ubiquitous computers, at regular time intervals the things-that-think could store the exact positioning of the bearer under compressed form and transmit this at a later time. It is clear that the sooner a high bandwidth network is installed and the more omnipresent computers become, the more frequently the global positioning of persons can be updated. This then facilitates the more detailed monitoring of individuals. Traffic monitoring which nowadays mainly monitors who communicates electronically with whom can then be extended to its full power.

The scenario worsens if one takes into consideration that modern technology replaces after a while — when it is no longer an expensive exclusivity — the old and the old technology is no longer produced, even if the new has several disadvantages. Indeed, the reliable and powerful Saturn V rocket (which placed a man on the moon, i.e. roughly 380,000 kilometers from earth) was replaced by the more expensive Space Shuttle (which can only travel to a few hundred kilometers from earth [6]). Also, commercial vacuum tube based radio sets are no longer produced, even though these are more resistant against EMP [14, 22] than the transistor based ones. So, if ubiquitous computing and Things That Think become more popular they will replace old technology such that it will be inevitable to wear clothing with chips, which may enable covert identification.

We remark that the authors of Things That Think [23] are *somewhat* aware of privacy related issues:

> As more and more things develop a sense of identity, it will be important to define standards for thingness ... The issue of standards is connected to the many cryptographic questions associated with guaranteeing privacy, security, and authenticity for communications and commerce.

Modern cryptography is not able to solve the several issues related to covert technology such as covert hardware and covert computation. Moreover, not any type of cryptosystem provides the desired privacy. If no freshness is used and if the monitoring agency is willing to give up accuracy, then the encrypted data will leak whether a person is traveling away from home or not, and how often a person travels to a certain (but unknown) destination. Moreover, even if cryptography would protect the privacy one can wonder whether the cryptographic protection will be escrowed [2, 15, 4], covertly-escrowed, or escrow-free?

4   Conclusion

We conclude by saying that modern chips are much too powerful and have so many transistors (several million [10, p. 61] nowadays) that using them in an ubiquitous way may pose an extreme danger to society, in particular it makes Orwell's 1984 Big Brother scenario technologically feasible in the next century. One should definitely restrict the use of chips in such articles as sneakers, belt buckles, tie clasps, books, magazines, newspapers, street signs, billboards, shop signs, etc. and if an item contains a chip, it should be clearly labeled. The question as to how one can guarantee that the few chips being used do not have covert technology, is not easy to answer. The development of covert technology to protect the right of individuals, such as copyright, may backfire and be used against individuals.

Acknowledgement

The author thanks Jean-Jacques Quisquater (University of Louvain) for having informed the author, before the author was working on subliminal channels, about the technology of flexible antenna and to point out that these fit into a cover of a book. The author also thanks him, Mike Burmester (University of London), Toshiya Itoh (Tokyo Institute of Technology), Kouichi Sakurai (Kyushu University), Gus Simmons, and Moti Yung (IBM) for several discussions about covert channels. He also thanks Moti Yung for pointing out the work of Mark Weiser.

References

1. Anderson, R.: Why cryptosystems fail. In Proceedings of the 1st ACM Conference on Computer and Communications Security (November 3–5, 1993) pp. 215–227
2. Beth, T.: Zur Sicherheit der Informationstechnik. Informatik-Spektrum 13 (1990) 204–215
3. Beth, T., Desmedt, Y.: Identification tokens — or: Solving the chess grandmaster problem. In Advances in Cryptology — Crypto '90, Proceedings (Lecture Notes in Computer Science 537) (1991) A. J. Menezes and S. A. Vanstone, Eds. Springer-Verlag pp. 169–176
4. A proposed federal information processing standard for an escrowed encryption standard (EES). Federal Register July 30, 1993
5. Desmedt, Y.: Is there an ultimate use of cryptography? In Advances in Cryptology, Proc. of Crypto '86 (Lecture Notes in Computer Science 263) (1987) A. Odlyzko, Ed. Springer-Verlag pp. 459–463
6. Encyclopedia of science & technology. McGraw-Hill New York 1992
7. Guterl, F.: Personal tech: Reinventing the PC. Discover 16 (1995) 42–47
8. Haigh, J. T., Kemmerer, R., McHugh, J., Young, W. D.: An experience using two covert channel analysis techniques on a real system design. IEEE Transactions on Software Engineering SE-13 (1987) 157–168
9. Hopcroft, J. E., Ullman, J. D.: Introduction to automata theory, languages, and computation. Addison-Wesley Reading, MA 1979
10. Hutcheson, G. D., Hutcheson, J. D.: Technology and economics in the semiconductor industry. Scientific American 274 (1996) 54–62
11. Kurak, C., McHugh, J.: A cautionary note on image downgrading. In Proceedings of the 8th Computer Security Applications Conference (December 1992)

12. Lampson, B. W.: A note on the confinement problem. Comm. ACM **16** (1973) 613–615

13. Lenstra, A. K., Manasse, M. S.: Factoring by electronic mail. In Advances in Cryptology, Proc. of Eurocrypt '89 (Lecture Notes in Computer Science 434) (1990) J.-J. Quisquater and J. Vandewalle, Eds. Springer-Verlag pp. 355–371

14. Lerner, E. J.: Electromagnetic pulses: potential crippler. IEEE Spectrum **18** (1981) 41–46

15. Micali, S.: Fair public-key cryptosystems. In Advances in Cryptology — Crypto '92, Proceedings (Lecture Notes in Computer Science 740) (1993) E. F. Brickell, Ed. Springer-Verlag pp. 113–138

16. Poras, P. A., Kemmerer, R. A.: Covert flow trees: a technique for identifying and analyzing covert storage channels. In Proc. of the 1991 IEEE Symposium on Security and Privacy (May 1991) IEEE Computer Society Press pp. 36–51

17. Quisquater, J.-J., Desmedt, Y. G.: Chinese lotto as an exhaustive code-breaking machine. Computer **24** (1991) 14–22

18. Ramsey, N. F.: Precise measurement of time. American Scientist **76** (1988) 42–49

19. Simmons, G. J.: The prisoners' problem and the subliminal channel. In Advances in Cryptology. Proc. of Crypto 83 (1984) D. Chaum, Ed. Plenum Press N.Y. pp. 51–67

20. Simmons, G. J.: Subliminal channels; past and present. European Trans. on Telecommunications **5** (1994) 459–473

21. Simmons, G. J.: Subliminal communication is easy using the DSA. In Advances in Cryptology — Eurocrypt '93, Proceedings (Lecture Notes in Computer Science 765) (1994) T. Helleseth, Ed. Springer-Verlag pp. 218–232

22. Teller, E.: Electromagnetic pulses from nuclear explosions. IEEE Spectrum (1982) 65

23. The TTT vision. http://ttt.www.media.mit.edu/vision.html

24. Weiser, M.: The computer for the 21st century. Scientific American **265** (1991) 94–104

25. White, S. R.: Covert distributed processing with computer viruses. In Advances in Cryptology — Crypto '89, Proceedings (Lecture Notes in Computer Science 435) (1990) G. Brassard, Ed. Springer-Verlag pp. 616–619

Covert Channels—A Context-Based View

Catherine Meadows and Ira S. Moskowitz

Information Technology Division, Mail Code 5543
Center for High Assurance Computer Systems
Naval Research Laboratory
Washington, DC 20375
USA

Abstract. In this paper we introduce a taxonomy of covert channels that is based on the context in which the covert channel occurs. This differs from the usual taxonomies, which are based upon the mechanisms employed by the covert channel. Our goal is to use a context-based taxonomy to aid in the understanding of the tradeoffs that are involved in building a secure system.

1 Introduction

Systems that process information at different sensitivity levels require a high degree of assurance. Since it is not practical to require this assurance of the system as a whole, the most commonly recommended practice is to task a small portion of the system with maintaining separation of sensitivity levels, while the remainder of the system requires a much lower level of assurance. Such separation is usually achieved by assigning untrusted portions of the system a sensitivity level, and allowing a component (which could be anything from a process to local-area network, depending upon the architecture) to only read data at its level or below, and to only write data at its level or above. However, concentrating the security responsibilities in one portion of the system introduces other risks. Suppose that an untrusted component operating at a high level H is able to affect the system in a way visible to a component operating at a lower or incomparable level L. The H component may be able to take advantage of this fact to construct a communication channel with the L component by which H data is encoded and passed along to the L component. Since both the H and L component are low-assurance, it is conceivable that Trojan horse code could have been inserted into both components to pass along information in this way. Such an illicit communication channel is known as a *covert channel*. Covert channels were first discovered by Lampson [Lam73] and have been the subject of much study ever since.

An extensive literature now exists on covert channels. Briefly, it can be divided into three parts: work on detecting covert channels, work on measuring them, and work on constructing countermeasures. What is lacking, however, is a general understanding of how and when these countermeasures should be used. There may be a number of ways of handling a covert channel. Some will eliminate the channel completely, but at a possible performance cost. Some will give better performance, but only decrease the *size* (this includes such metrics as Shannon's channel *capacity* and the *small message criterion* [MK94]) of the channel instead of eliminating it. [1] Even for two solutions that provide the same level of security, there may be tradeoffs between other aspects of system performance. Thus, in order to understand how best to mitigate the effects of a covert channel, it is necessary to understand its place in the system as whole. The intent of this paper is to provide assistance in doing so.

We propose a new taxonomy of covert channels in which covert channels are classified, not according to the *mechanisms they employ*, but according to the *context in which they occur*. Techniques for identifying and closing covert channels usually concentrate on examining a system at a very low level of abstraction. This makes sense, since covert channels occur in the parts of a system that the higher level specifications fail to describe or account for. However, when we are attempting to identify tradeoffs between covert channel capacities and other system requirements such as timeliness or reliability, such a low-level view may become inconvenient. This is because the way in which the covert channel is handled may affect these other system requirements. Covert channels usually arise in the context of necessary communication between system entities. For example, a common source of covert channels is the sharing of system resources such as memory between entities at different sensitivity levels. Entities need to be told whether or not the resource is available, but a high entity can use this fact to signal information to a low entity by periodically making the resource unavailable. Common solutions to this problem involve either partitioning the resource, and thus not allowing it to be used at its full capacity, or adding noise to the covert channel by making the resource unavailable from time to time. Clearly, if the low entity does not need a large amount of resources, but does need to have at least some resources always available, then the first approach is better. For example, say that the low entity needs to write an audit-log of failed transactions. The high entity also must write its failed transactions into an audit-log. If this audit-log is a shared file we have the obvious covert channel problems. Assuming that transactions failures are sparse, we simply dedicate a static allocation of the disk for the low audit-log. We further assume that the system administrator always reads data out of the low audit-log before this file can fill. Thus, we have eliminated the covert channel without affecting system functionality. If the low entity transaction failures are in fact large and numerous then this method would not work. Therefore, the context in which this covert channel appears is extremely important. Knowing the mechanisms by which this covert channel operates may suffice for analyzing its size, but it does not suffice for analyzing covert channel counter-measures.

In light of this it is necessary to take a step backwards and examine how the covert channel functions as part of the system as a whole. Does it occur as a part of some operation whose timeliness is of primary importance, or does it occur

---

[1] Note that techniques for reducing capacity usually take care of the small message criterion concerns also. Therefore, size can usually be taken as being synonymous with capacity.

as part of some operation that is necessary to ensure the system's reliability? In cases such as these, it is necessary to understand not only the covert channel itself, but the *context* in which the covert channel occurs. Therefore, in this paper we set forth a taxonomy of covert channels in terms of the context in which they occur, in particular, in terms of the kinds of services being provided in which the covert channel appears. We use our taxonomy to assist in placing covert channels in their proper contextual environment. We further use to this to create *enabling diagrams* which give a visual aid in the identification of covert channels based on their context, methods for mitigating the covert channels, and assistance in assessing the effects upon system performance/functionality.

As an example of the kind of problem we are dealing with, consider the covert channel described by Gasser in [Gas88, section 7.2.1] in which names and attributes of files stored at a high sensitivity level are not protected by mandatory access control, and thus can be read by processes operating at a low sensitivity level. This can clearly lead to a covert channel (as well as a potential overt channel!), since untrusted processes operating at a high sensitivity level have the ability to create and modify such attributes. But the way in which the covert channel is handled will depend upon the context in which the covert channel occurs. A number of possibilities present themselves, including the following:

1. The attributes are access control lists (ACLs), and a file at a given sensitivity level can only be created or modified by a process at that sensitivity level (that is, no write-ups). In this case, low security processes have no way of accessing the files either by reading or creating them, and so the access control lists are of no use to them. Thus the names and ACLs can be protected by mandatory access controls with no negative impact on the system.

2. The attributes are again access control lists, but a file at a given sensitivity level can be created or modified by a process at that level or below (that is, write-ups are allowed). There are several possible options here. First, the ACLs can protected by mandatory access controls and the low processes not told whether or not the write-up succeeded. Secondly, the ACLs can be protected by mandatory access controls, but a low process can be told that a write-up failed because the ACL did not give it permission to perform it. Thirdly, the ACL can remain unprotected. The first choice eliminates the covert channel, but at a potential cost to correct system performance, since if the write-up failed, the low process will not be informed. The third choice gives the best performance, but does nothing about the covert channel. The second choice can be seen as a tradeoff. The low process can determine whether or not a write-up is possible, but only by attempting to perform one. Since the low process is given information from an entity created by the high process, the covert channel is not eliminated, but it is transformed into a covert channel which can be more easily audited, since the only way the covert channel can be exploited is through repeated attempts at write-ups, which should be possible to flag.

3. The files are messages that will be encrypted and sent over an untrusted network, and the attributes are the addresses to which the files will be sent

once they are encrypted. In this case, the low process that will manage the sending of the encrypted messages needs to see the attributes in order to perform the service of sending the encrypted messages. In this case it is not possible to reduce the size of the covert channel by hiding the attributes from the low process.

4. The file attributes are file sizes. The low processes use the attributes to determine how much available memory is left in the system. The capacity of this covert channel can be reduced by releasing only an approximation of the sum of the file sizes instead of individual sizes. By using the sum instead of the individual sizes we have reduced the number of available output symbols in the covert channel and, by using an approximation of the size, we have introduced extra noise into the covert channel. The covert channel can be eliminated altogether by partitioning memory so that each sensitivity level is allocated a fixed amount, thus allowing the attributes to be protected by mandatory access controls. Knowledge of the context in which the covert channel appears can give us the proper guidance in mitigating the covert channel threat.

As we have noted knowledge of the mechanisms used by a covert channel, when taken by itself, is not enough to provide guidance as to the best techniques for handling it. One also needs to know the context in which the covert channel occurs. This is why we have proposed a new taxonomy of covert channels in which covert channels are classified, not according to the mechanisms they employ, as in the popular storage/timing channel categorizations originally proposed by Lampson [Lam73], but according to the context in which they occur. This taxonomy can be used to help the system designer decide which of the available techniques for reducing or avoiding covert channels will have the least adverse impact on system performance/functionality.

The philosophy behind our taxonomy is that covert channels arise as a result of the communication that takes place when one part of the system supplies a service to another part. Loosely speaking, we say that A *provides a service* to B if, by the result of some action of A, B is assisted in performing some operation. Thus, we classify covert channels in terms of the nature of the service provided. Once we have done this, we can figure which means of handling the covert channel will provide the least interference with that form of service.

2   The Taxonomy

2.1   Definitions

We begin by dividing a system into *entities*, which loosely correspond to objects in object-oriented modelling. An entity may have a number of *operations* associated with it. We do not attempt to give a precise definition of either an entity or operation, except to say that an entity must in some sense form a coherent whole, and to note that the result of an entity's performing an operation should result in the modification of some entity or entities in the system. An entity may be capable of modifying itself.

An entity can only perform the operations that are explicitly associated with it. Thus the notion of operation does not extend to cover any actions that might occur as the result of Trojan horse code included in the entity. However, the Trojan horse code could take advantage of the operations that are available to the entity to exploit a covert channel.

Entities may or may not be protected by the mandatory access control policy. If an entity is so protected, we assume either it exists at a single sensitivity level or that the entity is multilevel. If the entity is multilevel, we assume that it is trusted to obey the security policy, and we do not consider any covert channels that originate within the entity. If we wish to do so, we must break the entity into subentities.

We must not assume, however, that entities correspond to the subjects and objects in the Bell-LaPadula model [BL76]. Some entities may be of this form, but an entity may also be of a much coarser granularity. For example, it may be an untrusted system-high node in a network, or a collection of subjects and objects at the same sensitivity level.

Definition 1. We say that (A,F) is an *entity-operation pair* if F is an operation associated with entity A.

Entities supply services to each other. We define this more precisely as follows:

Definition 2. Let (A,G) and (B,F) be two entity-operation pairs. If B cannot perform F unless A performs G, we say (A,G) *enables* (B,F). If it is only sometimes the case that B cannot perform F unless A performs G, we say (A,G) *partially enables* (B,F). In either instance, we say that A *provides the service* G to B.

If (A,G) enables (B,F) we use the notation $(A,G) \rightarrow (B,F)$. If (A,G) partially enables (B,F) we use the notation (A,G) - - $\rightarrow$ (B,F). Note that we do not require that A perform G before B performs F; the execution can be concurrent. However, B should not be able to perform F before A performs G.

We are now ready to start writing about covert channels.

Definition 3. We say that a covert channel occurs in the context of an entity-operation pair (A,G) if eliminating A's ability to perform the operation G would eliminate the covert channel.

Since an operation may enable more than one entity-operation pair, a covert channel occurring in the context of that pair will likewise occur in the context of more than one pair. Thus we will need to examine each service in whose context the covert channel occurs when we attempt to figure out the best way to handle the covert channel.

To give an example, consider the classic secure reader-writer problem [RK79]. There are three entities, a low file, a low writer entity A, and a high reader entity B. In the traditional accounts of this covert channel the only operations considered are A's writing, B's reading, and the making of the file available for reading and writing. But, since we are approaching these problems from the point of view of the context in which they occur, we need to consider the context in which the reader-writer problem may occur. What services are being providing here? Presumably, A is writing the file so B can read it, and B will need to use the information A writes in some way. Thus we need to consider the operation or operations that define B's use of this data. There are thus four entity-operation pairs: (A,write_file), (B,read_file), (file,make_available), and (B,use_Adata), where the last describes whatever use B makes of the information A writes. Clearly, (file,make_available) enables (A,write_file) and (B,read_file). Moreover, (A,write_file) and (B,read_file) both enable (B,use_Adata).

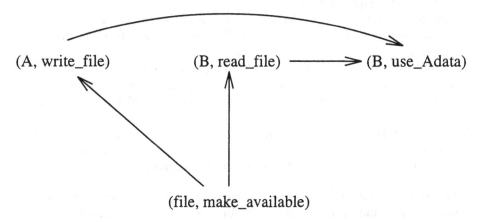

Figure 1: Secure Reader-Writer Problem

The covert channel arises in the following way: the entities cannot be reading and writing the file at the same time. Thus, there is a potential covert channel, since the operation that informs A of the availability of the file may give information about B's activities. Note that the covert channel thus occurs in the context of the three entity-operation pairs (A,write_file), (B,read_file), and (file,make_available). There are a number of ways of closing this covert channel or limiting its size. One is to always give the priority to the low write. Another is to keep one or more old copies of of the file around so that the high entity is always able to read at least one version of the file. Both have been well documented in the literature [AJJ92, KTS93, MJ93].

However, the way in which we handle the covert channel will depend mostly on the nature of the entity-operation pair (B,use_Adata), not on the other three pairs. If it is important that B sees everything that A writes, as may be true for audit data, then we may choose the option of keeping around old copies of the file. On the other hand, if it is important that B only sees the most up-to-date information, then we may choose the option of allowing B to see the actual file A writes to at the cost of possibly denying B access from time to time. Thus, we see that one cannot make a blanket statement about how to minimize information leakage from the secure reader-writer problem without understanding the context in which the covert channel appears. In order to understand how to handle the covert channel, we need to look at all operations enabled by the interaction between A, B, and the file and see how they would be affected.

2.2 Outline of the Taxonomy

We are now ready to give an outline of the taxonomy. This is presented as follows.

I. High-to-low service covert channels. These occur in the context of an entity-operation pair (A,F) where A is providing the service F to to an entity B, and A is at a higher sensitivity level than B.

II. Low-to-high service covert channels. These occur in the context of an entity-operation pair (A,F) where A is providing the service F to to an entity B, and A is at a lower sensitivity level than B.

III. Shared service covert channels. These occur in the context of an entity providing a service or services to two entities at different sensitivity levels. The entity providing the service may or may not be assigned a sensitivity level itself.

IV. Incomparable service covert channels. These occur in the context of an entity-operation pair (A,F) where A is providing the service F to to an entity B where the sensitivity levels of A and B are incomparable.

We note that *we* have yet to come across an example of an incomparable service channel, and it is included only for the sake of completeness. In the remainder of the paper, we will restrict ourselves to the discussion of the first three types of covert channels.

A given application can cause covert channels of more than one type to arise. Consider the example where a low entity A is attempting to send information to a high entity B by writing it to a file. This gives rise to the secure reader-writer problem, which is an example of a shared service channel, since it arises from the sharing of the file between A and B. However, suppose that it is important that B read everything that A writes. If the file becomes full and A needs to erase data so that it can write new data, how can it be assured that B has read the old data without opening a covert channel (see the discussions of the full buffer channel in [KM93, McD94])? This second covert channel is an example of a low-to-high service channel, since it occurs in the context of A supplying a service to B. As we have seen in the previous section, the choice we make for closing or limiting a covert channel can have an effect on how other services are provided, so it is important to consider both of these together.

One advantage of this taxonomy is that covert channels belonging to a particular class can be handled in similar ways. There are a number of different techniques in the literature for handling shared service channels. High-to-low channels generally involve the downgrading of data, so we can use the various techniques that have been developed for secure downgrading to handle some of these. Low-to-high channels usually arise in the context of the low entity's providing a reliable service to the high one, and so we can use techniques for handling covert channels that arise in this context to those. Once we have identified the various covert channels that arise as a result of a given situation, we can identify the type of each covert channel in the taxonomy, choose the relevant set of solutions, and then look at the covert channels in the context of the services provided and their interactions to choose the subset of each set of solutions that is appropriate for the application.

We can classify the various cases of the file attribute example discussed in the introduction according to our taxonomy as follows. The first access control list example involves no services; it can thus be eliminated without adversely affecting the system. The second access control list example is a case of a low-to-high service channel. The low entities are providing information to the high part of the system by writing up. The third example, the message header case, is a little harder to figure out. It appears at first to be a high-to-low service channel, since information about the message is being supplied to low entities so that they can perform the operation of sending the message. But the ultimate result of sending the message will be that it will be decrypted and read by some high entity. Thus we may also think of the message header channel as a low-to-high service channel. The information must be made available to the low entities in order that they may better supply the service of enabling messages to be sent between high entities.

Finally, the file size case is an example of both a high-to-low service channel and a shared service channel. It is a high-to-low service channel because the high security part of the system is performing a service to the low part by releasing the file sizes, and it is a shared service channel because it arises out of the fact that high and low entities are sharing the same memory resources. This allows us to tackle the covert channel either by controlling access to the resources themselves, or controlling information about the resources.

In the next three sections, we discuss the first three types of covert channels, and describe the various techniques that have been developed for each type. We then give an example of a system in which all three types of covert channels occur, and show how our taxonomy and analysis methodology applies.

2.3 Shared Service Channels

A shared service covert channel arises when an entity provides a service or services to entities at different sensitivity levels. Usually the supplying of the service to the high entity has an effect on the ability of the service-supplying entity to supply the service to the low entity. If that effect is visible to the low entity, we have a covert channel.

All covert channels have shared service aspects. Indeed, many techniques for detection of covert channels depend upon the identification of shared resources [Kem83]. Most techniques for closing or limiting the size of a covert channel depend upon making the resource less available. In this section we list some of the various techniques that have used for doing so.

Adding Noise to the Channel by Resource Exhaustion One way to lower the size of a shared service channel is to make the resource, or portions of it, unavailable from time to time. Since the low entity cannot tell what caused a resource to become unavailable, this has the result of reducing the size of the covert channel. This also has the side effect of making the resource less available.

Partitioning Another technique is to partition the resource, either by making the resource available to different levels at different times, or by making different portions of the resource available to different levels. This generally has a negative impact on system performance. However, a technique, called *probabilistic partitioning* [Gra93], allows one to trade off performance against capacity by using partitioning only at designated time intervals that are randomly determined.

Granting Priorities to Low Sensitivity Levels Still another technique, that can be used only when the sensitivity classes of the entities contending for the resource are always comparable, is to always give priority to the entity with the lower sensitivity label. This is the situation that arises when entities are contending for the right to read or write a data item. In such a case, more than one read can be going on at the same time, but not more than one write, and not both a read and a write. Since in many cases data can only be read by entities whose sensitivity dominates the level of that piece of data and written by entities whose level is equal to the level of that data, one can prevent a covert channel by always giving the low write priority. How this can be done is described by Reed and Kanodia in [RK79]. Their work has been extended to concurrency control in a database management context by McDermott and Jajodia in [MJ93].

Fuzzy Time Finally, we note that most shared service channels require a clock of some sort. Thus, another way of limiting capacity is to make clocks less available or reliable [Hu92]. Studies of the effectiveness of this approach have been performed by Gray [Gra93] and Trostle [Tro93].

2.4   High-to-low service channels

As discussed, a covert channel is a *high-to-low service channel* if it arises in the context of a portion of the system operating at a high sensitivity level providing a service to a portion operating at a low sensitivity level. Many of these cases arise when data that was classified at a high level is deemed to be no longer sensitive (either as a result of sanitization or passage of time) or to have been inappropriately classified, and is downgraded. In the interval between the time the data was entered and the time it was downgraded, it may have been possible for a Trojan horse in the high part of the system to have encoded other sensitive data in the data to be downgraded. Sensitive information may also be encoded in the rate at which the data is released, or possibly in replication of downgraded data.

One approach to such covert channels has been to have humans review all data to be downgraded. However, in today's systems, in which large amounts of very complex data may be handled and stored, such an approach has been shown to be no longer adequate. In [KM92] Kurak and McHugh have shown that, when the data items to be downgraded are large and complex, such as is the case for most digital images, it is possible to transmit information at an extremely fast rate in a way that is undetectable by a human reviewing the data to be downgraded.

In some cases, this may not be as serious a threat as it appears. Although high-to-low service channels can transmit a large amount of data, the operation used, downgrading, is relatively simple, and the main thing that needs to be checked is that the data to be downgraded was not changed in any unauthorized way. If the data was not supposed to be changed at all while it was in the system, this can be done fairly straightforwardly by taking a cryptographic checksum over it at the point at which it is entered, and verifying the checksum at the point at which it is downgraded.

An example of the application of such a technique is the case in which data is passed through a network containing low and high untrusted nodes. If a high node is used to forward a message from one low node to another, a Trojan horse might encode high data into the message when it is in the high-sensitivity node. This can be prevented by having a cryptographic checksum taken over the message at the point it enters the high node, and by having the checksum verified when the message leaves the high node.

Such an approach does not eliminate the covert channel. Information may still be encoded in the rate and in variations of the rate in which the downgraded information is produced, in replication and sequencing of information, and so forth. However, the use of replication and sequencing can be audited, and the size of the timing channel can be reduced by adding arbitrary delays. Adding noise to or auditing covert channels hidden in messages is much more difficult.

When the data may be changed within the system, or was originated within the system, the task is harder. Checksums may be used to ensure that data is not changed except when it is supposed to be changed, but it is difficult to ensure that, when data are changed, they are only changed in the manner intended. For this case we can consider the problem still unsolved, and thus one may still have to rely on human review, inadequate as it is in many cases.

2.5 Low-to-High Service Channels

Low-to-High service channels occur when a portion of the system operating at a low sensitivity level provides a service to a portion operating at a high sensitivity level. Such covert channels are more subtle than high-to-low channels, but their size can still be high. Information can be passed in a low-to-high channel in the following ways:

1. High's request for the service from Low;
2. High's message to Low that the service has been successfully completed (e.g., ACK) , and;
3. High's message to Low that the service has not been successfully completed (e.g., NAK) and must be reinitiated.

Most commonly, low-to-high service channels arise as a result of the need for a high part of the system to obtain information from a low part. Although the flow of the information from low to high is within the security policy, the information that must pass between high and low to ensure that the service is provided properly may be in violation of that property.

One such example, and probably the best known of low-to-high service channels, is the "distributed read" channel. This occurs when an untrusted single-level high node in a distributed system must read data from an untrusted single-level low node. Unlike in a stand-alone operating system, in which all accesses are mediated by a security kernel, the only way in which the high node can obtain the information is by presenting the query to the low node. Even if a trusted portion of the system passes on this request on the high node's behalf, it is still possible for a Trojan horse residing in the high node to encode sensitive data in the request. A discussion of this channel is given in [MN92].

There are a number of ways of avoiding the distributed read channel. One, of course, is to abandon the distributed architecture and return to the kernelized architecture. A less drastic approach is to use replication. In a replicated architecture all information stored at the low node would be transmitted to the high node. Thus, the high node would have a high-level copy of all data possessed by the low end. This is the approach used by the SINTRA project for databases [FM89] and for multilevel systems in general [FKM+94, FGK+95]. A similar approach has also been suggested by Proctor and Neumann [PN92].

Both the replicated and the kernelized architectures reduce the size of the distributed read channel by reducing the information passed in the request for data. In the replicated architecture, the request is eliminated altogether. In the kernelized architecture, the request still exists, but it is never presented directly to the low entity. This does not mean, however, that one does not have to do further work to eliminate or reduce the size of covert channels. In the kernelized architecture, the covert channel could result from the fact that, in order to maintain the integrity of the data (and therefore, the integrity of the service being provided by the low entity to the high one), it is necessary that a low entity not be able to write a file while a high entity is reading it. Means for eliminating this channel have been in existence for some time; for example, see [RK79], and solutions in a database context have been an area of active research [MJ93]. In the replicated architecture, a covert channel could result from the fact that, in order to maintain the integrity of the service provided by low to high, the low entity may need to know whether or not the high entity received the data that was sent to it. We will refer to it as the *reliable write-up problem*. This is a newer problem than the secure reader-writer problem, but in recent years an extensive literature has developed on the subject, see for example [KM93,

McD94, FGK+95, KML96]. In particular, Kang and Moskowitz [KM93, KM95] outlined a solution to the reliable write-up problem called the NRL Pump. The major covert channel threat in the reliable write-up problem is that low knows the timing of the high ACKs; thus a timing channel exists. The Pump places a buffer between the low and high entities. High acknowledgements are sent to the buffer, which, after adding noise according to the Pump algorithm, sends its own acknowledgements to the low entity. This splitting of the acknowledgement stream gives reliability and security in a manner that does not affect performance if no Trojan horse is present, because the ACK stream is "averaged" out so that the timing of the ACKs carries very little information down from High. Hence covert channel size is minimized.

We note that the distributed read channel, the secure reader/writer channel, and the reliable write-up channel may have more in common than initially appears, once we have looked at the *context* in which they occur. In some contexts of the secure reader/writer problem it may be necessary, in order to meet real-time requirements, that the high reads have priority over low writes, even though this leads to a covert channel. In other contexts it may be necessary to have assurance that the high reader see each version of the file. Thus, a case in which the low entity writes twice without the high entity being able to read the intervening version would not be allowed. Although this can be ensured by keeping around old copies of the file, there will come a point at which this is no longer practical. Thus it will be necessary to gain some assurance that the high entity has read the data. This is similar to the assurance that the high entity has received a message that is needed for the replicated approach. In such cases we conjecture that a modification of the Kang-Moskowitz approach may also be useful for the secure reader/writer problem in a kernelized architecture.

3 Case Study: A Network of System-High Components

In this section we present a case study of a network of system-high components. We note that none of the covert channels we present here are new; all have been discussed in the literature elsewhere, and many have a long history. What our methodology contributes is, not a new technique for finding covert channels, but a method for placing them in their context and understanding how the various methods for closing or controlling them affects the behavior of the system as a whole.

Consider a network of system-high components, as discussed in [KFM96]. The components may be at different sensitivity levels, but they all communicate across the same untrusted communication medium. The low level system is at L, and the high level system is at H. L components may send messages to H (which dominates L) components via the Pump, and H components may downgrade information and send it to L components. The communication medium itself is at level U dominated by L.

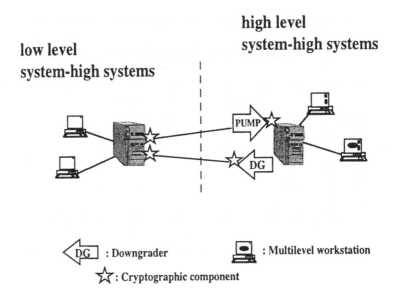

low level
system-high systems

high level
system-high systems

DG : Downgrader : Multilevel workstation
: Cryptographic component

Figure 2: A Network of System-High Components

Messages sent from L to H are stored in the Pump buffer at the receiving site. Messages cannot be received if the buffer is full, however, the Pump functions to keep the buffer from becoming full. Messages are encrypted when sent across the untrusted U level communication medium, but the message headers must be left unencrypted so the medium knows where to send them. Note that both the L to H communication and the H to L communication use encryption due to the untrusted nature of the medium.

Let us consider some of the various entity-operation pairs involved and the covert channels that may arise. In order to assist in the presentation, we will divide our analysis in two parts. First, we will look at channels between L and H as a result of L's communication with H. Secondly, we will look at some of the channels between U and L and U and H that arise as a result of the network's using a U communication medium. Keep in mind that the entity-operation pairs are given at a coarse level of granularity. The more finely we dissect the entity-operation pairs the more we learn about the context of the covert channels in our system. This is a similar situation to deciding what is the "state" in an automaton model of a computer system.

Some Channels Between L and H

The L component sends a message; thus, we have (Lcomp,send_mess). The Pump receives the messages from L, giving us (Pump,accept_mess). The Pump informs the L sender of the message whether or not the Pump's buffer was able to accept the message. Thus we have (Pump,ACK/NAK). (Blind write-up scenarios do not send this message back down from an intermediary buffer. This eliminates covert channel concerns but at the cost of reliability; see [McD94, MK96, FGK+95, Gol96].) When the L sender receives an ACK/NAK from the Pump, it will either decide that it has been received or resend the message, depending on whether it received an ACK or a NAK. Thus we have (Lcomp,finish_mess) and (Lcomp,resend_mess). Due to the handshake protocol of the Pump, a new message will not be sent from a L component until it has received an ACK. Note that the Pump can also be used with a windowing protocol that will allow more than one outstanding message. This will of course result in different operation-entity pairs. The H component retrieves messages from the buffer, which results in (Hcomp,retrieve_mess). So we see that (Pump,accept_mess) enables (Hcomp,retrieve_mess). However, since the Pump's buffer is able to accept messages from L as long as there is space in the buffer, we have that (Hcomp,retrieve_mess) partially enables (buffer,accept_mess). Because if the buffer fills it cannot accept a new message until H removes an old message. Our enabling diagram shows us the different covert channel/performance dependencies.

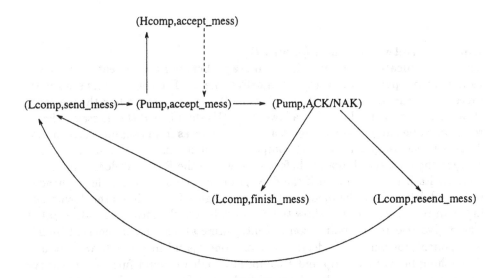

Figure 3: Enabling diagram of the channels between L and H

Let us consider the pairs (Lcomp,send_mess) and (Hcomp,retrieve_mess). As

before, the first pair enables the other. The covert channel that the Pump miti-
gates occurs in the context of (Lcomp,send_mess) as a low-to-high service channel. As before the covert channel occurs because the receiving component ac-
knowledges the receipt of the message.

How does the introduction of the Pump affect the covert channel? The pair
(Pump,ACK/NAK) enables (Lcomp,send_mess) because a message will not be
sent from the L component until it has received an ACK of the previous message.
Since (Pump,accept_mess) enables (Hcomp,retrieve_mess) we see that the Pump
is thus providing a service to both sender and receiver, so the covert channel
can also be interperted as a shared service channel. Assume one uses a method
other than the Pump, for example, blind write-up. That would simply eliminate
the communication between buffer and L component sender, as in [McD94].
This could interfere, not only with the service that the buffer is providing the L
sender, but the service that the L sender is providing to the H receiver. Thus,
our taxonomy further assists in highlighting possible performance/functionality
penalties associated with security counter-measures. As noted, the Pump in fact
does not cut out the ACK stream, but moderates it by judiciously adding noise
to the covert channel by modulating the communication between the buffer and
the L sender.

Channels Between U and (L and H)
The communication medium delivers messages between components. This gives
us the entity-operation pair (medium,deliver_mess). The components send messages across the network by either using the Pump or downgrading the message.
However, since the medium is at a lower level (U) than L or H the messages themselves must be encrypted to prevent any security leaks from tapping the medium.
Thus it is necessary for (L or H) component to first generate the message, then
encrypt the message (L does it before it is sent to the Pump, H does it after the
message itself is downgraded if the downgrading occurs), downgrade the header
to U, and deliver it to the medium. (Note that figure 2 only shows the downgrading from H to L, it does not show the downgrading of the message headers to U.)
These give rise to the pairs (component,gen_mess),(component,encrypt_mess),
(component,downgrade_header), and (component,send_mess). We are not distinguishing between Lcomp and Hcomp, although we could further our entity-
operation pairs to show this if we wished for a finer grained analysis. Similarly, by looking at the components sending to the Pump or downgrader we can
obtain the pairs (component,send_mess) and (component,retrieve_mess). Since
(medium,deliver_mess) enables both (component,send_mess) and
(component,retrieve_mess) the entity medium provides a service to both L and
H components.

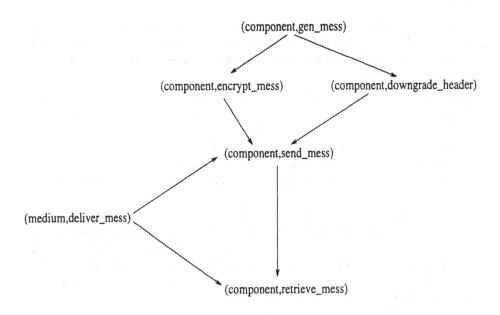

Figure 4: Enabling diagram-covert channels between U and (L and H)

We now consider the various covert channels occurring in the context of these services. These have been studied in depth in [PMM94], and we make extensive use of that work here. Since we are merely trying to illustrate the context of the covert channels, not to provide an exhaustive list, for reasons of space we do not discuss all the channels mentioned in that paper, especially ones concerned with the particular implementation used in [PMM94]. We also cover a few, such as the subliminal channel mentioned below, that could occur in some cases but would not be relevant to the implementation put forth in [PMM94].

First of all, we note that since the medium is providing a service to components operating at different sensitivity levels, it makes sense to look for a shared service channel. It is indeed possible that a H component could signal information to the U medium by flooding the network. Certainly without some sort of fairness criterion ([KML96, KM95, Mil95]), this is a real threat—it is also a denial of service threat!

The operations of the components in sending a message, namely gen_mess, encrypt_mess, downgrade_header, send_mess clearly enable the medium operation deliver_mess. Since the sensitivity level of the components dominates that of the message (which is now U), there are potential high-to-low service channels involved in each of these actions (L to U and H to U). We consider first the operation encrypt_mess. Certain cryptosystems possess *subliminal channels* [Sim83] by which the sender of the message can encode additional data which can be read by a third party who possesses some secret information, but which cannot even be detected otherwise.

We next consider the operation send_mess. There is also a channel occurring in this context, since a component could signal information to the untrusted medium by varying the rate at which messages are sent, or the order in which they are sent [PMM94].

We next consider the operation gen_mess. There is a covert channel occurring in this context as well, since a component could signal information to the medium by varying the length of messages [PMM94].

Finally, we consider the operation downgrade_header. There is considerable variation allowed in message headers; thus it is possible for the sender of the message to encode information in the header that could be read by the untrusted medium.

We now consider some of the possible solutions. The network flooding channel is a denial of service problem as well as a covert channel. Thus it would make sense to look at some of the techniques that have been developed for handling this sort of denial of service attack [Gli83, Mil95]. In these solutions users of a resource agree to make only certain demands upon it; if they do not keep to their agreements, they will be denied access to the resource. However, agreements of this sort may not be practical in some cases in which a component or components may have to make extensive use of the network in emergencies. Thus the nature of the service that the components are providing to the network must be taken into account.

We next consider possible subliminal channels in the encrypt_mess operation. Most subliminal channels apply to the case in which two parties are communicating via messages signed with a digital signature and are being monitored by a third party. The subliminal channel can be used by the communicating parties to send information in a way that is undetectable by the third party. Such subliminal channels often require knowledge of the signature key to be exploited. Since this paper confines itself to leakage from one sensitivity level to another, and since communication is only allowed if the sensitivity level of the recipient dominates the sensitivity level of the sender, these types of channels for the most part do not concern us. Indeed, if a cryptographic key belonging to a component becomes available to the untrusted medium, we have worse problems than covert channels! We note that there do exist some low-capacity subliminal channels that do not require knowledge of the signature key [Sim93]; these would merit further study.

The send_mess channels can be eliminated by fixing the order and rate at which messages are sent, as in [PMM94]. This may involve the insertion of dummy messages. Clearly, this can have a negative impact on network performance, both by increasing the time it takes to send a message, and by increasing the load on the network by the generation of dummy messages. Another possibility it to reduce the size of the channel by adding a trusted component that varies the rate at which the messages are sent out. This also of course may increase the time in which it takes a given message to be delivered. It is possible that such a solution might not be acceptable in emergency situations. Thus, there are some proposals for varying the degree at which noise is added depending upon the situation [BCJW94]. Again, how this will done will depend upon the services that the component sending the message is performing for the components receiving them. If the communication uses (or is forced to use) a handshake protocol, a Pump-like solution can be used to slave the transmission rate to a moving average of the reception rate, thus alleviating the covert channel threat. Further research is needed into this.

The gen_mess channel can be closed by requiring that all messages be of the same length [PMM94]. If this is unacceptable, another possibility is to reduce the capacity of the channel by adding random padding to messages.

The capacity of the message header channel can be reduced to some extent by restricting the format of the header as much as possible, and by controlling the context of every message. This solution has been explored in [PMM94].

Of course a full study would involve folding the the different types of channels together in one enabling diagram. The resulting diagram might be too large to present easily in a conference paper like this. However, it would allow one to make a more detailed study of how the covert channels come about, what methods would be appropriate for mitigating the covert channels, and what would be the effects upon system performance/functionality.

4 Conclusion

In this paper, we have examined covert channels from the point of view of the context in which they occur. We have shown how the context can affect the way in which covert channels are handled, and we have used that information to construct a preliminary taxonomy of covert channels based on context instead of mechanisms. For each category, we have identified the context, characterized the covert channels that usually occur in that context, and characterized the methods for dealing with the covert channel that are most relevant to that context.

We consider our work far from done; there are many factors still to be taken into account. For example, we have not yet considered the human factor at all. This can result in techniques that were considered acceptable from the purely performance point of view to become unacceptable; for example, in a recent talk at the National Computer Security Conference [KH92], Kramer gave an example in which a technique for closing a covert channel that was perfectly acceptable from the performance point of view was rejected by users as being too confusing. Such an example shows that there are still many variables to be taken into account in determining context that we have yet to explore. Other factors that we have touched upon but not explored in depth include ease of exploitation of the covert channel, ease of real-time detection, ease of post-facto detection, the value of the data at risk, and concern of the small message criterion over that of capacity.

It may also be useful to consider how our taxonomy interacts with taxonomies that divide up covert channels along other lines. For example, in [JS92] Sandhu and Jajodia divide covert channels into signaling channels, which appear in the system design, and covert channels, which do not appear until the system is implemented. Do any of our various kinds of service channels correspond to signaling channels, or is this definition orthogonal to ours? Our conjecture is that high-to-low and low-to-high channels, which involve direct communication between active entities, will usually occur at the higher level of abstraction, while shared service channels, which involve communication via a passive object, will occur at all levels, including the lowest. As of yet, however, we have no firm data on this.

There is also the question of how we can make our work more rigorous. For the present we have simply identified the various entities, operations, covert channels, and the relations between them in an informal way, and our analysis has been ad hoc. However, there has been a large amount of work on formal and semi-formal methods for identifying covert channels (see [McH] for a survey). It is possible that this could be incorporated into our framework and be used to provide a more formal underpinning. Dependency analysis, which has been used in the past to identify covert channels, seems like a particularly promising place to begin. Briefly, if X and Y are two resource attributes, and O is an operation performed on Y, we say that a dependency exists from X to Y if it is possible to learn something about the value X by observing Y both before and after O has been performed. Although our notion of entity is broader than the notion of system resource we can still note that in cases where it is meaningful to say so, if entity A performs a service to B, then a dependency exists from some attribute of A to some attribute of B. The converse is not necessarily true, as we say in the case of the file attribute example at the beginning of this paper. Thus one way to tie in our work with dependency analysis would be to first generalize the concept of dependency to entities, then to perform a dependency analysis of a system and identify covert channels, then to use the results of the dependency analysis to develop an enabling graph and identify the services performed, and finally to use the results of this analysis to eliminate covert channel dependencies that are not related to any service and to modify appropriately the dependencies that are related to a service. This would give rise to a unified method for identifying and managing covert channels.

References

[AJJ92]   P. Ammann, F. Jaeckle, and S. Jajodia. A two snapshot algorithms for concurrency control in secure multi-level databases. In *Proceedings of the 1992 Symposium on Research in Security and Privacy*, pages 204–215. IEEE Computer Society Press, May 1992.

[BCJW94] P. K. Boucher, R. K. Clark, E. D. Jensen, and D. M. Wells. Toward a multilevel-secure, best-effort real-time scheduler. In F. Cristian, G. Le Lann, and T. Lunt, editors, *Proceedings of Dependable Computing for Critical Applications 4*, pages 49–68. Springer-Verlag, 1994.

[BL76]   D.E. Bell and L.J. LaPadula. Secure computer system: Unified exposition and multics interpretation. Technical Report MTR-2997, The MITRE Corporation, Bedford, Massachusetts, March 1976. Available from the National Technical Information Service as report number: AD A023 588.

[FGK+95] J. N. Froscher, D. M. Goldschlag, M. H. Kang, C. E. Landwehr, A. P. Moore, I. S. Moskowitz, and C. N. Payne. Improving inter-enclave information flow for a secure strike planning application. In *Proceedings of the 11th Annual Computer Security Applications Conference*. IEEE Computer Society Press, December 1995.

[FKM+94] J. N. Froscher, M. H. Kang, J. P. McDermott, O. Costich, and C. E. Landwehr. A practical approach to high assurance multilevel secure computing service. In *Proceedings of the Tenth Annual Computer Security Applications Conference*, pages 2–11, December 1994.

[FM89] J. N. Froscher and C. A. Meadows. Achieving a Trusted Database Management System Using Parallelism. In *Database Security, II: Status and Prospects*, pages 151–160. North-Holland, Amsterdam, 1989.

[Gas88] Morrie Gasser. *Building a Secure Computer System*. Van Nostrand Reinhold Company Inc, New York, 1988.

[Gli83] Virgil Gligor. A note on the denial of service problem. In *Proceedings of the 1983 Symposium on Security and Privacy*, pages 139–149. IEEE Computer Society Press, 1983.

[Gol96] David M. Goldschlag. Several secure store and forward devices. In *Proceedings of the 3rd ACM Conference on Computer and Communication Security*, pages 129–137. ACM, New York, New York, 1996.

[Gra93] James W. Gray. On Introducing Noise into the Bus-Contention Channel. In *Proceedings of the 1993 IEEE Computer Society Symposium on Research in Security and Privacy*, pages 90–98. IEEE Computer Society Press, Los Alamitos, California, 1993.

[Hu92] Wei-Ming Hu. Reducing Timing Channels with Fuzzy Time. In *Proceedings of the 1992 IEEE Computer Society Symposium on Research in Security and Privacy*, pages 28–21. IEEE Computer Society Press, Los Alamitos, California, 1992.

[JS92] S. Jajodia and R. S. Sandhu. Eliminating Polyinstantiation Securely. *Computers and Security*, 11(6):547–562, October 1992.

[Kem83] Richard A. Kemmerer. Shared resource matrix methodology: A practical approach to identifying covert channels. *ACM Transactions on Computer Systems*, 1(3):256–257, August 1983.

[KFM96] Myong H. Kang, Judith N. Froscher, and Ira S. Moskowitz. A framework for MLS interoperability. Preprint, 1996.

[KH92] Frank E. Kramer and Steven M. Heffern. Implications of Monoinstantiation in a Polyinstantiated Environment. In *Proceedings of the 15th National Computer Security Conference*, pages 236–243. NIST/NCSC, Baltimore, MD, 1992.

[KM92] C. Kurak and J. McHugh. A Cautionary Note on Image Downgrading. In *Proceedings of the Eighth Annual Computer Security Applications Conference*, pages 153–159. IEEE Computer Society Press, Los Alamitos, California, 1992.

[KM93] Myong H. Kang and Ira S. Moskowitz. A Pump for rapid, reliable, secure communication. In *Proceedings of the First ACM Conference on Computer and Communications Security*, pages 119–129. ACM, November 1993.

[KM95] Myong H. Kang and Ira S. Moskowitz. A data Pump for communication. Memo Report 55-95-7771, Naval Research Laboratory, 1995.

[KML96] Myong H. Kang, Ira S. Moskowitz, and Daniel C. Lee. A Network Pump. *IEEE Transactions on Software Engineering*, pages 329–338, May 1996.

[KTS93]   T. F. Keefe, W. T. Tsai, and J. Srivastave. Database concurrency control in multilevel secure database management systems. *IEEE Transactions on Knowledge and Data Engineering*, 1993.

[Lam73]   Butler Lampson. A note on the confinement problem. *CACM*, 16(10):613–615, October 1973.

[McD94]   J. McDermott. The b2/c3 problem: How big buffers overcome covert channel cynicism in trusted database systems. In J. Biskup, M. Morgenstern, and C. E. Landwehr, editors, *Database Security, VIII: Status and Prospects*, pages 111–122, Amsterdam, 1994. Elsevier.

[McH]   John McHugh. Covert channel analysis: A chaper of the handbook for computer security certification of trusted systems. to appear.

[Mil95]   Jonathan Millen. Denial of service: A perspective. In F Cristian, G. Le Lann, and T. Lunt, editors, *Dependable Computing for Critical Applications 4*, pages 93–108. Springer-Verlag, 1995.

[MJ93]   J. McDermott and S. Jajodia. Orange locking: Channel-free database concurrency control via locking. In B. Thuraisingham and C. Landwehr, editors, *Database Security VI: Status and Prospects*, pages 267–284. North-Holland, 1993.

[MK94]   Ira S. Moskowitz and Myong H. Kang. Covert channels—Here to stay? In *Proceedings of COMPASS 94*, pages 235–243, NJ, 1994. IEEE Press.

[MK96]   Ira S. Moskowitz and Myong H. Kang. The Modulalted-Input Modulated-Output mode. In S. Demurjian and J. Dobson, editors, *Database Security IX—Proc. of the 9th annual IFIP TC11 Working Conference on Database Security (August 1995)*. Chapman Hall, 1996.

[MN92]   Catherine D. McCollum and LouAnna Notargiacomo. Distributed concurrency control with optional data replication. In C. E. Landwehr and S. Jajodia, editors, *Database Security, V: Status and Prospects*, pages 149–171. North-Holland, 1992.

[PMM94]   C. N. Payne, A. P. Moore, and D. M. Mihelcic. An experience modeling critical reqirements. In *Proceedings of COMPASS '94*, pages 245–256. IEEE Press, June 1994.

[PN92]   Norman E. Proctor and Peter G. Neumann. Architectural Implications of Covert Channels. In *Proceedings of the 15th National Computer Security Conference*, pages 236–243. NIST/NCSC, Baltimore, MD, 1992.

[RK79]   P. D. Reed and R. K. Kanodia. Synchronization with Eventcounts and Sequencers. *Communications of the ACM*, 22(2):225–124, February 1979.

[Sim83]   G. J. Simmons. The prisoners' problem and the subliminal channel. In *Proceedings of Crypto '83*. Plenum Press, 1983.

[Sim93]   G. J. Simmons. Subliminal communication is possible using the DSA. In *Proceedings of Eurocrypt '93*. Springer-Verlag, 1993.

[Tro93]   J. T. Trostle. Modelling a Fuzzy Time Systems. In *Proceedings of the 1993 IEEE Computer Society Symposium on Research in Security and Privacy*, pages 82–89. IEEE Computer Society Press, Los Alamitos, California, 1993.

Covert Channel Analysis for Stubs

Mark S. Anderson and Maris A. Ozols

Information Technology Division
Electronics and Surveillance Research Laboratory
DSTO, PO Box 1500
Salisbury, Australia

Abstract. This paper explains a range of techniques for covert channel control for the Stubs network security devices. The techniques deal with both timing and storage channels, and rely on a combination of channel elimination, reduction, and audit mechanisms. Although specific to the Stubs system, the techniques of analysis and control are adaptable to similar systems.

1 Introduction

Stubs are a set of retrofittable security devices developed by the Defence Science and Technology Organisation to allow controlled interconnection of highly sensitive networks to other, less secure networks. They have been developed to conform to a high degree of assurance. In fact, for some functions, they are targeted for evaluation to a level of at least E6 under the ITSEC assurance regime. They include NSA approved high grade crypto components.

To be fully effective in protecting the confidentiality of information, the Stubs devices, particularly the Gateway, must not only prevent the direct release of inappropriate information, but must also prevent the covert signalling of information. Since Stubs are designed to be retrofittable to untrusted components such as commercial off the shelf workstations, we are concerned that a Trojan Horse, which has been introduced into the system by whatever means, may try to subvert the intended security supplied by the Stubs device to covertly signal sensitive information to a cooperating process outside the relevant security domain, thus violating the release policy of the network. In many cases this is a serious threat, as the system's users and administrators may not even be aware of the Trojan Horse's existence. In addition, covert channels in some computer systems have extremely high capacity.

The purpose of the work in this paper is to examine the possible covert channels that may potentially exist in a Stubs protected network, and to analyse the capacity of each of these. Methods for eliminating the channels are explored, and in cases where this proves impossible or impractical, methods for reducing channel capacity, and/or auditing use of the channel, are examined.

We discuss three major approaches to controlling covert signalling channels in a typical configuration for the Stubs security device. Although these channels are specific to Stubs protected networks, the methods described here for analysing, reducing or eliminating them, have more general application.

The first approach deals with the manipulation of data which is authorised to "leave" the system, using timewindows to reduce timing channels. The second approach deals with certain covert channels which may be a result of the data itself, and eliminates them by use of a unique representation. A third approach, radically different to the second, is proposed for dealing with similar, but more general, threats.

2 Assumptions

To analyse the capacity of covert channels available to an attacker for signalling information across a Stub it is first helpful to identify the types of techniques available to signal the information. Our main interest centres on methods which allow information to be signalled across a Gateway Stub, since this represents an unauthorized release of potentially sensitive information. Fig. 1 depicts a model of a network protected by a set of Stubs devices. The only electronic connection to the "outside world" of the network is via the Gateway Stub. Hence our previous assertion that we will concentrate only on the passage of covert information via the Gateway.

There are several further assumptions that form the basis of this analysis of the covert channels. Firstly, the attacker has complete (logical, rather than physical) control of the secure network (other than the Stubs themselves), and thus can control which messages are passed to the Gateway, at what time they are passed, and can modify them as desired (Fig. 1.). While this situation may be unlikely in practice, worst-case scenario strengthens the validity of any desirable result we obtain from our analysis. It also allows an easier treatment of the covert channel analysis without invalidating the results for the purposes of making decisions at the security policy level.

The configuration and associated assumptions allow an attacker to introduce an arbitrary Trojan Horse into the secure network[1].

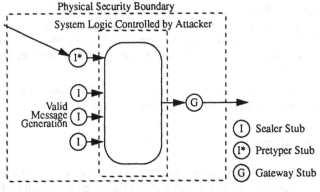

Fig. 1. Secure Network Configuration

---

[1] The astute reader will realise that the model depiction is not entirely accurate in that messages to be sealed must first get to the sealer. Typically this is through the network itself hence allowing an attacker to change the ordering of messages as a covert signalling path. This particular situation is extremely difficult to exploit due to each human expecting messages relevant to them in a specific order and any timing manipulation is severely distorted due to the unpredictable human review time period. For the purposes of this analysis, we assume the messages are generated local to the Sealer.

There are two main methods by which information is authorised for release through the gateway. The first is via the sealer Stub. Here information is presented to the Sealer for inspection. A trusted path exists from the sealer to a user situated at a terminal device, allowing that user to inspect the message held in the Sealer to ascertain whether it is suitable for release. If this is the case, the user orders the sealer to associate a tamperproof seal to the message. The message is then transported to the Gateway where the seal is inspected. If the seal still matches the message, the message is allowed to pass through the Gateway.

The second method of authorised release is via use of the pretyper. In a number of military networks, messages are received from other networks where the content and structure is easily parsed. The pretyper inspects messages and for those which satisfy an appropriate criteria a seal is generated which is recognisable by the Gateway.

We assume that seals are correctly generated. In the case of human generated seals, this means that each sealed message has been fully inspected by an operator and certified as correctly sealed.

A Pretyper Stub generating the seals poses no direct risk to the confidentiality of locally held data, since the input data comes from outside the security boundary. Since the pretyper generates a seal for the data before it enters the main security domain, any attack which may modify the data must happen outside the security domain. Thus the agent carrying out the attack (e.g. a Trojan Horse) is also outside the secure domain.

Since only messages with valid seals can pass through the Gateway, the attacker is left with no choice but to exploit the stream of valid messages as the only logical means for the transmission of covert information. The supply of valid sealed messages to the attacker is only limited by the rate at which such messages are generated on the secure network, since the attacker has (logical) control of the network.

Other limits on the attacker arise from the Stubs' design. The checksum algorithm is chosen such that it is computationally infeasible to alter a message while leaving the checksum unaltered. Thus altered messages will be detected by the Gateway Stub as having an invalid seal. As an added precaution, the checksum is constructed using a strong military grade encryption algorithm using a key not available to an attacker. Thus even if an attacker knows the checksum algorithm, the seal could not be successfully forged.

In the next section, we introduce the concept of "Time Windows", a tool for managing the capacity of covert timing channels, and analysing their size.

3 Time Windows

If the output of messages from a Gateway Stub is not regulated, an attacker can utilise a relatively large capacity covert channel through the Stub by controlling both the order and timing of the output messages.

In order to reduce this problem to manageable proportions, the concept of *time windows* is introduced. When a message is sealed, the time at which the seal was generated is attached to the message (and covered by the seal, to prevent tampering). This seal is then only valid for some defined length of time. With the additional constraint that no two messages may share any part of their time windows, covert signalling of data by re-ordering messages can be totally eliminated.

While time windows are nice in theory, there are some extra problems which arise in their implementation. The main one of these is that the Sealing and Gateway Stubs have different physical clocks. Even if these can be perfectly synchronised initially, they will drift with respect to each other as time passes. Eventually, the difference between the clocks will be sufficient to cause the Gateway Stub to reject messages which should be allowed to pass. How quickly this situation may occur in practice depends on the engineering tolerances of the clocks, the size of the allowed time windows and the time taken for a message to travel from the Sealer to the Gateway. This minimum time between required re-synchronisations is important, since the Stubs must be taken off-line and placed in Maintenance Mode for their clocks to be reset.

3.1 Required Length of Time Windows

Of interest is the required size of the time window. Assume that a message is sealed at time T_S and may then take up to T_M seconds to reach the Gateway. If the two clocks were perfectly synchronised, then the most stringent requirement that can be enforced is

$$T_G - T_M \leq T_S \leq T_G$$

where T_G is the time of arrival of the message at the Gateway. Now assume that the clocks may have drifted up to D seconds with respect to each other. Thus the Sealing Stub's clock may be D seconds behind the Gateway's and the earliest time which must be allowed becomes T_G-D-T_M. Alternatively, the Sealer's clock could be D seconds ahead of the Gateway's, so we must allow time stamps as late as T_G+D. Thus our expression above becomes

$$T_G - D - T_M \leq T_S \leq T_G + D$$

Assume that D is the total drift allowed between the two clocks. This means that each clock must have engineering tolerances such that it can drift at most D/2 over the required time period.

Thus for a maximum transmission time from Sealer to Gateway of T_M and a requirement to tolerate a relative clock drift of D seconds over some defined period of time, the time window must be at least $(2D + T_M)$ seconds long. If a longer window is used, greater clock drifts may occur without messages being rejected, or delays in transmission of messages to the Gateway may go unnoticed.

Note however that the maximum transmission time T_M cannot be enforced by this mechanism. If $T_G = T_S + 2$, it is impossible to tell whether the message took 2 seconds in transit and the clocks are perfectly synchronised or the message was in transit for only 1 second and the Sealer's clock is 1 second slower than the Gateway's. By a similar argument, any message which arrives at the Gateway in less than T_M will tolerate clock drifts larger than D.

4 Possible Covert Channels

We now consider each possible method of covert signalling data across a Gateway Stub, and discuss how best to constrain each channel if they cannot be eliminated.

Information can possibly be signalled across the Gateway by means of:

- encoding information in the actual data passed by the Stub.
  If this is done before the data is sealed, then it is assumed that the human reviewer will reject the message[2].
  Once the data has been sealed, it cannot be modified in any way without this tampering being detected. As discussed above, encoding data in a message would involve the attacker either modifying a message such that its checksum remained the same, or possessing enough knowledge to forge a valid seal (i.e., encrypted checksum) for the modified data. Both of these attacks are rendered infeasible by the choice of checksum and encryption algorithms, so this class of attack is not considered further.
- message ordering.
  Information could be transmitted through the Gateway by the ordering of the messages output. This could be done using either some portion of the message which is amenable to ordering (e.g. a date or time) or else by some property of the message itself (e.g., the length of the message).
  This class of attack is defeated by having the Gateway Stub impose a required ordering on the messages it transmits. In particular, if time windows are implemented such that only one message is valid during each time window and each message has only one valid time window, the ordering of output messages is totally defined and no information can be transmitted covertly using this channel.
- positioning of the message within the time window.
  Even given that messages must be presented to the Gateway within a specified time window, an attacker could still signal information based on the positioning of the message within that time window. For example, a message appearing at the start of the time window would carry a different meaning to one appearing at the end of its window.
  To defeat this class of attack, it is possible for the Gateway to not immediately re-signal the message after its seal has been validated, but rather wait for the expiration of the time window. At this time, if there is a valid message to transmit this can be done. In this fashion, the message is output to the external domain at precisely the same time, regardless of when it arrived at the Gateway, thus eliminating the covert channel. Note that this makes use of the fact that only one message is allowed per time window.
  This solution forces another requirement onto the Stub, namely that processing of the output message, if any, must take priority over processing incoming messages.

---

[2] Pretypers are not of concern here, since they take their input from outside the secure domain, hence an attacker there has no access to secure data. For the purposes of the initial analysis, we assume that a user can detect any covert information in data and thus reject it before sealing. In a later section on the discussion of complex text, this assumption is relaxed.

If this is not the case, the attacker in the secure domain could signal information by either presenting more input data when the output was meant to occur, or not doing so. This would be visible to the outside domain as a slight delay in the output of the message if the extra data was input.

If this solution is not adopted, a constraint on the minimum length of each time window is introduced. This is discussed in detail below.

- selective deletion of messages and associated message characteristics.

  If messages can reliably be expected to be transmitted at certain times (e.g. when a Pretyper Stub is used on regularly arriving traffic), the attacker in the secure domain can signal information by either allowing or not allowing the message to reach the Gateway. While we cannot prevent this attack, it can be detected by procedural means, as described later. This problem is also much less exploitable with human-generated seals, since a required message may not be available to the attacker at the right time. It is possible to signal information by selectively deleting messages based on such criteria as the length of the message, its type, whether it is longer or shorter than the previously sent message, etc. The outside attacker can then deduce the information based on the messages that are allowed through. This type of attack cannot be stopped under our assumptions, but since significant numbers of messages must not be allowed to pass through the Gateway, exploitation of such channels can detected from the audit trail.

In the last two cases, information can be signalled by controlling which messages are allowed to reach the Gateway within their correct time window. Since we are assuming that the attacker has complete control over the network (other than the Stubs), this type of attack cannot be prevented. The Stubs' audit trails are, however, sufficient that these types of attack can be detected by analysis of the audit data. To limit the possible damage from such an attack, we rely on procedural mechanisms. All the signalling mechanisms of concern involve stopping or delaying transmission of significant numbers of messages. It is thus possible to compare the timestamps associated with messages which reached the Gateway within their allowed time window with the timestamps used to generate seals. This information is available in the currently defined audit trails. If all the messages were presented to the Gateway at the correct time, everything is working well, and the covert channels of concern are probably not being employed. If there are a significant number of timestamps used to generate seals (recorded on the Sealers' audit trails) which were not presented to the Gateway, or were presented after the timewindow expired, then there is either a problem with the network (e.g. congestion) or one of these channels is being exploited. In either case, further exploration by the Security Administrator is warranted to isolate and remove the problem.

The frequency with which the audit trail needs analysis depends on the specific implementation. For extremely secure operation, it may be required that use of such a covert channel be detected within minutes, whereas for less secure sites, once per day or even once per week may be acceptable. One critical factor in making this decision is the amount of information which may be compromised through these covert channels. This can be determined using information theory.

4.1 Formal Analysis of Channel Capacity

It is assumed for this analysis that only one message can be output per time window, and that each time window has constant length L, and that they are non-overlapping. If time windows have varying lengths, L must be taken as the shortest possible one, since this represents the worst case.

Throughout this section the analysis is of the covert channel between a single Sealer/ Gateway pair. To obtain the covert capacity for the entire network, one may add the individual channel rates for all such pairs, although this will be a worst-case value, as in general the receiving attacker may not be able reliably to attribute messages to their Sealers.

We also assume in this section that Sealer Stubs will not apply their seal until the timewindow for the previous message has expired. This ensures that on this Sealer/ Gateway channel, the timewindows have the properties of being disjoint (i.e. not overlapping).

Using notation from "Communication Systems" by Carlson [1], the capacity of a discrete channel is given by

$$C = sC_S \tag{1}$$

where C is the channel capacity, s is the symbol rate for the channel (i.e., number of signalling events per time unit) and C_S is the information transferred per signalling event.

Only one message may be output by the Gateway Stub during each time window of length L, so we have

$$s = \frac{1}{L} \tag{2}$$

for the maximum rate, as each message is a signalling event. C_S is defined by Carlson as the average information $I(X, Y)$, which is derived from the probability that a symbol x_i was transmitted given that a symbol y_j was received. More specifically,

$$I(X;Y) = \sum_{x, y} P(x_i, y_j) \log \left(\frac{P(x_i|y_j)}{P(x_i)} \right) \tag{3}$$

where log represents logarithms to the base 2.

If we assume that there are n possible signals which the attacker may send, and that they are all equally likely to be sent, then we can derive that

$$C_S = \log n \tag{4}$$

for an error-free channel. This capacity is reduced in the case where the transmitted symbol need not be received correctly. For instance, if for any symbol transmitted, it could be either corrupted during transmission and so received as one of two incorrect symbols (assume each symbol is equally likely to occur, with probability a for each), or it could be received correctly (with probability $(1 - 2a)$) then we find that the highest channel capacity possible is

$$C_S = \log\left(\frac{n}{3}\right) \tag{5}$$

which occurs when $a = 1/3$ (i.e., each of the three possible symbols is equally likely to be received). Further possible errors on the channel further reduce the capacity, up to the limiting case where, regardless of the symbol transmitted, any valid symbol is equally likely to be received. In this case

$$C_S = \log\left(\frac{n}{n}\right) = 0 \tag{6}$$

and so there is no information flow.

4.1.1   Message Characteristic Channels

We consider the case where the Gateway Stub does not reorder messages it receives for transmission outside the secure domain. Given this assumption, it is difficult to introduce errors into channels which rely on quantities such as message lengths, or the presence or absence of a message. This first analysis therefore assumes that the channel is error-free, and reasons about security on that basis.

Given time windows of length L, and a symbol alphabet containing n symbols, the maximum channel capacity is given by

$$C = \frac{\log n}{L} \tag{7}$$

As an example, to control a channel to under 1 bit per second, this would require

$$L \geq \log n \tag{8}$$

where there are n different symbols available to the attacker.

While the theoretical channel capacity increases with an increased size of alphabet available to the attacker, this is not necessarily useful in practice. Unless there are a large number of messages being generated with a wide diversity of whatever characteristic is being used to signal information, the attacker may be forced to wait for an extended period for the correct message to become available. This reduces the covert information flow, and also requires deletion of all other message traffic for this period, which makes the attack more likely to be detected.

Another useful feature of the derived channel capacity is that capacity only increases with the logarithm of the alphabet size. Thus to double the capacity of the covert channel for a fixed size of time window, the attacker must square the size of the alphabet (i.e., the attacker must now be able to send n^2 distinct symbols rather than just n). As described above, this can be difficult to achieve in practice.

To determine the best sized time windows requires a knowledge of the expected traffic through the Stub. This is used to determine what characteristics of messages (e.g. length) could be used to signal information, and thus the alphabet size n available to the attacker. An estimate for the length of time window desired can then be used in the equation above to determine the worst case channel capacity, and the proposed frequency of audit analyses can then be used to determine how much information may be lost before the channel usage is discovered. If the result is unacceptable, either the time window needs to be increased (fewer messages allowed through the Stub results in less carrier for covert information) or the frequency of audit analysis should be increased (to enable earlier detection of channel usage) to achieve the desired result.

4.1.2 Time Window Channels

As another example, consider the possible signalling capacity available to an attacker if the Gateway Stub does not delay transmission of messages until the end of the time window, but passes them on immediately. Information may then be passed by means of the message's position within its allowed time window. While such a channel will be noisy in practice, we initially consider the worst case of a noiseless channel.

4.1.2.1 Noiseless Channels

The assumptions from the previous example are still valid, so the channel capacity is

$$C = \frac{\log n}{L} \tag{9}$$

for an alphabet of size n. Assuming that the Stub has an output clock frequency of H_S, then there are $(H_S \cdot L)$ distinguishable times at which the message may appear, so this is the alphabet size. The capacity then becomes

$$C = \frac{\log (H_S L)}{L} \tag{10}$$

To control this channel to under B bits per second then requires

$$\frac{\log (H_S L)}{L} \leq B \tag{11}$$

Since L is positive (being a time period), this requires that

$$H_S L \leq 2^{B \cdot L} \tag{12}$$

The variable of interest in this inequality is "L", the length of the time window. For values of H_S less than some critical value, the inequality holds for all values of L. Unfortunately, this critical value can be shown to be

$$H_S^* = e \cdot B \cdot ln2 \tag{13}$$

(where ln represents the natural logarithm function) which for small allowable capacity (e.g. 1 bit per second) gives unrealistically small values of H_S. In practical cases, H_S will thus be above this critical value, in which case there are two values of L for which equality will hold, and the required inequality will not hold for any value of L between these two values. The lower limit occurs at approximately

$$L_1 = \frac{1}{H_S} \tag{14}$$

which is clearly an impractical time window since messages cannot be propagated from the sealing Stub to the Gateway in less than one clock cycle. Thus to satisfy our capacity constraint the time window must be set at greater than the upper limit L_2, which satisfies

$$H_S L_2 = 2^{B \cdot L_2} \tag{15}$$

This equation can be solved numerically, and for an allowed channel capacity of 1 bit per second and a clock speed of 1 MHz to equate to a data transmission capacity of 1 Mb/s, forces $L_2 = 24.5$ secs. Increasing the clock speed to 10 MHz makes $L_2 = 28.1$ secs. Even the longer of these two time windows allows more than 128 messages per hour (or approximately 92300 messages per month) to pass through the Gateway Stub. In the absence of Pretyper Stubs generating seals, this limitation may be quite acceptable, as all seals must be generated by a human. If Pretypers are being used, action to remove this class of channel as described earlier may be warranted if these limits cause problems.

4.1.2.2 Message Batching

Another technique which can be used to increase the throughput of a Gateway Stub is to combine several messages into a single batch for transmission through the Gateway. Within each batch of messages there is a well-defined ordering (based on, say, the timestamp on each message) so that no covert information transmission is possible by reordering messages within a batch. The entire batch of messages is then presented to the Gateway for transmission in some time window. Because the entire batch is now the bearer of any covert information, rather than individual messages, the above analysis is still valid, except that limits expressed as "messages per hour" above become "batches per hour".

Clearly, a Trojan Horse process inside the security domain could attempt to signal information by modulating the number of messages in each batch (if a batch is created every x time units) or the time between batches (if a batch is created every time n messages are available). As described earlier, these techniques involve delay or deletion of a significant number of messages, so the exploitation of such covert channels will be visible when the audit data is analysed.

A variation on this, where a batch is created when the correct number of messages become available, would be for the Trojan Horse to fill up a batch with a number of messages with missing or bad seals. The channel would then consist of the process outside the security domain monitoring the number of messages in each batch that made it through the Gateway. Again, since messages with missing or invalid seals are audited, exploitation of this channel will become obvious very quickly when the audit data is analysed.

4.1.2.3 Noisy Channels

The situation improves even further in the presence of noise on the channel. It can be shown, from equation (3) above, that if there are k erroneous values which may be received equi-probably, as well as the correct value, then the maximum channel capacity possible is

$$C = \frac{1}{L}\log\left(\frac{H_S \cdot L}{k+1}\right) \qquad (16)$$

From this equation, it can be seen that introduction of noise is equivalent to having a slower clock in the Stub. This fact can be used to achieve large reductions in the length of the required time window. For example, if the Gateway Stub introduces an uncertainty in the timing of the output of half a second, so $k = H_S/2$, the required time window L becomes much smaller (e.g. around 5 secs for a 1 bit per second allowed channel). If there is even more noise, the effective H_S may even be smaller than the critical value defined by equation (13), which would remove the time window restriction completely. For instance, this is the case if we set $k = H_S$ for an allowed 1 bit per second channel. This corresponds to the Gateway delaying messages for up to one second.

5   Analysis of Bits per Message

As noted by Moskowitz and Kang [4], covert channel capacity may be measured either on a per time interval basis C (as in the previous section), or on a per channel usage basis C_S. In this section we briefly consider the per channel usage capacity of the channels discussed above, and the connection with the time windows and the volume of messages.

Some assumptions in force in the previous section may be relaxed. There is no longer a need to consider each Scaler/Gateway channel individually, and there is no need to insist that the time windows be disjoint. Hence a Scaler may seal a document before the time window has expired for previously scaled documents. We will assume noiseless channels.

The alphabet for each scaled message consists of the possibility of not sending the document, plus the times at which the document may be exported. Hence the capacity is

$$C_S = \log(1 + H_S \cdot L) \qquad (17)$$

giving the number of bits of data per scaled document in this timing channel.

Note that the per usage capacity increases as the time window length increases, although only logarithmically. This contrasts with the capacity C analysed previously, where increased time window length decreases the channel capacity per time unit, due to the disjoint time windows forcing the signalling rate to decrease linearly.

To use reduction of the per usage capacity (for example, by reducing time windows) to control covert channel flow, some control of the signalling rate (i.e the volume of scaled documents) is desirable. As the scaled messages are generated by users, or by the pretypers, the attacker does not have a direct means for increasing the usage rate, although a clever attacker may be able to find ways to induce users to seal more documents. Any significant increases in the number of scaled messages can be quickly detected by the audit mechanisms.

More direct means can be found for controlling the signalling rate. The Gateway may be configured so that only a certain number of messages per some time unit may be exported, or the Stubs Sealers may limit the rate at which documents are sealed (this is the effect of the requirement of disjoint time windows). If the Gateway only allows the export of n sealed documents each hour, the capacity is

$$C = \frac{n \cdot C_s}{3600} = \frac{n \cdot \log\left(1 + H_s \cdot L\right)}{3600} \tag{18}$$

So for a time window of 1 second, and a desired maximum covert capacity of 1 bit per second, a clock speed of 1 MHz allows $n = 180$, while a clock speed of 10MHz allows a maximum of $n = 154$ messages per hour.

It is important to realise that although these values seem quite good, they are averaged over the hour. Messages are allowed to occur in bursts, and during those bursts the covert channel capacity could be much higher. This is a good example where a *small message criterion* [4], giving consideration of the potential damage caused by short (but timely) covert messages, may be needed in addition to providing a requirement on the permitted average covert channel capacity.

6   Covert Channels in Complex Text

The previous discussions have focused on messages with no inherent covert channels within the message itself. However, if we consider the case where messages may include word processed files such as those produced by many graphical based editors, then it becomes clear that it is quite possible for a variety of large covert channels to be exploited. Such channels are called *storage channels* [4].

The aims behind visual verification are to avoid unintentional release of inappropriate information, and to detect any visible covert channels. Although some visible covert channels may be difficult to detect, a major problem is to remove *invisible* covert channels, i.e. those which cannot possibly be detected by visual inspection.

It is important to realise that although the techniques of this section may prove that a given kind of representation of complex text may eliminate invisible covert channels, it does not attempt to eliminate channels which, although theoretically visible, may be extremely hard to detect.

Invisible covert channels occur when documents can be represented in multiple ways internally but which have an identical visual representation. The choice of which particular representation to use provides the channel to the attacker.

The basic problem is that visual inspection of a document D_0 requires the human reviewer to inspect $f(D_0)$, where f is the function mapping the representation of the document onto the monitor screen. Unfortunately there may be other documents D_1, D_2,... such that $f(D_0) = f(D_1) = f(D_2) = ...$ The attacker may choose one of these alternate representations (which thus form the attacker's alphabet), and as they all map to the same image on the screen the covert channel is not visible to the viewer (it has been filtered out by f). The actual document D_j selected by the attacker is then sealed and released, and the covert information interpreted by the receiver.

Suppose we can prove that for all D_i, D_j that $f(D_i) \neq f(D_j)$ whenever $D_i \neq D_j$, so for each possible image which is visually verified, there is, at most, one document which can generate it. Hence no new covert channels can be introduced which are not detectable in the visual verification. A function with this property is called *one-to-one* (or 1-1). Proving that the visual presentation function *f* is 1-1 on the set of releasable documents is the fundamental technique used in this section, and guarantees that any covert channels in a released document have some visual effect.

The covert channels involved may be very large. For example, if backspaces are explicitly represented in the text, then an arbitrarily large piece of covert text may be inserted, and then rendered invisible by following it with backspaces. For example, the strings:

"This<space>"

and

"This<space>secret<del><del><del><del><del><del>"

both have the same pixel representation: "This ".

More subtle channels may use different fonts and font sizes on empty strings, or on strings where such modifications cannot be detected. For example, the following binary encoding using <bold> and <italic> is completely invisible and therefore undetectable:

"<bold><bold><italic><bold><plain>This<space>"

Again the problem is that the display function is not 1-1 on these representation - a single image "This " has many internal representations.

The analysis below will show how such invisible covert channels can be entirely eliminated, while still using a simple and efficient internal representation of the document.

The analysis will involve a two step process, the overall result being to show that for each visual representation of the text there is a *unique* internal representation which can generate it. The first step is to show that each stream of characters has only one internal representation. The second step is to show that distinct streams of characters will always result in distinct patterns of pixels on the screen, as this is what is actually visually verified.

The way in which this can be implemented in the Stubs system, is that the filtering transformation of the document into its unique internal representation (thus removing the invisible covert channels) can be done by *untrusted* software. All that is required is a trusted checker which ensures that the rules defining the class of unique internal representations are satisfied by the filtered document. If the untrusted filter leaves invisible covert channels in the code, the document will be rejected by the trusted checker, while if it introduces other changes to the text, these will result in visible changes to the document which can then be rejected by the user. A diagram represents the steps of process in Figure 2:

108

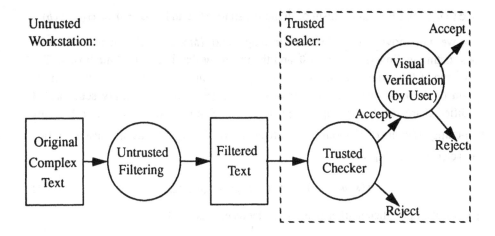

Fig. 2. The steps in covert channel filtering

6.1 Internal Representation to Modified Character Sequence

In our analysis we introduce a set M of *modifiers*, and a set C of *characters*. An example of a modifier might be <14Pt, Times-Roman, Bold, RegularVariation>. The set C may be viewed as the set of printable ASCII characters.

A pair $(m, c) \in M \times C$ is called a *modified character*. Once an internal representation of a document has been represented as an element of $(M \times C)^*$ finite sequence of modified characters, the pixel representation of each modified character may be easily calculated, and concatenated for display onto the screen.

The modified character sequence is a very inefficient way of representing a document, as every character is provided with its own explicit modifier. In most documents characters are modified in only a few ways, and consecutive characters very frequently have the same modifier. The internal representation is intended to exploit these properties to provide a more compact representation of most documents.

Let $C^\dagger$ denote the set of all sequences of one or more characters. Define an *internal representation* to be a finite sequence of pairs $(m_i, c_i) \in M \times C^\dagger$ such that for no i does $m_i = m_{i+1}$, and denote the set of such sequences, IR. The function φ can now be defined to map from IR to modified character sequences. The function is defined as:

$$\varphi(\Pi(m_i, \Pi c_{ij})) = \Pi(\Pi(m_i, c_{ij})) \tag{19}$$

In the notation the Π operator forms the concatenated product of its indexed terms, abbreviating a sequence of elements. For example, here is an illustration of how φ works, distributing each modifier over its character sequence:

$$\varphi((m_1, c_{11}c_{12})(m_2, c_{21}c_{22}c_{23})) = (m_1, c_{11})(m_1, c_{12})(m_2, c_{21})(m_2, c_{22})(m_2, c_{23}) \tag{20}$$

Note that φ, is a homomorphism of monoids, so for all a and b, $\varphi(ab) = \varphi(a)\varphi(b)$.

First we will show that the function φ maps onto $(M \times C)^*$. This will be done by constructing the inverse function θ and then proving that it is indeed the inverse. The definition of θ is somewhat more elaborate as it requires a recursive definition on the length of the modified character stream. Firstly let θ map the empty sequence of modified characters to the empty sequence in IR . Suppose now that $s(m_n, c_n)$ is any non-empty sequence of modified characters, with (m_n, c_n) as the last modified character. If s is empty then

$$\theta(s(m_n, c_n)) = \theta((m_n, c_n)) = (m_n, c_n) \tag{21}$$

If s is not empty, then neither is $\theta(s)$, so let us express it as

$$\theta(s) = t(m_k, \Pi c_{kj}) \tag{22}$$

We can now do the inductive step in the definition of θ :

$$\theta(s(m_n, c_n)) = \begin{cases} t(m_k, (\Pi c_{kj}) c_n) & \text{if } (m_k = m_n), \\ \theta(s)(m_n, c_n) & \text{otherwise} \end{cases} \tag{23}$$

To show that φ is onto we will show that $\varphi(\theta(s)) = s$ for all s . Firstly if s is empty, or a single modified character, then $\varphi(\theta(s)) = s$ is trivially true. So consider the case where $s = s_1(m_n, c_n)$ and s_1 is not empty. The argument works by induction on the length of the sequence, so we may assume that $\varphi(\theta(s_1)) = s_1$. So there must exist elements such that:

$$\theta(s_1) = t(m_k, \Pi c_{kj}) \tag{24}$$

We now do a cases analysis, depending on whether $m_k = m_n$. If the modifiers are not equal then

$$\begin{aligned} \theta(s) &= \theta(s_1(m_k, c_n)) \\ &= \theta(s_1)\theta((m_k, c_n)) \end{aligned} \tag{25}$$

and therefore, using the fact that φ is a homomorphism,

$$\begin{aligned} \varphi(\theta(s)) &= \varphi(\theta(s_1))\varphi(\theta((m_k, c_n))) \\ &= s_1(m_k, c_n) = s \end{aligned} \tag{26}$$

In the case where $m_k = m_n$ we have $\theta(s) = t(m_k, (\Pi c_{kj}) c_n)$ (using the inductive definition) and so

$$\varphi(\theta(s)) = \varphi(t)\,\varphi((m_k, (\Pi c_{kj})\,c_n))$$
$$= \varphi(t)\,(\Pi\,(m_k, c_{kj}))\,(m_n, c_n)$$
$$= \varphi(\theta(s_1))\,(m_k, c_n) \tag{27}$$
$$= s_1\,(m_k, c_n) = s$$

Having established that φ is onto we need to show that it is also one-to-one (1-1). A direct algebraic argument could be used to do this, similar to the onto proof above. However here we will demonstrate an alternate technique based on counting.

Let the length of an IR be defined as the length of the modified character stream which it maps to. Then we can count the total number of internal representations with a given length, and the total number of modified character sequences of that length. If these numbers are equal then the sets have the same (finite) cardinality, and an onto map must therefore also be 1-1.

It is very easy to calculate the number of modified character sequences of length n; it simply $|M|^n|C|^n$.

For counting the number of elements of IR with length n, first consider the choice of the characters sequence (without modifiers), which gives $|C|^n$ choices. The internal representation is formed by inserting modifiers between characters, to break the stream into pieces. Between any two characters either no modifier is inserted or one of $|M| - 1$ modifiers distinct from the most recently used; this gives $|M|$ choices before each character (the first character is preceded by an unrestricted choice of modifier, but it is mandatory, so still $|M|$ possibilities arise). Hence there are $|M|^n|C|^n$ different internal representations with length n.

Modifications of the above argument may easily be made. For example, spaces can be introduced as a new special character which is considered identical, irrespective of the modifier. Combined with restrictions on IR - for example that the first character of a sequence modified is not a space - the cardinality of the sets can again be shown to be equal, guaranteeing that the function is 1-1, and that no covert channel exist in the IR representations, which are not already present in the modified character sequences. Similar arguments can be made special characters, such as tabs, page breaks, justification markers, etc.

6.2   Modified Character Stream to Pixel Map

The second stage is to prove that the map from modified character sequences to pixels is 1-1. Although this may intuitively seem easy, in practice it can be difficult to prove. If all the fonts used are to the same fixed width, then a given pixel representation may be easily cut into characters, and using the bitmap for each character (provided they are different for all modified characters) then the inverse map may be defined, and 1-1 mapping may be proved.

Note that it is unjustified to assume that distinct commercial fonts will have distinct characters representations. Some characters may have identical representation in each font (for example the full stop ".") while occasionally a character in one font, may be identical to another character in a quite different font (for example capital "I" and lower-case "l" may be identical in a pair of sans serif fonts).

In the general case it is difficult to be sure where one character finishes and another begins. An example of the kind of problem which can occur is illustrated in Fig. 3.:

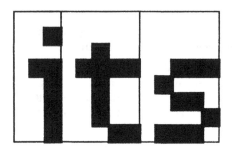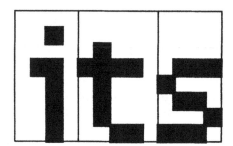

Fig. 3. Covert Channels in the Pixel Mapping

One approach is to ensure that all characters begin with a black pixel, and finish with a single, pixel-wide, vertical strip of white pixels (such a strip must also not be permitted elsewhere in a character). The difference of the two can be used to automatically calculate the partition into characters, and the usual techniques for proving that the map is 1-1 are applicable. A few indispensable characters may fail to satisfy these requirements (in particular the space character), and so special, ad hoc methods are required to define the means for their detection and correct (i.e. unique) partitioning.

One of the difficulties with the above approach is that the modified character may in itself be extremely complex, i.e. a diagram. The strategy for dealing with this situation is again, to form a one to one and onto mapping. One way that this can be achieved is by demanding that diagrams can only be represented by a bitmap. This strategy, while stripping out invisible covert channels, does have its limitations. For example, the power of having an editable diagram via vector based drawings is lost. In addition, while invisible channels are eliminated, there is still a fair amount of scope for storage channels which are not discernable to the visual inspection process. This matter is further discussed in the next section.

7   Blind Man's Filter

In this section, we discuss a technique for stripping out covert information from complex documents which is radically different to the approach described for complex text. Note that it is intended to introduce the functionality of the approach and not to provide an exhaustive analytical discourse in this particular paper.

While the approach discussed in the previous section is interesting in that we can prove that no new covert information can be introduced into the complex text portion of a document, there are still a number of avenues which may be exploited to pass covert information. The first is of course via diagrams and graphics. Another method involves visible changes in font etc. These types of channels, while not invisible channels, may not be discernable channels. It is outside the scope of this particular paper to delve into the quantification of specific risks on whether certain situations require covert channel control of one form or another. Here, we focus on the techniques available for various cases.

The major problem with subtle visible covert channels is that they are subtle to the human checker. What would be desirable is some sort of automated filter which was "blind" to the covert information when transferring the data. Just as the human user fails to register the human data, so we also wish that the filter did not see it and therefore not transfer the covert data. We call a filter which has this kind of property a Blind Man's Filter (BMF). It is blind to information which the user cannot discern. The next question which obviously springs to mind is how to construct such a filter and how effective it might be. In order to open the discussion on how to construct a BMF, we focus our attention on a method which is used extensively to strip out covert channels when transferring data from a high system to a low system. This venerable method involves printing the information on paper, checking it, and then rescanning the information back into the computer system. This method has the desirable effect of placing strong constraints on covert channels which exploit bitmap properties and white space hiding.

The BMF we have in mind is one where the output of a screen display is captured by a camera. The resolution of the camera must be less than that of the display. In addition, the scanning action of the camera must ensure that it does not reliably map one to one to pixels on the output. As a further mechanism for reducing covert channel capacity, software which may be used to attempt to recognise the scanned image can only accept a single or limited set of fonts.

Again, while the BMF does not guarantee the total elimination of covert channels, it does place very strong constraints on their exploitation. It does this by mimicing the same effects obtained by printing and rescanning: less data is needed to represent the required semantic information on a piece of paper with a given resolution, than that available for representation in a bitmap on a computer. In other words, by printing the information such as text on paper, the printing process "flattens" the bitmap for representation. If the messages being passed through the filter are well structured, then OCR software can have its parameters set to rescan the messages while preserving the overt information reliably.

If visual inspection is done on the output of the BMF, an attacker may signal by making changes to the original text (say, modulating between single and double spaces) which are mistaken by the human reviewer for the "noise" introduced by the BMF, but which are robust enough to pass through the BMF. Hence, visual inspection must occur prior to the BMF being applied. (Optionally, additional visual inspection could also be carried out after the BMF.)

8   History and Related Work

The original timing covert channel analysis was presented to the Allied TTCP XTP-1 forum in 1992 by M. Anderson.

The "message pump" subsequently developed at Naval Research Laboratories [3], has a similar problem to the timing problem in Stubs, as it requires the release of acknowledgements from high to low users. The means taken there to reduce timing channels is to have the pump buffer these acknowledgements, and then introduce a randomly generated delay to the times at which the acknowledgements are forwarded to the low users.

Covert channels have been an important factor in computer security for some time, and a number of studies have been carried out. Hu [2] provides a good description of a number of timing channels similar to the ones we have been reasoning about. A useful survey is the work by Moskowitz and Kang [4], especially for the consideration of timing channels.

9   Conclusion

It can be seen from the above examples that the Stubs have been designed in such a way as to remove many covert channels. Those few which remain can be controlled through implementing effective operational procedures such as correct choice of operating parameters combined with effective and regular analysis of the audit data generated. Done properly, such techniques allow the rigorous control of covert channel capacities in the presence of arbitrary Trojan Horses.

The techniques discussed earlier of timewindows, unique representation of complex text, and the Blind Man's Filter (BMF), are relatively simple and general and could be adapted to other information security systems. They are not to regarded as "silver-bullets" to eliminate all covert channelling problems, but as additional tools for the designer of secure systems.

10   Acknowledgements

Although the concepts in this paper are the authors' work, considerable acknowledgement is due to Dr. Ken Hayman. Before leaving DSTO, he reviewed and modified the original covert timing channel analysis presented to the Allied TTCP XTP-1 forum in 1992 by M. Anderson, in order to recast it in a more rigorous manner. This work appears in elements of sections 2, 3, and 4 of the paper.

We also thank Ira Moskowitz who provided comments on the paper, and presented it at the Workshop when the authors were unfortunately unable to attend.

11   References

[1] Carlson. Communication Systems, 1986.

[2] Wei-Ming Hu. Reducing Timing Channels with Fuzzy Time. In *Proceedings of the Security and Privacy Conference.* 8-20, Oakland, CA, 1991.

[3] Myong H. Kang and Ira S. Moskowitz. A pump for rapid, reliable, secure communication. In *Proc. of the 1st ACM Conference on Computer and Communication Security.* 119-129, Fairfax, VA, November 1993.

[4] Ira S. Moskowitz and Myong H. Kang. Covert Channels - Here to Stay? In *Proc. of the Ninth Annual Conference on Computer Assurance (Compass'94):* 235-243, Gaithersburg, MD, June 1994.

Anonymous Addresses and Confidentiality of Location

Ian W. Jackson

Cambridge University Computer Laboratory /
Olivetti Research Limited, Cambridge

Abstract

We describe a scheme which will allow location information from devices like active badges to be collected by an agent controlled by the user, hiding the user's location from the network infrastructure, so that the user may distribute the information about their location as they see fit.

1. Introduction

Suppose a location information system which involves something like active badges – small devices worn by users which communicate with sensors in a building to locate people.[2]

Many people, especially employees of large companies not noted for concern with things like employee privacy, are reluctant to accept this kind of technology because they fear that the management will use them to 'spy' on them.

To alleviate this fear I believe that it is necessary to give users strong control over the information gathered by such a system.

This control should continue to be effective even when large portions (but not all) of the computing infrastructure have been 'compromised', in the sense that the people who run them are doing monitoring.

Here is an outline of a possible solution to this problem.

2. Users' agents

Possible the most flexible way of achieving the goal is to allow the user to maintain, on systems controlled by themselves or those that they trust, an 'agent' which is the only entity that has direct access to the information about their location. Anyone wanting the user's location must ask their agent.

The agent may be quite remote from the sensors doing the actual tracking.

How does the user's agent keep track of the user's location, without allowing other parts of the system to do so ? Ideally the badge (or other device carried by the user) would be able to send unobserved and unintercepted a message directly to the user's agent. The sensor then simply sends the user's agent the location data. Unfortunately this is impractical as it stands. Spread-spectrum radio might be an option, but would be rather large to implement in a badge-like device, and in any case restrictions on the types of devices and the ways of gathering location information are undesirable.

3. Anonymous address labels

Instead, I have borrowed some ideas from the cryptographically-based anonymous message schemes, as described by Chaum [1]. Messages are sent via a series of remailers, all of whom must be compromised for a message to be traceable (other than by traffic analysis).

The badge sends to the sensor an 'address label', which the sensor can use to communicate with the user's agent without knowing where that agent is or whose it is.

The address label consists of a key with which to encrypt the location data, the name (or network address) of the next remailer, and an piece of encrypted instructions which is to be interpreted by that next remailer. This latter will usually consist of another address label.

The sending badge constructs the address label by repeated encapsulation, and broadcasts it for the benefit of any sensors present.

Each sensor which receives it use the label to send a message containing the location of the sighting.

Each remailer strips off, uses and discards one layer of addressing encapsulation. At each stage the key from that stage's address label is used to reencipher the data, so that the destination receives a multi-layered encrypted message.

Address labels have to be constructed so that many different labels can be found for a single path or destination - this is so that the address label doesn't become an alternative means of identifying the user. Preferably, each transmission from a badge will use a different label.

4. Protocols

4.1. Public key done by badge

Each remailer receives a message in two parts. The second part is the message itself (possibly already encrypted, perhaps more than once).

The first part is encrypted, using the remailer's public key. It contains a symmetric key with which to encrypt the data, and information which can be added to the message to allow the final recepient to determine that key (the key must change with each new label, so that it cannot be used to trace the user and is not so easily compromised). The first part also contains the name of the next hop destination, as well as an encrypted lump that the next hop (presumably) knows how to unpick.

I propose to generate the 'hop session key', which is used to re-encrypt the data, by encrypting a nonce under a key shared between the badge and the agent. By encrypting the nonce in two different ways we can give the remailer the session key as well as allow the remailer to pass on without understanding information that will allow the agent to recover the session key.

Let us call the badge B and the user's agent A. Supposing that remailer P receives:

$$\{\{N_{B,P}\}_{K_{AB}}, \{f(N_{B,P})\}_{K_{AB}}, Q, \{stuff\ for\ Q\}_{K_Q}\}_{K_P} \qquad \boxed{D}$$

Here the left hand box is the "anonymous address label", and the right hand side is the data to be sent.

It then sends to Q (which is either the next remailer or A, the final destination, but P doesn't need to know which):

$$\{stuff\ for\ Q\}_{K_Q} \qquad \{N_{B,P}\}_{K_{AB}}, \{D\}_{\{f(N_{B,P})\}_{K_{AB}}}$$

A can now recover the original D by decrypting $N_{B,P}$, applying f (which might be some simple function such as exclusive or with a fixed bit-pattern), and hence deriving the key $\{f(N_{B,P})\}_{K_{AB}}$.

Before a message as shown above arrives at the first remailer it is assembled by the sensor. The sensor (S) is receives from the badge data equivalent to that used by a remailer (ie, *stuff for S*, which includes amongst other things P and $\{stuff\ for\ P\}_{K_P}$). This data need not be encrypted, if we do not trust the sensor and do not want to spend effort encrypting things for it which we could better spend encrypting things for a more trusted party. S encrypts the location L using the rules for D above, and sends the result to P.

At the last stage, where $Q = A$, *stuff for Q* is merely B's name, so that A knows which of the possibly many badges it is handling is involved. A strips off the many levels of encryption to recover the original D, ie L, the location.

4.2. No public key in badge

Public key cryptography has disadvantages for very small mobile entities; it requires much computational effort, and the messages it produces are large.

The required aspect of public key cryptography is the fact that many senders can encrypt messages to the same recipient in such a way that none of the senders can read each other's messages, nor can they relate different messages from the same sender. We can achieve much the same effect by using symmetric key cryptography with large numbers of different keys.

The recipient issues {nonce,key} pairs on request; these are constructed so that the recipient can derive the key from the nonce easily, but the nonces are unpredictable, and noone else can see the relationship between nonces and keys that they haven't explicitly been sent:

$$N_{Xi} = \{i\}_{K_{xx}} ; K_{Xi} = \{f(i)\}_{K_{xx}}$$

We can now rewrite the remailing function using these pairs. Supposing that remailer P receives:

$$\boxed{N_{Pi}, \{N_{Ak}, K_{Ak}, Q, N_{Qj}, \{stuff\,for\,Q\}_{K_{Qj}}\}_{K_{Pi}}} \quad \boxed{D}$$

It then sends to Q:

$$\boxed{N_{Qj}, \{stuff\,for\,Q\}_{K_{Qj}}} \quad \boxed{N_{Ak}, \{D\}_{K_{Ak}}}$$

4.3. Delivery of keys to badge

The above scheme requires that the badge have a stock of anonymous address labels for its user's agent. Since the labels now only contain symmetric keys and symmetric key encrypted data they are a lot smaller - just over 3 times the key size per hop - and the badge is now no longer required to manipulate them. This means we can do away with the complication surrounding $N_{B,P}$ and K_{AB}.

Instead, we have the agent collect {nonce,key} pairs from the remailers, construct address labels for itself, and send them to the badge. It needs a way of sending the labels to the badge, anonymously.

We have to use public key cryptograpy here, in order to bootstrap the symmetric keys. Supposing that remailer Q receives

$$\{P, \{stuff\,for\,P\}_{K_P}\}_{K_Q}$$

it sends to P:

$$\{stuff\,for\,P\}_{K_P}$$

This is similar to the electronic mail remailers – the sender (here the user's agent) is responsible for constructing the message and nesting the encryptions.

4.4. Request for {nonce,key} pairs

Finally, we need a protocol for the user's agent to request {nonce,key} pairs. This has to be done anonymously too. We use the 'reverse' anonymity mechanism to transmit the request, and the anonymous address label scheme itself to return the reply.

When a remailer P receives:

$$\{ \boxed{ N_{Qj} , \{stuff\,for\,Q\}_{K_{Qj}} } , N_{Ak} , K_{Ak} , n \}_{K_P}$$

it replies, via Q, with:

$$\boxed{ N_{Qj} , \{stuff\,for\,Q\}_{K_{Qj}} } , \boxed{ N_{Ak} , \{ N_{P(i+1)} , K_{P(i+1)} \cdots N_{P(i+n)} , K_{P(i+n)} \}_{K_{Ak}} }$$

4.5. Freshness

The descriptions above do not include any timestamps or other means of producing freshness. However, because the user's agent knows when each of the requests for address labels was sent it can discard stale replies, and also stale address labels.

This is another improvement over the public-key based protocol, which would need the introduction of clocks or perhaps some kind of challenge-response.

4.6. Limitations and practicality

There are a number of unresolved issues here. In particular, problems will arise when the badge is out of touch for a long time and runs out of address labels. The usual tradeoff between security and functionality exists here: the badge can go off-air (or transmit much less frequently), until it is 'refilled' (perhaps by the user pressing a button to indicate that they're willing to have their location known), or it can reuse old labels in the hope that this will allow the agent to find it and send it some new ones.

I have not done a convincing formal analysis of the protocols, looking for weaknesses.

There will be a certain vulnerability to traffic analysis. The key setup messages will provide cover traffic for the actual badge data, but they do tend to be rather large. In order to solve this problem it will probably be necessary to make explicit provision for cover traffic; this, combined with a certain degree of regular queueing of messages (rather than sending them instantaneously) may help.

5. 'Advanced' applications

5.1. 'Who is at location L ?'

It will frequently be the case that an enquirer will want to ask questions about locations, rather than users. How, then, will they know which agent(s) to ask ?

Such enquiries can be sent to the sensors in the relevant area. The sensors can keep a list of recently-seen address labels, and forward the enquiry to all of those agents. Each agent can then choose whether and how to reply (possibly anonymising the reply, for example to say 'there is someone here but they won't tell you who they are').

References

[1] David Chaum. Untraceable electronic mail, return addresses, and digital pseudonyms. *Communications of the ACM* **24/2**, 84–88 (1981).

[2] Roy Want, Andy Hopper, Veronica Falcao, Jonathon Gibbons. The Active Badge location system. *ACM Transactions on Information Systems* **10/1**, 91–102 (January 1992).

[3] A. Pfitzmann B. Pfitzmann M. Waidner. ISDN-Mixes: Untraceable communications with very small bandwidth overhead. In *GI/ITG Conference on Communication in Distributed Systems, Mannheim* pages 451–463 February 1991.

MIXes in Mobile Communication Systems: Location Management with Privacy[*]

Hannes Federrath, Anja Jerichow, Andreas Pfitzmann

University of Dresden,
Institute of Theoretical Computer Science, D-01062 Dresden, Germany

{feder, jerichow, pfitza}@inf.tu-dresden.de

Summary. This paper introduces a new technique for location management in cellular networks. It avoids the recording of moving tracks of mobile subscribers. The described procedures are derived from the well known untraceable MIX network and the distributed storage of location information according to GSM networks.

1   Terminology

The served area of a cellular radio network is usually divided into location areas. Location areas are comprised of one or several radio cells. The mark (address) of a location area is the Location Area Identification (LAI).

To address a Mobile Station (MS) in the case of an incoming call, the mobile network needs to know the current location area in order to broadcast the connection request.[1]

The location management is comprised of the procedures location update and handover.

The location update consists of all procedures for location management in the stand-by state of an MS, whereas the handover handles an MS moving during a call.

2   Storage of Location Information

To register the location of an MS, the network operator can maintain a Home Location Register (HLR) at a *central place* in the network. The HLR keeps track of the actual LAI of the MS.

In the case of a (mobile terminated) call the subscriber A calls the Mobile Subscriber Integrated Services Digital Network Number (MSISDN) of the mobile subscriber B. The mobile network reads the current LAI and routes the call to the responsible Base Transceiver Station (BTS). Then the BTS broadcasts a connection request in all cells of the location area (see Fig. 1).

---

[*]   We thank the Gottlieb-Daimler - and Karl-Benz Foundation, Ladenburg (Germany) and the German Science Foundation (DFG) for their financial support. For suggestions and discussions, we thank Elke Franz, Ulrich Hensel, Dogan Kesdogan, Jan Müller, Leslie & Christian "ChriRo" Rook and Ivonne Voigt.

[1]   The technique "broadcast over the whole served area" is not discussed in this paper! In 3rd generation mobile networks (Universal Mobile Telecommunication System, UMTS and Future Public Land Mobile Telecommunication Network, FPLMTN) the globally covered area does not allow broadcast. However, broadcasts in some parts of the globe require location management again.

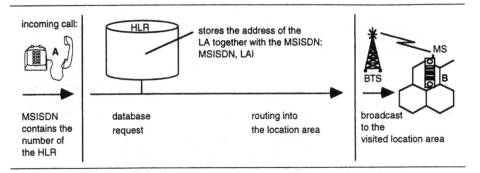

Fig. 1: Call setup with central storage of location information

If the MS is moving into another location area, the HLR is addressed and informed of the new LAI. This location update causes a signalling load on the air-interface and the fixed mobile network. In case of long distances between the visited location area and the HLR, the load in the fixed mobile network is immense.

The solution of this problem is *two-stage storage*: The additional Visitor Location Register (VLR) stores the actual LAI while the HLR (hierarchically) holds the address of the VLR (A_{VLR}).

If the location area changes without leaving the VLR area, only the VLR record has to be updated. If the MS moves to a new VLR area, the HLR record has to be updated. The signalling load in the fixed mobile network is reduced by this technique. However, the complexity of the network management increases. The location management described above is used in the Global System for Mobile Communication (GSM) [GSM_93] (see Fig. 2).

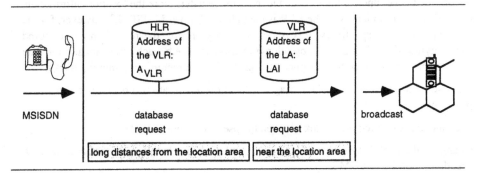

Fig. 2: Call setup with two-stage storage of location information in HLR and VLR

A generalized form of the two-stage storage is the *multi-stage storage* of location information (see Fig. 3). The registers Ri (with i=1..n) store hierarchical location information.

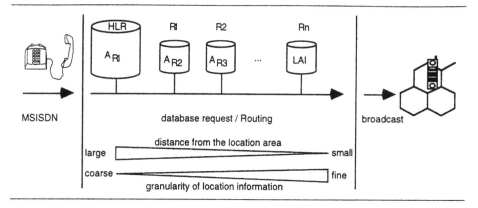

Fig. 3: Generalized multi-stage storage of location information

Consequently, the additional database requests require an even more expensive call setup. The costs for database updates in the case of long distances from the location area are decreased and the signalling load may be reduced.

3 Recording Moving Tracks of Mobile Subscribers

Unfortunately, the above mentioned measures do not prevent the ability of the network operator to record moving tracks. There are two reasons for this problem:

Firstly, the operators of the registers (HLR, VLR, Ri) cooperate with one another. This cooperation is necessary for call setup but implies the hazards of an easier linkability of the distributed location information.

Secondly, it is yet unclear under which identity the registers store the location information. Clearly, the stored identity in the HLR is the publicly known MSISDN.[2] However, for the VLR and the Ri respectively, this is not necessary. There, the records may be stored pseudonymously.[3] Changing the pseudonym periodically, e.g. each time a location update is performed on the stage Ri, complicates considerably the recording of moving tracks.

The use of pseudonyms for the storage of location information, however, creates new problems:

Each incoming call requires a link between the pseudonymous records.

Changing the pseudonym should lead to the unlinkability between the old and the new pseudonym of the same MS.

---

[2] For internal purposes, the MS has another number, the International Mobile Subscriber Identity (IMSI). In the procedures described in this paper, we assume that MSISDN and IMSI are equivalent identities. For a uniform presentation of all described procedures, we use only the MSISDN!

[3] If they are not stored under a pseudonym, but under the identity of the mobile subscriber (MSISDN), the MS is traceable by the VLR (and the Ri respectively). The moving track will become more detailed with increasing i. Otherwise, only a pseudonym is traceable.

4 Measures that Prevent the Creation of Moving Tracks

Generally, the "creation of moving tracks in mobile communication" can be prevented as follows:

1) *Avoidance of location information* and broadcast covering the entire served area (see [FJKP_95]),

2) *Trustworthy maintenance of location information* (see [Pfit_93, Hets_93, FJKP_95]), e.g. in a trusted Fixed Station (trusted FS, e.g. the fixed telephone of the mobile subscriber in the fixed network),

3) *"covered" storage of location information* — the scope of this paper.

In particular, the solutions 2) and 3), however, require further measures depending on the varying strength of an attacker. These measures are:

i) Protection of the communication relations between the components of the fixed network (see [PfWa_87, PfPW_91]),

ii) Protection against locating by means of electromagnetic radio waves (see [FeTh_95, FJKP_95]).

The measure *i)* works against a strong attacker who can observe all communications in the network, e.g. transactions between BTS', VLRs and HLR. Since the BTS' serve particular areas, indirect locating is possible. In order to achieve protection against observation, the untraceable MIX network [Chau_81, PfWa_87, PfPW_91] and special addressing attributes, "implicit addresses", can be used.

Measure *ii)* is important because the source of the waves corresponds to the location of the sending mobile station. Special modulation methods, e.g. Direct Sequence Spread Spectrum (DS/SS) and Code Division Multiple Access (CDMA) reduce the abilities for locating.

5 A New Centralized Procedure for Location Management with Privacy

In the following sections we are going to describe a new "covered" form of the location information (LAI) stored in the HLR database. The new procedure is firstly described for the centralized storage of location information and will afterwards be generalized to the multi-stage storage.

The situation without protection can be described as follows. In the HLR, a database record «MSISDN, LAI» is stored. For each incoming call, the mobile network routes the connection request to the responsible Mobile Switching Centre (MSC) which arranges to broadcast the call setup message to the location area.

Before a MS can recognize its call setup message (in Fig. 4 call_setup_msg[4]), it must be addressed using an implicit address concealing the MS' identity.

This method is similarly applied in GSM networks. A frequently changing pseudonym – the Temporary Mobile Subscriber Identity (TMSI) – ensures the privacy on the air-interface against outsider attacks. The TMSIs are assigned by the network.

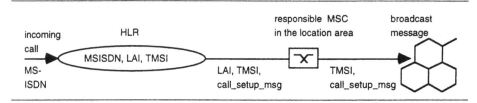

Fig. 4: Call setup with centralized storage of location information (more detailed than Fig. 1)

Below, we describe the new procedures for location registration and call setup with covered LAI. The LAI is *stored not in its plain form, but in its covered form instead*, denoted by {LAI}.

5.1 Premises and Assumptions

Throughout this paper, an MIX network [Chau_81, PfWa_87, PfPW_91] is assumed. Consequently, all statements in the literature concerning the organization, operation and efficiency of MIXes are to be applied to the new procedures.

For clarification, we assume that an encryption key has been exchanged between the MS and the fixed part of the mobile network to encrypt *all* messages on the air-interface. This encryption is omitted in the following formulas.

In asymmetric (public key) cryptosystems we assume an *indeterministic cryptosystem*, i.e. equal plaintext blocks are encrypted to different ciphertext blocks!

Furthermore, we only describe the most necessary messages in the following "protocols". For better comprehension we use characteristic examples instead of the general formal notation.

5.2 Location Registration and Location Update

Whereas before the network has taken the routing information from the LAI, now the MS needs to create the routing information itself.

---

[4] Provided that all messages (e.g. call_setup_msg and location_registration_msg) are unique and network wide standardized messages – a kind of service primitives – used by all subscribers for a service request.

For the covered location registration, the MS formulates for the {LAI} a so called *untraceable return address* (example for a cascade of three MIXes M1, M2 and M3):

$$\{LAI\} := A_{M1}, c_{M1}(k_{M1}, A_{M2}, c_{M2}(k_{M2}, A_{M3}, c_{M3}(k_{M3}, TMSI))).[5]$$

A_{M1}, A_{M2} and A_{M3} denote the addresses of the MIXes M1, M2 and M3; their public keys are denoted by c_{M1}, c_{M2} and c_{M3}, respectively. The sending in every MIX, i.e. call_setup_msg, is encoded by the (symmetric) keys k_{M1}, k_{M2} and k_{M3}.

The implicit address for the broadcast on the air-interface is denoted by TMSI. Our algorithms allow only the MS to create the TMSI. In the following section, additional properties of the TMSI are required.

The location registration message LR to the Home Location Register is

$$LR := MSISDN, \{LAI\}, location\_registration\_msg.$$

The MS uses the MIX network to protect the LR message (and consequently its source):

$$\{LR\} := A_{M3}, c_{M3}(A_{M2}, c_{M2}(A_{M1}, c_{M1}(A_{HLR}, LR))).$$

Since an *indeterministic* cryptosystem was assumed, there is no need to encode random bits into {LR}. The indeterministic encryption is necessary to prevent the following attack to a MIX network: The attacker could simply encrypt the outgoing messages of a MIX Mi using its public key c_{Mi} and matching it to the incoming messages!

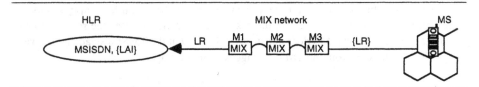

Fig. 5: Location registration with central and covered storage of the location information

The HLR stores the covered return address {LAI} instead of the plain LAI.

Because the TMSI is encoded in the {LAI}, it does not need to be stored explicitly.

In case of a location update, the HLR is informed of the new {LAI}, and the old {LAI} expires.

It is important to know that (according to the MIX functionality "ignore repeats of messages") each {LAI} can only be used once.[6] This means that after a transaction caused by the HLR a new {LAI} is needed. For permanent reachability of the MS, it transmits a new {LAI} after each transaction or a set of {LAI}s for more sophisticated interactions.

---

[5] The symbol k_x with some subscript x will always denote a key of the symmetric cryptosystem, c_x and d_x public and private keys of the asymmetric cryptosystem; encryptions and decryptions of a message N are denoted by $k_x(N)$, $k_x^{-1}(N)$, $c_x(N)$, and $d_x(N)$, resp. The subscript denotes the owner of the key.

[6] The MIX ignores repetitions of sent messages in order to prevent replay attacks. The deterministic decryption of these messages would "uncover" the relation between the incoming and outgoing messages.

5.3   Call Setup (mobile terminated)

In the case of an incoming call, the stored record of the MSISDN is read. The {LAI} contains the address A_{M1} of the first MIX. Beyond this point, the HLR has no routing information for the message call_setup_msg!

MIX M1 finds the address A_{M2} and k_{M1} to encode the call_setup_msg. The encoding of the message is the (symmetric) encryption k_{M1}(call_setup_msg).

Through the MIXes M1, M2 and M3, the encoded message

$$\{call\_setup\_msg\} := k_{M3}(k_{M2}(k_{M1}(call\_setup\_msg)))$$

is generated. It is addressed with the TMSI and broadcasted to the location area.

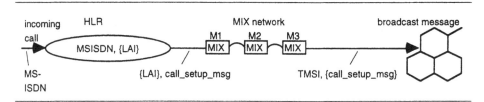

Fig. 6: Call setup with central and covered storage of the location information

The MS decodes the message {call_setup_msg} by decrypting with k_{M3}, k_{M2} and k_{M1}. Therefore, it must store or reconstruct these keys. The TMSI indicates the relation to an {LAI}. This means that the MS does not store the {LAI} but the TMSI instead and derives the k_{Mi} (i=1..3) directly from the TMSI as suggested in this paper.

6   Efficiency

The use of MIX networks leads to a message expansion. However, the bandwidth on the air-interface is limited. The following section proposes optimizations of the ideas described above.

6.1   Trusted Base Transceiver Station (trusted BTS)

Because of the small bandwidth on the air-interface, the BTS could act as an extension of the MS, and it could generate and transmit the {LAI}s. In this case, the BTS must be trustworthy to the MS, i.e. it is identified and authenticated as a trusted BTS.

To reduce the ability of locating (by means of the radio waves), this organizational condition is possibly acceptable. Consequently, the MIX functionality works only in the fixed network.

6.2   Generating {LAI} Sets

As mentioned above, each {LAI} can only be used once. Therefore, it is desirable to hold a set of {LAI}s in the HLR.

A further measure for reducing the bandwidth on the air-interface in location update situations is to reference existing[7] {LAI}s of different location areas with a short index. Of course, the transfer of the {LAI}s to the HLR requires more bandwidth than plain method described above. Moreover, additional memory capacity is needed in the HLR.

The problem of limited bandwidth does not exist if the MS is roaming in an area with low traffic or if the MS is "connected" to the fixed network.[8] In these situations the MS can transmit {LAI} sets to the HLR. A similar situation is given by the end of an existing connection (e.g. a normal call). The existing radio channel could be used to transmit some {LAI}s.[9]

The following types of {LAI} sets can be distinguished:

a) {LAI} sets of the present roaming area. This variant is restricted to the MS staying within a single location area. These {LAI} sets can be transmitted at the end of a call connection.

b) {LAI} sets of different roaming areas previously visited by the MS. In this variant, it is assumed that an MS revisits these areas.

c) {LAI} sets of different areas preferred by the MS to be visited. This variant requires intelligent mobility analysis strategies in the MS.

In particular, b) and c) may increase the efficiency of the location management (especially location update).

It is not necessary to transmit the short indices while transmitting the {LAI} sets. With the help of a globally known hash function h, the index (i.e. the hash value) of a {LAI} is calculated by $h(\{LAI\})$ and stored together with the {LAI}. The hash value must be sufficiently long to avoid collisions of indices.

The MS must also store the hash value $h(\{LAI\})$. It is not necessary to store the {LAI} itself, but the relation to the location area must be stored. Furthermore, the MS must store the accompanying TMSI (and possibly the k_{Mi}).

If the {LAI} is already stored in the HLR while a location is being updated, the MS transmits only the index of the {LAI}.

---

[7]   stored in the HLR

[8]   The mobile networks of the 3rd generation (Universal Mobile Telecommunication System, UMTS, and Future Public Land Mobile Telecommunication Network, FPLMTN) distinguish between home, business, and public environments with different mobility levels and bandwidths.

[9]   In this way, another problem may be solved. The disconnection of several MS' occurs simultaneously if discrete time slots (e.g. the full minute and the 30th second of a minute) are used. Thereby the linkability of subscriber actions is reduced.

6.3   Trusted Fixed Station (trusted FS)

If a trusted Fixed Station (trusted FS) is installed instead of, or in addition to, a telephone in the fixed network, the short "plain" LAI can be transmitted to the trusted FS. The covered {LAI}s can be generated in the trusted FS and transmitted to the HLR. Of course, the MS must know the TMSIs and the k_{Mi}!

However, the strength of the proposed procedures is that a trusted FS is unnecessary, at least from the security and privacy point of view.[10] This offers new opportunities to "decentralize" the procedures which will be demonstrated in the following sections.

7   Multi-staged Storage of Location Information with Pseudonyms but without MIXes

The following measures reduce the signalling load during the location update process under central storage of location information if the distance between the HLR and the location area is large.

We put the situation described in Fig. 3 into a concrete form in terms of privacy aspects. For example, we use a 3-stage storage (Ri with i=0..2) of location information (see Fig. 7).

7.1   Call Setup (mobile terminated)

For a mobile subscriber with a MSISDN, the HLR (also denoted as R0) stores the address of the next register (A_{R1}) which, in turn, stores the location information of the mobile subscriber. The HLR also stores a pseudonym P1 which is not linkable to anything.[11]

The register R1 uses the pseudonym P1 to store the address of the next register (here A_{R2}) and a pseudonym P2.

The register R2 uses the pseudonym P2 to store the LAI and the implicit address TMSI for the broadcast message on the air-interface.

This system results in a pseudonymously chained list which describes the location information for the MS. When a call comes in, the chaining is processed.

For the security of the described procedure, we assume that not all Ri conspire together as one attacker. The HLR plays a special role in that. Without cooperation from anyone it can assign coarse location information to the MSISDN, provided the address of R1 represents a location (respectively a served area similar to the VLR in GSM networks).

The message call_setup_msg is unique in the whole network. As a result, no linkability is possible via call_setup_msg! In this way, we can take advantage of this "small (signalling) message space".

---

[10] There are other proposals using a trusted FS that may be more efficient than our procedures (see [KFJP_95, FJKP_95]). However, in this proposals the trusted FS is *necessary for security and privacy*!

[11] It can be computed by a true random generator.

Replay attacks are another problem. An attacker who does not control all Ri can intercept a connection request message and send it to the Ri again. Because of the deterministic process, the Ri would create the same output message, and the "path" of the message would be recognizable. Therefore, each pseudonym may only be used once (similar to a {LAI} in the previous sections).

A solution for this problem is a modification of the pseudonyms, either after each use or periodically.

If a global time base T is used, the pseudonyms switch forward at each time step. In this case the switching does not depend on the transactions. If the switching is processed by a globally known cryptographic function f, the MS must send an initial value P_{init} for the location update, or location registration where P_{init} can be a random number. The pseudonyms are calculated according to the rule $Pi := f(T, P_{init})$.

Alternatively, the switch of the pseudonyms is calculated by the successor function $Pi' := f(Pi, k_{Pi})$ from the current pseudonym Pi. The required "secrets" (keys) k_{Pi} are only known to the two Ri, which use a common pseudonym (e.g. R0 and R1 regarding P1; R1 and R2 regarding P2).

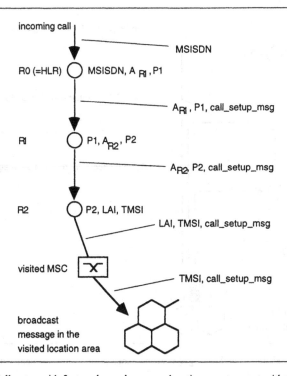

Fig. 7: Call setup with 3-staged pseudonymous location management without MIXes

7.2   Location Registration and Location Update

The terms "location registration" and "location update" are used in this paper for the process through which the registers Ri are informed of the records they must store. If the distance to the location area decreases with increasing i, the signalling load will be reduced.

For location registration and location update, the MS must know the potentially usable Ri. It is desired that the MS can them select from many Ri on all stages. This diversity achieves the independence of the Ri. An anonymous directory service – e.g. the "blinded read operation" described in [CoBi_95] – could be a proper solution for gathering information about favorable Ri. Using this service, the MS can read the directory entries for the visited area in an anonymous and unobservable manner.

For a location update, only the MS decides which records must be updated in which Ri. The MS decides when it must change to another register.

An MIX network (sender anonymity scheme) is also used for the unlinkability between the sender (i.e. the MS) and recipient (i.e. the registers Ri).

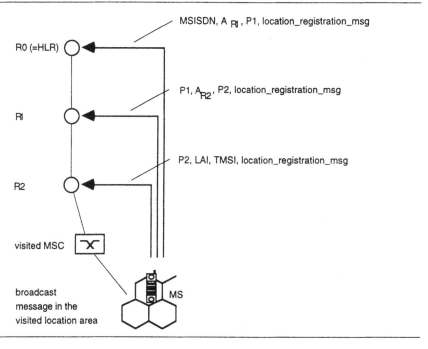

Fig. 8: Location registration with 3-staged pseudonymous location management without MIXes

8   Multi-staged Location Management with Pseudonyms and MIXes

So far, we have assumed that the Ri do not conspire (work together) as one attacker. In reality, this would be too hard to achieve because many available registers can belong to one network operator.

If an attacker can observe all communication in the entire network, he can moreover recognize all communication relations if no untraceable network is used.

The registers store the signalling messages, wait until other connection messages are received, and then sends them out in one batch. This system reduces the linkability of signalling messages.

The use of an MIX network makes multi-staged location management applicable without the above mentioned limitations of security.

Here, each Ri stores an untraceable return address {Ri+1} generated by the MS. Ri+1 and Pi+1 are included in {Ri+1}. Thus, neither Ri+1 nor Pi+1 is recognizable by the register Ri. Even if all Ri conspire, they are not in a position to uncover the location of the MS.[12]

8.1   Call Setup (mobile terminated)

An incoming call is processed in the following way (example for the three registers R0, R1 and R2, see Fig. 9).

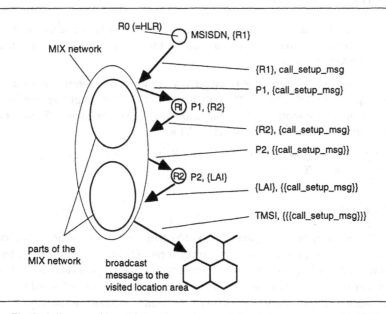

Fig. 9: Call setup with multi-staged pseudonymous location management with MIXes

---

[12] Untraceable return addresses *force* the registers Ri to use the MIX network.

The HLR (R0) sends a connection request message call_setup_msg – "addressed" with covered {R1} into the MIX network.

The register R1 receives P1 and the encoded message {call_setup_msg} and passes the message {call_setup_msg} to the MIX network – prefixed with the untraceable return address {R2}.

The register R2 receives P2, and the "re-encoded" message {{call_setup_msg}} sends {{call_setup_msg}} into the MIX network again – addressed with the covered {LAI}.

Finally, the MS receives the TMSI and the three times covered connection request message {{{call_setup_msg}}}.

The MS must decode this message with all k_{Mi} used "along" its path through the MIX network.

The procedure is described assuming a "classic" MIX network[13]. If no linkable information is contained in the (signalling) messages, as is assumed in the above sections, the expensive change of encoding in the MIXes is unnecessary. Passing the messages (without encoding) through the MIXes would be sufficient to ensure security. However, the MIXes need to know that the incoming messages are signalling messages without any linkability. For the use of a common classic MIX network, the described form with encoding is useful.

8.2   Security and Efficiency

Even if all registers would conspire as one attacker, they would not even be able to trace the messages they send to themselves, because of the use of untraceable return addresses generated by the MS.

The security of our procedures – that is the privacy of the location information – depends on the security of the MIX network. The only purpose of using the registers is to increase the efficiency of the location management (similar to GSMs functional division of the location management between the HLR and the VLR).

The use of MIXes geographically close to the Ri is recommended to prevent an unnecessary reduction of efficiency.

9   Conclusions

The outlined procedures do not require a trustworthy fixed station for location management without recordable moving tracks of mobile subscribers. The security of the procedures is based on the security of asymmetric (public key) cryptography, whereas the procedures at best are complexity theoretically secure. The design principle "diversity" – realized in the multi-stage storage of the location information – was used to increase the security.

---

[13] Store incoming messages, discard repeats, change encodings and reorder them, and put them out as a single batch.

It is interesting to note that the recipient anonymity scheme (i.e. untraceable return addresses) is not directly used to hold the recipient (the MS) anonymously. After all, the HLR "knows" the identity of the mobile subscriber – the MSISDN. The untraceable return addresses are only used to hide the routing information and thereby the location of the MS in cellular networks.

It is worth stating at this point that the use of MIXes in this paper refers only to signalling processes in mobile communications. The efficient use of MIX networks to protect the communication relations (and the exchange of user data) between fixed stations in fixed networks is described in the literature (e.g. in [PfPW_91]); however, its use in mobile communications corresponds to these measures to a great extend.

Finally, the small bandwidth on the air-interface conflicts with the increasing signalling overhead of the new procedures. The construction and use of a trusted BTS (see section 6.1) may be the remedial action.

The application of the procedures to mobile networks using only personal mobility – i.e., the mobile subscriber has no mobile station but can use his personal communication environment at all fixed terminals – however, seems possible because a broadband network (but no air-interface) is used.

10 References

Chau_81   D. Chaum: Untraceable Electronic Mail, Return Addresses, and Digital Pseudonyms; Communications of the ACM 24/2 (1981) 84-88.

CoBi_95   D. A. Cooper, K. P. Birman: Preserving Privacy in a Network of Mobile Computers; 1995 IEEE Symposium on Research in Security and Privacy, IEEE Computer Society Press, Los Alamitos 1995, 26-38.

FeTh_95   H. Federrath, Jürgen Thees: Schutz der Vertraulichkeit des Aufenthaltsorts von Mobilfunkteilnehmern; Datenschutz und Datensicherung, DuD 6/95, 338-348.

FJKP_95   H. Federrath, A. Jerichow, D. Kesdogan, A. Pfitzmann: Security in Public Mobile Communication Networks; Proc. of the IFIP TC 6 International Workshop on Personal Wireless Communications, Verlag der Augustinus Buchhandlung Aachen, 1995, 105-116.

GSM_93   ETSI: GSM Recommendations: GSM 01.02 - 12.21; February 1993, Release 92.

Hets_93   T. Hetschold: Aufbewahrbarkeit von Erreichbarkeits- und Schlüsselinformation im Gewahrsam des Endbenutzers unter Erhaltung der GSM-Funktionalität eines Funknetzes; GMD-Studien Nr. 222, Oktober 1993.

KFJP_96   D. Kesdogan, H. Federrath, A. Jerichow, A. Pfitzmann: Location Management Strategies increasing Privacy in Mobile Communication Systems; in: Information Systems Security. Facing the information society of the 21st century. Proc. of the IFIP SEC '96 12th International Information Security

Conference 21 - 24 May, 1996, Island of Samos, Greece, Chapman & Hall, 1996.

Pfit_93   A. Pfitzmann: Technischer Datenschutz in öffentlichen Funknetzen; Daten-schutz und Datensicherung, DuD 17/8 (1993), 451-463.

PfPW_91   A. Pfitzmann, B. Pfitzmann, M. Waidner: ISDN-MIXes – Untraceable Communication with Very Small Bandwidth Overhead; Proc. IFIP/Sec'91, May 1991, Brighton, North-Holland, Amsterdam 1991, 245-258.

PfWa_87   A. Pfitzmann, M. Waidner: Networks without user observability; Computers & Security 6/2 (1987) 158-166.

Hiding Routing Information

David M. Goldschlag, Michael G. Reed, and Paul F. Syverson

Naval Research Laboratory, Center For High Assurance Computer Systems,
Washington, D.C. 20375-5337, USA, phone: +1 202.404.2389, fax: +1 202.404.7942,
e-mail: {*last name*}@itd.nrl.navy.mil.

Abstract. This paper describes an architecture, *Onion Routing*, that
limits a network's vulnerability to traffic analysis. The architecture provides anonymous socket connections by means of proxy servers. It provides real-time, bi-directional, anonymous communication for any protocol that can be adapted to use a proxy service. Specifically, the architecture provides for bi-directional communication even though no-one but
the initiator's proxy server knows anything but previous and next hops
in the communication chain. This implies that neither the respondent
nor his proxy server nor any external observer need know the identity
of the initiator or his proxy server. A prototype of *Onion Routing* has
been implemented. This prototype works with HTTP (World Wide Web)
proxies. In addition, an analogous proxy for TELNET has been implemented. Proxies for FTP and SMTP are under development.

1 Introduction

This paper presents an architecture that limits a network's vulnerability to traffic analysis. We call this approach *Onion Routing*, because it relies upon a layered object to direct the construction of an anonymous, bi-directional, real-time
virtual circuit between two communicating parties, an *initiator* and *responder*.
Because individual *routing nodes* in each circuit only know the identities of adjacent nodes (as in [1]), and because the nodes further encrypt multiplexed virtual
circuits, studying traffic patterns does not yield much information about the
paths of messages. This makes it difficult to use traffic analysis to determine
who is communicating with whom.

Onion Routing provides an anonymous socket connection through a proxy
server. Since proxies are a well defined interface at the application layer [12, 11],
and many protocols have been adapted to work with proxy servers in order to
accommodate firewalls, Onion Routing can be easily used by many applications.
Our prototype works with HTTP (World Wide Web) proxies. In addition, a
proxy for TELNET has been implemented.

Traffic analysis can be used to help deduce who is communicating with whom
by analyzing traffic patterns instead of the data that is sent. For example, in
most networks, it is relatively easy to determine which pairs of machines are
communicating by watching the routing information that is part of each packet.
Even if data is encrypted, routing information is still sent in the clear because
routers need to know packets' destinations, in order to route them in the right

direction. Traffic analysis can also be done by watching particular data move through a network, by matching amounts of data, or by examining coincidences, such as connections opening and closing at about the same time.

Onion Routing hides routing information by making a data stream follow a path through several nodes en route to its destination. The path is defined by the first node, which is also a proxy for the service being requested (e.g., HTTP requests). Therefore, this Proxy/Routing Node is the most sensitive one, so sites that are concerned about traffic analysis should also manage a Proxy/Routing Node. We will see later that it is important that this Proxy/Routing Node also be used as an intermediate routing node in other virtual circuits. Although the compromise of all routing nodes compromises the hiding, one uncompromised routing node is sufficient to complicate traffic analysis. Figure 1 illustrates the topology of an Onion Routing network with five nodes, one of which (W) is the Proxy/Routing node for the initiator's site.

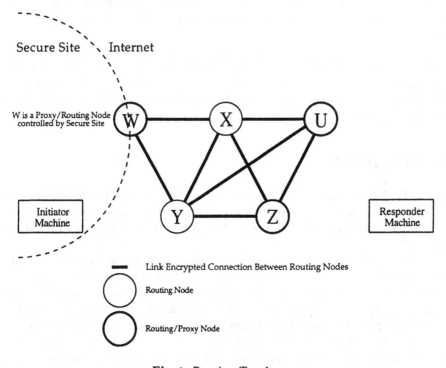

Fig. 1. Routing Topology.

The goal of Onion Routing is not to provide anonymous communication. Parties are free to (and usually should) identify themselves within a message. But the use of a public network should not automatically give away the identities and locations of the communicating parties. For example, imagine a researcher who uses the World Wide Web to collect data from a variety of sources. Although each piece of information that he retrieves is publicly known, it may be possible for an outside observer to determine his sensitive interests by studying the patterns in his requests. Onion Routing makes it very difficult to match his HTTP requests to his site.

Anonymous re-mailers [5, 6] attempt to limit the feasibility of traffic analysis by providing an anonymous store and forward architecture. To prevent replay attacks, re-mailers keep a log of sent messages. These two characteristics make the anonymous re-mailer approach unsuitable for HTTP applications, as HTTP requests would both generate an enormous log and require bi-directional communication. Anonymous ISDN [8] has even more severe real-time and bi-directional requirements than HTTP, but, the architecture of an ISDN network is considerably different from the architecture of the Internet [4].

Onion Routing provides bi-directional communication, without requiring that the responder know the initiator's identity or location. Individual messages are not logged. In addition, Onion Routing is easily adapted to electronic mail. Messages can include *Reply Onions* that permit a later reply to the sender without knowing his address and without keeping the original virtual circuit open.

The rest of the paper is organized in the following way: Section 2 presents background information. Section 3 describes the *Onion*, the object that directs the construction of the virtual circuit. Section 4 describes the construction and use of these virtual circuits. Section 5 describes the vulnerabilities in the Onion Routing architecture. Section 6 presents some concluding remarks.

2 Background

Chaum [1] defines a layered object that routes data through intermediate nodes, called *mixes*. These intermediate nodes may reorder, delay, and pad traffic to complicate traffic analysis. Some work has been done using mixes in ATM networks [3].

Anonymous Remailers like [5, 6] use mixes to provide anonymous e-mail services and also to invent an address through which mail can be forwarded back to the original sender. Remailers work in a store and forward manner at the mail application layer, by stripping off headers at each mix, and forwarding the mail message to the next mix. These remailers provide confirmation of delivery.

In [8], mixes are used to provide untraceable communication in an ISDN network. In a phone system, each telephone line is assigned to a particular local switch (i.e., local exchange), and switches are interconnected by a (long distance) network. Anonymous calls in ISDN rely upon an anonymous connection within each switch between the caller and the long distance network, which is obtained by routing calls through a predefined series of mixes. The long distance endpoints of the connection are then mated to complete the call. (Notice that observers can tell which local switches are connected.) This approach relies upon two unique features of ISDN switches. Since each phone line has a subset of the switch's total capacity pre-allocated to it, there is no (real) cost associated with keeping a phone line active all the time, either by making calls to itself, to other phone lines on the same switch, or to the long distance network. Keeping phone lines active complicates traffic analysis because an observer cannot track coincidences.

Also, since each phone line has a control circuit connection to the switch, the switch can broadcast messages to each line using these control circuits. So, within a switch a truly anonymous connection can be established: A phone line makes an anonymous connection to some mix. That mix broadcasts a token identifying itself and the connection. A recipient of that token can make another anonymous connection to the specified mix, which mates the two connections to complete the call.

Our goal of anonymous socket connections over the Internet differs from anonymous remailers and anonymous ISDN. The data is different, with real-time constraints more severe than mail, but somewhat looser than voice. Both HTTP and ISDN connections are bidirectional, but, unlike ISDN, HTTP connections are likely to be small requests followed by short bursts of returned data. In a local switch capacity is pre-allocated to each phone line, and broadcasting is efficient. But broadcasting over the Internet is not free, and defining broadcasts domains is not trivial. Most importantly, the network topology of the Internet is more akin to the network topology of the long distance network between switches, where capacity is a shared resource. In anonymous ISDN, the mixes hide communication within the local switch, but connections between switches are not hidden. This implies that all calls between two businesses, each large enough to use an entire switch, reveal which businesses are communicating. In Onion Routing, mixing is dispersed throughout the Internet, which improves hiding.

3 Onions

To begin a session between an initiator and a responder, the initiator's proxy identifies a series of routing nodes forming a route through the network and constructs an *onion* which encapsulates that route. Figure 2 illustrates an onion constructed by the initiator's Proxy/Routing Node W for an anonymous route to the responder's Proxy/Routing Node Z through intermediate routing nodes X and Y. The initiator's proxy then sends the onion along that route to establish a virtual circuit between himself and the responder's proxy.

The onion data structure is composed of layer upon layer of encryption wrapped around a payload. Leaving aside the shape of the payload at the very center, the basic structure of the onion is based on the route to the responder that is chosen by the initiator's proxy. Based on this route, the initiator's proxy encrypts first for the responder's proxy, then for the preceding node on the route, and so on back to the first routing node to whom he will send the onion. When the onion is received, each node knows who sent him the onion and to whom he should pass the onion. But, he knows nothing about the other nodes, nor about how many there are in the chain or his place in it (unless he is last). What a

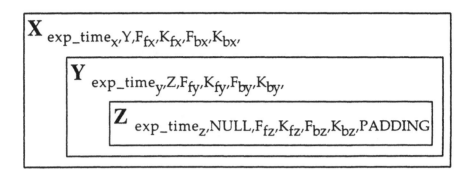

Fig. 2. A Forward Onion.

node P_x receives looks like this

$$\{exp\_time, next\_hop, F_f, K_f, F_b, K_b, payload\}_{PK_x}$$

Here PK_x is a public encryption key for routing node P_x, who is assumed to have the corresponding decryption key.[1] The decrypted message contains an expiration time for the onion, the next routing node to which the payload is to be sent, the payload, and two function/key pairs specifying the cryptographic operations and keys to be applied to data that will be sent along the virtual circuit. The forward pair (F_f, K_f) is applied to data moving in the forward direction (along the route that the onion is traveling) the backward pair (F_b, K_b) is applied to data moving in the opposite direction (along the onion's reverse route).[2] (If the receiving node is the responder's proxy, then the *next_hop* field is *null*.) For any intermediate routing node the payload will be another onion. The expiration time is used to detect replays, which pairs of compromised nodes could use to try to correlate messages. Each node holds a copy of the onion until *exp_time*. If he receives another copy of the same onion within that time he simply ignores it. And, if he receives an onion that has expired, he ignores that as well.

Notice that at each hop the onion shrinks as a layer is peeled off. To avoid compromised nodes inferring route information from this monotonically diminishing size, a random bit string the size of the peeled off layer is appended to the end of the *payload* before forwarding. No proxy except the last will know how much of the *payload* he receives is such padding because he won't know where

---

[1] Depending on certain assumptions about the fields in each onion layer, a naive RSA implementation of the simple public key encryption implied by our notation could be vulnerable to an attack as described in [7]. In our implementation, this potential vulnerability is illusory since the public key is only used to encrypt a secret key, and that secret key is used to encrypt the remainder of the message using an efficient symmetric algorithm. This also makes for a more efficient implementation than the simple, straightforward implementation using only public keys.

[2] Specifying two pairs of functions unifies the virtual circuits that are constructed by forward and reply onions. See section 3.3.

he is in the chain. He simply 'decrypts' the padding along with the rest of the onion. Even a constant size onion might be traced unless all onions are the same size, so we fix the size of the onion. To maintain this constant size to hide the length of the chain from the responder's proxy, the initiator's proxy will pad the central *payload* according to the size of the onion, i.e., the number of hops. So, when any onion arrives at the responder's proxy it will always have the same amount of padding, either added initially or en route.

3.1   Creating the circuit

The goal in sending the onion is to produce virtual circuits within link encrypted connections already running between routing nodes.[3] More details will be given in section 4. An onion occurs as the data field in one of the presently described 'messages'. Such messages contain a circuit identifier, a command (*create*, *destroy*, and *data*), and data. Any other command is considered an error, and the node who receives such a message ignores that message except to return a *destroy* command back through that virtual circuit. The *create* command accompanies an onion. When a node receives a create command along with an onion, he chooses a virtual circuit identifier and sends another *create* message containing this identifier to the next node and the onion (padded with his layer peeled off). He also stores the virtual circuit identifier he received and virtual circuit identifier he sent as a pair. Until the circuit is destroyed, whenever he receives data on the one connection he sends it off on the other. He applies the forward cryptographic function and key (obtained from the onion) to data moving in the forward direction (along the route the onion traveled) and the backward cryptographic function and key to data moving in the opposite direction (along the onion's reverse route). The virtual circuit established by the onion in figure 2 is illustrated in figure 3:

Data sent by the initiator over a virtual circuit is "pre-crypted"[4] repeatedly by his proxy by applying the inverse of all the forward cryptographic operations specified in the onion, innermost first. Therefore, these layers of cryptography will be peeled off as the data travels forward through the virtual circuit. Data sent by the responder is "crypted" once by his proxy and again by each previous node in the virtual circuit using the backward cryptographic operation specified at the corresponding layer of the onion. The initiator's proxy applies the inverse of the backward cryptographic operations specified in the onion, outermost first, to this stream, to obtain the plaintext.

3.2   Loose Routing

It is not necessary that the entire route be prespecified by the initiator's proxy. He can instruct various nodes along the route to choose their own route to the

---

[3] Onions could be used to carry data also, but since onions have to be tracked to prevent replay, this would introduce a large cost.

[4] We define the verb *crypt* to mean the application of a cryptographic operation, be it encryption or decryption, where the two are logically interchangeable.

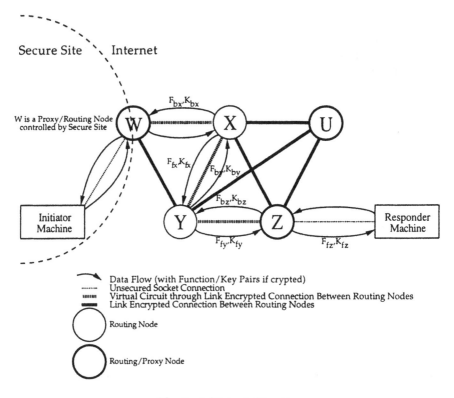

Fig. 3. A Virtual Circuit.

next prespecified node. This can be useful for security, adding more hops to the chain. It could also be used if the initiating proxy does not know a complete, connected route to the responder but believes that the node where any break occurs can construct a route to the next node. Or, loose routing can be used to handle connection changes that occur of which the initiator was unaware. Also, since onions are all of fixed size, there is a fixed maximum length to the route from the initiator's proxy to the responder's proxy. Loose routing allows us to increase the size of that maximum for the same fixed onion size. Why this is so should become clear presently.

It is also possible to iterate the loose routing process, allowing nodes on the added route to themselves add to the chain. Obviously, we need a mechanism to prevent the chain from lengthening indefinitely. This can be incorporated into the onion structure. An onion for a system that allows for loose routing is as follows:

$$\{exp\_time, next\_hop, max\_loosecount, F_f, K_f, F_b, K_b, payload\}_{PK_x}$$

If the node receiving this onion decides to loose-route the onion, he prepares a new onion with up to *max_loosecount* layers. The payload of this onion is simply the onion he received with PK_x changed for the last (innermost) node he added to the chain. In other words, he behaves as an initiator's proxy except that his payload is itself already an onion. (This node behaves like an initiator's proxy with respect to data also, since he must repeatedly pre- and post- crypt data that moves along the diverted route.) To keep the onion a constant length he must truncate the payload by an amount commensurate with the layers he has added to the onion. The initiating proxy must anticipate the amount of padding (both present initially and any added and/or truncated en route) that will be on the central payload at the time loose routing occurs to allow for this truncation. Failure to pre-pad correctly or ignoring an onion's fixed size will result in a malformed onion later in the route. The total of the *max_loosecount* values occurring in the added layers plus the number of added layers must be less than or equal to the *max_loosecount* value that the adding node received.

3.3 Reply Onions

There are applications in which it would be useful for a responder to send back a reply after the original circuit is broken. This would allow answers (like e-mail replies) to be sent to queries that were not available at the time of the original connection. As we shall see presently, this also allows the responder as well as the initiator to remain hidden. The way we allow for these delayed replies is by sending a reply onion to accompany the reply. Like the forward onion, it reveals to each node en route only the next step to be taken. It has the same structure as the forward onion and is treated the same way by nodes en route. Intermediate nodes processing an onion cannot differentiate between forward and reply onions. Furthermore, the behavior of the original initiator and responder proxies are the same, once the circuit is formed.

The primary difference between a forward and a reply onion is the innermost payload. The payload of the forward onion can be effectively empty (containing only padding). The reply onion payload contains enough information to enable the initiator's proxy to reach the initiator and all the cryptographic function and key pairs that are to crypt data along the virtual circuit. The initiator's proxy retrieves the keys from the onion. Figure 4 illustrates a reply onion constructed by the initiator's Proxy/Routing Node W for an anonymous route back to him starting at the responder's Proxy/Routing Node Z through intermediate routing nodes Y and X:

There is no difference between virtual circuits established by reply onions and forward onions, except that in circuits established by reply onions intermediate routing nodes appear to think that forward points toward the initiator's proxy. But since the behavior of intermediate routing nodes is symmetric, this difference is irrelevant. The terminal Proxy/Routing nodes, however, have the same behavior in circuits established by forward and reply onions. Therefore, a figure of the virtual circuit formed by the reply onion illustrated in figure 4 would be identical to the virtual circuit illustrated in figure 3 even though the circuit was formed by the reply onion moving from the responder's proxy node to the

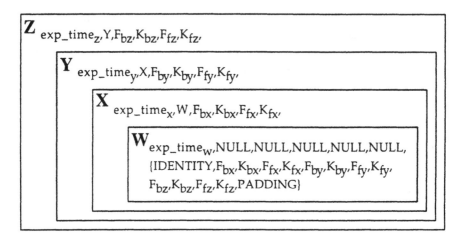

Fig. 4. A Reply Onion.

initiator's proxy node. Internally to the intermediate nodes, the forward crypto-graphic functions are applied to data moving in the direction that the circuit was established, and the backward cryptographic functions are applied to data moving in the opposite direction. The location of the terminal Proxy/Routing Nodes are in this sense reversed, with the initiator's proxy at the end of the circuit and the responder's proxy at the beginning of the circuit. However, the behavior of the initiator and responder proxies is identical to their behavior in the virtual circuit formed by a forward onion. This is the reason for having forward and backward function/key pairs at each layer of the onion.

Like a forward onion, a reply onion can only be used once. When a node receives an onion it is kept until it expires, and any onion received is compared to detect replay. If a replay is detected, it is treated as an error and ignored. Since reply onions can only be used once, if multiple replies are desired, multiple reply onions must be sent. Of course, they need not all follow the same return route; although they may. If replies are only likely to be forthcoming if they are anonymous, one or more reply onions can be broadcast. Anyone can then reply with an unused onion. If he can maintain anonymity from or in cooperation with the responder's proxy for that reply onion, then he can do so anonymously.

4 Implementation

The easiest way to build our system without requiring the complete redesign and deployment of new client and server software is to make use of existing proxy technologies. Historically, proxy technologies have been used to create tunnels through a firewall. The use of proxy technologies requires that the client applications be 'proxy aware'. The widespread deployment of firewalls on the Internet has created the demand for such proxy aware applications, which software manufacturers are rushing to meet.

In the firewall setting, a system administrator will set up a proxy server on the firewall machine which will be responsible for forwarding requests from the protected domain out onto the open Internet, and maintain a return path for the response to the request. A proxy server can be divided into two parts: the front end that receives and parses the request, and the back end that processes the request and returns the results back to the requester. Classically, the front and back ends are the same process running on one machine.

Under our system we will use a traditional proxy front end and back end, but, they will be separate processes on separate machines with a tunnel connecting them. In this manner, our Proxy/Routing Nodes will look no different to the client and server software than any other proxy server. A couple of assumptions will hold for the remainder of this paper: 1) Proxy/Routing Nodes and intermediate routing nodes know about each other in advance of their operation, and 2) public key certificates for each node have been securely distributed to all others prior to operation.

All nodes are connected by link encrypted connections which multiplex many virtual circuits between initiator and responder proxy nodes. These connections are link encrypted in an odd way (for efficiency). All messages moving through these connections are of fixed size and have two components, header and payload fields. Header fields contain the virtual circuit identifier and the command and are link encrypted using a stream cipher [10]. Since all payload fields will be encrypted via other mechanisms (public keys or onion keys), they need not be link encrypted.

There are three commands that nodes understand. The first is to *create* a virtual circuit. At each node, a virtual circuit has two connections. Data arriving on one is passed along on the other. The circuit is defined by the labels for these two connections. Creating a virtual circuit is the process of defining these labels for each node along the route. For the first Proxy/Routing Node, one connection is a link to the initiator, and the other is a link to the next routing node. The Proxy/Routing Node creates an onion defining the sequence of intermediate routing nodes to the responder's Proxy/Routing Node. It breaks the onion up into payload sized chunks and transmits these chunks in order to the next node with a control field containing both the label of the connection and a *create* command. Each subsequent node reassembles the onion and peels off a layer from the onion which reveals the next node in the route and two cryptographic function/key pairs. Before acting on the *create* command, the node checks whether the onion has expired or is a replay. To check for replay, the node consults a table of unexpired onions. If the onion is valid, it is inserted into the table, and the node then labels a new connection to the next node and passes the peeled and padded onion in a similar sequence of messages to the next node. It also updates a table containing the labels and cryptographic function/key pairs associated with the new virtual circuit. The appropriate (forward or backward) function/key pair should be used to crypt data moving along that circuit. The responder's Proxy/Routing Node, recognizing that the onion is empty, will partially update its tables. As with standard proxies the next *data* message along this circuit will identify the responder.

The second command is *data*. The second role of the initiator's Proxy/Routing Node is to pass a stream of data from the initiator along the virtual circuit together with other control information for the responder's Proxy/Routing Node. To do this, he breaks the incoming stream into (at most) payload sized chunks, and repeatedly pre-crypts each chunk using the inverse of the cryptographic operations specified in the onion, innermost first. The function/key pairs that are applied, and the virtual circuit identifier of the connection to the next node are obtained from a table. The header field for each payload is the label of the connection and a *data* command. Each subsequent node looks at its table, obtaining the cryptographic function/key pair associated with the circuit (for the appropriate direction) and the virtual circuit identifier of the connection to the next node. It then peels off a layer of cryptography and forwards the peeled payload to the next node. Once the data reaches the responder's proxy, its final cryption will produce the plaintext that is to be processed or forwarded to the responder.

The *data* command can also be used to move data from the responder's Proxy/Routing Node to the initiator's Proxy/Routing Node. The responder's Proxy/Routing Node obtains the cryptographic function/key pair and the virtual circuit identifier for the next node from its tables, and crypts the stream. It breaks the crypted stream into payload sized chunks and forwards them to the next node with the appropriate control field. Each subsequent node further stream crypts each payload using the appropriate function/key associated with that virtual circuit. Once a messages arrives at the initiator's Proxy/Routing Node he looks at his table and applies the inverse of the backward cryptographic operations specified in the onion, outermost first, to this stream to obtain the plaintext. The plaintext is forwarded to the initiator.

The third command is *destroy* which is used to tear down a virtual circuit when it is no longer needed or in response to certain error conditions. Notice that *destroy* messages can be initiated by any node along a virtual circuit, and it is a node's obligation to forward the *destroy* messages in the appropriate directions. (A node initiating a *destroy* message in an active virtual circuit forwards it in both directions. A node that receives a *destroy* message passes it along in the same direction.) The payload of a *destroy* command is empty padding. Nonetheless, this payload is still crypted with the appropriate function/key pair. In addition to the *destroy* command, the control field contains the virtual circuit identifier of the recipient of the *destroy* command. Upon receipt of a *destroy* command a node deletes the table entries associated with that virtual circuit.

5   Vulnerabilities

Onion Routing is not invulnerable to traffic analysis attacks. With enough data, it is still possible to analyze usage patterns and make educated guesses about the routing of messages. Also, since our application requires real time communication, it may be possible to detect the near simultaneous opening of socket connections on the first and last proxy servers revealing who is requesting what information. However, these sorts of attacks require the collection and analysis of huge amounts of data by external observers.

Other attacks depend upon compromised Proxy Servers and Routing Nodes. If the initiator's proxy is compromised then all information is revealed. In general it is sufficient for a single routing node to be uncompromised to complicate traffic analysis. However, a single compromised routing node can destroy connections or stop forwarding messages, resulting in denial of service attacks.

Onion Routing uses expiration times to prevent replay attacks. It is curious that, unlike timestamps, the vulnerability due to poorly synchronized clocks here is a denial of service attack, instead of a replay attack. If a node's clock is too fast, otherwise timely onions will appear to have already expired. Also, since expiration times define the window during which nodes must store used onions, a node with a slow clock will end up storing more information.

If the responder's proxy is compromised, and can determine when the unencrypted data stream has been corrupted, it is possible for compromised nodes earlier in the virtual circuit to corrupt the stream and ask which responder's proxy received uncorrupted data. By working with compromised nodes around a suspected initiator's proxy, one can identify the beginning of the virtual circuit. The difficulty with this attack is that once the data stream has been corrupted, it will remain corrupted (because we use a stream cipher), limiting further analysis.

In order for Onion Routing to be effective, there must be significant use of all the nodes, and Proxy Nodes must also be intermediate routing nodes. Choosing the appropriate balance between efficient use of network capacity and security is a hard problem both from a theoretical and practical standpoint. Theoretically, it is difficult to calculate the value of the tradeoff. For more security, network traffic must be relatively constant. This requires sending dummy traffic over a connection when traffic is light and buffering data when traffic is heavy. If traffic is very bursty and response time is important, smoothing out network traffic requires wasting capacity. If however, traffic is relatively constant, additional smoothing may not be necessary. From a practical point of view, the Internet may not provide the control necessary to smooth out traffic: unlike ATM, users do not own capacity on shared connections. The important observation, however, is that Onion Routing forms an architecture within which these tradeoffs can be made and explored.

6   Conclusion

Onion Routing is an architecture that hides routing information while providing real-time, bi-directional communication. Since it provides a virtual circuit that can replace a socket connection, Onion Routing can be used in any protocol that can be adapted to use a proxy service. Although our first use is in HTTP and TELNET, it is easy to imagine other applications. In e-mail, for example, Onion Routing would create an anonymous socket connection between two sendmail daemons. This contrasts with Anonymous Remailers, where each remailer provides a single hop in a chain of mail forwarding. In this sense, in Onion Routing, the rerouting of messages is independent of the type of message.

Other extensions are also possible and integrate nicely with the proxy approach to anonymity. For example, to create a completely anonymous conversation between two parties, each party would make an anonymous connection to some anonymity server, which mates connections sharing some token. This approach, similar to IRC servers, can also be used if the responder does not trust the initiator, especially with (broadcast) reply onions. The responder builds his own (trusted) connection to some anonymity server, and asks that anonymity server to build another connection to the initiator using a reply onion and to mate the two connections. Each party is therefore protected by a route that he determined.

In Onion Routing the encryption burden on connected intermediate nodes is less than the burden of link encryption on routers. In link encryption, each packet is encrypted by the sender and decrypted by the recipient. In Onion Routing the header and payload of each message are crypted separately: the header is encrypted and decrypted using the connection's key, and the payload is crypted (only by the recipient) using the appropriate function/key pair associated with the virtual circuit.

Our goal here is not to provide anonymous communication, but, to place identification where it belongs. The use of a public network should not automatically reveal the identities of communicating parties. If anonymous communication is undesirable, it is easy to imagine filters on the endpoint machines that restrict communication to signed messages.

Onion Routing will only be effective in complicating traffic analysis if its Proxy and Routing Nodes become widespread and widely used. There is an obvious tension between anonymity and law enforcement. If this tension is resolved in favor of law enforcement, it would be straightforward to integrate a key escrow system within the onion, which would make routing information available to the lawful authorities.

7 Acknowledgements

Discussions with many people helped develop the ideas in this paper. We would like to thank Ran Atkinson, Markus Jakobbsen, John McLean, Cathy Meadows, Andy Moore, Moni Naor, Holger Peterson, Birgit Pfitzmann, Michael Steiner, and the anonymous referees for their helpful suggestions.

References

1. D. Chaum. *Untraceable Electronic Mail, Return Addresses, and Digital Pseudonyms,* Communications of the ACM, v. 24, n. 2, Feb. 1981, pages 84-88.
2. D. Chaum, *The Dining Cryptographers Problem: Unconditional Sender and Recipient Untraceability,* Journal of Cryptology, 1/1, 1988, pages 65-75.

3. S. Chuang. *Security Management of ATM Networks*, Ph.D. thesis, in progress, Cambridge University.

4. D. E. Comer. *Internetworking with TCP/IP, Volume 1: Principles, Protocols, and Architecture*, Prentice-Hall, Engelwood Cliffs, New Jersey, 1995.

5. L. Cottrell. *Mixmaster and Remailer Attacks*, http://obscura.obscura.com/~loki/remailer/remailer-essay.html

6. C. Gulcu and G. Tsudik. *Mixing Email with* Babel, 1996 Symposium on Network and Distributed System Security, San Diego, February 1996.

7. A. Pfitzmann and B. Pfitzmann. *How to Break the Direct RSA-implementation of MIXes*, Advances in Cryptology-EUROCRYPT '89 Proceedings, Springer-Verlag, Berlin, 1990, pages 373-381.

8. A. Pfitzmann, B. Pfitzmann, and M. Waidner. *ISDN-Mixes: Untraceable Communication with Very Small Bandwidth Overhead*, GI/ITG Conference: Communication in Distributed Systems, Mannheim Feb, 1991, Informatik-Fachberichte 267, Springer-Verlag, Heildelberg 1991, pages 451-463.

9. A. Pfitzmann and M. Waidner. *Networks Without User Observability*, Computers & Security, 6/2 1987, pages 158-166.

10. B. Schneier. *Applied Cryptography: Protocols, Algorithms and Source Code in C*, John Wiley and Sons, 1994.

11. W. R. Stevens. *TCP/IP Illustrated, Volume 3: TCP for Transactions, HTTP, NNTP, and the UNIX Domain Protocols*, Addison-Wesley, Reading, Mass., 1996.

12. L. D. Stein. *How to Set up and Maintain a World Wide Web Site: The Guide for Information Providers*, Addison-Wesley, Reading, Mass., 1995.

The Newton Channel

Ross Anderson[1], Serge Vaudenay[2], Bart Preneel[3] and Kaisa Nyberg[4]

[1] Computer Laboratory, Pembroke Street, Cambridge, CB2 3QG
[2] Ecole Normal Supérieure — DMI, 45 rue d'Ulm, 75230 Paris, France
[3] KU Leuven — ESAT-COSIC, Kardinaal Mercierlaan 94, B-3001 Heverlee, Belgium
[4] Finnish Defence Forces, PO Box 919, FIN-00101 Helsinki, Finland

Abstract. Simmons asked whether there exists a signature scheme with a broadband covert channel that does not require the sender to compromise the security of her signing key. We answer this question in the affirmative; the ElGamal signature scheme has such a channel. Thus, contrary to popular belief, the design of the DSA does not maximise the covert utility of its signatures, but minimises them. Our construction also shows that many discrete log based systems are insecure: they operate in more than one group at a time, and key material may leak through those groups in which discrete log is easy. However, the DSA is not vulnerable in this way.

1 Introduction

Many digital signature schemes have the property that the signer of a message can hide some information in the signature that can be recovered by a third party, and that the presence of this hidden information cannot even in principle be detected in any given instance of the signature. These channels were discovered by Simmons, who called them subliminal channels [7].

The problem originally arose in the context of nuclear arms limitation treaty verification. The USA and the USSR had decided to place certain sensors in each other's nuclear facilities in order to share certain agreed sensor information, and needed integrity controls to prevent information being manipulated in order to provide false evidence that a test did or did not take place [8]. In addition, both parties wanted to be sure that the integrity mechanisms could not be abused to transmit other, prohibited, information.

This was a special concern with systems used to monitor not just the occurrence of nuclear tests, but the numbers of fielded nuclear weapons. If a Russian sensor designed to relay merely the presence or absence of an American missile in a silo could covertly communicate the silo's location, then this information could have been used to facilitate a first strike. One of the early designs for equipment to verify treaty compliance had just such a weakness: the sensor's location could have been transmitted using a subliminal channel in an early authentication scheme based on discrete logarithms [7].

To see how such channels work, consider the ElGamal signature scheme [3]. Let p be a prime number such that finding discrete logs in F_p^* is hard, let g

be a generator of F_p^*, let $x \in \{1, ..., p-1\}$ be a user's secret signing key, let $y = g^x$ be her published signature verification key, let $k \in \{1, ..., p-1\}$ (with $\gcd(k, p-1) = 1$) be a message key and M the message to be signed. Then the ElGamal signature on M is (r, s) where

$$r = g^k \pmod{p} \tag{1}$$

$$s = (M - xr)/k \pmod{p-1} \tag{2}$$

The two previously known covert channels in this scheme are:

1. a broadband channel in which the signer shares her signing key with the message recipient, allowing k to be trivially recovered using equation (2). We can thus encode a covert message directly in k;
2. a narrowband channel in which she tries out many values of k until she manages to force a number of bits of r to encode the covert message c. Thus she might wish to encode a ten bit message in the low order bits of r, and try successive values of k until she got lucky. This would take about a thousand tries on average, and in general the covert bandwidth in bits per signature is about the binary logarithm of the number of computations that the signer is willing to perform.

Even the narrowband channel would have been sufficient for a sensor in a missile silo to encode a few bits of information, and over time this information could have revealed its physical location. Narrowband covert channels could also be used to leak cryptographic key material, and in fact any compact secret; a government might, for example, hide a few bits of information about a citizen's arrest record, HIV status or political reliability in the signature on an identity card.

So covert channels are important in a number of applications. However, neither of the above channels is ideal: the signer must either compromise her signing key or accept severe computational limitations on the usable covert bandwidth. This led Simmons to ask whether there is a better scheme — with a broadband covert channel that does not require the sender to compromise the security of her signing key.

2 Our Construction

The ElGamal scheme possesses just such a channel. We assume that the modulus $p = qm + 1$ where m is smooth and extracting discrete logarithms is hard in the subgroup of F_p^* of order q that is generated by g^m. If the covert message we wish to convey is c, we can set

$$k \equiv c \pmod{m} \tag{3}$$

In other words, we set $k = c + k'm$ for some randomly chosen k'. Now, when the recipient gets the signature (r, s), he forms r^q and solves for z the equation

$$(g^q)^z \equiv r^q \pmod{p} \tag{4}$$

This is feasible since the order of the subgroup of F_p^* generated by g^q is smooth. Using the Pohlig-Hellman decomposition [4] in combination with Pollard's rho method [5], this will require time $O(\sqrt{B})$ where B is the smoothness bound (the largest prime factor of m). We will then have

$$c \equiv z \pmod{m} \tag{5}$$

and the covert message can thus be recovered.

Note that the discrete log calculation needs to be done only once. Given z, we can recover the signing key mod m using equation (2), so further messages can be decoded trivially using equation (2).

This channel is a broadcast one, in the sense that anyone may perform the discrete log calculation and recover x mod m. However, we can also create narrowcast channels, in which the covert message c is only available to parties who possess some previously shared secret. In particular, if $p - 1 = mq_1q_2 + 1$, and the discrete logarithm problem is hard in the groups of order q_1 and q_2, then the signer can keep her signing key secret modulo q_1 but reveal its value modulo q_2 to the intended recipient of covert messages. She can now communicate her covert message c as k mod q_2.

In short, when we use the ElGamal signature scheme with g a generator of Z_p^*, we are signing simultaneously in a number of different groups that correspond to the factors of $p - 1$. Our signing key can be secure in some of these, shared with certain parties in others, and will be available to everyone modulo the smooth part of $p - 1$. This smooth part will be at least 2, and where p is a randomly chosen prime, it will be about $\log_2 B$ (see for example [11]).

3 Tailoring the Channel

Of course, the prime p can be chosen so as to provide any desired combination of broadcast and narrowcast channels. A prime that is optimal for broadcast in ElGamal signatures was given in the original specification of the Digital Signature Algorithm: this had $(p - 1)/q = 2^{70}3^{46}5^{30}7^{25}11^{20}$ [1], yielding a broadcast channel of about 352 bits.

The current DSA standard [2] suggests a different pair of primes, namely

$p = $ 11106950485250668473896599553110864943642757210461774008701010
23825839678874642481120264311896935336016195066787729193595754779
56779496046310058460953487227

and

$q = 1016505656888901462990072961821000258491855382166\text{9}$

The factors of $(p-1)/q$ have been found by Paul Leyland and are:

2

$q_1 = 4196363948260739557$

$q_2 = 420810174371644789390718287\text{3}$

$q_3 = 30938244015097155307491012957530738401924312738978350828490\text{7}$

Using this prime p for ElGamal signatures would provide a secure signature in the groups of order q and q_3; and either of these could be subverted to provide a narrowcast covert channel. There will also be a broadcast channel of somewhat over 160 bits per signature, as the signing key can be recovered in the groups whose orders are 2 (trivially), q_1 (for about 2^{34} computations) and q_2 (for about 2^{47} computations).

It should be clear from this example how to select p for any desired combination of broadcast and narrowcast covert channel capacity. In the case of a randomly chosen prime p, it can be shown that the expected length in bits v of the product of all prime divisors $\leq B$ is approximately equal to $\log_2 B$ [11]. Thus the subliminal channel requires an effort of $O(2^{v/2})$ to communicate v bits, where the previously known narrowband channel needed about 2^v. Moreover, v has a large variance: for one in 100 1024-bit primes, one obtains a value of v which is about four times larger than the expected value [11]. In any case, the values of p and q in the current DSA specification are not particularly out of the ordinary.

Since this channel was discovered by the authors while they were guests of the Isaac Newton Institute of Mathematical Sciences in Cambridge, we hereby name it 'the Newton channel'.

4 Discussion

The Newton channel arises when a digital signature is performed in a composite group with the property that the key in one or more of its subgroups is shared with the recipient. This sharing can be explicit, in the case of the narrowband channel, or implicit in the case where third parties can simple compute the key in the relevant group or groups.

It is clear that the Newton channel can be avoided by operating in a group of prime order. In the example above, we could replace g by $g^{(p-1)/q}$ (or $g^{(p-1)/q_3}$), and indeed this is the approach taken by DSA (see [6] for more information on this algorithm and its background). When the DSA was first proposed, claims were made that it appeared to have been designed to maximise the covert channel capacity [9]. This claim was denied at the time by a senior NSA official [10], and we can now see that he was right: the DSA does not maximise the covert utility of a signature, but minimises it — by eliminating the Newton channel.

Our methods have implications for security as well as covertness: anyone can recover both the message key k and the signing key x modulo m. In fact, in a typical discrete log based cryptosystem, we would expect to be able to recover all key material modulo the smooth component of the group order. It would be imprudent of a designer to allow such severe key leakage, as many random number generators show regularities due to resonances, implementation bugs and the like. An ElGamal scheme using the p and q originally proposed with the DSA would be leaking over two thirds of each key. In many implementations, this could be enough to mount an attack.

This, and other, security considerations will be discussed in more detail in a future paper. For the meantime, we recommend that designers of ElGamal and Diffie-Hellman type systems should always use groups of prime order unless there are good reasons not to.

5 Conclusions

We have answered Simmons' question by demonstrating that the ElGamal signature scheme has a broadband covert channel, the Newton channel, that does not require the sender to compromise the security of her signing key. However, Simmons' conjecture that such schemes did not exist was not entirely mistaken, since the bandwidth of the Newton channel in bits per signature is exactly equal to the number of bits that the signer is prepared to compromise of her signing key. So it may well be that Simmons' conjecture holds with a more precise formulation; we express no opinion on this.

We have also established that, contrary to popular belief, the design of the DSA does not maximise the covert utility of its signatures, but minimises them. Our construction also shows that many discrete log based systems are insecure, while the DSA is not vulnerable in this way. Given the authorship of the DSA, these are perhaps the results that one might have expected.

Acknowledgement: The authors are grateful to the Isaac Newton Institute, 20 Clarkson Road, Cambridge, for hospitality while this research was being conducted; to the National Fund for Scientific Research (Belgium), which sponsored the third author; and last but not least to Paul Leyland for factoring $p - 1$.

References

1. 'A Practical RSA Trapdoor', R Anderson, in *Electronics Letters* v 29 no 11 (27 May 1993) p 995
2. 'Digital Signature Standard,' *Federal Information Processing Standard (FIPS) Publication 186*, National Institute of Standards and Technology, US Department of Commerce, Washington D.C., May 1994
3. 'A Public Key Cryptosystem and a Signature Scheme based on Discrete Logarithms', T ElGamal, *IEEE Transactions on Information Theory, v 31, no 4 (1985) pp 469–472*

4. 'An Improved Algorithm for Computing Logarithms over $GF(p)$ and its Cryptographic Significance', SC Pohlig, ME Hellman, *IEEE Transactions on Information Theory, v 24, no 1 (Jan 78) pp 106–110*

5. 'Monte Carlo Methods for Index Computation (mod p), ' JM Pollard, *Mathematics of Computation, v 32 no 143 (Jul 78) pp 918–924*

6. *'Applied Cryptography'*, B Schneier (2nd edition), Wiley 1995

7. 'Subliminal Channels; Past and Present', GJ Simmons, *European Transactions on Telecommunications v 5 no 4 (Jul/Aug 94) pp 459–473*

8. 'How to Insure That Data Acquired to Verify Treaty Compliance are Trustworthy', GJ Simmons, *Contemporary Cryptology* (IEEE, 1992) pp 617–630

9. 'Subliminal Communciation is Easy Using the DSA', GJ Simmons, *Advances in Cryptology - EUROCRYPT 93*, Springer LNCS v 765 pp 218–232

10. Comment made from the floor at Eurocrypt 93, B Snow

11. 'On Diffie-Hellman Key Agreement with Short Exponents', PC van Oorschot, MJ Wiener, *Advances in Cryptology - EUROCRYPT 96*, Springer LNCS v 1070 pp 332–343

A Progress Report on Subliminal-Free Channels

Mike Burmester*, Yvo G. Desmedt**, Toshiya Itoh***, Kouichi Sakurai†,
Hiroki Shizuya‡, Moti Yung§

Abstract. Subliminal channels are closely related to covert channels and are used to hide secret information. They abuse the communications resource. Subliminal channels can be introduced in many cryptographic systems, and exploit the inherent randomness of the systems. For example, secret information can be hidden in the randomness of the authenticators of an authentication system. Similarly secret information can be hidden in the randomness (of the prover or verifier) of both zero-knowledge proof systems and signature systems.

To establish a subliminal channel the cryptosystem is *abused*, that is, used in a different way and for a different purpose than intended by its designer. A particularly obnoxious type of subliminal channel may be activated by abortive halting.

For state-of-the-art security, it may be desirable to detect, and if possible prevent, subliminal channels. In this paper we address the problem of whether it is possible to develop (and if so, how) appropriate techniques for detecting or preventing the use of such channels. Several such techniques have already been proposed in the literature, and are suitable for many systems. We review these. We also consider recent developments, in particular with regards to the formal security requirements and their impact on research.

Key Words: Subliminal-freeness, authentication, identification, zero-knowledge proofs, secret sharing, untraceability, divertibility.

* Department of Mathematics, Royal Holloway – University of London, Egham, Surrey TW20 OEX, U.K., m.burmester@rhbnc.ac.uk
** Department of EE & CS, University of Wisconsin, Milwaukee, P.O. Box 784, WI 53201 Milwaukee, U.S.A., Milwaukee, WI 53201, U.S.A., desmedt@cs.uwm.edu Supported by NSF NCR9004879.
*** Department of Information Processing, Interdisciplinary Graduate School of Science and Engineering, Tokyo Institute of Technology, Midori-ku, Yokohama 226, Japan, titoh@ip.titech.ac.jp
† Department of Computer Science and Communication Engineering, Kyushu University, 6-10-1 Hakozaki, Higashi-ku, Fukuoka 812-81, Japan, sakurai@csce.kyushu-u.ac.jp
‡ Education Centre for Information Processing, Tohoku University, Kawauchi, Aoba-ku, Sendai 980-77, Japan, shizuya@ecip.tohoku.ac.jp
§ IBM T.J. Watson Research Centre, Yorktown Hights, NY 10598, U.S.A., moti@watson.ibm.com

1   Introduction

In 1983, Gus Simmons observed that covert (embedded) data could be hidden within the authenticator of an authentication system [29]. He called this hidden (embedded) channel a *subliminal channel*. The capacity of this channel was not large (a few bits per authenticator), but as Simmons disclosed 10 years later [36, p. 459–462], the potential impact on treaty verification and on the national security of the USA could have been catastrophic. The second Strategic Arms Limitation Treaty (SALT II) between the former USSR and the USA allowed both nations to authenticate their messages. While it was not possible to hide covert (embedded) data in the messages which were standardized (and could be controlled by the other nation), this was not the case with the authenticators. The capacity of this channel was enough to reveal which silos were loaded with nuclear missiles and which were not. This information would have been crucial to whichever power contemplated a first strike.

Subliminal channels are closely related to covert channels. Both are used to send hidden information. Lampson [26] defined covert channels as channels which are not intended for information transfer. With this definition, subliminal channels may be regarded as a special kind of covert channels. However this view is not shared by everybody [29]. Subliminal channels are usually established during the execution of a cryptographic protocol (the cover protocol) and involve either information theoretic techniques or computational complexity techniques, but not engineering implementation methods. Covert channels can be established using any technique, but usually involve implementation aspects such as timing channels and storage channels. A well known example of a timing channel uses the start-time, or the duration of an implementation (CPU time). Examples of storage channels include the modulation of disc space, and the hiding of secret data in the least significant bits of pictures.

Designing systems which are free from the standard covert channels is not sufficient in itself: one has to make certain that subliminal channels cannot be introduced [30, 29, 36]. Subliminal channels can be introduced in many cryptosystems (the cryptosystems are used as covers). They are established by running the cryptosystems on a different program from that specified by their designer, and for a different purpose. We shall refer to this as an *abuse*.

State-of-the-art security may require that subliminal channels be detected and if possible prevented. In this paper we address this problem. We consider whether it is possible to develop appropriate techniques for preventing and detecting the use of such channels. A number of basic techniques have already been proposed and are suitable for many systems. We discuss these and recent developments, in particular with regard to the formal security requirements and their impact on research. In the rest of this section we review briefly the main results in the literature on abuse-free systems.

At Crypto 87 Desmedt, Goutier and Bengio presented the first subliminal-free zero-knowledge proof system [15]. In 1988 Desmedt presented abuse-free protocols for several cryptosystems, such as coin flipping, distribution of public keys, signatures, authentication systems, and zero-knowledge proof systems [12].

Later, some weaknesses were found in the original definition of abuse-freeness [16]. To overcome these, Desmedt and Yung proposed a new definition. This was used to analyze unconditionally secure authentication systems [16]. The notion of divertibility for proof systems was introduced by Okamoto and Ohta [27] and is closely related to abuse-freeness. In this case however, the warden is invisible to either the prover or the verifier, i.e. is transparent. Okamoto and Ohta proved that any commutative random self-reducible relation has a divertible zero-knowledge proof system [27]. This result was extended to all languages in *NP*, and to the subliminal-free scenario, by Burmester and Desmedt [6]. Itoh, Sakurai and Shizuya proved that graph non-isomorphism and all languages in *IP* [24] have divertible zero-knowledge proofs by using a different definition for divertibility. Several problems were later found in these proof systems and modifications are being made by Burmester, Desmedt, Itoh, Sakurai and Shizuya [7].

2 Making a good definition

One of the difficulties in laying the foundations of a discipline is to find an appropriate model which captures our intuitive understanding of its primitives. Setting up such a model for subliminal-freeness has turned out to be much harder than originally thought. Early attempts failed in many respects, and protocols which were claimed to be subliminal-free are not so. Indeed the notion of a subliminal-freeness is quite elusive, as we shall see. The difficulty is to define its scope and its limitations.

In this section we shall analyze the notion of subliminal-freeness. Our approach will build on what has already been done. We will start with the early definitions in the literature and discuss their weaknesses. These will be used to get a better understanding of the notion of subliminal-freeness. Then we will modify the definition, focusing on those aspects which reflect the intuitive meaning of subliminal-freeness.

To motivate our analysis, we first consider a simple example of a public key distribution system in which a subliminal channel is introduced [11]. Suppose that a party P agrees with a party Q *before* the public key distribution system is set up, on a particular 500 bit prime p. Later, when the public keys are being distributed, P selects an appropriate 500 bit prime q which contains the hidden secret P wants to send to Q. P then broadcasts the modulus $n = pq$. From this, Q can easily compute the 500 bit prime q. In this application, P is using the public key distribution system to establish a subliminal channel and is not concerned about leaking the factorization of n to Q. Observe that it is impossible for any third party (even with unlimited resources) to detect this subliminal channel.

We now describe our model. We require a warden W whose task it is to detect subliminal channels. We also specify the cryptosystem: whether it is an authentication system, a signature system, a proof system, etc. We say that a system A is an $s(L)$-*system* [12], if s is a predicate such that $s(x, A)$ is true for all x in a language $L \subset \{0,1\}^*$. For example, if A is an authentication system and $s(m, \mathbf{A})$ is the predicate "$\mathbf{A}(m)$ is an authenticator of the message m", then $\mathbf{A}$ is an $s(L)$-*system* if $s(m, \mathbf{A})$ is true for all messages m in L.

The warden W may be regarded as an adversary. The reason for this is that, in our model, the goal of the 'honest' participants may be to establish a subliminal channel. This channel is therefore a design feature of the program of the participants. The goal of W is to prevent the participants from using it.

Inherent to any subliminal channel are the *history tapes*. All parties have them, including the warden, if he is active. These contain information which is acquired either before the system is set up, or during its executions. This information can serve many purposes. For example the participants may use it to abuse the system, whereas the warden can use it to prevent this. So with the $s(L)$-system $\mathbf{A}$ we have the languages, $L_w = \{(x, h_w) \mid x \in L, |h_w| = |x|^c, c \text{ constant}\}$ for the warden, and $L_p = \{(x, h_p) \mid x \in L, |h_p| = |x|^c, c \text{ constant}\}$ for each participant P. Here $|x|$ is the binary length of x, h_w is the history of W, and h_p is the history of participant P. If the warden is passive then $L_w = L$. We now are in a position to give our first tentative definition for subliminal-free systems, which we give informally.

Tentative Definition 1. [12] An $s(L)$-system $\mathbf{A}$ is *abuse-free* if, *when* it is replaced by any other $s(L)$-system $\mathbf{A}'$ then: if the warden cannot distinguish the strings (the view) that the participants receive while $\mathbf{A}'$ is executed from those received while $\mathbf{A}$ is executed on L_w, *then* neither can participant P distinguish them on L_p, for all participants P. That is, if $\mathbf{A} = (A, W, B)$ and $\mathbf{A}' = (A', W, B')$ and if the warden cannot distinguish the strings (the view) that the participants receive, then neither can B' distinguish the strings it receives in (A, W, B') from those in (A', W, B'), nor can A' distinguish the strings it receives in (A', W, B) from those in (A', W, B').

To detect subliminal channels during the execution of $\mathbf{A}$, the warden eavesdrops on the communication, and controls it if necessary. Participants who send, or who expect to receive, hidden information execute the program $\mathbf{A}'$. They use their history to distinguish the hidden information.

We have focused on detection, not prevention. The reason for this is that for prevention, if one of the participants deviates completely from the specifications of the protocol (e.g. aborts), then the warden would have to replace him for the rest of the protocol. This requirement is *too* strong, and may not be possible to achieve. A weaker form of prevention would allow the warden to stop the protocol, if a subliminal is detected. However, the fact itself that the protocol was halted reveals some information to the other participants.

The first definition suffers in several respects. The most important one is that it does not address the indistinguishability of the strings that the warden W sees properly. To illustrate this, and the methodology used to design subliminal-free systems, we describe briefly an authentication scheme for the Simmons' prisoners scenario [29], which is abuse-free according to our first definition, but which nevertheless fails to prevent subliminal messages from being sent.

Two prisoners T (Terence) and R (Raisa) exchange authenticated messages in the presence of a warden W. W can read all their messages, and check the authenticators. T and R want to exchange secret information but do not want W to detect this. So they send their messages in the clear, and hide secret information in the randomness (the cover) of their authenticators. For simplicity we shall assume that the message to be authenticated is one bit b. In the initialization phase (before T, R were incarcerated), T and R exchange privately two random strings $C_0, C_1 \in [0, 2^{2\ell} - 1]$, $C_0 \neq C_1$, where ℓ is the security parameter. These will be the authenticators. In the transmission phase, T sends a bit b together with the authenticator C_b to the warden W. W chooses a number $n \in [2^\ell, 2^{\ell+1} - 1]$, and sends b and n to R. Raisa then sends $z = C_b \bmod n$ to the warden W who checks if this is correct. If so, W sends the authenticator C_b to R.

Clearly W cannot substitute the bit b. Furthermore W cannot impersonate P because the number z does not provide enough information (from an information theoretic point of view) for this purpose. Let us now discuss abuse-freeness, using our first definition. To send a subliminal message Terence would have to send some $C_b' \neq C_i$. However only $1/n \leq 1/2^\ell$ of such numbers C_b' would fail to be detected by the warden.

Now consider a variation in which T, R agree in the initialization phase to exchange two pairs (C_0^0, C_1^0), (C_0^1, C_1^1). Then, if T wants to send the subliminal (embedded) bit B_T to R, he sends the bit b together with the authenticator $C_b^{B_T}$ to W. R tosses a coin B_R, and sends $z_{B_R} = C_b^{B_R} \bmod n$ to W. If $B_T \neq B_R$, then W will detect the abuse. But if $B_T = B_R$, W will fail to detect it, despite the fact that T has succeeded in sending the bit B_T to R. Nevertheless W will distinguish the strings that T, R exchange, as a random variables, from those they exchange when there is no abuse with probability $1/2$. The problem is that half the times the warden will fail to detect the abuse. This motivates the following modification of our first definition, which we describe informally.

Tentative Definition 2. [5] An $s(L)$-system $\mathbf{A}$ is *subliminal-free* if, when it is replaced by any other $s(L)$-system $\mathbf{A}'$, either the warden almost always detects the subliminal channel, or if he does not, the participants cannot distinguish (as in Definition 1) the strings they receive while $\mathbf{A}'$ is executed from those they receive while $\mathbf{A}$ is executed on L_p.

There are still some problems with this definition. Clearly we only need to focus on the *conditional view* of the participants, i.e. what they 'see' when W has failed to detect an abuse. The rest should not concern us. Let W set a detection bit w to 1 if he detects an abuse, 0 otherwise. The conditional view of the participants when $\mathbf{A}$ (or $\mathbf{A}'$) is executed consists of all the strings the participants receive together with their random coin tosses *given that* $w = 0$.

However there is another problem. What if the $s(L)$-system $\mathbf{A}$ is 'badly' designed and delivers more than it is supposed to? For example $\mathbf{A}$ may be *designed* to support a subliminal channel. Even though this may not be included in the specification s, our definition of $s(L)$-systems does not require that the systems be 'minimal' with respect to their specifications. We now address this issue. Informally, we say that an $s(L)$-system $\mathbf{A}$ is *minimal* [17] if all participants receive no more than strictly specified by the specification s when **A** is executed. Minimality is based on zero-knowledge and minimal-knowledge [23, 21] and involves simulation. Depending on the type of simulation, we have *perfect, statistical* or *computational* minimality. We are now in a position to give a definition for subliminal-free systems which reflects our intuition.

Definition 3. [17] An $s(L)$-system **A** is *subliminal-free* if the following hold.

- **Fairness:** When **A** is executed then almost always $w = 0$.
- **Minimality:** **A** is a minimal.
- **Detectability:** If **A** is replaced by any other $s(L)$-system **A$'$** then either W will almost always detect the abuse, or, if he does not, then the conditional view (when $w = 0$) of the participants while **A$'$** is executed, cannot be distinguished from that while **A** is executed on L_p.

We have *perfect, statistical* or *computational* subliminal-freeness depending on the minimality and the distinguishability of the warden.

3 Discussion

As is well known in system theory, modeling real life can be quite complex, if not impossible, since the primitives involved are synthetic and may not be amenable to analysis. For this reason we can never be sure that Definition 3 properly reflects our intuitive understanding of the notion of subliminal-freeness (which our first definition clearly failed to).

As an illustration of how subtle and elusive the notion of subliminal-freeness can be, we describe the signature scheme proposed in [11] which was claimed to be subliminal-free, but which is not (see also the discussion on the composition of subliminal-free protocols in §3.1 and §3.5). This scheme is based on the Feige-Fiat-Shamir signature scheme [18, 20]. We first describe briefly this last scheme. Let $n = pq$ be a product of two primes p, q, $p \equiv q \equiv 3 \,(\mathrm{mod}\,4)$, and QR_n be the the set of quadratic residues modulo n. The public key is $(n, I_1, \ldots, I_k)$, where $I_j = s_j^{-2} \bmod n$, $s_j \in \mathrm{QR}_n$. Let m be the message to be signed. The signer S picks random residues $r_i \in \mathrm{QR}_n$, takes $x_i = r_i^2 \bmod n$, and computes the first kt bits e_{ij} of $f(m, x_1, \ldots, x_k)$, where f is an appropriate function. The signature of m consists of: m, $(n, I_1, \ldots, I_k)$, the kt bits e_{ij}, and $y_1, \ldots, y_t$, where $y_i = r_i \prod_{e_{ij}=1} s_j \bmod n$. The verifier checks the signature by computing $z_i = y_i^2 \prod_{e_{ij}=1} I_j \bmod n$ and verifying that the first kt bits of $f(m, z_1, \ldots, z_k)$ are e_{ij}.

We now describe the modified scheme. Assume that the signer S has a public-key. The warden W selects random residues $\rho_i \in \mathrm{QR}_n$, $i = 1, \ldots, t$, and sends to S commitments for these (using an appropriate commitment scheme). Then S picks random $r_i \in \mathrm{QR}_n$, computes $x_i = r_i^2 \bmod n$, $i = 1, \ldots, t$, and sends these to W. Now W 'opens' his commitments and gives S the values ρ_i. The signer S checks that these are correct and if so, computes $x_i' = x_i \rho_i^2 \bmod n$. The signature is obtained as in the Feige-Fiat-Shamir scheme with x_i' replacing the x_i. It is easy to see that the modified signature scheme satisfies the requirements of Definition 1. Indeed the x_i' which determine the signature are uniformly distributed in QR_n, whatever distribution S assignes to the x_i. So the distribution of the signature is indistinguishable from the uniform distribution, provided that the signing process is completed. If not, the warden W will distinguish the strings.

However this scheme is not subliminal-free. To prove this we consider a powerful technique for establishing subliminal channels: *abortive halting* [14]. Suppose that the signer S and a verifier V agree in advance, when the system is set up, that the last bit of all signatures of S should be 0. Then each time that S has to sign a message he makes certain that the last bit is 0, by halting if it is not. The verifier V will distinguish subliminal signatures from ordinary signatures and thus a subliminal channel is established. Definition 3 addresses this particular aspect of the view of V (which Definition 1 failed to): namely the conditional view of V ($w = 0$), when there is no halting and no abuse is detected. This consists of the subliminal signatures. For subliminal-freeness these should be indistinguishable from ordinary signatures.

3.1 Impact of the new definition

Cleve [8] observed in 1986 that abortive halting could be used in the Blum coin-flipping protocol [4] to control the distribution of the outcome. Although it not intended to be used to establish subliminal channels, its scope is quite extensive and it applies to any protocol in which two parties independently influence the outcome of an event.

As a result, several protocols in the literature which claim to be subliminal-free (and which satisfy the requirements of Definition 1) are not. With these, during the execution of the protocol, one party succeeds in sharing with another party a message with some randomness (eg, the x_i' in the modified signature scheme in §3). Then, halting when a particular pattern occurs in the randomness of the message will influence the conditional view (when there is no halting) of the other party, and thererefore will establish a subliminal channel. Similarly, the composition of probabilistic subliminal-free protocols is not subliminal-free, as will be illustrated in §3.5.

In the following sections we review the literature. We first consider the protocols which are not subliminal-free, and for which we do not know any way to make them subliminal-free. Then we consider protocols which remain subliminal-free (using Definition 3). Finally we consider the protocols which we can fix.

3.2 Protocols which are not subliminal-free

- All (probabilistic) signature schemes presented in [10, 9, 12] and in [33, 35] (the signer and verifier end up sharing strings with some randomness).
- All the public key generating schemes in [9, 11, 12].

3.3   Protocols which are subliminal-free

- The zero-knowledge proof for quadratic residuocity in [15].
- The zero-knowledge proof for Commutative Random Self-Reducibility in [27].
- The zero-knowledge proof for graph isomorphism in [6].
- The unconditional authentication scheme in [16].
- The secret sharing scheme in [13].

3.4   Protocols which can be fixed

- The zero-knowledge proofs for NP in [6] (we need homomorphic commitment schemes whose parameters are selected by an oracle as in [6, Theorem 1]; Theorem 2 and Corollary 2 in [6] are incorrect). A corrected protocol is given in [7].
- The zero-knowledge proof for graph non-isomorphism in [24] (see [7]).
- The zero-knowledge authentication scheme in [10] – only proven secure against generic chosen plaintext attacks (this can be fixed by using commitments with unconditionally secure privacy in the protocol of [10, top p. 29]).
- The coin flipping protocols in [10, 11, 9, 12]. In the following section we show one way to fix them.

3.5   A subliminal-free coin-flipping protocol

We present in this section a modified version of the coin-flipping protocol of Blum [4] which is subliminal-free.

Let A (Alice) and B (Bob) be the parties who want to flip a coin over the telephone. We shall assume that both A and B have limited computing resources. Our protocol will use a homomorphic bit-commitment scheme f. Bit commitment schemes are probabilistic functions: they take as input a bit b and coin tosses r, and output a number $f(b)$ (in general a string) which is the commitment for the bit b. We assume that it is hard to find b given only $f(b)$ (for privacy), and that it is hard to find coin tosses such that $f(0) = f(1)$ (to prevent lying). A commitment $f(b)$ is opened by revealing the bit b and the coin tosses r. For homomorphic commitments, we also assume that given $f(b), f(b')$, with coin tosses r, r', the product $f(b) \cdot f(b')$ is a commitment for $b \oplus b'$ (the xor sum) whose coin tosses can easily be computed given b, b', r, r'. An example of such a commitment scheme is given in [3, pp. 176] (for this commitment scheme privacy is unconditionally secure).

The protocol is described in Fig. 1. In this, Alice commits the bit b to the warden, who in turn commits the bit $b \oplus q$ to Bob. Observe that $f(b) \cdot f(q) = f(b \oplus q)$, because the commitment scheme is homomorphic. Bob then reveals his bit b' to the warden, and the warden commits the bit $q \oplus b'$ to Alice. Finally Alice opens her commitment to the warden, and after checking it, the warden opens his commitment to both Alice and Bob.

In this protocol both Alice and Bob get the coin flip $q \oplus b \oplus b'$ only at the end of the protocol, by which time halting will have no influence on the conditional

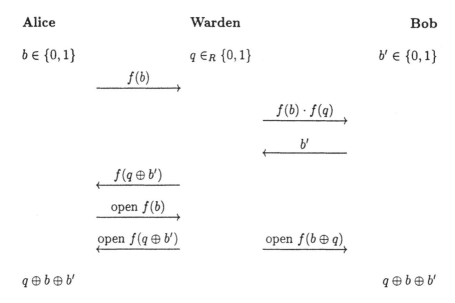

Fig. 1. A subliminal-free coin-flipping protocol.

view of the outcome. Halting earlier does not influence the conditional outcome (i.e. the view when $w = 0$), because then the warden detects the abuse. Since Alice and Bob use a secure bit commitment scheme, and since their bits b, b' are xor-ed by the warden with the random bit q, there is no way that they can find out anything about the committed bits before they are opened by the warden.

In this protocol we assume that both Alice and Bob have limited resources. We could allow for one of them, say Alice, to have unlimited resource, provided she uses a homomorphic commitment scheme which is unconditionally secure against lying (the encryption scheme in [22, p. 281] will do). The warden will then have to use a scheme which guarantees unconditional privacy (the scheme in [3, pp. 179] will do), otherwise Alice can find the committed bit of the warden.

It is easy to see that running this twice, in succession, is not subliminal-free. Indeed at the end of the first run, both parties share the bit $q \oplus b \oplus b'$. Suppose that the parties have agreed to the subliminal bit e before the coin-flipping protocol is set-up (e on their history tape). Then if Alice halts when $e \neq q \oplus b \oplus b'$, after the first run, then Bob will always get the coin flip e for the first round.

4   Future research

It seems that it is impossible to make subliminal-free signature schemes which use randomness, but this has not been proven. Also no subliminal-free protocol exists so far for making public keys and it is not known whether one can be made.

The abortive halting attack against protocols which were originally thought to be subliminal-free introduces a subliminal channel with a very low capacity, roughly 1/2 bit (in fact $1/\ln(2) \cdot 2^{-1/\ln(2)}$ bit [14]). In practice protocols which only support subliminal channels with very small capacity may be acceptable. The problem is that the state-of-the-art research on subliminal-freeness has focussed on an all, or nothing approach. A quantitative approach seems much more difficult. Indeed, we do not know of any method to prove that the abortive halting channel is the only one that can be used against signature schemes such as those proposed in [10, 9, 12, 33, 35]. Other subliminal channels with a larger capacity may exist. Moreover, it seems not easy to define a computational complexity equivalent for the information theoretical notion of capacity [28]. Indeed, the invention of public key by Diffie and Hellman [19] has demonstrated that the traditional measure of information is insufficient. For example, how much information, from a computational point of view, in a secret key corresponds to a public key?

References

1. Bellare, M., Goldreich, O.: On defining proofs of knowledge. In Advances in Cryptology — Crypto '92, Proceedings (Lecture Notes in Computer Science 740) (1993) E. F. Brickell, Ed. Springer-Verlag pp. 390–420.
2. Bengio, S., Brassard, G., Desmedt, Y. G., Goutier, C., Quisquater, J.-J.: Secure implementations of identification systems. Journal of Cryptology 4 (1991) 175–183.
3. Brassard G., Chaum D., Crépeau C.: Minimum disclosure proofs of knowledge Journal of Computer and System Sciences, vol. 37 (2), 1988, pp. 156–189.
4. Blum, M.: Coin flipping by telephone — A protocol for solving impossible problems. Digest of papers COMPCON82, *IEEE Computer Society*, 1982, pp. 133–137
5. Burmester, M., Desmedt, Y., Yung, M.: Subliminal-free channels: a solution towards covert-free channels. In Symposium on Computer Security, Threats and Countermeasures (1991) pp. 188–197.
6. Burmester, M. V. D., Desmedt, Y.: All languages in NP have divertible zero-knowledge proofs and arguments under cryptographic assumptions. In Advances in Cryptology, Proc. of Eurocrypt '90 (Lecture Notes in Computer Science 473) (1991) I. Damgård, Ed. Springer-Verlag pp. 1–10.
7. Burmester, M., Desmedt, Y., Itoh, T., Sakurai, K., and Shizuya, H.: Divertible and subliminal-free zero-knowledge proofs of languages. Submitted 1993, under revision.
8. Cleve R.: Limits on the security of coin flips when half the processors are fault.*Proceedings of the eighteenth annual ACM Symp. Theory of Computing, STOC*, 1986, pp. 364–369.
9. Desmedt Y.: Protecting against Abuses of Cryptosystems in Particular in the Context of Verification of Peace Treaties. Sequences (Combinatorics, Compression. Security, and Transmission), R. M. Capocelli, Ed, Springer-Verlag, 1990, pp. 394–405.
10. Desmedt, Y.: Subliminal-free authentication and signature. In Advances in Cryptology, Proc. of Eurocrypt '88 (Lecture Notes in Computer Science 330) (May 1988) C. G. Günther, Ed. Springer-Verlag pp. 23–33.

11. Desmedt, Y.: Abuses in cryptography and how to fight them. In Advances in Cryptology — Crypto '88, Proceedings (Lecture Notes in Computer Science 403) (1990) S. Goldwasser, Ed. Springer-Verlag pp. 375–389.

12. Desmedt, Y.: Making conditionally secure cryptosystems unconditionally abuse-free in a general context. In Advances in Cryptology — Crypto '89, Proceedings (Lecture Notes in Computer Science 435) (1990) G. Brassard, Ed. Springer-Verlag pp. 6–16.

13. Desmedt, Y.: Subliminal-free sharing schemes. Proceedings 1994 IEEE International Symposium on Information Theory, Trondheim, Norway, 1994, p. 490.

14. Desmedt, Y.: Simmons' Protocol is not free of subliminal channels. To be presented at the 9th IEEE Computer Security Foundations Workshop, County Kerry, Ireland, June 10–12, 1996, to appear in the proceedings.

15. Desmedt, Y., Goutier, C., Bengio, S.: Special uses and abuses of the Fiat-Shamir passport protocol. In Advances in Cryptology, Proc. of Crypto '87 (Lecture Notes in Computer Science 293) (1988) C. Pomerance, Ed. Springer-Verlag pp. 21–39.

16. Desmedt, Y., Yung, M.: Unconditional subliminal-freeness in unconditional authentication systems. In Proceedings 1991 IEEE International Symposium on Information Theory (Budapest, Hungary, June 24–28, 1991) p. 176. Full paper in preparation.

17. Desmedt, Y., Yung, M.: Minimal cryptosystems and defining subliminal-freeness. In Proceedings 1994 IEEE International Symposium on Information Theory (Trondheim, Norway, June 27–July 1, 1994) p. 347.

18. Feige, U., Fiat, A., Shamir, A.: Zero knowledge proofs of identity. Journal of Cryptology 1 (1988) 77–94.

19. Diffie W., Hellman, M. E.: New directions in cryptography. IEEE Trans. Inform. Theory, vol. IT–22 (6), pp. 644–654 1976.

20. Fiat, A., Shamir, A.: How to prove yourself: Practical solutions to identification and signature problems. In Advances in Cryptology, Proc. of Crypto '86 (Lecture Notes in Computer Science 263) (1987) A. Odlyzko, Ed. Springer-Verlag pp. 186–194.

21. Galil, S., Haber, S., Yung, M.: Minimum-knowledge interactive proofs for decision problems. *Siam J. Comput.*, vol. 18, pp. 711–739, August 1989.

22. Goldwasser, S., Micali S.: Probabilistic Encryption. *Journal of Computer and System Sciences,* vol. 28 (2), pp. 270–299, 1984.

23. Goldwasser, S., Micali, S., Rackoff, C.: The knowledge complexity of interactive proof systems. *Siam J. Comput.*, vol. 18, pp. 186–208, February 1989.

24. Itoh, T., Sakurai, K., Shizuya, H.: Any language in IP has a divertible ZKIP. In Advances in Cryptology — Asiacrypt '91, Proceedings (Lecture Notes in Computer Science 739) (1993) H. Imai, R. L. Rivest, and T. Matsumoto, Eds. Springer-Verlag pp. 382–396.

25. Jones, T. C., Seberry, J.: Authentication without secrecy. ARS Combinatoria 21 (1986) 115–121.

26. Lampson B. W.: A note on the confinement problem. *Comm. ACM*, vol. 16 (10), pp. 613–615, 1973.

27. Okamoto, T., Ohta, K.: Divertible zero knowledge interactive proofs and commutative random self-reducibility. In Advances in Cryptology, Proc. of Eurocrypt '89 (Lecture Notes in Computer Science 434) (1990) J.-J. Quisquater and J. Vandewalle, Eds. Springer-Verlag pp. 134–149.

28. Shannon, C. E.: A Mathematical Theory of Communications. Bell System Techn. Jour., vol. 27, pp. 623–656 1948.

29. Simmons, G. J.: The prisoners' problem and the subliminal channel. In Advances in Cryptology. Proc. of Crypto 83 (1984) D. Chaum, Ed. Plenum Press N.Y. pp. 51–67.

30. Simmons, G. J.: Verification of Treaty Compliance-Revisited. Proc. of the 1983 IEEE Symposium on Security and Privacy, *IEEE Computer Society Press*, Oakland, 1983, pp. 61–66.

31. Simmons, G. J.: The subliminal channel and digital signatures. In Advances in Cryptology. Proc. of Eurocrypt 84 (Lecture Notes in Computer Science 209) (1985) T. Beth, N. Cot, and I. Ingemarsson, Eds. Springer-Verlag, Berlin pp. 364–378.

32. Simmons, G. J.: The secure subliminal channel (?). In Advances in Cryptology: Crypto '85, Proceedings (Lecture Notes in Computer Science 218) (1986) H. C. Williams, Ed. Springer-Verlag pp. 33–41.

33. Simmons, G. J.: An introduction to the mathematics of trust in security protocols. In Proceedings: Computer Security Foundations Workshop VI (1993) IEEE Computer Society Press. pp. 121–127.

34. Simmons, G. J.: The subliminal channels in the U.S. digital signature algorithm (DSA). In Proceedings of the 3rd Symposium on: State and Progress of Research in Cryptography (February 15–16, 1993) W. Wolfowicz, Ed. pp. 35–54.

35. Simmons, G. J.: Cryptanalysis and protocol failures. Commun. ACM **37** (1994) 56–65.

36. Simmons, G. J.: Subliminal channels; past and present. European Trans. on Telecommunications **5** (1994) 459–473.

Modeling Cryptographic Protocols and Their Collusion Analysis

Steven H. Low
Department of EEE
University of Melbourne
Australia
slow@ee.mu.oz.au

Nicholas F. Maxemchuk
Bell Laboratories
Murray Hill, NJ 07974
USA
nfm@allegra.att.com

Abstract. As network applications such as electronic commerce proliferate, complex communications protocols that employ cryptographic building blocks, such as encryption and authentication, will become more common. We view a cryptographic protocol as a process by which information is transferred among some users and hidden from others. The collusion property of a protocol measures how well it hides information. The collusion problem determines whether a subset of users can discover, through collusion, the information that is designed to be hidden from them during or after a protocol's execution. We introduce a model for a general multiparty cryptographic protocol and its collusion analysis. The model has two components, one modeling the protocol phase and the other the subsequent collusion phase. We derive a necessary and sufficient condition under which such collusion is possible. Based on this characterization we design an algorithm that checks whether the condition is satisfied, and when it is, computes an efficient collusion process.

1 Introduction

As networked applications such as electronic commerce and digital library proliferate complex communications protocols employing cryptographic building blocks, such as encryption and authentication, are being developed to provide privacy as well as security. For instance [20] presents ways to use communications networks to separate and hide information while satisfying the need of a group of communicating parties for (different parts of) the information. It is useful to assess how well a cryptographic protocol hides information. In this paper we consider one aspect of it, the collusion property of a cryptographic protocol.

This is motivated by our earlier work [18, 19] and [20] in which we designed multiparty communications protocols to protect privacy in credit card and health-care systems. In the credit card system, for instance, the protocol uses standard cryptographic techniques to hide different pieces of transaction information from different parties involved in the transaction so that at the end of a credit card transaction, no single party except the cardholder can associate the cardholder's identity with where or what she purchases. Moreover it takes all but one party to collude in order to compromise the cardholder's privacy.

For our purposes, a cryptographic protocol is a process by which some information is transferred among some users and hidden from others. The collusion problem determines whether it is possible for a *subset* of users to discover, through collusion, the information that is to be hidden from them after a protocol has been executed. Typically a user does not know the identity of other users involved in the multiparty protocol except those it needs to directly communicate with. It must start from what it can learn from all the messages it possesses to seek possible colluders. Different parts of a messages may be encrypted with different keys, some of which it cannot decrypt. As collusion proceeds more and more messages can be decrypted, revealing more information and candidate colluders. If *all* protocol users can collude the problem is trivial, but when only a subset of them can collude they may not be able to uncover a target set of information. In this paper we will give the condition under which successful collusion is possible and provide an algorithm to construct a sequence of collusions that uncover the target information set when one exists.

Cryptographic protocols are notoriously hard to design and their correctness is harder to prove [29]. Numerous cryptographic protocols have been published and later found to contain security flaws, see, e.g., [24, 6, 25, 30, 28, 21, 23, 3]. As surveyed in [23] these often subtle failures do not require eroding the integrity of the underlying cryptoalgorithm and hence are weaknesses of the protocols. Often the soundness of a cryptographic protocol is evaluated by having experts attempt to find flaws in the protocol. When flaws are found the protocol is modified and then the cycle repeats. Very useful rules of thumb for prudent designs have been distilled from such experiences [1, 2]. Yet, examples abound in the literature that have survived extensive and intensive scrutiny, only to have been shown later to contain a protocol failure. They clearly demonstrate the need for formal methods to verify cryptographic properties of protocols.

One of the earliest such efforts is [8, 7] in which algebraic methods are used to model and analyze the security of a class of public key protocols. A logic is introduced in [3] to formally describe the beliefs of users involved in an authentication protocol and their evolution as communication proceeds, and is later extended in [11]. A third approach models security protocols as transition systems and analyzes them using existing tools in hardware and software specification and verification. In [15], for example, the cryptographic protocol and the means by which an intruder attacks it are described in a formal specification language and a symbolic execution tool is then used to 'walk through' the protocol to detect vulnerabilities. Recently, software tools have been built to perform mechanical and formal analysis of cryptographic protocols based on these models [22, 15, 21]; see also [14]. As network applications such as electronic commerce and networked publishing proliferate, complex multiparty protocols that employ cryptographic building blocks will become more common. Their cryptographic properties can only be fully analyzed using formal methods.

We are interested in the possibility of collusion either during or after protocol execution. In §2 we introduce a novel model for this purpose. The model has two components, one modeling a multiparty cryptographic protocol and the other modeling the subsequent collusion. Roughly, the collusion problem determines whether it is possible for a subset of users to discover a target set of information through a sequence of message exchanges among them. A solution to the problem, called a *collusion path*, is a specific sequence of message exchanges that uncovers the target set of information. As we will see below, the problem is equivalent to a reachability analysis on a large transition system, exhaustive search on which is infeasible.

By exploiting the structure of collusion paths we show in §3 that the existence of a solution can be determined by examining just the initial knowledge of all the colluders (which is also the initial state in the transition system from which reachability analysis should start). This eliminates the need to explore the large transition system.

Based on this characterization we present in §4 an algorithm to check whether a collusion problem has a solution, and when it does, computes a simple collusion path.

In §5 we conclude and describe two extensions.

There are three important differences between our work and earlier work on formal analysis of cryptographic protocols. First, previous work [8, 7, 3, 11, 22, 15, 21] mostly verifies the security of a protocol, i.e., whether it fulfills its intended function. Given a secure protocol, we are concerned with how well it protects privacy. Second, as explained in §2.4, a collusion problem is defined on a transition system, and hence can in principle be solved by exhaustive reachability search, as done in [22, 15, 21]. By exploiting the special structure of the collusion problem, however, our algorithm (in §4) is much more efficient. We reduce the search on the state space of the transition system, which can have $2^{|U|(|U|-1)}$ reachable states, to a search on a graph with $|U|$ nodes, where $|U|$ is the number of colluders. This reduction in time complexity is important as large multiparty cryptographic protocols become common. Third, in the formulation of the collusion problem, we do not consider, as most previous work does, *active* saboteurs as formalized in [8]. Inclusion of active saboteurs in the formulation is an interesting open problem. We note that our algorithm supplements, and can be incorporated into, existing protocol analysis tools such as those in [22, 15, 21].

All proofs, omitted here, can be found in [17] along with more detailed development entensions. An application of the algorithm here to a proposed cryptographic protocol can be found in [19].

2 Model and Problem Formulation

In this section we present a model for a cryptographic protocol and one for its collusion analysis, and formulate the collusion problem.

The protocol execution phase and the subsequent collusion phase are modeled as separate transition systems in which the system state keeps track of the knowledge of all users involved. The state evolves as users communicate by exchanging messages. With a slight modification the collusion problem can be formulated on just one transition system instead of two as done here; see [17, 19].

The model for cryptographic protocols is presented here because it may be of independent interest.

2.1 Notation

For any set A, $|A|$ denotes the number of elements in A, 2^A denotes the collection of subsets of A, and A^* denotes its Kleen closure.

Our environment is described by the triple (U_p, D, K) where

1. U_p is a finite set of protocol users;
2. D is a finite set of data;
3. K is a finite set of encryption keys.

Define the *information set* as the set of every possible encryption and clear text combination of every piece of information in the system:

$$I := K^*(U_p \cup D \cup K)$$

For example, if $d \in U_p \cup D \cup K$ and $k_i \in K$, then d, $k_1(d)$, $k_2 k_1(d)$ are all in I.

If $d \in U_p \cup D \cup K$ and $k \in K$ then $k(d)$ denotes the encryption of d with k. A string $k_n \cdots k_1$ represents successive application of keys $k_1, \ldots, k_n$ in order. We use ϵ to denote the identity key: for any d, $\epsilon(d) = d$. We assume that K contains the identity key ϵ.

For any key k, k^{-1} denotes its inverse with the cancellation rule $k^{-1} k = k k^{-1} = \epsilon$. For example, The keys k and k^{-1} are identical in secret-key cryptosystems, but not in public-key crypotsystems. When we refer to a string γ of keys, we always assume that γ is in reduced form that cannot be further simplified by application of the cancellation rule.

If $A = \{k^{-1}, k(d)\}$ then the key k^{-1} can be used to decrypt $k(d)$ and hence A is 'equivalent to' $\{k, d\}$. In general if $A \subseteq I$ then A can be reduced to an 'equivalent' set by application of the cancellation rule. We abstractly describe this transformation by the function $\Delta : 2^I \to 2^I$. Δ represents the decryption of a set $A \subseteq I$ of information by the keys included in A such that if $k_1 \cdots k_n(d) \in \Delta(A)$ then $k_1^{-1} \notin \Delta(A)$. The specific form of Δ depends on the underlying cryptosystem. In general the decryption is an iterative process because when the information is decrypted by the keys that are available, additional keys may become visible, which make it possible to further decrypt the information. Whenever we refer to a subset of I we always assume that it is in this reduced form.

A *transition system* is a triple $\Theta = (Q, \Sigma, \delta)$, where Q is a set of states, Σ is a finite set of transition labels, and $\delta : Q \times \Sigma \to Q$ is a transition (partial) function. For example, a finite state machine is a special transition system in which Q is finite. A *path* is a sequence of transitions. A concatenation of two paths θ and ρ is denoted $\theta \rho$.

Finally, we use $(y_j, j \in J)$ to denote a vector with components y_j, j spanning the index set J; the jth component y_j is sometimes denoted $y.j$.

2.2 Protocol System

A protocol is executed by a set of users who exchange information by transmitting messages. The users who can use the information is controlled by encrypting the information with a set of keys. In each step of the protocol a sender $s \in U_p$ transfers a message, containing a subset of $U_p \cup D \cup K$, to a receiver $r \in U_p$. Each element in the message is encrypted by a string of keys in K, and may contain pieces that r can decrypt, those that r cannot decrypt, as well as keys that can decrypt part of r's current information. Each message is made unique to prevent replay attack. We refer to a message by a unique message number. The receiver's knowledge is increased by the content of the message. Moreover, the sender and the receiver share a unique message that can be used for collusion purposes, as we will see below. A user's knowledge is the set of information and the set of messages that it possesses, and is modified as protocol proceeds. The protocol specifies all possible sequences of message exchanges that are allowed and the evolution of the users' knowledge. Protocol execution terminates when the users' knowledge reaches a certain prespecified pattern. For example, in an on-line payment protocol, e.g. [9, 18, 19], execution is complete when the store receives confirmation from its bank that funds has been transferred from the customer's account to the store's account. We now make these notions precise.

The *knowledge set* is the combination of the messages and information:

$$W := 2^N \times 2^I$$

where N is the set of unique message identifiers and I is the information set. An element $w = (w.N, w.I)$ of W represents a user's knowledge. It has two components: the first component $w.N \subseteq N$ represents all the messages the user has seen, and the second component $w.I \subseteq I$ represents all the information the user knows. As noted above $w.I$ is in reduced form. User u's knowledge is denoted $w_u \in W$. We naturally assume that a user knows its own identity: $u \in w_u.I$ for all $u \in U_p$.

The messages that are exchanged form a *message set* M, a subset of W. For each $m \in M$, $m.N$ is a singleton corresponding to the unique message number, and $m.I$ is the information exchanged. Hence every message in M is distinct.

The users exchange messages and as a result their knowledge is changed. A protocol specifies all possible sequences of message exchanges that are allowed and how the users' knowledge evolve. It is modeled by a transition system $\Phi = (W^{|U_p|}, \Sigma_p, \delta_p)$, where

1. The state of the system $w = (w_u, u \in U_p) \in W^{|U_p|}$ is the knowledge possessed by every user.
2. The transitions $\Sigma_p \subseteq U_p \times U_p \times M$ are the possible message exchanges between all of the users. An event $(s, r, m) \in \Sigma_p$ represents the transfer of message m from user s to user r. Every transition involves a different (unique) message, i.e., if (s, r, m) and (s', r', m') are distinct transitions in Σ_p, then m and m' differ at least in $m.N$ and $m'.N$.

3. The transition function $\delta_p : W^{|U_p|} \times \Sigma_p \rightarrow W^{|U_p|}$ describes how the knowledge of the sender and the receiver is transformed by an event.

The transition function δ is a partial function because of two obvious constraints: a sender cannot transfer a message to a receiver unless the sender knows the receiver and can compose the message from its current information, i.e., for each $w = (w_u, u \in U_p)$ and each $\sigma = (s, r, m)$, $\delta_p(w, \sigma)$ is defined *only if*

$$r \in w_s.I \quad \text{and} \quad m.I \subseteq (w_s.I \cap K)^*(w_s.I) .$$

When a message is transferred between a sender and a receiver, the knowledge of other users is unchanged, and the only change in the sender's information set is a unique message number that is shared with the receiver. The shared message number is important in the collusion stage. Specifically, when a transition $\sigma = (s, r, m)$ is made from the current state w, the next state $w' = \delta_p(w, \sigma)$ is defined by

$$
\begin{aligned}
w'_y &= w_y, && \text{if } y \neq s, \; y \neq r \\
w'_s.N &= w_s.N \cup m.N, & w'_s.I &= w_s.I \\
w'_r.N &= w_r.N \cup m.N, & w'_r.I &= \Delta(w_r.I \cup m.I) \cup \{s\}.
\end{aligned}
$$

The application of the function Δ guarantees that the information component of a receiver's knowledge is always in the unique reduced representation.

Definition 1. A protocol is a triple $(\Phi, w(0), F)$ where Φ is a transition system described above, $w(0)$ is the initial state, and F is a set of final states. The initial and final states are the knowledge possessed by all of the users. i.e., $w(0) \in W^{|U_p|}$ and $F \subseteq W^{|U_p|}$.

Here $w(0)$ describes the users' knowledge at the beginning of a protocol run. A protocol run is completed when Φ enters a state in F.

Once specified as a transition system, a protocol can be checked for various logical properties such as safety, absence of deadlock, livelock or unspecified transitions, using several techniques; see for example [13]. Its security can also be verified using existing tools, e.g., those described in [22, 15, 21]. We focus in this paper only on the collusion property.

2.3 Collusion System

The collusion problem determines whether a subset of users can discover the information that is being hidden from them. They discover the hidden information by combining the information that they possess. Combining information is modeled as sending additional messages among the subset of users, and looks very much like the model for the original protocol.

It is not always possible for two users to collude. In order for s to send a message to r, s must know r, as in the protocol. In addition they must share a common, unique piece of information pertaining to the protocol run in question.

To motivate this requirement consider as an example the intermediary cx in [4] that forwards a piece of data to its recipient r in order to hide the identity of its sender s from r:

1. $s \longrightarrow cx : k_{cx}(r, k_r(d))$
2. $cx \longrightarrow r : k_r(d)$

In the above s encrypts the (encrypted) data $k_r(d)$ and the recipient's identity r with a key k_{cx} that can only be decrypted by the intermediary cx and sends them to cx (message 1). Note that the data d is also encrypted with a key k_r that can only be decrypted by the recipient r. The intermediary cx then forwards the encrypted data to r (message 2), thus hiding the identity of the sender s from r. After the above steps are carried out, cx knows $w_{cx} := (\{\text{message 1, message 2}\}, \{s, cx, r, k_{cx}^{-1}, k_r(d)\})$ and r knows $w_r := (\{\text{message 2}\}, \{cx, r, k_r^{-1}, d\})$. For r to discover s, r must learn the information in w_{cx}. In a large system however cx may have forwarded a large number of messages to the same recipient r in a short period of time and they have collected a large number of w_{cx} and w_r, corresponding to different protocol runs. Hence to combine the information in w_{cx} and w_r of the *same* protocol run, cx and r must share a unique piece of information pertaining to that protocol run. The unique message that is exchanged between cx and r serves this purpose. Since different w_{cx} (or w_r) contain different message identifiers, shared unique message identifiers can be used to pair up w_{cx} and w_r that belong to the same protocol run: only w_{cx} and w_r that share a unique message identifier ('message 2' in the above) can be combined. Variants of this simple protocol have been the building blocks of large cryptographic protocols to provide privacy in broadband networks [27, 26], in credit card transactions [18, 19], and in mobile networks [10], where traffic volumes are high. We will comment on the limitation and describe a relaxation of this requirement in §5 below. We now define the collusion model.

In the collusion model, we have an environment (U_p, U_c, D, K), where (U_p, D, K) is the environment in which the protocol is defined and $U_c \subseteq U_p$ is the subset of users who are colluding.

The information set I and the knowledge set W of the colluders in U_c are the same as in the original protocol: $I = K^*(U_p \cup D \cup K)$ and $W = 2^N \times 2^I$.

Since users in U_c collude by exchanging messages, we model the collusion process by a transition system $\Theta = (W^{|U_c|}, \Sigma_c, \delta_c)$, the same way as we did with a protocol. Here, a state in $W^{|U_c|}$ describes the colluders' knowledge, an event in $\Sigma_c = U_c \times U_c$ describes the transfer of information from one user to another to attempt to extract the hidden information at the receiver, and the transition function δ_c describes the transformation of colluders' knowledge as a result of the message exchange. The sender s always transfers its complete knowledge $w_s = (w_s.N, w_s.I)$. When the current state is $w = (w_u, u \in U_c)$ and a transition $\sigma = (s, r)$ is made, the receiver's knowledge is expanded to include that of the sender. The next state, $w' := \delta(w, \sigma)$, is defined by:

$$w'_y = w_y, \quad \text{if } y \neq r \tag{1}$$

$$w'_r.N = w_r.N \cup w_s.N, \quad w'_r.I = \Delta(w_r.I \cup w_s.I) \tag{2}$$

For each state $w = (w_u, u \in U_c)$ and event $\sigma = (s, r)$, the transition $\delta_c(w, \sigma)$ is defined if and only if

$$r \in w_s.I \quad \text{and} \quad w_s.N \cap w_r.N \neq \phi \tag{3}$$

i.e., if and only if the sender knows the receiver and they share a unique message. This condition can be generalized to include the case where two users can collude as long as they know each other; see §5. We call an event $\sigma = (s, r)$ in Σ *enabled in state w* if the transition $\delta(w, \sigma)$ is defined; we often say that σ is *enabled* when the state from which the transition is made is understood. A path is *valid* if every transition on the path is enabled.

Note that the set of users that can collude can increase as users collude and information is combined. For instance a user may learn in the course of collusion the identity of another user and a message identifier shared with that user, enabling them to collude.

A collusion system is thus similar to a protocol system. Both describe all possible sequences of message exchanges and the evolution of the users' knowledge. The essential differences are in the enabling condition for a transition and the message exchanged. In a protocol a transition is enabled as long as the sender knows the receiver, while in the collusion system, the sender and receiver must also share a unique message that has been exchanged during the protocol phase. In the protocol, the message consists of a subset of the sender's knowledge, while in the collusion system, the message is everything the sender knows.

We summarize our model in the following definition.

Definition 2. Given an environment (U_p, U_c, D, K), a collusion system is the (unique) transition system $\Theta = (W^{|U_c|}, \Sigma_c, \delta_c)$ defined above.

2.4 Problem Formulation

The collusion problem is to determine if a subset of users can combine their information, by passing messages, and extract the hidden information after the protocol is completely *or* partially executed. It is defined in the same environment (U_p, U_c, D, K) as a collusion system $\Theta = (W^{|U_c|}, \Sigma_c, \delta_c)$.

Collusion problem

Given an initial state $w(0) \in W^{|U_c|}$ and a target set of unencrypted information $T \subseteq U_p \cup D \cup K$, does there exists a valid path ρ in Θ from $w(0)$ such that, in the final state $w(\rho)$, there is a colluder $c \in U_c$ whose information contains T, i.e., $w_c(\rho).I \supseteq T$?

We call the valid path in the definition of the collusion problem a *collusion path*. We next make two assumptions, one on the initial state $w(0)$ of the collusion system Θ, and the other on the decryption function Δ.

First, the collusion problem is defined on the collusion system Θ and is apparently independent of the protocol system. However we are interested in the possibility of collusion during or after protocol execution. This means that the initial state $w(0)$ in the collusion problem cannot be arbitrary, but must correspond to a reachable state in the protocol system. In particular in state $w(0)$,

(u, v) is enabled if and only if colluders u and v share a unique message that has been exchanged during the protocol phase. Therefore, u and v must know each other in $w(0)$ and (v, u) must also be enabled:

$$\exists n \in w_u(0).N \cap w_v(0).N \quad \Rightarrow \quad v \in w_u(0).I \quad \text{and} \quad u \in w_v(0).I. \qquad (4)$$

Second, we make the natural assumption that the order in which a user receives information is immaterial. The final combined and reduced information is the same. This is expressed formally as the following property we require of the function Δ: for any A, A' in I,

$$\Delta(\ \Delta(A) \cup A'\ ) \ = \ \Delta(A \cup A'). \qquad (5)$$

The set of reachable states in Θ is a subset of all possible combinations of all colluders' initial knowledge $w(0)$. It is finite, but can contain up to $2^{|U_c|(|U_c|-1)}$ states. For the anonymous credit card protocol analysed in [19], $U_c = 8$ giving a reachable space of $\sim 7 \times 10^{16}$ states. A straightforward reachability analysis on the transition system Θ, such as breadth-first-search or depth-first-search, is infeasible. A clever technique to perform exhaustive reachability analysis on finite state machines, a special case of transition systems, is described in [12]. A novel algorithm is reported in [16] that performs simultaneously reachability analysis and minimization of a transition system that is specified through a compact representation without explicitly constructing first the whole system graph. The algorithm in reference [16] can be applied directly to the collusion system to determine the reachable blocks starting from $w(0)$. These techniques however apply to general transition systems and does not exploit the special structure of the collusion problem. In particular, any event permuted path leads to the same final state, provided that the permutation remains a valid path (see (6–7) below and comments thereafter). As a consequence of this property, in exploring the state space $W^{|U_c|}$, we can skip the many different intermediate states reached by permuting the events in a path ρ, once we have obtained the state reached by ρ itself. Indeed, by exploiting this property, we can determined whether a solution exists and constructs one when it does just from the initial state $w(0)$ alone, thus eliminating the need to search Θ altogether, as we shall show.

3 Solution Structure

For the rest of this paper, fix an environment (U_p, U_c, D, K), an initial state $w(0)$ and a target information set T. In this section we explain the structure of collusion paths and arrive at an exact characterization of when the collusion problem has a solution (Theorem 2 below). In the next section we present an efficient algorithm to solve the collusion problem, based upon this result. Proofs for the results in this and the next sections are omitted and can be found in [17].

The structure of a collusion path on the transition system Θ can be better exhibited in terms of a *collusion graph* we now explain. Consider a path $\rho =$

$(s_1, r_1) \cdots (s_n, r_n)$. We may also use ρ to refer to the set of events $\rho = \{(s_t, r_t)\}_1^n$ in the path, or the set of colluders $\rho = \{s_t, r_t\}_1^n$; the meaning should be clear from the context. Hence by '$(s, r) \in \rho$' and '$c \in \rho$', we mean $(s, r) = (s_t, r_t)$ and $c = s_t$ or r_t, respectively, for some t.

A path in Θ can be equivalently specified by a *labeled graph* $G = (V, E)$ where V are the nodes and $E = \{(u, v, t) \mid u, v \in V, t \in \{1, \ldots, |E|\}\}$ is a set of directed edges from node u to node v labeled by t. The nodes represent colluders involved in the path and the edges represent messages among the colluders. The label on an edge indicates its relative transmission time. It is an important consideration because some events are not enabled until other messages have been transmitted. There can be multiple edges between two nodes in the same direction with different labels, corresponding to the same sender-receiver pair appearing multiple times in the path. Let $\rho(G)$ be the path in Θ defined by a sequentially labeled graph G such that each edge $(u, v, t) \in E$ corresponds to the event (u, v) and is the t-th event in $\rho(G)$. Similarly, let $G(\rho) = (V(\rho), E(\rho))$ be the unique labeled graph defined by ρ in Θ, such that $V(\rho) = \{c \in \rho\}$ and $E(\rho) = \{(u, v, t) \mid (u, v) = (s_t, r_t) \in \rho\}$.

Definition 3. A labeled graph G is a *valid* graph if $\rho(G)$ is a valid path; it is a *collusion graph* if $\rho(G)$ is a collusion path.

Suppose we have a valid path $\rho = (s_1, r_1) \cdots (s_n, r_n)$ and the associated labeled graph $G(\rho) = (V, E)$. A *timed path* (with respect to ρ) from node x to node y is a directed path in $G(\rho)$

$$(x, u_1, t_1) \cdots (u_{k-1}, y, t_k)$$

starting at x and terminating at y such that $1 \le t_1 < \cdots < t_k \le n$. If there is a timed path from x to y, we call x a *timed ancestor* of y. Let $A(\rho; y, t)$ denote the set of all timed ancestors of node y, with respect to ρ, such that the labels on timed paths connecting these timed ancestors to y are all *strictly less* than t. An example is given in Figure 1. We sometimes omit ρ in the notation $A(\rho; c, t)$ when ρ is clear from the context.

If there is a timed path from s to r, the initial knowledge $w_s(0)$ of s is transferred to r after ρ is executed. For any $s' \notin A(\rho; r, |\rho| + 1)$, there is no timed path from s' to r and the initial knowledge is not transferred to r. Assumption (5) on Δ implies that for any valid path ρ, for any r, the state after the path is executed is:

$$w_r(\rho).N = \cup_{s \in A(\rho; r, |\rho|+1)} w_s(0).N \tag{6}$$

$$w_r(\rho).I = \Delta \left(\cup_{s \in A(\rho; r, |\rho|+1)} w_s(0).I \right). \tag{7}$$

In particular, a colluder r knows in state $w(\rho)$ the decrypted union of the initial information of all, and only, its timed ancestors.

This implies that the final state $w(\rho)$ is the same if we permute the events in ρ, as long as the permutation remains a valid path. Different permutations visit different intermediate states on the state space $W^{|U_c|}$. Since they are not

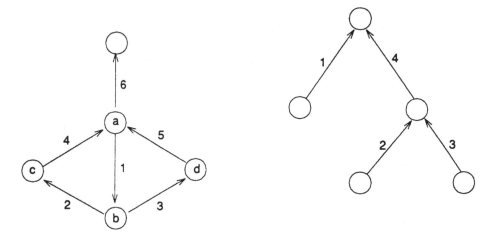

Fig. 1. Collusion graphs. A timed path in the left collusion graph is $(a, b, 1)$ $(b, c, 2)$ $(c, a, 4)$. Timed ancestors are $A(a, 5) = \{a, b, c\}$ or $A(a, 6) = \{a, b, c, d\}$.

as important as the final state, this suggests solving the collusion problem not by exploring $W^{|U_c|}$ but by building a collusion graph. The advantage is that the collusion graph has at most $|U_c|$ nodes while the state space has $2^{|U_c|(|U_c|-1)}$ states.

We are only interested in minimal collusion paths, those on which no colluder can be omitted in order to complete the path in the same relative order. Denote by $\rho - (s_t, r_t)$ the (not necessarily valid) path

$$(s_1, r_1) \cdots (s_{t-1}, r_{t-1})(s_{t+1}, r_{t+1}) \cdots (s_n, r_n)$$

obtained by deleting (s_t, r_t) from $\rho = (s_1, r_1) \cdots (s_n, r_n)$.

Definition 4. A collusion path $\rho = \{(s_t, r_t)\}_1^n$ is *minimal* if for all $j \in \{1, \ldots, n\}$, $\rho - (s_j, r_j)$ is not a collusion path. A collusion graph G is *minimal* if $\rho(G)$ is a minimal collusion path.

A non-minimal collusion path can always be made minimal by removing redundant transitions and keeping the relative order of the remaining transitions, i.e., if $\rho = \{(s_t, r_t)\}_1^n$ is a collusion path that is not minimal, then for some $t_1, \ldots, t_k$, $\rho - (s_{t_1}, r_{t_1}) - \cdots - (s_{t_k}, r_{t_k})$ is a minimal collusion path.

Our first result explains the structure of a minimal collusion graph.

Theorem 1 *Suppose $G = (V, E)$ is a minimal collusion graph and $\rho(G) = (s_1, r_1) \cdots (s_n, r_n)$. Every node u except r_n has at least one outgoing transition; moreover every outgoing transition from node u is on a timed path to r_n.*

The theorem and (7) imply that $w_{r_n}(\rho).I$ that contains the target information T is the decrypted union of the initial information of every colluder in ρ. Hence, to solve the collusion problem, it is necessary and sufficient to find a set of colluders whose *initial* information in state $w(0)$, when combined, yields T and to find a way for all of them to communicate their information to the same colluder.

Because of the collusion prerequisite (3) it turns out that such a set of colluders must have exchanged messages among them in the protocol phase and can be determined from the initial state $w(0)$.

To state this result precisely, define $F = (U_c, E(w(0)))$ as a graph, depending on the initial state $w(0)$, that contains all colluders as its nodes. There is an edge (u, v) in $E(w(0))$ if and only if (u, v) is enabled in the initial state $w(0)$. As noted earlier (condition (4)), in state $w(0)$, (u, v) is enabled if and only if (v, u) is also enabled, since they must have exchanged a unique message during the protocol phase. Hence we can take F to be an undirected graph with each edge representing two directed edges in opposite directions.

The next theorem characterizes exactly the condition under which the collusion problem has a solution, in terms of the graph F and hence of $w(0)$ and T. This avoids exploring the collusion system Θ. A 'connected component' of a graph is a subgraph in which there is a path connecting any two nodes.

Theorem 2 *The collusion problem has a solution if and only if there is a connected component $F' = (V, E)$ of the undirected graph F such that $\Delta(\cup_{u \in V} w_u(0).I) \supseteq T$.*

4   A Solution

In this section we present an algorithm that determines whether the collusion problem has a solution, and if so, produces a collusion path.

By Definition 3 the collusion problem has a solution if and only if there is a collusion graph. In general a collusion graph can take the form of any directed graph. Theorem 3 says that if the collusion problem has a solution then there must exist a collusion graph which is a simple path[1].

Theorem 3 *The collusion problem has a solution if and only if there is a collusion path with the simple structure*

$$\rho = (u_0, u_1)(u_1, u_2) \cdots (u_{n-1}, u_n)$$

where u_i are all distinct, or equivalently, $G(\rho)$ is a simple path.

Theorems 2 and 3 suggest the following algorithm to solve the collusion problem. It first constructs the graph F that describes all transitions that are initially enabled in state $w(0)$. Then it finds each connected component $F' = (V, E)$ of F using breadth-first search while, at the same time, constructing a possible collusion path with the structure given in Theorem 3. The path has visited every node in the connected component when the search on the connected

---

[1] A *simple path* in a graph is a path that contains no loop.

component is complete. Hence the last recipient on the path knows the combined knowledge of every colluder in the connected component (by (7)):

$$\Delta(\cup_{u \in V} w_u(0).I).$$

This combined knowledge is then checked to see if it contains the target information set T. A collusion path is found if it does; otherwise the search is repeated on a different connected component of F. When all connected components have been found without producing a collusion path, Theorem 2 guarantees that none exists.

The algorithm maintains several data structures. The adjacent lists $Adj[v]$ represent the graph F. The variable $discovered[v]$ stores the status of a node v in F. It is initialized to be NO and becomes YES after node v is discovered in the breadth-first search. Q is a queue of nodes and HEAD$[Q]$ is the node at the head of the queue. A node is appended to the end of Q when it is first discovered and removed from the queue when all its neighbors have been discovered. The variable ρ stores the path under construction and *last* stores the last node visited by ρ. The algorithm extends ρ, whenever possible, by a directed edge from *last* to a newly discovered node.

Algorithm

Input: An initial state $w(0)$ and a target information set T.

Output: A collusion path ρ if the collusion problem has a solution; NIL otherwise.

1.   Construct graph $F = (U_c, E)$ from $w(0)$
2.   For each $v \in U_c$, $discovered[v] \leftarrow$ NO
3.   For each $s \in U_c$
            If $discovered[s] =$ NO, then SEARCH(s)
4.   Return (NIL)

SEARCH(s)

1. $discovered[s] \leftarrow$ YES
2. $\rho \leftarrow$ NIL; $last \leftarrow s$; $Q \leftarrow \{s\}$
3.   While $Q \neq \phi$
            $u \leftarrow$ HEAD$[Q]$
            For each $v \in Adj[u]$
                    If $discovered[v] =$ NO
                    then $\rho \leftarrow \rho \cdot (last, v)$; $last \leftarrow v$
                    $discovered[v] =$ YES;   append v to the end of Q
            Remove u from Q
4.   If $\Delta(\cup_{u \in \rho} w_u(0).I) \supseteq T$, then Return$(\rho)$

In the algorithm, the function SEARCH(s) is an adaptation of a breadth-first search. It finds a connected components of F that contains the node s. For a formal proof of its correctness, see, e.g., [5]. The function SEARCH(s) also constructs a path ρ while it scans the connected component, by adding an edge from the last node of the current ρ to a new node when the new node is first discovered. For a proof that the constructed path ρ is valid, see [17]. It has visited every node in the connected component when the entire connected component has been scanned. The algorithm then checks whether the initial information of all nodes on the path ρ can be combined to uncover T. If so, the algorithm stops and outputs the collusion path ρ. Otherwise, it repeats the search on a different connected component of F. If all connected components of F have been searched without producing a collusion path then the algorithm returns NIL. We summarize.

Theorem 4 *If the collusion problem has a solution, Algorithm 1 returns a collusion path ρ; otherwise, it returns* NIL.

5 Conclusion and Extensions

Complex cryptographic protocols are rapidly being developed to provide security and privacy in networked applications. We propose a 'collusion property' as a measure of how well a cryptographic protocol protects privacy. We have introduced a model for cryptographic protocols and one for their collusion analysis. We have defined formally the collusion problem. We have derived the condition under which a collusion path exists and presented an algorithm that checks whether the condition is satisfied and when it is, computes a collusion path.

We now describe two extensions. First the modeling assumption (3) excludes the possibility of collusion between two users who share a unique piece of data, e.g, two banks may have the unique social security number of a customer and hence can combine their knowledge about the customer as long as one knows the other, even if they don't share a unique message. This restriction can be relaxed by defining a subset $L \subseteq U_p \cup D \cup K$ in the environment to be unique in this sense, i.e., two users s and r can collude in state w if and only if $r \in w_s.I$ and at least one of the following conditions is satisfied:

$$w_s.N \cap w_r.N \neq \phi$$
$$w_s.I \cap w_r.I \cap L \neq \phi$$

i.e., if they either share a unique message or an element of L. Note that if L is defined to be U_c then s can send its knowledge to r simply if s knows r. Hence the extension includes as a special case the possibility of collusion without the need of any shared unique information between colluders. With this relaxation the condition under which a collusion path exists is no longer a simple expression as given in Theorem 2, but it can still be determined from just the initial state $w(0)$ using an iterative algorithm whose first iteration embodies the condition in Theorem 2; see [17].

Second suppose a cost is incurred when a pair of users collude. Given the collusion costs associated with each pair of colluders it is desirable to determine a collusion path that incurs the least cost, when one exists. The collusion path computed by the algorithm in §4 is generally not a least-cost one. As presented the algorithm constructs a collusion path that visits *every* node in a connected component of F even when a subset of the colluders suffices. We show in [17] however that determining a least-cost collusion path is NP-hard.

References

1. Martin Abadi and Roger M. Needham. Prudent engineering practice for cryptographic protocols. SRC Research Report 125, DEC, June 1994.
2. Ross Anderson and Roger Needham. Robustness principles for public key protocols. *Advances in Cryptology - CRYPTO'95*, August 1995.
3. Michael Burrows, Martin Abadi, and Roger Needham. A logic of authentication. *ACM Transactions on Computer Systems*, 8(1):18–36, February 1990.
4. David L. Chaum. Untraceable electronic mail, return addresses, and digital pseudonyms. *Communications of the ACM*, 24(2):84–88, February 1981.
5. Thomas H. Cormen, Charles E. Leiserson, and Ronald L. Rivest. *Introduction to Algorithms*. The MIT Press, 1993.
6. D. E. Denning and G. M. Sacco. Timestamps in key distribution protocols. *Communications of the ACM*, 24(8):533–536, August 1981.
7. D. Dolev, S. Even, and R. M. Karp. On the security of Ping-Pong protocols. *Information and Control*, 55:57–68, 1982.
8. Danny Dolev and Andrew C. Yao. On the security of public key protocols. *IEEE Transactions on Information Theory*, IT-29(2):198–208, March 1983.
9. Semyon Dukach. SNPP: A Simple Network Payment Protocol. In *Proceedings of the Computer Security Applications Conference*, San Antonio, TX, November 1992.
10. Hannes Federrath, Anja Jerichow, and Andreas Pfitzmann. Mixes in mobile communication systems: Location management with privacy. *Proc. Workshop on Information Hiding*, May 1996.
11. Li Gong, Roger Needham, and Raphael Yahalom. Reasoning about belief in cryptographic protocols. *Proceedings of the 1990 IEEE Symposium on Security and Privacy*, pages 234–248, May 1990.
12. Gerard J. Holzmann. An improved protocol reachability analysis technique. *Software - Practice and Experience*, 18(2):137–161, February 1988.
13. Gerard J. Holzmann. *Design and Validation of Computer Protocols*. Prentice-Hall, 1991.
14. R. Kemmerer, C. Meadows, and J. Millen. Three systems for cryptographic protocol analysis. *Journal of Cryptology*, 7:79–130, Spring 1994.
15. Richard A. Kemmerer. Analyzing encryption protocols using formal verification techniques. *IEEE Journal on Selected Areas in Communications*, 7(4):448–457, May 1989.
16. David Lee and Mihalis Yannakakis. Online minimization of transition systems. *Proceedings of 24th Annual ACM Symposium on the Theory of Computing*, pages 264–274, May 1992.

17. S. H. Low and N. F. Maxemchuk. Collusion in cryptographic protocols. Technical report, University of Melbourne, Department of Electrical & Electronic Engineering, 1996.

18. S. H. Low, N. F. Maxemchuk, and S. Paul. Anonymous credit cards. *Proceedings of the 2nd. ACM Conference on Computer and Communications Security*, November 2-4 1994.

19. S. H. Low, N. F. Maxemchuk, and S. Paul. Anonymous credit cards and its collusion analysis. *IEEE/ACM Transactions on Networking*, December 1996.

20. N. F. Maxemchuk and S. H. Low. The use of communications networks to increase personal privacy. *Proceedings of Infocom'95*, pages 504-512, April 1995.

21. Catherine Meadows. A system for the specification and analysis of key management protocols. *Proceedings of the 1991 IEEE Symposium on Security and Privacy*, pages 182-195, May 1991.

22. Jonathan K. Millen. The Interrogator: A Tool for Cryptographic Protocol Security. *Proceedings of the 1984 IEEE Symposium on Security and Privacy*, pages 134-141, May 1984.

23. Judy H. Moore. Protocol failures in cryptosystems. *Proceedings of the IEEE*, 76(5):594-602, May 1988.

24. Roger M. Needham and Michael D. Schroeder. Using encryption for authentication in large networks of computers. *Communications of the ACM*, 21(12):993-999, December 1978.

25. Roger M. Needham and Michael D. Schroeder. Authentication revisited. *ACM Operating System Review*, 21(1):7-7, January 1987.

26. A. Pfitzmann, B. Pfitzmann, and M. Waidner. ISDN-MIXes – Untraceable Communications with very Small Bandwidth Overhead. *Proc. IFIP/Sec'91*, pages 245-258, May 1991.

27. A. Pfitzmann and M. Waidner. Networks without user observability. *Computers and Security*, 6(2):158-166, 1987.

28. G. J. Simmons. How to (selectively) broadcast a secret. *Proceedings of the 1985 IEEE Symposium on Security and Privacy*, pages 108-113, May 1985.

29. G. J. Simmons. Proof of soundness (integrity) of cryptographic protocols. *Journal of Cryptology*, 7(2):69-77, Spring 1994.

30. M. Tatebayashi, N. Matsuzaki, and D. B. Newman. Key distribution protocol for digital mobil communication systems. In G. Brassard, editor, *Advances in Cryptology – CRYPTO'89*, volume 435 of *Lecture Notes in Computer Science*, pages 324-333. Springer-Verlag, New York, 1991.

A Secure, Robust Watermark for Multimedia

Ingemar J. Cox[1], Joe Kilian[1], Tom Leighton[2] and Talal Shamoon[1*]

[1] NEC Research Institute, 4 Independence Way, Princeton, NJ 08540
Email: ingemar—joe—talal@research.nj.nec.com
[2] Mathematics Department and Laboratory for Computer Science, MIT, Cambridge, MA 02139.
Email: ftl@math.mit.edu

Abstract. We describe a digital watermarking method for use in audio, image, video and multimedia data. We argue that a watermark must be placed in perceptually significant components of a signal if it is to be robust to common signal distortions and malicious attack. However, it is well known that modification of these components can lead to perceptual degradation of the signal. To avoid this, we propose to insert a watermark into the spectral components of the data using techniques analogous to spread sprectrum communications, hiding a narrow band signal in a wideband channel that is the data. The watermark is difficult for an attacker to remove, even when several individuals conspire together with independently watermarked copies of the data. It is also robust to common signal and geometric distortions such as digital-to-analog and analog-to-digital conversion, resampling, and requantization, including dithering and recompression and rotation, translation, cropping and scaling. The same digital watermarking algorithm can be applied to all three media under consideration with only minor modifications, making it especially appropriate for multimedia products. Retrieval of the watermark unambiguously identifies the owner, and the watermark can be constructed to make counterfeiting almost impossible. Experimental results are presented to support these claims.

1 Introduction

The proliferation of digitized media (audio, image and video) is creating a pressing need for copyright enforcement schemes that protect copyright ownership. Conventional cryptographic systems permit only valid keyholders access to encrypted data, but once such data is decrypted there is no way to track its reproduction or retransmission. Conventional cryptography therefore provides little protection against data piracy, in which a publisher is confronted with unauthorized reproduction of information. A digital watermark is intended to complement cryptographic processes. It is a visible, or preferably invisible, identification code that is permanently embedded in the data, that is, it remains present within the data after any decryption process. In the context of this

---

* Authors in alphabetical order

work, data refers to audio (speech and music), images (photographs and graphics), and video (movies). It does not include ASCII representations of text, but does include text represented as an image. A simple example of a digital watermark would be a visible "seal" placed over an image to identify the copyright owner. However, the watermark might contain additional information, including the identity of the purchaser of a particular copy of the material.

In order to be effective, a watermark should be:

Unobtrusive The watermark should be perceptually invisible, or its presence should not interfere with the work being protected.

Robust The watermark must be difficult (hopefully impossible) to remove. Of course, in theory, any watermark may be removed with sufficient knowledge of the process of insertion. However, if only partial knowledge is available, for example, the exact location of the watermark within an image is unknown, then attempts to remove or destroy a watermark by say, adding noise, should result in severe degradation in data fidelity before the watermark is lost. In particular, the watermark should be robust to

> **Common signal processing** The watermark should still be retrievable even if common signal processing operations are applied to the data. These include, digital-to-analog and analog-to-digital conversion, resampling, requantization (including dithering and recompression), and common signal enhancements to image contrast and color, or audio bass and treble, for example.

> **Common geometric distortions (image and video data)** Watermarks in image and video data should also be immune from geometric image operations such as rotation, translation, cropping and scaling.

> **Subterfuge Attacks: Collusion and Forgery** In addition, the watermark should be robust to collusion by multiple individuals who each possess a watermarked copy of the data. That is, the watermark should be robust to combining copies of the same data set to destroy the watermarks.
>
> Further, if a digital watermark is to be used as evidence in a court of law, it must not be possible for colluders to combine their images to generate a different valid watermark with the intention of framing a third-party.

Universal The same digital watermark algorithm should apply to all three media under consideration. This is potentially helpful in the watermarking of multimedia products. Also, this feature is conducive to implementation of audio and image/video watermarking algorithms on common hardware.

Unambiguous Retrieval of the watermark should unambiguously identify the owner. Further, the accuracy of owner identification should degrade gracefully in the face of attack.

Previous digital watermarking techniques [21, 22, 5, 4, 20, 17, 16, 2, 12, 13, 1, 19] are not robust, and the watermark is easy to remove. In addition, it is unlikely that any of the earlier watermarking methods would survive common signal and geometric distortions. The principal reason for these weaknesses is that previous methods have not explicitly identified the perceptually most significant components of a signal as the destination for the watermark. In fact, it is often the case that the perceptually significant regions are explicitly avoided. The reason for this is obvious – modification of perceptually significant components of a signal results in perceptual distortions much earlier than if the modifications are applied to perceptually insignificant regions. Hence, for example, the common strategy of placing a watermark in the high frequency components of a signal's spectrum.

The key insight of this paper is that in order for it to be robust, the watermark *must* be placed in perceptually significant regions of the data despite the risk of potential fidelity distortions. Conversely, if the watermark is placed in perceptually insignificant regions, it is easily removed, either intentionally or unintentionally by, for example, signal compression techniques that implicitly recognize that perceptually weak components of a signal need not be represented.

The perceptually significant regions of a signal may vary depending on the particular media (audio, image or video) at hand, and even within a given media. For example, it is well known that the human visual system is tuned to certain spatial frequencies and to particular spatial characteristics such as line and corner features. Consequently, many watermarking schemes that focus on different phenomena that are perceptually significant are potentially possible. In this paper, we focus on perceptually significant *spectral* components of a signal.

Section 2 begins with a discussion of how common signal transformations, such as compression, quantization and manipulation, affect the frequency spectrum of a signal. This motivates why we believe that a watermark should be embedded in the data's perceptually significant frequency components. Of course, the major problem then becomes how to insert a watermark into perceptually significant components of the frequency spectrum without introducing visible or audible distortions. Section 2.2 proposes a solution based on ideas from spread spectrum communications.

The structure of a watermark may be arbitrary. However, Section 3 provides an analysis based on possible collusion attacks that indicates that a binary watermark is not as robust as a continuous one. Furthermore, we show that a watermark structure based on sampling drawn from multiple i.i.d Gaussian random variables offers good protection against collusion.

Of course, no watermarking system can be made perfect. For example, a watermark placed in a textual image may be eliminated by using optical character recognition technology. However, for common signal and geometric distortions, the experimental results of Section 4 strongly suggest that our system satisfies *all* of the properties discussed in the introduction, and displays strong immunity to a wide variety of attacks, though more extensive experiments are needed to confirm this. Finally, Section 5 discusses possible weaknesses and enhancements to the system.

188

2 Watermarking in the Frequency Domain

In this section, we first discuss how common signal distortion affect the frequency spectrum of a signal. This analysis supports our contention that a watermark must be placed in perceptually significant regions of a signal if it is to be robust. Section 2.2 proposes inserting a watermark into the perceptually most significant components of the spectrum using spread spectrum techniques.

2.1 Common signal distortions and their effect on the frequency spectrum of a signal

In order to understand the advantages of a frequency-based method, it is instructive to examine the processing stages that an image (or sound) may undergo in the process of copying, and to study the effect that these stages could have on the data, as illustrated in Figure 1. In the figure, "transmission" refers to the

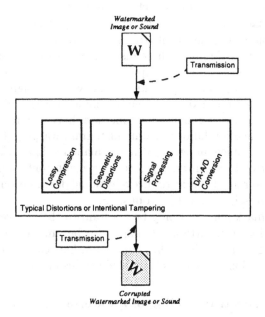

Figure 1. Common processing operations that a media document could undergo

application of any source or channel code, and/or standard encryption technique to the data. While most of these steps are information lossless, many compression schemes (JPEG, MPEG etc.) can potentially degrade the data's quality, through *irretrievable* loss of data. In general, a watermarking scheme should be resilient to the distortions introduced by such algorithms.

Lossy compression is an operation that usually eliminates perceptually non-salient components of an image or sound. If one wishes to preserve a watermark in the face of such an operation, the watermark must be placed in the perceptually significant regions of the data. Most processing of this sort takes place in the frequency domain. In fact, data loss usually occurs among the high frequency components. Hence, the watermark must be placed in the *significant* frequency components of the image (or sound) spectrum.

After receipt, an image may endure many common transformations that are broadly categorized as geometric distortions or signal distortions. Geometric distortions are specific to images and video, and include such operations as rotation, translation, scaling and cropping. By manually determining a minimum of four or nine corresponding points between the original and the distorted watermark, it is possible to remove any two or three dimensional affine transformation [7]. However, an affine scaling (shrinking) of the image leads to a loss of data in the high frequency spectral regions of the image. Cropping, or the cutting out and removal of portions of an image, also leads to irretrievable loss of data. Cropping may be a serious threat to any spatially based watermark such as [5] but is less likely to affect a frequency-based scheme, as shown in Section 4.5.

Common signal distortions include digital-to-analog and analog-to-digital conversion, resampling, requantization, including dithering and recompression, and common signal enhancements to image contrast and/or color, and audio frequency equalization. Many of these distortions are non-linear, and it is difficult to analyze their effect in either a spatial or frequency based method. However, the fact that the original image is known allows many signal transformations to be undone, at least approximately. For example, histogram equalization, a common non-linear contrast enhancement method, may be removed substantially by histogram specification [9] or dynamic histogram warping [6] techniques.

Finally, the copied image may not remain in digital form. Instead, it is likely to be printed, or an analog recording made (onto analog audio or video tape). These reproductions introduce additional degradation into the image that a watermarking scheme must be robust to.

The watermark must not only be resistant to the inadvertant application of the aforementioned distortions. It must also be immune to intentional manipulation by malicious parties. These manipulations can include combinations of the above distortions, and can also include collusion and forgery attacks.

2.2 Spread spectrum coding of a watermark

The above discussion makes it clear that the watermark should *not* be placed in perceptually insignificant regions of the image or its spectrum since many common signal and geometric processes affect these components. For example, a watermark placed in the high frequency spectrum of an image can be easily eliminated with little degradation to the image by any process that directly or indirectly performs low pass filtering. The problem then becomes how to insert a watermark into the most perceptually significant regions of an spectrum without such alterations becoming noticeable. Clearly, any spectral coefficient may be altered, provided such modification is small. However, very small changes are very susceptible to noise.

To solve this problem, the frequency domain of the image or sound at hand is viewed as a *communication channel*, and correspondingly, the watermark is viewed as a signal that is transmitted through it. Attacks and unintentional signal distortions are thus treated as noise that the immersed signal must be immune to. While we use this methodology to hide watermarks in data, the same rationale can be applied to sending any type of message through media data.

Rather than encode the watermark into the least significant components of the data, we originally conceived our approach by analogy to spread spectrum communications [18]. In spread spectrum communications, one transmits a narrowband signal over a much larger bandwidth such that the signal energy present in any single frequency is imperceptible. Similarly, the watermark is spread over very many frequency bins so that the energy in any one bin is very small and certainly undetectable. Nevertheless, because the watermark verification process knows of the location and content of the watermark, it is possible to concentrate these many weak signals into a single signal with high signal-to-noise ratio. However, to confidently destroy such a watermark would require noise of high amplitude to be added to *all* frequency bins.

Spreading the watermark throughout the spectrum of an image ensures a large measure of security against unintentional or intentional attack: First, the spatial location of the watermark is not obvious. Furthermore, frequency regions should be selected in a fashion that ensures severe degradation of the original data following any attack on the watermark.

A watermark that is well placed in the frequency domain of an image or a sound track will be practically impossible to see or hear. This will always be the case if the energy in the watermark is sufficiently small in any single frequency coefficient. Moreover, it is possible to increase the energy present in particular frequencies by exploiting knowledge of masking phenomena in the human auditory and visual systems. Perceptual masking refers to any situation where information in certain regions of an image or a sound is occluded by perceptually more prominent information in another part of the scene. In digital waveform coding, this frequency domain (and, in some cases, time/pixel domain) masking is exploited extensively to achieve low bit rate encoding of data [11, 8]. It is clear that both the auditory and visual systems attach more resolution to the high energy, low frequency, spectral regions of an auditory or visual scene [11]. Further, spectrum analysis of images and sounds reveals that most of the information in such data is located in the low frequency regions.

Figure 2 illustrates the general procedure for frequency domain watermarking. Upon applying a frequency transformation to the data, a *perceptual mask* is computed that highlights perceptually significant regions in the spectrum that can support the watermark without affecting perceptual fidelity. The watermark signal is then inserted into these regions in a manner described in Section 3.2. The precise magnitude of each modification is only known to the owner. By contrast, an attacker may only have knowledge of the possible range of modification. To be confident of eliminating a watermark, an attacker must assume that each modification was at the limit of this range, despite the fact that few such modifications are typically this large. As a result, an attack creates visible (or audible) defects in the data. Similarly, unintentional signal distortions due to compression or image manipulation, must leave the perceptually significant spectral components intact, otherwise the resulting image will be severely degraded. This is why the watermark is robust.

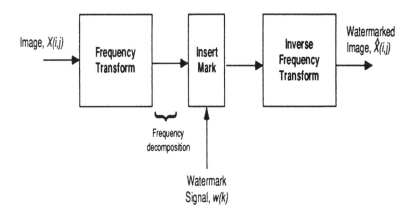

Figure 2. Immersion of the watermark in the frequency domain

In principle, any frequency domain transform can be used. However, for the experimental results of Section 4 we use a Fourier domain method based on the discrete cosine transform (DCT) [15], although we are currently exploring the use of wavelet-based schemes as a variation. In our view, each coefficient in the frequency domain has a *perceptual capacity*, that is, a quantity of additional information can be added without any (or with minimal) impact to the perceptual fidelity of the data. To determine the perceptual capacity of each frequency, one can use models for the appropriate perceptual system or simple experimentation.

In practice, in order to place a length n watermark into an $N \times N$ image, we computed the $N \times N$ DCT of the image and placed the watermark into the n highest magnitude coefficients of the transform matrix, excluding the DC component. [1] For most images, these coefficients will be the ones corresponding to the low frequencies. Reiterating, the purpose of placing the watermark in these locations is because significant tampering with these frequency will destroy the image fidelity well before the watermark.

In the next section, we provide a high level discussion of the watermarking procedure, describing the structure of the watermark and its characteristics.

---

[1] More generally, n randomly chosen coefficients could be chosen from the $M, M \geq n$ most perceptually significant coefficients of the transform.

3 Structure of the watermark

We now give a high-level overview of our a basic watermarking scheme; many variations are possible. In its most basic implementation, a watermark consists of a sequence of real numbers $X = x_1, \ldots, x_n$. In practice, we create a watermark where each value x_i is chosen independently according to $N(0,1)$ (where $N(\mu, \sigma^2)$ denotes a normal distribution with mean μ and variance σ^2). We assume that numbers are represented by a reasonable but finite precision and ignore these insignificant roundoff errors. Section 3.1 introduces notation to describe the insertion and extraction of a watermark and Section 3.3 describes how two watermarks (the original one and the recovered, possibly corrupted one) can be compared. This procedure exploits the fact that each component of the watermark is chosen from a normal distribution. Alternative distributions are possible, including choosing x_i uniformly from $\{1, -1\}, \{0, 1\}$ or $[0, 1]$. However, as we discuss in Section 3.5, using such distributions leaves one particularly vulnerable to attacks using multiple watermarked documents.

3.1 Description of the watermarking procedure

We extract from each document D a sequence of values $V = v_1, \ldots, v_n$, into which we insert a watermark $X = x_1, \ldots, x_n$ to obtain an adjusted sequence of values $V' = v'_1, \ldots, v'_n$. V' is then inserted back into the document in place of V to obtain a watermarked document D'. One or more attackers may then alter D', producing a new document D^*. Given D and D^*, a possibly corrupted watermark X^* is extracted and is compared to X for statistical significance. We extract X^* by first extracting a set of values $V^* = v_1^*, \ldots, v_n^*$ from D^* (using information about D) and then generating X^* from V^* and V.

Frequency-domain based methods for extracting V and V^* and inserting V' are given in Section 2. For the rest of this section we ignore the manipulations of the underlying documents.

3.2 Inserting and extracting the watermark

When we insert X into V to obtain V' we specify a scaling parameter α which determines the extent to which X alters V. Three natural formulae for computing V' are:

$$v'_i = v_i + \alpha x_i \tag{1}$$

$$v'_i = v_i(1 + \alpha x_i) \tag{2}$$

$$v'_i = v_i(e^{\alpha x_i}) \tag{3}$$

Equation 1 is always invertible, and Equations 2 and 3 are invertible if $v_i \neq 0$, which holds in all of our experiments. Given V^* we can therefore compute the inverse function to derive X^* from V^* and V.

Equation 1 may not be appropriate when the v_i values vary widely. If $v_i = 10^6$ then adding 100 may be insufficient for establishing a mark, but if $v_i = 10$

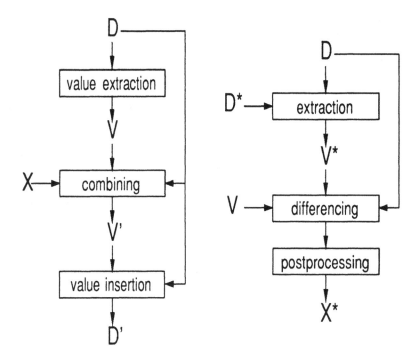

Figure 3. Encoding and decoding of the watermark string

adding 100 will distort this value unacceptably. Insertion based on Equations 2 or 3 are more robust against such differences in scale. We note that Equations 2 and 3 give similar results when αx_i is small. Also, when v_i is positive then Equation 3 is equivalent to $\lg(v_i') = \lg(v_i) + \alpha x_i$, and may be viewed as an application of Equation 1 to the case where the logarithms of the original values are used.

Determining multiple scaling parameters A single scaling parameter α may not be applicable for perturbing all of the values v_i, since different spectral components may exhibit more or less tolerance to modification. More generally one can have multiple scaling parameters $\alpha_1, \ldots, \alpha_n$ and use update rules such as $v_i' = v_i(1 + \alpha_i x_i)$. We can view α_i as a relative measure of how much one must alter v_i to alter the perceptual quality of the document. A large α_i means that one can perceptually "get away" with altering v_i by a large factor without degrading the document.

There remains the problem of selecting the multiple scaling values. In some cases, the choice of α_i may be based on some general assumption. For example, Equation 2 is a special case of the generalized Equation 1 ($v_i' = v_i + \alpha_i x_i$), for $\alpha_i = \alpha v_i$. Essentially, Equation 2 makes the reasonable assumption that a large value is less sensitive to additive alterations than a small value.

In general, one may have little idea of how sensitive the image is to various values. One way of empirically estimating these sensitivities is to determine the distortion caused by a number of attacks on the original image. For example, one might compute a degraded image D^* from D, extract the corresponding values $v_1^*, \ldots, v_n^*$ and choose α_i to be proportional to the deviation $|v_i^* - v_i|$. For greater robustness, one should try many forms of distortion and make α_i proportional to the average value of $|v_i^* - v_i|$. As alternatives to taking the average deviation one might also take the median or maximum deviation.

One may combine this empirical approach with general global assumptions about the sensitivity of the values. For example, one might require that $\alpha_i \geq \alpha_j$ whenever $v_i \geq v_j$. One way to combine this constraint with the empirical approach would be to set α_i according to

$$\alpha_i \sim \max_{j \mid v_j \leq v_i} |v_j^* - v_j|.$$

A still more sophisticated approach would be to weaken the monotonicity constraint to be robust against occasional outliers.

In all our experiments we simply use Equation 2 with a single parameter $\alpha = 0.1$. When we computed JPEG-based distortions of the original image we observed that the higher energy frequency components were not altered proportional to their magnitude (the implicit assumption of Equation 2). We suspect that we could make a less obtrusive mark of equal strength by attenuating our alterations of the high-energy components and amplifying our alterations of the lower-energy components. However, we have not yet performed this experiment.

3.3 Evaluating the similarity of watermarks

There are a number of ways that one can evaluate the similarity between two watermarks. A traditional correlation measure can be used, for example, or variants such as the t-distribution and Fisher's z transform. Below, we outline an alternative similarity metric, primarily to establish that a false positive judgement is highly unlikely, i.e. an innocent party is unlikely to be wrongly accused of copying.

It is highly unlikely that the extracted mark X^* will be identical to the original watermark X. Even the act of requantizing the watermarked document for delivery will cause X^* to deviate from X. We measure the similarity of X and X^* by

$$\text{sim}(X, X^*) = \frac{X^* \cdot X}{\sqrt{X^* \cdot X^*}}. \tag{4}$$

We argue that large values of $\text{sim}(X, X^*)$ are significant by the following analysis. Suppose that the creators of document D^* had no access to X (either through the seller or through a watermarked document). Then, even conditioned on any fixed value for X^*, each x_i will be independently distributed according to $N(0, 1)$. The distribution on $X^* \cdot X$ may be computed by first writing it as $\sum_{i=1}^{n} x_i^* x_i$, where x_i^* is a constant. Using the well-known formula for the distribution of a linear combination of variables that are independent and normally distributed, $X^* \cdot X$ will be distributed according to

$$N(0, \sum_{i=1}^{n} x_i^{*2}) = N(0, X^* \cdot X^*)$$

Thus, $\text{sim}(X, X^*)$ is distributed according to $N(0, 1)$. We can then apply the standard significance tests for the normal distribution. For example, if X^* is created independently from X then it is extremely unlikely that $\text{sim}(X, X^*) > 6$. Note that slightly higher values of $\text{sim}(X, X^*)$ may be required when a large number of watermarks are on file.

Robust statistics The above analysis required only the independence of X from X^*, and did not rely on any specific properties of X^* itself. This fact gives us further flexibility when it comes to preprocessing X^*. We can process X^* in a number of ways to potentially enhance our ability to extract a watermark. For example, in our experiments on images we encountered instances where the average value of x_i^*, denoted $E_i(X^*)$, differed substantially from 0, due to the effects of a dithering procedure. While this artifact could be easily eliminated as part of the extraction process, it provides a motivation for postprocessing extracted watermarks. We found that the simple transformation $x_i^* \leftarrow x_i^* - E_i(X^*)$ yielded superior values of $\text{sim}(X, X^*)$. The improved performance resulted from the decreased value of $X^* \cdot X^*$; the value of $X^* \cdot X$ was only slightly affected.

In our experiments we frequently observed that x_i^* could be greatly distorted for some values of i. One postprocessing option is to simply ignore such values, setting them to 0. That is,

$$x_i^* \leftarrow \begin{cases} x_i^* & \text{if } |x_i^*| > \text{tolerance} \\ 0 & \text{Otherwise} \end{cases}$$

Again, the goal of such a transformation is to lower $X^* \cdot X^*$. A less abrupt version of this approach is to normalize the X^* values to be either $-1, 0$ or 1, by

$$x_i^* \leftarrow \text{sign}(x_i^* - E_i(X^*)).$$

This transformation can have a dramatic effect on the statistical significance of the result. Other robust statistical techniques could also be used to suppress outlier effects [10].

A natural question is whether such postprocessing steps run the risk of generating false positives. Indeed, the same potential risk occurs whenever there is any latitude in the procedure for extracting X^* from D^*. However, as long as the method for generating a set of values for X^* depends solely on D and D^*, our statistical significance calculation is unaffected. The only caveat to be considered is that the bound on the probability that one of $X_1^*, \ldots X_k^*$ generates a false positive is the sum of the individual bounds. Hence, to convince someone that a watermark is valid, it is necessary to have a published and rigid extraction and processing policy that is guaranteed to only generate a small number of candidate X^*.

3.4 Choosing the length, n, of the watermark

The choice of n dictates the degree to which the watermark is spread out among the relevant components of the image. In general, as the number of altered components are increased the extent to which they must be altered decreases. For a more quantitative assessment of this tradeoff, we consider watermarks of the form $v'_i = v_i + \alpha x_i$ and model a white noise attack by $v^*_i = v'_i + r_i$ where r_i are chosen according to independent normal distributions with standard deviation σ. For the watermarking procedure we described below one can recover the watermark when α is proportional to $\sigma/\sqrt{n}$. That is, by quadrupling the number of components used one can halve the magnitude of the watermark placed into each component. Note that the sum of squares of the deviations will be essentially unchanged.

However, when one increases the number of components used there is a point of diminishing returns at which the new components are randomized by trivial alterations in the image. Hence they will not be useful for storing watermark information. Thus the best choice of n is ultimately document-specific.

3.5 Resilience to multiple-document (collusion) attacks

The most general attack consists of using t multiple watermarked copies $D'_1, \ldots, D'_t$ of document D to produce an unwatermarked document D^*. We note that most schemes proposed seem quite vulnerable to such attacks. As a theoretical exception, Boneh and Shaw [3] propose a coding scheme for use in situations in which one can insert many relatively weak 0/1 watermarks into a document. They assume that if the ith watermark is the same for all t copies of the document then it cannot be detected, changed or removed. Using their coding scheme the number of weak watermarks to be inserted scales according to t^4, which may limit its usefulness in practice.

To illustrate the power of multiple-document attacks, consider watermarking schemes in which v'_i is generated by either adding 1 or -1 at random to v_i. Then as soon as one finds two documents with unequal values for v'_i one can determine v_i and hence completely eliminate this component of the watermark. With t documents one can, on average, eliminate all but a 2^{1-t} fraction of the components of the watermark. Note that this attack does not assume anything about the distribution on v_i. While a more intelligent allocation of ± 1 values to the watermarks (following [14, 3]) will better resist this simple attack, the discrete nature of the watermark components makes them much easier to completely eliminate. Our use of continuous valued watermarks appears to give greater resilience to such attacks. Interestingly, we have experimentally deter-

Figure 4. "Bavarian Couple" courtesy of Corel Stock Photo Library.

Figure 5. Watermarked version of "Bavarian Couple".

mined that if one chooses the x_i uniformly over some range, then one can remove the watermark using only 5 documents. We believe a Gaussian distribution is somewhat stronger.

Using a probabilistic analysis, it can be shown that any attack on Gaussian watermarks must make use of $\Omega(\sqrt{n/\ln n})$ watermarks in order to have any chance of destroying the watermark. (This is provided only that the original image to be protected comes from a Gaussian distribution and that the second moment of the deviation of the new image from the original is small compared to n.) Hence, Gaussian watermarks are better than uniform watermarks, particularly when n is large.

4   Experimental Results

In order to evaluate the proposed digital watermark, we first took the "Bavarian Couple"[2] image of Figure (4) and produced the watermarked version of Figure (5)

4.1   Experiment 1: Uniqueness of watermark

Figure (6) shows the response of the watermark detector to 1000 randomly generated watermarks of which only one matches the watermark present in Figure (5). The positive response due to the correct watermark is very much stronger that the response to incorrect watermarks, suggesting that the algorithm has very low false positives (and false negative) response rates.

---

[2] The common test image "Lenna" was originally used in our experiments and similar results were obtained. However, questions of taste aside, Playboy Inc. refused to grant copyright permission for electronic distribution.

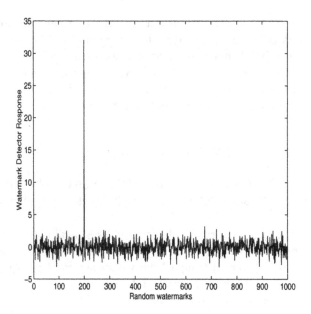

Figure 6. Watermark detector response to 1000 randomly generated watermarks. Only one watermark (the one to which the detector was set to respond) matches that present in Figure (5).

4.2 Experiment 2: Image Scaling

The watermarked image was scaled to half its original size, Figure (7a). In order to recover the watermark, the quarter-sized image was re-scaled to its original dimensions, as shown in Figure (7b), in which it is clear that considerable fine detail has been lost in the scaling process. This is to be expected since subsampling of the image requires a low pass spatial filtering operation.

Figure 7. (a) Low pass filtered, 0.5 scaled image of "Bavarian Couple", (b) re-scaled image showing noticeable loss of fine detail.

The response of the watermark detector to the original watermarked image of Figure (5) was 32.0 which compares to a response of 13.4 for the re-scaled version of Figure (7b). While the detector response is down by over 50%, the response is still well above random chance levels suggesting that the watermark is robust to geometric distortions. Moreover, it should be noted that 75% of the original data is missing from the scaled down image of Figure 7.

4.3 Experiment 3: JPEG Coding Distortion

Figure (8) shows a JPEG encoded version of "Bavarian Couple" with parameters of 10% quality and 0% smoothing, which results in clearly visible distortions of the image.

The response of the watermark detector is 22.8, again suggesting that the algorithm is robust to common encoding distortions. Figure (9) shows a JPEG encoded version of "Bavarian Couple" with parameters of 5% quality and 0% smoothing, which results is very significant distortions of the image. The response of the watermark detector in this case is 13.9, which is still well above random.

Figure 8. JPEG encoded version of "Bavarian Couple" with 10% quality and 0% smoothing.

Figure 9. JPEG encoded version of "Bavarian Couple" with 5% quality and 0% smoothing.

4.4 Experiment 4: Dithering Distortion

Figure (10) shows a dithered version of "Bavarian Couple". The response of the watermark detector is 5.2 again suggesting that the algorithm is robust to common encoding distortions. In fact, more reliable detection can be achieved simply by removing any non-zero mean from the extracted watermark, as discussed in Section 3.3. In this case the detection value is 10.5.

Figure 10. Dithered version of "Bavarian Couple".

4.5 Experiment 5: Clipping

Figure (11a) shows a clipped version of the watermarked image of Figure (5) in which only the central quarter of the image remains. In order to extract the watermark from this image, the missing portions of the image were replaced with portions from the original **unwatermarked** image of Figure (4), as shown in Figure (11b). In this case, the response of the watermark is 14.6. Once again,

Figure 11. (a) Clipped version of watermarked "Bavarian Couple", (b) Restored version of "Bavarian Couple" in which missing portions have been replaced with imagery from the original unwatermarked image of Figure (4).

this is well above random even though 75% of the data has been removed.

Figure (12a) shows a clipped version of the JPEG encoded image of Figure (8) in which only the central quarter of the image remains. As before, the missing portions of the image were replaced with portions from the original **unwatermarked** image of Figure (4), as shown in Figure (12b).

In this case, the response of the watermark is 10.6. Once more, this is well above random even though 75% of the data has been removed and distortion is present in the clipped portion of the image.

4.6   Experiment 6: Print, Xerox and Scan

Figure (13) shows the bavarian image after (1) printing, (2) xeroxing, then (3) scanning at 300 dpi using UMAX PS-2400X scanner, and finally (4) rescaled to a size of 256 × 256. Clearly, this image suffers from several levels of distortion that accompany each of the four stages. High frequency pattern noise is especially noticeable. The detector response to the watermark is 4.0. However, if the non-zero mean is removed and only the sign of the elements of the watermark are used, then the detector response is 7.0, which is well above random.

Figure 12. (a) Clipped version of JPEG encoded (10% quality, 0% smoothing) "Bavarian Couple", (b) Restored version of "Bavarian Couple" in which missing portions are replaced with imagery from the original unwatermarked image of Figure (4).

Figure 13. Printed, xeroxed, scanned and rescaled image of "Bavarian Couple".

4.7 Experiment 7: Attack by Re-watermarking Watermarked Images

Figure (14) shows an image of "Bavarian Couple" after five successive watermarking operations, i.e. the original image is watermarked, the watermarked image is watermarked, etc. This may be considered another form of attack in which it is clear that significant image degradation eventually occurs as the process is repeated. This attack is equivalent to adding noise to the frequency bins containing the watermark. Interestingly, Figure (16) shows the response of the detector to 1000 randomly generated watermarks, which include the five watermarks present in the image. Five spikes clearly indicate the presence of the five watermarks and demonstrate that successive watermarking does not interfere with the process.

Figure 14. Image of "Bavarian Couple" after five successive watermarks have been added.

Figure 15. Image of "Bavarian Couple" after averaging together five independently watermarked copies.

4.8   Experiment 8: Attack by Collusion

In a similar experiment, we took five separately watermarked images and averaged them to form Figure (15) in order to simulate a simple collusion attack. As before, Figure (17) shows the response of the detector to 1000 randomly generated watermarks, which include the five watermarks present in the image. Once again, five spikes clearly indicate the presence of the five watermarks and demonstrate that simple collusion based on averaging a few images is ineffective.

5   Conclusion

A need for electronic watermarking is developing as electronic distribution of copyright material becomes more prevalent. Above, we outlined the necessary

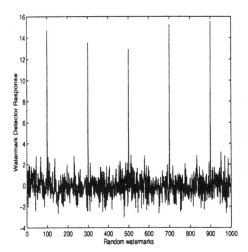

Figure 16. Watermark detector response to 1000 randomly generated watermarks (including the 5 specific watermarks) for the watermarked image of Figure (14). Each of the five watermarks is clearly indicated.

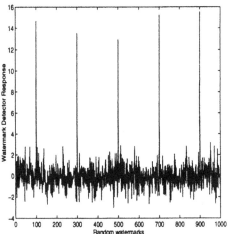

Figure 17. Watermark detector response to 1000 randomly generated watermarks (including the 5 specific watermarks) for the watermarked image of Figure (15). Each of the five watermarks is clearly detected, indicating that collusion by averaging is ineffective.

characteristics of such a watermark. These are: fidelity preservation, robustness to common signal and geometric processing operations, robustness to attack, and applicability to audio, image and video data.

To meet these requirements, we proposed a watermark whose structure consisted of 1000 randomly generated numbers with a Normal distribution having zero mean and unity variance. A binary watermark was rejected based on the fact that it is much less robust to attacks based on collusion of several independently watermarked copies of an image. The length of the watermark is variable and can be adjusted to suit the characteristics of the data. For example, longer watermarks might be used for an image that is especially sensitive to large modifications of its spectral coefficients, thus requiring weaker scaling factors for individual components.

The watermark is then placed in the perceptually *most* significant components of the image spectrum. This ensures that the watermark remains with the image even after common signal and geometric distortions. Modification of these spectral components results in severe image degradation long before the watermark itself is destroyed. Of course, to insert the watermark, it is necessary to alter these very same coefficients. However, each modification can be extremely small and, in a manner similar to spread spectrum communication, a strong narrowband watermark may be distributed over a much broader image (channel) spectrum. Conceptually, detection of the watermark then proceeds by adding all of these very small signals, and concentrating them once more into a signal with high signal-to-noise ratio. Because the magnitude of the watermark at each location is only known to the copyright holder, an attacker would have to add much more noise energy to each spectral coefficient in order to be sufficiently confident of removing the watermark. However, this process would destroy the image.

In our experiments, we added the watermark to the image by modifying 1000 of the more perceptually significant components of the image spectrum. More specifically, the 1000 largest coefficients of the DCT (excluding the DC term) were used. Further refinement of the method would identify perceptually significant components based on an analysis of the image and the human perceptual system and might also include additional considerations regarding the relative predictability of a frequency based on its neighbors. The latter property is important to consider in order to minimize any attack based on a statistical analysis of frequency spectra that attempts to replace components with their maximul likelihood estimate, for example. The choice of the DCT is not critical to the algorithm and other spectral transforms, including wavelet type decompositions are also possible. In fact, use of the FFT rather than DCT may prefereble from a computational perspective.

It was shown, using the "Bavarian Couple" image, that the algorithm can extract a reliable copy of the watermark from imagery that has been significantly degraded through several common geometric and signal processing procedures. These include, zooming (low pass filtering), cropping, lossy JPEG encoding, dithering, printing, photocopying and subsequent rescanning.

More experimental work needs to be performed to validate these results over a wide class of data. Application of the method to color images should be straightforward though robustness to certain color image processing procedures should be investigated. Similarly, the system should work well on text images, however, the binary nature of the image together with its much more structured spectral distribution need more work. Furthermore, application of the watermarking method to audio and video data should follow in a straightforward fashion, although, attention must be paid to the time varying nature of these data. A more sophisticated watermark verification process may also be possible using methods developed for spread spectrum communications.

Larger system issues must be also addressed in order for this system to be used in practice. For example, it would be useful to be able to prove in court that a watermark is present without publically revealing the original, unmarked document. This is not hard to accomplish using secure trusted hardware; an efficient purely cryptographic solution seems much more difficult. It should also be noted that current proposal only allows the watermark to be extracted by the owner, since the original unwatermarked image is needed as part of the extraction process. This prohibits potential users from querying the image for ownership and copyright information. This capability may be desirable but appears difficult to achieve with the same level of robustness. However, it is straightforward to provide if a much weaker level of protection is acceptable and might therefore be added as a secondary watermarking procedure. Finally, we note that while the proposed methodology is used to hide watermarks in data, the same process can be applied to sending other forms of message through media data.

Acknowledgements

The authors thank Larry O'Gorman of AT&T Bell Laboratories for bringing this problem to our attention, Harold Stone for advice on image transforms and Sebastien Roy for testing the robustness of the watermark.

References

1. E. H. Adelson. Digital signal encoding and decoding apparatus. Technical Report 4,939,515, United States Patent, 1990.
2. W. Bender, D. Gruhl, and N. Morimoto. Techniques for data hiding. In *Proc. of SPIE*, volume 2420, page 40, February 1995.
3. Dan Boneh and James Shaw. Collusion-secure fingerprinting for digital data. In *Advances in Cryptology: Proceedings, CRYPTO '95*. Springer-Verlag, 1995.
4. J. Brassil, S. Low, N. Maxemchuk, and L. O'Gorman. Electronic marking and identification techniques to discourage document copying. In *Proc. of Infocom'94*, pages 1278–1287, 1994.
5. G. Caronni. Assuring ownership rights for digital images. In *Proc. Reliable IT Systems, VIS'95*. Vieweg Publishing Company, 1995.
6. I. J. Cox, S. Roy, and S. L. Hingorani. Dynamic histogram warping of images pairs for constant image brightness. In *IEEE Int, Conf. on Image Processing*, 1995.
7. O. Faugeras. *Three Dimensional Computer Vision: A Geometric Viewpoint*. MIT Press, 1993.
8. Allen Gersho and Robert Gray. *Vector Quantization and Signal Compression*. Kluwer Academic Publishers, Boston, 1992.
9. R. C. Gonzalez and R. E. Woods. *Digital Image Processing*. Addison-Wesley, 1993.
10. P. J. Huber. *Robust Statistics*. John Wiley and Sons, 1981.
11. N. Jayant, J. Johnston, and R. Safranek. Signal compression based on models of human perception. *Proc IEEE*, 81(10), 1993.

12. E. Koch, J. Rindfrey, and J. Zhao. Copyright protection for multimedia data. In *Proc. of the Int. Conf. on Digital Media and Electronic Publishing*, 1994.

13. E. Koch and Z. Zhao. Towards robust and hidden image copyright labeling. In *Proceedings of 1995 IEEE Workshop on Nonlinear Signal and Image Processing*, June 1995.

14. F. T. Leighton and S. Micali. Secret-key agreement without public-key cryptography. In *Proceedings of Crypto*, 1993.

15. J.S Lim. *Two-Dimensional Signal Processing*. Prentice Hall, Englewood Cliffs, N.J., 1990.

16. B. M. Macq and J-J Quisquater. Cryptology for digital tv broadcasting. *Proc. of the IEEE*, 83(6):944–957, 1995.

17. K. Matsui and K. Tanaka. Video-steganography. In *IMA Intellectual Property Project Proceedings*, volume 1, pages 187–206, 1994.

18. R. L. Pickholtz, D. L. Schilling, and L. B. Millstein. Theory of spread spectrum communications - a tutorial. *IEEE Trans. on Communications*, pages 855–884, 1982.

19. W. F. Schreiber, A. E. Lippman, E. H. Adelson, and A. N. Netravali. Receiver-compatible enhanced definition television system. Technical Report 5,010,405, United States Patent, 1991.

20. K. Tanaka, Y. Nakamura, and K. Matsui. Embedding secret information into a dithered multi-level image. In *Proc, 1990 IEEE Military Communications Conference*, pages 216–220, 1990.

21. L. F. Turner. Digital data security system. Patent IPN WO 89/08915, 1989.

22. R. G. van Schyndel, A. Z. Tirkel, and C. F. Osborne. A digital watermark. In *Int. Conf. on Image Processing*, volume 2, pages 86–90. IEEE, 1994.

Modulation and Information Hiding in Images

Joshua R. Smith and Barrett O. Comiskey

{jrs, elwood}@media.mit.edu
Physics and Media Group
MIT Media Lab
20 Ames Street
Cambridge, MA 02139
USA

Abstract. We use concepts from communication theory to character-ize information hiding schemes: the amount of information that can be hidden, its perceptibility, and its robustness to removal can be modeled using the quantities channel capacity, signal-to-noise ratio, and jamming márgin. We then introduce new information hiding schemes whose pa-rameters can easily be adjusted to trade off capacity, imperceptibility, and robustness as required in the application. The theory indicates the most aggressive feasible parameter settings. We also introduce a tech-nique called *predistortion* for increasing resistance to JPEG compression. Analogous tactics are presumably possible whenever a model of antici-pated distortion is available.

1 Introduction

In this paper, we discuss schemes for imperceptibly encoding extra information in an image by making small modifications to large numbers of its pixels. Potential applications include copyright protection, embedded or "in-band" captioning and indexing, and secret communication.

Ideally, one would like to find a representation that satisfies the conflict-ing goals of not being perceivable, and being difficult to remove, accidentally or otherwise. But because these goals *do* conflict, because it is *not* possible to simultaneously maximize robustness and imperceptibility, we will introduce a framework for quantifying the tradeoffs among three conflicting figures of merit useful for characterizing information hiding schemes: (1) capacity (the number of bits that may be hidden and then recovered) (2) robustness to accidental removal, and (3) imperceptibility. We will then present new information hiding schemes that can be tailored to trade off these figures of merit as needed in the particular application. For example, capacity may be more important in a captioning application, robustness may be most desired for copyright protec-tion schemes, and imperceptibility might be favored in a secret communication scenario.

1.1 Information theoretic view of the problem

We view an image in which extra information has been embedded as an approximately continuous (in amplitude), two-dimensional, band-limited channel with large average noise power. The noise is the original unmodified image, which we will refer to as the *cover image,* and the signal is the set of small modifications introduced by the hider. The modifications encode the *embedded message.* We will refer to the modified, distribution image as the *stego-image,* following the convention suggested at the Information Hiding Workshop. From this point of view, any scheme for communicating over a continuous channel—that is, any modulation scheme—is a potential information hiding scheme, and concepts used to analyze these schemes, such as channel capacity, ratio of signal power to noise power, and jamming margin can be invoked to quantify the trade-offs between the amount of information that can be hidden, the visibility of that information, and its robustness to removal.

1.2 Relationship to other approaches

In our framework, it becomes obvious why *cover image escrow* hiding schemes such as those presented in [CKLS] and [BOD95] have high robustness to distortion. In cover image escrow schemes, the extractor is required to have the original unmodified cover image, so that the original cover image can be subtracted from the stego-image before extraction of the embedded message. Because the cover image is subtracted off before decoding, there is no noise due to the cover image itself; the only noise that must be resisted is the noise introduced by distortion such as compression, printing, and scanning. While the image escrow hiding schemes must respect the same information theoretic limits as ours, the noise in their case is very small, since it arises solely from distortions to the stego-image.

In our view, image escrow schemes are of limited interest because of their narrow range of practical applications. Since the embedded message can only be extracted by one who possesses the original, the embedded information cannot be accessed by the user. For example, it would not be possible for a user's web browser to extract and display a caption or "property of" warning embedded in a downloaded image. The need to identify the original image before extraction also precludes oblivious, batch extraction. One might desire a web crawler or search engine to automatically find all illegal copies of any one of the many images belonging to, say, a particular photo archive, or all images with a certain embedded caption, but this is not possible with cover image escrow schemes (at least not without invoking computer vision). Finally, even assuming that the cover image has been identified and subtracted out, the proof value of such a watermark is questionable at best, since an "original" can always be constructed a posteriori to make any image appear to contain any watermark. The only practical application of cover image escrow schemes we have been able to identify is fingerprinting or traitor tracing[Pfi], in which many apparently identical copies of the cover image are distributed, but the owner wants to be able distinguish among them in order to identify users who have been giving away illegal copies.

The hiding methods presented in this paper are *oblivious*, meaning that the message can be read with no prior knowledge of the cover image. Other oblivious schemes have been proposed [BGM91, Cor95], but the information-theoretic limits on the problem have not been explicitly considered. We make comparisons between our hiding schemes and these other oblivious schemes later in the paper.

In the next section, we will estimate the amount of information that can be hidden (with minimal robustness) in an image as a function of signal-to-noise ratio. The bulk of the paper is a description of some new hiding schemes that fall short but are within a small constant factor of the theoretical hiding capacity. In the implementations of these schemes presented in this paper, we have chosen capacity over robustness, but we could have done otherwise. In the conclusion, we return to the discussion of modeling the trade offs between hiding capacity, perceptibility, and robustness using the quantities channel capacity, signal-to-noise, and process gain.

2 Channel Capacity

By Nyquist's theorem, the highest frequency that can be represented in our cover image is $\frac{1}{2}\frac{cycle}{pixel}$. The band of frequencies that may be represented in the image ranges from $-\frac{1}{2}\frac{cycle}{pixel}$ to $+\frac{1}{2}\frac{cycle}{pixel}$, and therefore the bandwidth W available for information hiding is $2 \times \frac{1}{2}\frac{cycle}{pixel} = 1\frac{cycle}{pixel}$.

For a channel subject to Gaussian noise, the channel capacity, which is an upper bound on the rate at which communication can reliably occur, is given by [SW49]

$$C = W \log_2(1 + \frac{S}{N})$$

Since the bandwidth W is given in units of pixel^{-1} and the base of the logarithm is 2, the channel capacity has units of bits per pixel. For some applications (particularly print) it might be desirable to specify the bandwidth in units of millimeters^{-1}, in which case the channel capacity would have units of bits per millimeter.

This formula can be rewritten to find a lower bound on the $\frac{S}{N}$ required to achieve a communication rate C given bandwidth W. Shannon proved that this lower bound is in principle tight, in the sense that there exist ideal systems capable of achieving communications rate C using only bandwidth W and signal-to-noise $\frac{S}{N}$. However, for practical systems, there is a tighter, empirically determined lower bound: given a desired communication rate C and an available bandwidth W, a message can be successfully received if the signal-to-noise ratio is at least some small *headroom factor* α above the Shannon lower bound. The headroom α is greater than 1 and typically around 3. [She95]

$$\frac{S}{N} \geq \alpha \left(2^{\frac{C}{W}} - 1\right)$$

In information hiding, $\frac{S}{N} < 1$, so $\log_2(1 + \frac{S}{N})$ may be approximated as $\frac{S/N}{\ln 2}$ or about $1.44\frac{S}{N}$.[She95] Thus $\frac{S}{N} \geq \frac{\alpha}{1.44}\frac{C}{W}$. So in the low signal-to-noise regime relevant to information hiding, channel capacity goes linearly with signal-to-noise.

The average noise power of our example cover image was measured to be 902 (in units of squared amplitude). For signal powers 1, 4, and 9 (amplitude^2), the channel capacity figures are 1.6×10^{-3} bits per pixel, 6.4×10^{-3} bits per pixel, and 1.4×10^{-2} bits per pixel. In an image of size 320×320, the upper bound on the number of bits that can be hidden and reliably recovered is then $320^2 C$. In our cover image of this size, then, using gain factors of 1, 2, and 3 (units of amplitude), the Shannon bound is 160 bits, 650 bits, and 1460 bits. With a headroom factor of $\alpha = 3$, we might realistically expect to hide 50, 210 or 490 bits using these signal levels.

3 Modulation Schemes

In the modulation schemes we discuss in this paper, each bit b_i is represented by some basis function ϕ_i multiplied by either positive or negative one, depending on the value of the bit. The modulated message $S(x, y)$ is added pixel-wise to the cover image $N(x, y)$ to create the stego-image $D(x, y) = S(x, y) + N(x, y)$. The modulated signal is given by

$$S(x, y) = \sum_i b_i \phi_i(x, y)$$

Our basis functions will always be chosen to be orthogonal to each other, so that embedded bits do not equivocate:

$$< \phi_i, \phi_j >= \sum_{x,y} \phi_i(x, y) \phi_j(x, y) = nG^2 \delta_{ij}$$

where n is the number of pixels and G^2 is the average power per pixel of the carrier.

In the ideal case, the basis functions are also uncorrelated with (orthogonal to) the cover image N. In reality, they are not completely orthogonal to N; if they were, we could hide our signal using arbitrarily little energy, and still recover it later.

$$< \phi_i, N >= \sum_{x,y} \phi_i(x, y) N(x, y) \approx 0$$

For information hiding, basis functions that are orthogonal to typical images are needed; image coding has the opposite requirement: the ideal is a small set of basis functions that approximately spans image space. These requirements come in to conflict when an image holding hidden information is compressed: the ideal compression scheme would not be able to represent the carriers (bases) used for hiding at all.

The basis functions used in the various schemes may be organized and compared according to properties such as total power, degree of spatial spreading (or localization), and degree of spatial frequency spreading (or localization). We will now explain and compare several new image information hiding schemes, by describing the modulation functions ϕ_i used.

3.1 Spread Spectrum Techniques

In the spectrum-spreading techniques used in RF communications[Dix94, SOSL94], signal-to-noise is traded for bandwidth: the signal energy is spread over a wide frequency band at low SNR so that it is difficult to detect, intercept, or jam. Though the total signal power may be large, the signal to noise ratio in any band is small; this makes the signal whose spectrum has been spread difficult to detect in RF communications, and, in the context of information hiding, difficult for a human to perceive. It is the fact that the signal energy resides in all frequency bands that makes spread RF signals difficult to jam, and embedded information difficult to remove from a cover image. Compression and other degradation may remove signal energy from certain parts of the spectrum, but since the energy has been distributed everywhere, some of the signal should remain. Finally, if the key used to generate the carrier is kept secret, then in the context of either ordinary communications or data hiding, it is difficult for eavesdroppers to decode the message.

Three schemes are commonly used for spectrum spreading in RF communications: direct sequence, frequency hopping, and chirp. In the first, the signal is modulated by a function that alternates pseudo-randomly between $+G$ and $-G$, at multiples of a time constant called the chiprate. In our application, the chiprate is the pixel spacing. This pseudo-random carrier contains components of all frequencies, which is why it spreads the modulated signal's energy over a large frequency band. In frequency hopping spread spectrum, the transmitter rapidly hops from one frequency to another. The pseudo-random "key" in this case is the sequence of frequencies. As we will see, this technique can also be generalized to the spatial domain. In chirp spreading, the signal is modulated by a chirp, a function whose frequency changes with time. This technique could also be used in the spatial domain, though we have not yet implemented it.

3.2 Direct-Sequence Spread Spectrum

In these schemes, the modulation function consists of a constant, integral-valued gain factor G multiplied by a pseudo-random block ϕ_i of $+1$ and -1 values. Each block ϕ_i has a distinct location in the (x, y) plane. In both versions of direct sequence spread spectrum we have considered, the blocks ϕ_i are non-overlapping (and therefore trivially orthogonal); they tile the (x, y) plane without gaps. Because distinct basis functions ϕ_i do not overlap in the x and y coordinates, we do not need to worry about interference and can write the total power

$$P \equiv \sum_{x,y}^{X,Y} (\sum_i Gb_i\phi_i(x, y))^2 = \sum_i^{X,Y} \sum_{x,y} (Gb_i\phi_i(x, y))^2 = G^2 XY = nG^2$$

The definition holds in general, but the first equation only holds if the ϕ_i tile the (x, y) plane without overlaps. Non-integral values of power can be implemented by "dithering": choosing step values

$$g \in (-G), (-G+1), \ldots, (-1), (0), (1), \ldots, (G-1), (G)$$

with probabilities $p(g)$ such that the average power $G^2 = \sum_g p(g)g^2$.

The embedded image is recovered by demodulating with the original modulating function. A TRUE (+1) bit appears as a positive correlation value; a FALSE (−1) bit is indicated by a negative correlation value. We have found the median of the maximum and minimum correlation values to be an effective decision threshold, though it may not be optimal. For this scheme to work, at least one value of the embedded image must be TRUE and one FALSE. In the version of direct sequence data hiding presented in [Cor95], a similar problem is avoided by including 0101 at the beginning of each line.

A more sophisticated scheme would be to use a "dual-rail" representation in which each ϕ_i is broken in two pieces and modulated with $(-1)(1)$ to represent FALSE and $(1)(-1)$ to represent TRUE. Then to recover the message, each bit can be demodulated twice, once with $(-1)(1)$ and once with $(1)(-1)$. Whichever correlation value is higher gives the bit's value. This dual rail scheme also has advantages for carrier recovery.

Bender et al.'s Patchwork algorithm[BGM91] for data hiding in images can be viewed as a form of spread spectrum in which the pseudo-random carrier is sparse (is mostly 0s) and with the constraint that its integrated amplitude be zero enforced by explicit construction, rather than enforced statistically as in ordinary spread spectrum schemes.

In the Patchwork algorithm, a sequence of random pairs of pixels is chosen. The brightness value of one member of the pair is increased, and the other decreased by the same amount, G in our terminology. This leaves the total amplitude of the image (and therefore the average amplitude) unchanged. To demodulate, they find the sum $S = \sum_{i=1}^{n} a_i - b_i$, where a_i is the first pixel of pair i, and b_i is the second pixel of pair i. Notice that because addition is commutative, the order in which the pixel pairs were chosen is irrelevant. Thus the set of pixels at which single changes are made can be viewed as the non-zero entries in a single two-dimensional carrier $\phi(x, y)$. Bender et al. always modulate this carrier with a coefficient $b = 1$, but $b = -1$ could also be used. In this case, the recovered value of s would be negative. If the same pixel is chosen twice in the original formulation of the Patchwork algorithm, the result is still a carrier $\phi(x, y)$ with definite power and bandwidth. Thus Patchwork can be viewed as a special form of spread spectrum (with extra constraints on the carrier), and evaluated quantitatively in our information-theoretic framework.

Fully Spread Version We have implemented a "fully spread" version of direct sequence spread spectrum by chosing a different pseudo-random ϕ_i for each value of i. This fully spreads the spectrum, as the second figure in the second column of Figure 2 shows. The figure shows both space and spatial frequency representations of the cover image, the modulated pseudo-random carrier, and the sum of the two, the stego-image.

To extract the embedded message (to demodulate), we must first recover the carrier phase. If the image has only been cropped and translated, this can be accomplished by a two dimensional search, which is simple but effective.

The point at which the cross-correlation of the stego-image and the carrier is maximized gives the relative carrier phase. We have implemented this brute force carrier phase recovery scheme, and found it to be effective. Rotation or scaling could also be overcome with more general searches.

Once the carrier has been recovered, we project the stego-image onto each basis vector ϕ_i:

$$o_i = <D, \phi_i> = \sum_{x,y} D(x,y)\phi_i(x,y)$$

and then threshold the o_i values. We have used the median of the maximum and minimum o_i value as the threshold value. Note that for this to work, there must be at least one $b_i = -1$ and one $b_i = +1$. Above we discussed more sophisticated schemes that avoid this problem. Figure 2 shows the original input to be embedded, the demodulated signal recovered from the stego-image, the threshold value, and the recovered original input.

Tiled Version This scheme is identical to the "fully spread" scheme, except that the same pseudo-random sequence is used for each ϕ_i. The ϕ_i differ from one another only in their location in the (x, y) plane. Unlike the fully spread version, which is effectively a one-time pad, some information about the embedded icon is recoverable from the modulated carrier alone, without a priori knowledge of the unmodulated carrier. This information appears as the inhomogeneities in the spatial frequency plane of the modulated carrier visible in Figure 3. If a different icon were hidden, the inhomogeneity would look different. One advantage of the tiled scheme is that carrier recovery requires less computation, since the scale of the search is just the size of one of the ϕ_i tiles, instead of the entire (x, y) plane. Given identical transmit power, this scheme seems to be slightly more robust than the "fully spread" scheme.

These two spread spectrum techniques are resistant to JPEGing, if the modulated carrier is given enough power (or more generally, as long as the jamming margin is made high enough). With carrier recovery, the two direct sequence schemes are resistant to translation and some cropping. However, unlike the frequency hopping scheme that we will describe below, the direct sequence basis functions are fairly localized in space, so it is possible to lose some bits to cropping.

Predistortion In addition to simply increasing the signal to improve compression immunity, Figure 4 illustrates a trick, called *predistortion*, for increasing the robustness of the embedded information when it is known that the image will be, for example, JPEG compressed. We generate the pseudo-random carrier, then JPEG compress the carrier by itself (before it has been modulated by the embedded information and added to the cover image), and uncompress it before modulating. The idea is to use the compression routine to filter out in advance all the power that would otherwise be lost later in the course of compression.[1] Then the gain can be increased if necessary to compensate for the power lost to compression. The once JPEGed carrier is invariant to further JPEGing using the same quality factor (except for small numerical artifacts).[2] Figure 4 shows both the space and spatial frequency representation of the JPEG compressed carrier. Note the suppression of high spatial frequencies. Using the same power levels, we achieved error-free decoding with this scheme, but had several errors using the usual fully spread scheme without the pre-distortion of the carrier. Tricks analogous to this are probably possible whenever the information hider has a model of the type of distortion that will be applied. Note that this version of predistortion cannot be applied to our next scheme, or to the version of direct sequence spread spectrum in [Cor95], because in these schemes carriers overlap in space and therefore interfere.

3.3   Frequency Hopping Spread Spectrum

This scheme produces perceptually nice results because it does not create hard edges in the space domain. However, its computational complexity, for both encoding and decoding, is higher than that of the direct sequence schemes.

Each bit is encoded in a particular spatial frequency; which bit of the embedded message is represented by which frequency is specified by the pseudo-random key. In our trial implementation of frequency hopping spread spectrum, however, we have skipped the pseudo random key, and instead chosen a fixed block of 10 by 10 spatial frequencies, one spatial frequency for each bit. One advantage of the frequency hopping scheme over the direct sequence techniques is that each bit is fully spread spatially: the bits are not spatially localized at all. This means that the scheme is robust to cropping and translation, which only induce phase shifts.

An apparent disadvantage of the frequency hopping scheme is that because the functions overlap in the space domain, the time to compute the modulated carrier appears to be kXY, where k is the number of bits, instead of just XY, the time required for the direct sequence schemes. However, the Fast Fourier Transform (more precisely, a Fast Discrete Cosine Transform) can be used to implement this scheme, reducing the time to $XY \log_2 XY$. This is a savings if $\log_2 XY < k$. In our example, $\log_2 320 \times 320 = 16.6$ and $k = 100$, so the FFT is indeed the faster implementation.

Figure 5 illustrates the frequency hopping modulation scheme. The results, shown in figure 6, are superior to the direct sequence schemes both perceptually

---

[1] By compressing the carrier separately from the image, we are treating the JPEG algorithm as an operator that obeys a superposition principle, which it does in an approximate sense defined in the Appendix.

[2] It should be apparent from the description of JPEG compression in the Appendix that the output of the JPEG operator (or more precisely, the operator consisting of JPEG followed by inverse JPEG, which maps an image to an image) is an eigenfunction and in fact a fixed point of that operator, ignoring small numerical artifacts.

and in terms of robustness to accidental removal. There is little need to threshold the output of the demodulator in this case. However, encoding and decoding require significantly more computation time.

This scheme survived gentle JPEGing[3] with no predistortion, as illustrated in figure 7.[4]

A disadvantage of this scheme for some purposes is that it would be relatively easy to intentionally remove the embedded message, by applying a spatial filter of the appropriate frequency. A more secure implementation of the scheme would disperse the frequencies from one another, to make this sort of filtering operation more difficult. The main disadvantage of this scheme relative to the direct sequence schemes is that, even using the FFT, its computational complexity for encoding and decoding is greater ($XY \log XY$ rather than XY).

4 Discussion

We have suggested that information and communication theory are useful tools both for analyzing information hiding, and for creating new information hiding schemes. We showed how to estimate the signal-to-noise needed to hide a certain number of bits given bandwidth W. A shortcoming of our channel capacity estimate is that we used the capacity formula for a Gaussian channel, which is not the best model of the "noise" in a single image, as a glance at any of the frequency domain plots in the figures will reveal. The Gaussian channel has the same power at each frequency, but clearly these images do not, especially after compression. A more refined theory would use a better statistical model of the image channel, and would therefore be able to make better estimates of the signal-to-noise needed to hide a certain number of bits. This would also lead to better hiding schemes, since the signal energy could be distributed more effectively.

The scheme we have called "frequency hopping" is superior perceptually, and in terms of robustness to accidental removal, to the direct sequence schemes with which we experimented. Direct sequence may be less vulnerable to intentional removal, and wins in terms of computational complexity.

Assuming that the Gaussian channel approximation discussed above is not too misleading, our capacity estimates suggest that there exist significantly better schemes than we have presented, capable of hiding several hundred bits in an image in which we hid one hundred. Hybrid modulation/coding schemes such as

---

[3] All the JPEG compression reported here was done in Photoshop using the "high quality" setting.

[4] In fact, it is not possible to predistort in the frequency hopping scheme: because the basis functions overlap, the resulting interference pattern depends strongly on the particular values of the bits being encoded. There is no single pattern onto which we can project the stego-image to recover the embedded data; we must (naively) project it onto a sequence of vectors, or (more sophisticated) use the FFT. In either case the idea of predistortion does not apply, at least not in the same way it did in the non-overlapping direct sequence schemes.

trellis coding are a promising route toward higher hiding densities. But better models of channel noise (the noise due to cover images themselves, plus distortion) would lead immediately to better capacity estimates, and better hiding schemes.

In all the practical examples in this paper, we have tried to hide as much information as possible using a given signal-to-noise. However, keeping signal-to-noise and bandwidth fixed, communication rate can instead be traded for robustness to jamming. The quantities known as jamming margin and processing gain in spread spectrum communication theory are helpful in capturing this notion of robustness.

Processing gain is the ratio $\frac{W}{M}$ of available bandwidth W to the bandwidth M actually needed to represent the message. Jamming margin, the useful measure of robustness, is the product of signal-to-noise and processing gain. If the actual signal-to-noise ratio is $\frac{S}{N}$, then the jamming margin or effective signal-to-noise ratio $\frac{E}{J}$ after demodulation is given by $\frac{E}{J} = \frac{W}{M}\frac{S}{N}$. So robustness may be increased either by increasing signal-to-noise (at the cost of perceptibility, as we will explain in more detail below), or by decreasing the size of the embedded message (the capacity), which increases the processing gain. For example, in the case of our direct sequence schemes, the processing gain increases when we hide fewer bits because each bit can be represented by a larger block. The Patchwork hiding scheme referred to earlier sacrifices communication rate entirely (hiding just one bit) in order to buy as much robustness as possible.

Signal-to-noise ratio provides a rough estimate of perceptibility, because, all other things being equal, the higher the signal-to-noise, the more visible the modulated carrier will be. However, keeping signal-to-noise constant, some carriers—particularly those with mid-range spatial frequencies, our experience so far suggests—will be more more perceptible than others. So the crudest model of perceptibilty is simply signal-to-noise ratio; a plausible refinement might be the integral over all spatial frequencies of the signal-to-noise as a function of frequency weighted by a model of the frequency response of the human visual system. Methods for quantifying visibility to humans might be a new theoretical avenue to explore, and developing systematic methods for minimizing the visibility of hidden signals is certainly a challenge to information hiding practice. The pre-distortion technique demonstrated in this paper can be viewed as a first step in this direction, in the sense that successful compression schemes comprise implicit, algorithmic models of the human visual system (the ideal compression scheme would encompass a complete model of the human visual system). It will be interesting to watch the development of information hiding schemes and their co-evolutionary "arms race" with compression methods in the challenging environment of the human visual system.

A Approximate superposition property for JPEG operator

An operator O obeys superposition if $O\{f + g\} - (O\{f\} + O\{g\}) = 0$. Each coefficient generated by the JPEG operator J satisfies $-1 \leq J\{f + g\} - (J\{f\} + J\{g\}) \leq 1$. In other words, JPEGing a pair of images separately and then adding them yields a set of coefficients each of which differs by no more than one quantization level from the corresponding coefficient found by adding the images first and then JPEGing them (using the same compression parameters in both cases).

The proof is simple. For a gray scale image, the unquantized JPEG coefficients S_{ij} are found by expanding each 8×8 block in a cosine basis. The final quantized coefficients a_{ij} are found by dividing each S_{ij} by a quantization factor q_{ij} (where each q_{ij} is greater than one, since the purpose of the JPEG representation is to decrease the file size), and rounding toward zero[BH93]:

$$a_{ij} = \lfloor \frac{S_{ij}}{q_{ij}} \rfloor$$

The cosine expansion is a linear operation, and therefore obeys superposition, so (as long as $q_{ij} > 1$) we need only show that for any real numbers f and g, $-1 \leq \lfloor f + g \rfloor - \lfloor f \rfloor - \lfloor g \rfloor \leq 1$. Without loss of generality, we may take f and g to be non-negative and less than one, since the integer parts F and G of f and g satisfy $\lfloor F + G \rfloor - \lfloor F \rfloor - \lfloor G \rfloor = 0$. So, for such an f and g, $0 \leq f + g < 2$. There are now two cases to consider. If $0 \leq f + g < 1$, then $\lfloor f + g \rfloor - \lfloor f \rfloor - \lfloor g \rfloor = 0 - 0 - 0 = 0$. If $1 \leq f + g < 2$ then $\lfloor f + g \rfloor - \lfloor f \rfloor - \lfloor g \rfloor = 1 - 0 - 0 = 1$. Since $f + g < 2$, these are the only two cases. The case of f and g negative is analogous, yielding a discrepancy of either -1 or 0. The discrepancy in the case that f and g have opposite sign is less than in the same sign case. Therefore each a_{ij} coefficient produced by the JPEG operator satisfies our approximate superposition principle, $-1 \leq J\{f + g\} - (J\{f\} + J\{g\}) \leq 1$. Since each a_{ij} coefficient has a discrepancy of $+1$, 0, or -1, each S_{ij} has a discrepancy of $+q_{ij}$, 0, or $-q_{ij}$. Thus the total power of the deviation from superposition (in either the spatial frequency or pixel representation, by Parseval's theorem) is bounded above by $\sum_{ij} q_{ij}^2$. This explains why JPEGing the carrier separately from the cover image is a reasonable predistortion tactic.

Note that the more aggressive the compression (the larger the q_{ij} values), the larger the discrepancies, or deviations from superposition.

Acknowledgments

This research was performed in the laboratory of Neil Gershenfeld. The authors thank him for his advice and support. The second author thanks Joe Jacobson for his support. We thank Walter Bender, Dan Gruhl, and the News in the Future Consortium for introducing us to the problem of data hiding. We acknowledge the other members of the Physics and Media group, especially Joe Paradiso and Tom Zimmerman, for helpful conversations about modulation techniques. Maggie Orth made useful suggestions about the proof of the approximate superposition principle.

This work was supported in part by the MIT Media Lab's News in the Future Consortium, a Motorola Fellowship, the Hewlett-Packard Corporation, Festo Corporation, Microsoft, Compaq Computer Corporation, and the MIT Media Lab's Things That Think consortium.

References

[BGM91] W. Bender, D. Gruhl, and N. Morimoto. Techniques for data hiding. In *Proceedings of the SPIE*, pages 2420–2440, San Jose, CA, February 1991.

[BH93] M.F. Barnsley and L.P. Hurd. *Fractal Image Compression*. AK Peters, Ltd., Wellesley, Massachusetts, 1993.

[BOD95] F.M. Boland, J.J.K. O'Ruanaidh, and C Dautzenberg. Watermarking digital images for copyright protection. In *Proceedings, IEE International Conference on Image Processing and its Application*, Edinburgh, 1995.

[CKLS] I. Cox, J. Kilian, T. Leighton, and T. Shamoon. A secure, robust watermark for multimedia. *This volume*.

[Cor95] Digimarc Corporation. Identification/authentication coding method and apparatus. *U.S. Patent Application*, June 1995.

[Dix94] R.C. Dixon. *Spread Spectrum Systems with Commercial Applications*. John Wiley and Sons, New York, 1994.

[Pfi] B. Pfitzmann. Trials of traced traitors. *This volume*.

[She95] T.J. Shepard. *Decentralized Channel Management in Scalable Multihop Spread-Spectrum Packet Radio Networks*. PhD thesis, Massachusetts Institute of Technology, July 1995.

[SOSL94] M.K. Simon, J.K. Omura, R.A. Scholtz, and B.K. Levitt. *The Spread Spectrum Communications Handbook*. McGraw-Hill, New York, 1994.

[SW49] C.E. Shannon and W.W. Weaver. *The Mathematical Theory of Communication*. The University of Illinois Press, Urbana, Illinois, 1949.

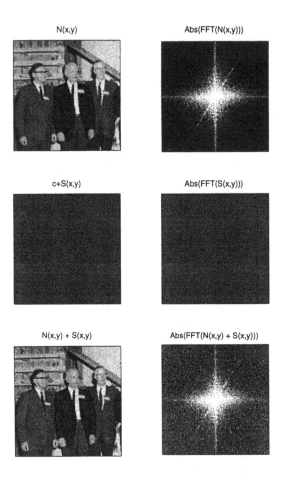

Fig. 1. "Fully Spread" version of direct sequence spread spectrum. The left column shows (from top to bottom) the space representation of the cover image, the modulated carrier, and the stego-image. The right column is the spatial frequency representation of the same three functions. The cover image has six bits of gray scale $(0-63)$, and the power per pixel of this particular cover image, that is, the noise power per pixel, is $902 \approx 30^2$. The carrier alternates between $+2$ and -2 in this figure, so the signal power per pixel is $2^2 = 4$. We have added a constant c to the carrier to map the values into a positive gray scale.

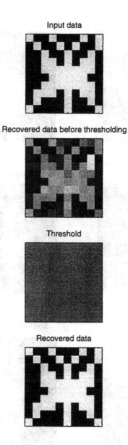

Fig. 2. Demodulation of Fully Spread Scheme. Top: 100 bit input data icon to be embedded. Second: normalized values after demodulation. Third: threshold value. Bottom: Original input recovered by comparing demodulated values to threshold.

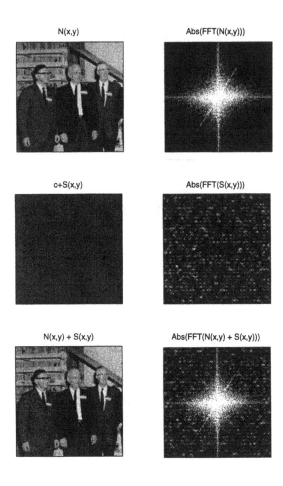

Fig. 3. Tiled version of spread spectrum modulation scheme. Note the inhomogeneities in the spatial frequency view of the modulated carrier. As in the fully spread scheme, the noise power per pixel (the average power of the cover image) is 902, and the carrier ranges between +2 and −2, for a signal power of 4 per pixel.

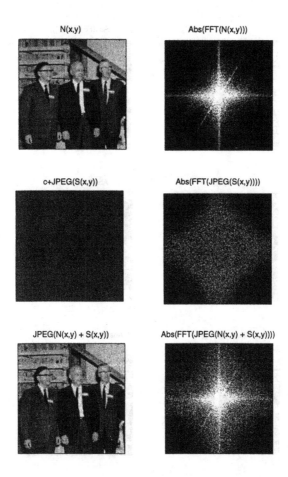

N(x,y) Abs(FFT(N(x,y)))

c+JPEG(S(x,y)) Abs(FFT(JPEG(S(x,y))))

JPEG(N(x,y) + S(x,y)) Abs(FFT(JPEG(N(x,y) + S(x,y))))

Fig. 4. Predistortion of carrier by JPEG compression to compensate for distortion from anticipated JPEG compression. The usual direct sequence carrier has been compressed and uncompressed before being used to modulate and demodulate. JPEG compression of the same quality factor will not alter the carrier further. The original average carrier power was 16; after JPEGing the carrier by itself, the average carrier power dropped to 8.8.

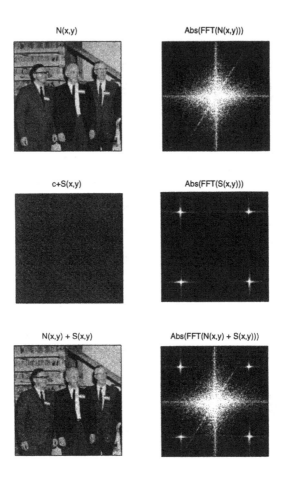

Fig. 5. Frequency Hopping spread spectrum. Average signal power = 9.1 (units of amplitude squared), and average noise power = 902.

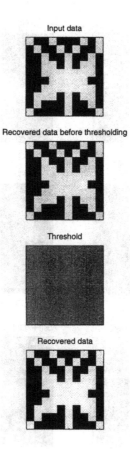

Fig. 6. Demodulation of Frequency Hopping spread spectrum.

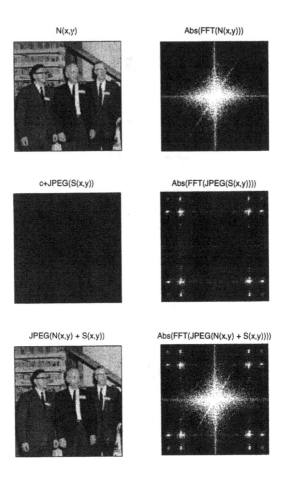

Fig. 7. Frequency Hopping spread spectrum, with JPEGed stego-image. The stego-image D was created, JPEGed at high quality, uncompressed, and then demodulated. To estimate the amount of signal lost to compression, we measured the average power of jpeg$(N + S) - N$ and found its value to be 5.6; the power in the carrier S was 9.1, as Figure 5 showed. The carrier shown for illustration purposes in the figure, labeled $c + JPEG(S(x, y))$, is in fact JPEG$(N + S) - N$. The carrier used to create the stego-image was in fact $S(x, y)$.

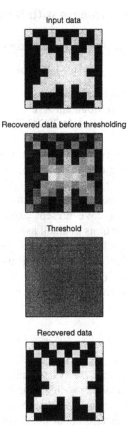

Fig. 8. Demodulation of Frequency Hopping spread spectrum, with JPEGed stego-image. The compression took its toll: contrast this output figure with the one from figure 6, which was so robust it needed no thresholding.

Watermarking Document Images with Bounding Box Expansion

Jack Brassil and Larry O'Gorman

{jtb|log}@bell-labs.com

Bell Laboratories
700 Mountain Ave.
Murray Hill, NJ 07972 USA

Imperceptible displacements of text objects has been shown to be a successful technique for hiding data in document images. In this paper we extend our earlier work to show how the height of a bounding box enclosing a group of text words can be used to increase the density of information hidden on a page. We present experimental results which show that bounding box expansions as small as 1/300 inch can be reliably detected, even after the distortions introduced by noisy image reproduction devices such as plain paper copiers. Digital watermarks based on this technique can be used with electronically disseminated documents for applications including copyright protection, authentication, and tagging.

1. Introduction

Traditional publishers seek access to the vast numbers of potential information consumers connected to computer networks such as the global Internet. However, many information providers remain reluctant to distribute their intellectual property electronically, in part due to their concerns about the unauthorized redistribution of their copyrighted materials. We have previously proposed a collection of techniques to discourage unauthorized copying of document images [1]. These techniques use digital watermarks created by imperceptible displacements of text objects in document images. Many other research groups are also successfully studying the use of digital watermarks in various media, including text, color image, audio and video [2, 3, 4, 5, 6, 7, 8, 9, 10]. In addition, a number of software companies have initiated efforts to pursue commercial applications of watermarks [11, 12, 13, 14, 15].

In this paper we introduce a new scheme to watermark binary document images containing text. Each document recipient receives either a paper or electronic document containing a set of *marks* constituting a unique fingerprint [16]. Each mark corresponds to the expansion of the height of a logical "bounding box" enclosing a group of adjacent characters (i.e. a text *block*) on a line. A bounding box is the smallest rectangle that encloses the block. We show how to encode documents imperceptibly with bounding box expansions, and demonstrate that this hidden information can be reliably recovered from degraded document images.

In the next section we briefly review our previous approaches to watermarking document images. Section 3 details our new approach to encoding and decoding documents with bounding box expansions. We also discuss troublesome image defects that characterize "noisy" document reproduction devices, as well as our approaches to circumventing these distortions. Section 4 presents experimental results that show that hidden information can be recovered from even rather poor quality document reproductions. The final section summarizes our work.

2. Background on Document Image Marking

The bounding box expansion technique described here complements our earlier work on watermarking electronic document images. In our initial work the vertical displacement of an entire text line formed a mark representing a single hidden information bit [1]. Figure 1 shows an example of a vertically shifted line.

> the Internet aggregates traffic flows from many end systems. Understanding
> effects of the packet train phenomena on router and IP switch behavior
> will be essential to optimizing end-to-end efficiency. A range of interesting

Figure 1 - Vertical shifting of a text line. The first and third lines are unshifted; the second line has been shifted by 1/300 inch. Can you tell if it has been moved up or down?

We observed that vertical line displacements of 1/300 inch and less were generally not noticed by readers of paper documents. This is true despite the fact that the human visual system can readily discern small deviations from uniform line spacing (i.e. *leading*). Empirical investigation found encoding and decoding procedures that were highly reliable, even surviving the effects of noisy document copying such as facsimile transfer and recursive plain paper copying. That is, marks were preserved even as the document moved from the electronic domain to paper, and back again. Indeed, marks endured even as documents became barely legible. Though highly reliable, a limitation of the line shifting technique is that a single simple document page is typically limited to approximately 20 bits of hidden information.

To increase the hidden information density while decreasing perceptibility, we next studied marks based on the horizontal displacement of individual text words [17].

> the Internet aggregates traffic flows from many end systems. Understanding
> the Internet aggregates traffic flows from many end systems. Understanding

Figure 2 - Horizontal shifting of words on a text line. The first contains no shifted words; on the second line the 2nd, 4th, 6th and 8th words are each horizontally displaced by 1/300 inch. Line length remains unchanged.

Small changes to interword spacing are, for practical purposes, not noticed by readers. Figure 2 shows two identical lines of text formatted slightly differently; a reader does not perceive that either is correctly or incorrectly formatted. We found that displacing words afforded approximately an order of magnitude increase in information density (i.e. approximately 200 bits/page), at the expense of a modest decrease in decoding reliability for degraded documents.

We have also considered robust combinations of both marking techniques [18]. Using both horizontal and vertical displacements simultaneously was suggested by empirical observations of the effects of of common paper document handling. The type and magnitude of defects introduced by devices such as plain paper copiers can be dramatically different along the paper width and length. The defects arising from movement of paper (e.g. a sheet feeder) or imperfect device mechanics (e.g. worn rollers) are often of greater magnitude in one direction than the other.

In the next section we describe a marking technique relying on even smaller displacements of smaller textual elements.

3. Encoding and Decoding Documents

Our proposed document marking scheme works by effectively increasing the height of a *collection* of adjacent characters (or words) on a text line. That is, a mark is inserted by manipulating text to increase the size of the logical bounding box enclosing a block. There are several possible approaches to achieving this expansion. For example, one can directly add a small number of pixels to the endlines of characters with ascenders or descenders. Alternatively, one can vertically displace either specific characters or entire words off the logical text baseline (Figure 3). If chosen carefully, a text block containing at least one vertically shifted character and one unshifted character will have a larger bounding box than if left unshifted.

Either one of the approaches to increasing bounding box height might be preferred for a particular application; we consider the latter approach in the remainder of this paper. Further, we will focus on vertical displacements of entire words or groups of adjacent words, which we believe to be less obvious to the casual reader than displacements of characters within words. Note of course that any block of adjacent characters may be selected for displacement; it is not necessary for blocks to have edges corresponding to text word boundaries. Also note that bounding box width adjustments can be used as a mark. This can be implemented, for example, by *track kerning*, which is the uniform adjustment of space between characters in a text block.

the impact it has on information providers and users. Over 100 speakers and 100
the impact it has on information providers and users. Over 100 speakers and 100
the impact it has on information providers and users. Over 100 speakers and 100

Figure 3 - Illustration of marks inserted by lifting words off the baseline. The first line contains no shifted words; the second and third lines contain 3 words each shifted by 1/600 and 1/300 inch, respectively.

Our basic document image encoding scheme is simple; for each mark one or more adjacent words on an encodable text line is selected for displacement, according to a selection criteria we discuss below. The words immediately before and after the shifted word(s) typically remain unshifted. A block of words on the text line either immediately above or below a line with shifted word(s) is also left untouched. We will use the heights of characters in these unshifted blocks as "reference heights" to facilitate decoding.

Not all text lines in a document lend themselves to encoding, such as a short line ending a paragraph. For lines deemed encodable, the choice of preferred text words to shift must be made carefully, for several reasons. The human visual system does remarkably well at identifying text set off with respect to the logical baseline. However, our experience suggests that displacements of 1/600 inch and less on a printed page are generally not noticed by casual readers, even with serif fonts exhibiting a clearly defined baseline. Larger displacements of text can be realized imperceptibly in steps, such as by both raising one word slightly, and lowering a second (non-adjacent) word slightly. That is, 2 opposite sense displacements of 1/600 inch within a block can be used to subtly increase a bounding box height by 1/300 inch. Use of sans serif fonts, or even purposely introducing image defects — perhaps by plain paper copying a document prior to distribution — further lessens a reader's ability to detect text set off the baseline.

A second reason why shifted text words must be chosen carefully is varying character heights within a given font. Note that shifting certain characters within a word, or even words within a block, need not increase bounding box height. While it is obvious that the Cap height and x-height are not identical, encoders must consider font specific details including the difference between Cap height and ascender height, and the presence of baseline overshoot. Hence one must examine the specific characters in a block of words to ensure that a vertical displacement will in fact expand the desired bounding box. Careful selection of text elements to displace is desirable for aesthetic reasons as well; words having characters with ascenders and descenders help obscure the perceived baseline location. Since serif fonts present well defined baselines, it is desirable to avoid displacing a block whose first and last characters have distinct "feet" on the baseline (e.g. the character 'm' in Times-Roman).

Our experience in implementing encoders suggests that their construction is relatively straightforward; see [17] and [19] for implementation details. In these implementations we have encoded Postscript documents (i.e. before rendering an image). Using a Postscript document facilitates the sort of adaptive encoding we have described above.

3.1 Decoder

For the purposes of this discussion, we assume that a degraded paper copy of a watermarked document is recovered. We seek to identify the unique embedded fingerprint. The recovered page is scanned at 1200 dpi at an 8-bit depth and is subject to the following image processing operations — cropping, binarization, inversion and deskewing. Deskewing typically requires special attention, which we will examine in the next section.

The simplest approach to detecting a vertically displaced text block is by direct measurement and comparison with the height of a reference text block. For simplicity we assume that the reference block height is identical to the height of the hypothetically shifted text block *prior* to any displacement. Each block height is measured by calculating a *projection profile*, which is the sum of the number of "on" pixels along each horizontal scan line within the block on the binarized image. The number of scan lines between the first and last nonzero-valued profile element represents the block height, in pixels. The reference text block is generally extracted from the text line immediately above or below the block to be measured. Such a line frequently suffers from similar small scale image defects (i.e. edge raggedness) and large scale defects (i.e. skewing, baseline curvature) as the region of the line containing the shifted block.

Consider first the original image (i.e. prior to any distribution and degradation). We assume that the reference block height in the original image is known and equals y_u^0 pixels. Suppose that a block shift expands a bounding box height by α pixels. Now consider a recovered, degraded version of the distributed image. Let the measured bounding box heights of the shifted and reference blocks on the recovered image be given by y_s and y_u pixels, respectively. The decision rule used to determine if a text block height has been increased is

$$\begin{aligned} if \quad y_s - y_u &> 0.5 \; \alpha \; y_u/y_u^0 : \quad \textit{decide block shifted} \\ \textit{otherwise} & \qquad\quad : \quad \textit{decide block unshifted.} \end{aligned} \tag{1}$$

The decision rule of Eq. 1 is optimal if the following conditions are satisfied; equal likelihood that blocks are shifted or unshifted, linear scaling of page length, and the cumulative "noise" affecting bounding box heights being additive and well represented by independent and identically distributed random variables. Empirical evidence suggests that the cumulative affects of the many distortions affecting the image can be approximately modeled in this way [1].

The recovered image scaling factor, y_u/y_u^0, is generally sufficiently close to unity that it can be ignored. In practice this means that it is generally not necessary to maintain a library of reference block bounding box heights for distributed images (assuming that they are identical to the unshifted block heights). All information necessary for decoding is found on the recovered image.

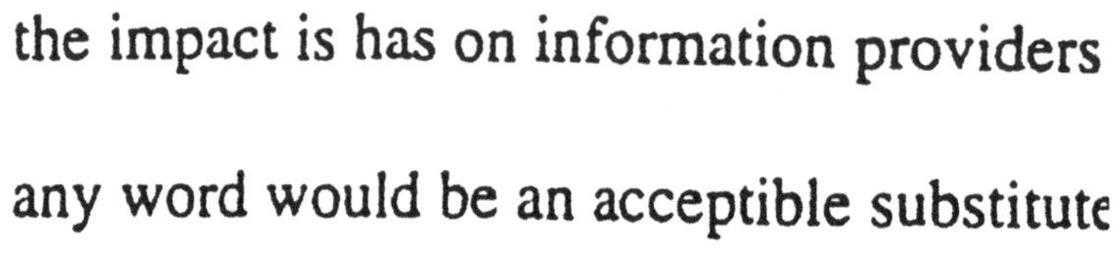

the impact is has on information providers

any word would be an acceptable substitute

Figure 4 - A third generation plain paper copy of a page. The second, fourth and sixth words on the first line were vertically displaced by 1/300 inch. No words on the 2nd line are displaced.

Though the above paragraphs describe the decoding procedure used throughout the remainder of this paper, our experience suggests that detecting even smaller displacements will likely require a more sophisticated technique. One possible approach would be based on calculating the relative vertical separation between *centroids* of the profiles of shifted and unshifted blocks, and comparing them to those in an original unshifted document image. We intend to examine this approach in future work.

4. Experimental Results

To test whether marked yet degraded document images could be decoded reliably, we created samples of encoded lines. We first printed a single page at 600 dpi containing two lines. The second word of the first line was lifted off the text baseline by 1/300 inch (i.e. 2 pixels printed at 600dpi), and the second line without a shifted block was printed immediately below the first. We then recursively copied the printed page 3 times on a plain paper copier, creating the 3rd generation copy shown in Figure 4. For this test case we tried to place the paper on a flatbed scanner with some care to avoid significant skewing (i.e. rotation). Note that both lines are similarly affected by a variety of image defects, including severe baseline curvature near the right margin.

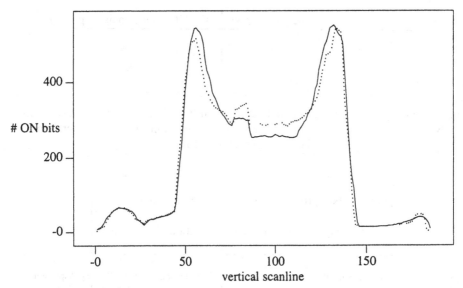

Figure 5 - The cumulative affect of plain paper copying is shown in this overlay of vertical projection profiles; the unshifted line of Figure 4 is shown before (solid) and after (dotted) copying. The two peaks correspond to the location of the text midline and baseline.

We cropped text from the two text lines in the 3rd generation copy image, being sure to capture the first three words on the first line. We correctly detected the bounding box expansion in this cropped image with relative ease, using the simple decoding method described in the previous section. The block profile heights of the shifted and unshifted lines in the original image were 184 and 180 pixels, respectively. The block profile heights of the shifted and unshifted lines in the recovered image (Figure 4) were 185 and 182 pixels, respectively. Hence, by applying the decision rule of Eq. 1, the single bit encoded in the first three words was correctly decoded. We were pleased to find that our simple decoding technique worked adequately, with no need to perform additional image processing operations such as noise removal or character thinning.

Figure 6 - A close look at small scale defects affecting characters in a second generation plain paper copy.

In a second experiment we studied the more gradual approach to encoding, namely by expanding the text block height through 2 small displacements. Figure 7 shows a line containing words shifted both up and down by 1/600 inch, creating a block of text with a 1/300 inch bounding box height expansion (i.e. $\alpha = 4$ pixels at 1200 dpi). Once again we created 3 generations of plain paper copies. On each copy we extracted the encoded block on the first line, and the text immediately below it on the second line. Figure 8 shows the cropped 3rd generation copy image. For each generation copy we applied the simple decoding approach discussed in the previous section, and we measured the following profile heights:

Copy #	Shifted block height (pixels)	Unshifted block height (pixels)
0	192	187
1	193	187
2	192	187
3	192	189

Here the 0th copy refers to the printed page, which itself is a corrupted representation. Clearly the height extension information remains preserved in each copy generation; the single bit was correctly decoded on each generation copy.

this will be a promising information extraction tool

before we quickly begin the new operation. Suppose that

Figure 7 - Example of the gradual marking technique. The first line contains the following displacements; the first word is shifted up by 1/600 inch, and the 4th and 5th words are shifted down by by 1/600 inch. All other words on the line sit on the text baseline. All words on the second line remain unshifted as well.

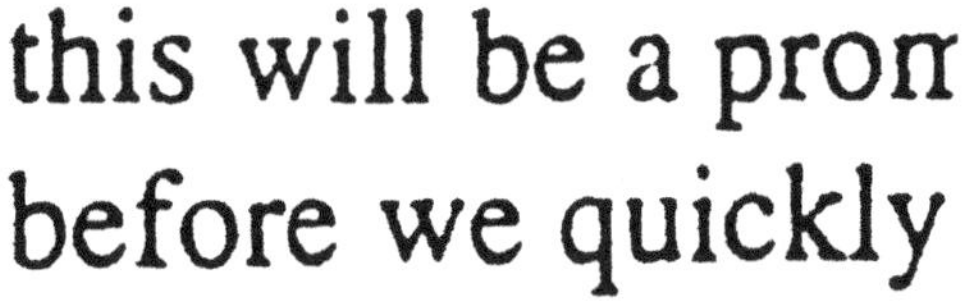

this will be a prom
before we quickly

Figure 8 - A third generation plain paper copy of the beginning of the lines of Figure 7.

Other tests we performed have indicated that the most troublesome image defect to contend with is severe baseline skewing. It is clear that even a slight rotation of text lines can cause a bounding box expansion to be undetectable. This is the case because a skewed text block can cause the measured profile height to either increase or decrease. Further, the same rotation of an encoded text block and a reference text block will generally alter their measured profile heights differently. Indeed, one profile height could decrease while the other increases.

Our experiments suggest that decoding is extremely sensitive to horizontal line skew and skew correction. Proper deskewing of an image ordinarily introduces a small profile height error, perhaps a single pixel. But it is not difficult to imagine that our encoding — lifting text off the baseline — can lead to a skew angle miscalculation and poor deskewing algorithm operation. The proper approach to deskewing encoded text will require additional research and testing.

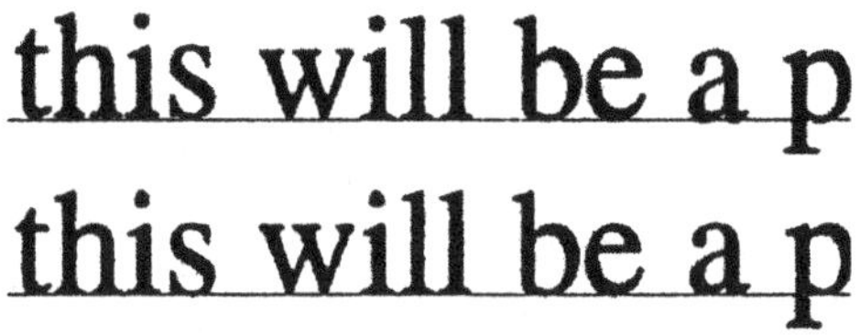

this will be a p
this will be a p

Figure 9 - Part of a scanned printed page containing a line with shifted words, and a line with no shifted words. On the first line, the first word is shifted up by 1/600 inch, and the 4th and 5th words (partly obscured) is shifted down by 1/600th inch. Note the presence of baseline overshoot in characters such as 'e'.

5. Concluding Remarks

We have proposed a new approach to fingerprinting document images. The approach can be used in conjunction with other document marking techniques (e.g. horizontal word shifting) and promises to increase the density of information that can be hidden on a single document page. We have also empirically verified that the marks can survive transfer to paper media, as well as a modest degree of degradation introduced by plain paper copying.

Possible applications of this technology include copyright protection of electronically distributed documents. However, as with our earlier proposals, a technically sophisticated attacker can remove the marks from a document image without substantially reducing presentation quality. Lower quality, derivative documents can also be produced with relative ease with technologies such as OCR.

Nonetheless, we continue to believe that the effort required to develop software tools to remove watermarks from a wide range of document types is easily underestimated. Unlike unformatted text documents, document images can be uniquely watermarked for a large number of recipients. Those wishing to distribute unformatted text might consider distributing images instead. The principal expense is the additional costs of distributing a larger size document.

Like other researchers we invoke a communication system model for detecting the presence of marks in document images. The underlying communications system differs markedly from traditional ones. Consider for example the "communication channel" modeling plain paper copying. It is certainly possible to assert that, at some level of detail, the channel is both time-varying and nonlinear on various spatial scales, with multiplicative noise. The complexity of such a system makes the detection problem both interesting and challenging.

Acknowledgement - Thanks to Steven Low and Nicholas Maxemchuk for many helpful discussions and major contributions to encoding and decoding techniques.

References

1. J. Brassil, S. Low, N. Maxemchuk, L. O'Gorman, "Electronic Marking and Identification Techniques to Discourage Document Copying," *Proceedings of IEEE INFOCOM'94*, vol. 3, Toronto, June 1994, pp. 1278-1287. Also in *IEEE Journal on Selected Areas in Communications*, vol. 13(8), October 1995, pp. 1495-1504.

2. W. Bender, D. Gruhl, N. Morimoto, "Techniques for Data Hiding," *Proceedings of the SPIE*, 2420:40, San Jose, CA, Feb. 1995, pp. 1-10.

3. E. Koch, J. Rindfrey, E. Zhao, "Copyright Protection for Multimedia Data," *Proc. of the International Conference on Digital Media and Electronic Publishing*, Leeds, UK, December 1994.

4. K. Tanaka, Y. Nakamura, K. Matsui, "New Integrated Coding Schemes for Computer Aided Facsimile," *First International Conference on Systems Integraion*, IEEE Computer Society, Morristown, NJ, April 1990, pp. 275-281.

5. G. Caronni, "Assuring Ownership Rights for Digital Images," Proceedings of Reliable IT Systems' (verlaessliche IT-Systeme) VIS '95, H.H. Brueggemann and W. Gerhardt-Haeckl (Ed.), Vieweg Publishing Company, Germany, 1995.

6. S. Brin, J. Davis, H. Garcia-Molina, "Copy Detection Mechanisms for Digital Documents," *ACM SIGMOD 1995*, 1995.

7. D. Boneh, J. Shaw, "Collusion-Secure Fingerprinting for Digital Data," Princeton University Technical Report #486, 1994.

8. R.G. van Schyndel, A.Z. Tirkel, C.F. Osborne, "A Digital Watermark," *IEEE Int. Conf. Image Processing '94*, Austin, Texas.

9. I. J. Cox, J. Killian, T. Leighton, T. Shamoon, "Secure Spread Spectrum Watermarking for Multimedia," *NEC Research Technical Report 95-10*, 1995.

10. F.M. Boland, J.J.K. O'Ruanaidh, C. Dautzenberg, "Watermarking Digital Images," *Irish DSP and Control Colloquium*, Belfast, 1995.

11. IBM Vatican Digital Library Project, http://www.software.ibm.com/is/dig-lib/vatican.html.

12. Digital Information Commodities Exchange (DICE) Co., http://digital-watermark.com/.

13. Highwater Designs Ltd., http://www.highwaterfbi.com/.

14. ARIS Technologies, Inc., mailto:rdg@aristech.com.

15. Digimarc Corp., http://www.digimarc.com/.

16. N. R. Wagner, "Fingerprinting," *Proceedings of the 1983 Symposium on Security and Privacy*, IEEE Computer Society, April 1983, pp. 18-22.

17. J.T. Brassil, S.H. Low, N.F. Maxemchuk, L. O'Gorman, "Hiding Information in Document Images," *Proceedings of the 1995 Conference on Information Sciences and Systems*, Johns Hopkins University, March 1995, pp. 482-489.

18. S.H. Low, N.F. Maxemchuk, J.T. Brassil, L. O'Gorman, "Document Marking and Identification Using both Line and Word Shifting", *Proceedings of Infocom'95*, April 1995.

19. J. Brassil, A. Choudhury, D. Kristol, A. Lapone, S. Low, N. Maxemchuk, L. O'Gorman, "SEPTEMBER: Secure Electronic Publishing Trial", *IEEE Communications Magazine*, vol. 34, no. 5, May 1996.

The History of Subliminal Channels

Gustavus J. Simmons

Trinity College, Cambridge and Box 365, Sandia Park, NM 87047

When Ross sent me a letter a month or so ago saying, "I think it will be of considerable interest if you told the story of how the modern subject, that is to say subliminal channels, began with treaty verification", I was a little hesitant about accepting the invitation since I'd already spoken several times on this subject; afraid that I'd be repeating myself. I accepted, however, rationalizing that few in this audience would have heard my other talks. This morning as Ross spoke about subliminal channels drawing on their origins in treaty verification, I became concerned that I would be repeating not only myself, but Ross as well. Then Yvo spoke this afternoon describing in detail the "Prisoners' Problem", a setting I had devised to allow me to get around classification problems and to present the concept of subliminal channels at Crypto '83, and it became apparent that I would be repeating Yvo as well. As luck would have it, though, Jack Brassil has just run 20 minutes over time and into the time allocated for my talk. These circumstances combined give me a chance to repeat one of my favorite stories.

Fifteen years ago, when public key cryptography was still new, the AAAS (The American Association for the Advancement of Science) asked me to organize a panel session for their annual meeting to present this new topic to their attendees. I invited two brilliant young number theorists, Len Adleman and Hugh Williams, names whom most of you will recognize, and a couple of other people to take part in the panel. The panel sat on a stage at the front of the room with a very large audience out front. Since I was Chairman, I was to be the last speaker. Len Adleman was much taken in those days with the topic that I happened to be talking about at that time which was treaty verification and the intriguing problems of information integrity involved.

I think Len spoke first, and instead of talking about RSA and the number theoretic basis of public key cryptography as I had expected him to do, he spoke about treaty verification and the associated problems . He covered the topic very well —- which was what I was going to talk about! Hugh Williams was the next to the last speaker, and he spoke – at great length – about hard problems in number theory, factorization, class numbers etc. and their potential applicability to cryptography. As his time ran out, as Chairman, I pushed the clock over in front of him and indicated that he had only a minute or so to go. He pushed the clock back down the table to me. This comedy routine was repeated several times: I would push the clock in front of him and he'd push the clock back. Finally when Hugh finished — fifteen or twenty minutes over his time — I got up and said to the audience; "Since Len has given my talk and Hugh has used my time, are there any questions?" Apropos the present; Since Ross has given my talk, and Jack has used a portion of my time, are there any questions?

What I would like to do in the time remaining this afternoon, probably for the last time for me, is tell you in more detail than I have done on previous occasions how subliminal channels came to be discovered.

In the Carter administration (we're going back 20 years to 1976–80), the President had two major defense initiatives that he was determined to push through during his presidency. One of these was the ratification of the SALT 2 treaty, which depended critically on what was then a radical notion: that the United States and the Soviet Union would co-operate with each other to the extent that each party would make it possible for the other by national means (that's a euphemism for satellites) to verify the number of strategic (intercontinental) missiles that the other had in place. The primary object of the treaty was to limit the number of strategic missiles that each side could legitimately field. In order for the treaty to be acceptable, though, there had to be some means for each party to verify that the other was complying with its terms. So on the one hand this treaty depended on each party co-operating with the other to make that possible, but on the other it had to be assumed that either party would cheat if they could do so without risk of detection.

The other initiative of the Carter administration, you may recall, was what in retrospect seems a rather silly thing, but at the time seemed serious; a scheme for making the land-based Minuteman missile system survivable against a first strike by intercontinental ballistic missiles. This was 1976 — coincidentally, the time that public key cryptography came on the scene — when the accuracy of delivery of intercontinental missiles had improved to the point where it was no longer possible to make a missile silo survive a targeted nuclear warhead just by hardening it more. The accuracy of missile delivery systems had gotten to the point where they could with high probability destroy the missiles in individual silos, and MIRV (multiple warheads with terminal guidance) had made it feasible to target individual silos. As a matter of fact, it was a popular saying in the defense community at the time that "This is the last generation of land missiles" and subsequent developments have proven this statement to have been approximately true.

The scheme the Carter administration was pushing was often referred to in the popular press as a "missile shell game". In a Minuteman field they were going to prepare a thousand silos and have a hundred missiles that would shuttle about amongst these emplacements. Unlike Ross said, it wasn't under the cover of darkness or clouds that they'd move them; there were to be "transportainers" — great trucks — that would continuously and randomly move around visiting all of the silos in a field. The transportainers would back up to a silo, go through the motions of loading or unloading a missile, and then trundle at 5 miles an hour, like the shuttle transport, to another silo and repeat the procedure. It was even envisioned that they would take on a dummy load — perhaps of water in tanks — so that from the exterior it would be impossible to tell whether the load was dummy or real. The idea was that since even from close range it would be impossible to tell whether a missile was being put in or taken out of the silo, after a period of time any knowledge an enemy might have had at the beginning as to which silos had missiles in them would have been dissipated and their certainty about which silos were occupied and which were empty would have vanished. An opponent (the Soviet Union presumably) could only guess at whether a particular silo was occupied or not. Consequently, all 1000 silos would have had to be targeted in order to be confident of destroying all 100 of the Minutemen. Since this dilution of the effectiveness of a first strike wasn't considered to be cost effective, it was thought that this would ensure the survival of an adequate force for a second strike.

So here we have these two competing and apparently mutually exclusive requirements. On the one hand the SALT 2 treaty required the United States to provide a way for the Soviet Union to verify how many silos were occupied. On the other hand, there was this elaborate scheme to conceal which ones were occupied. Incidentally, this might have been done using statistical techniques as was later negotiated to verify the MRBM (medium range ballistic missile) treaty. The Russians could have been allowed to say "We want to have a look in those twenty silos" and then estimate on the basis of how many out of the twenty silos they had chosen had missiles in them the expected number of occupied silos in the field.

But the level of suspicion in those days was such that this wasn't acceptable. In order for the treaties to go forward, there had to be a deterministic scheme whereby the Soviet Union could exercise their right to challenge and see how many missiles were in the field. If this was done by opening the lids of the silos so they could see from their satellites which ones were occupied, all the uncertainty that had been generated over a long period of time by shuffling the missiles around amongst the silos would be lost. The result would have been that the US would be back at ground zero, and it would be a long time before there had been sufficient potential moves by the transportainers that the Russians would be sufficiently uncertain again as to which silos were occupied.

This is the setting of the Carter administration's problem. They had a dilemma of the first order. On the one hand they needed to be able to com-pellingly respond to the Soviet Union's challenge as to how many Minuteman silos were occupied, but the survival of the force depended on not revealing whether any particular silo was occupied. The Department of Defense, put up for bid to the defense contractor community in the United States a request for a solution to this; i.e. to devise a way you could compellingly convince the Russians of how many silos were occupied without revealing the status of any particular silo.

The winning contractor was TRW — Thompson-Ramo-Wooldridge. They worked with the National Security Agency to devise a scheme that was believed to solve this problem. Parts of it I won't address here, but the essential premise was there were a number of sensors which, if they could be emplaced in a silo, could reliably tell whether there was a missile in the silo or not. These were gravimetic sensors, tilt sensors, etc. Both parties accepted that there were sensors or combinations of sensors that could do this, but the problem was that the data acquired by these sensors (after all there is only one critical bit involved —

"occupied" or "not occupied") had to be protected so that it couldn't be forged and couldn't be falsely attributed.

In other words the Russians should not be able to go to the United Nations and say "The Americans are cheating" and be able to present information that we couldn't disavow, showing that we were violating the terms of the treaty. Similarly, the US should not be able to generate information that would deceive the Russians into believing silos are empty when they are occupied, etc. There are a long list of requirements which I won't recite in their entirety here. In the paper that I mentioned [1], the complete list of requirements for all of the parties is given. An obvious one is that neither side should be able to forge messages that would be accepted as authentic. The Russians might wish to, so they could falsely accuse the United States of cheating. We certainly would wish to be able to, so that we could field more missiles than we had to account for.

Requests had to be timely, otherwise we could merely interrogate the silo when there was no missile in it and save the response until the Russians issued a challenge, and then give them one saying the silo was empty when in fact it was occupied. An important portion of the anticipated treaty was that there would only be a limited number of challenges allowed each party, so that the Soviet Union couldn't say every day that they wanted to get a report on the Minuteman missile field. Hence, it was also important that we could only cause the transducers to respond when the Russians requested it, so that we couldn't exhaust their stock of challenges, when they hadn't issued them. I refer you to a paper of mine that appeared in European Transactions on Telecommunications for a complete discussion of the various competed needs of all of the parties [1].

Now Whit (Diffie) will be surprised to learn, since he knows that I can't remember anything and that I've thrown away all items of historical interest in my personal files, that I found a critical set of vugraphs from that period describing the proposed solution that resulted. These are briefing charts (figures 1–5, appendix) prepared by the TRW project manager, for a briefing to his upper management reporting on a briefing he'd given at NSA. They describe in some detail the TRW scheme and obviously are referring to a briefing TRW had just made to NSA. I don't remember his name since I only met him once when he came to Sandia to brief us – for reasons I'll explain momentarily – on the TRW study. This is part of my failing memory: I was lucky to find the vugraphs he gave us after the briefing!

What I discovered when I first saw the TRW study is historically interesting. Furthermore, it's going to be fun to describe, since it allows me to pillory the National Security Agency, one of my favorite pastimes. There is an ex-NSA man in the audience today (Robert Morris), so he may take umbrage at this. I need to explain a couple of things here. NSA saw no difficulty with the crypto processing that I'm going to talk about, because it had all been developed jointly with them, but I should emphasize that these vugraphs were used by the TRW program manager in reporting back to his management. This line down here (mentioning that Sandia should be brought in), I need to explain (figure 5). It was suggested to TRW by NSA that Sandia be asked to look at the transducer package as an extension of the Sandia code storage study in which we had developed very secure tamper proof and/or tamper sensing container technology.

We weren't asked to look at anything having to do with the crypto. That would have been unlikely then or now. The code storage study was a Sandia program to secure the enabling information for nuclear weapons in tamper resistant containers, the idea being that even though someone had unauthorised possession of the container it should be essentially impossible that they could get at the information inside. Sandia was also asked to supply some of the transducers, such as an incredibly sensitive motion sensor we had developed for a nuclear weapons application to make it impossible to undetectably move the transducer packages after they were activated. These were to be active transducer containers, and so what they had in mind was that Sandia would apply this technology to protect the transducer package: the collection of instruments that could tell if there was a missile in the silo or not and also that a response had been generated by the equipment in a particular container. I'll go through what the response consisted of later.

Sandia was asked to come in on the program, sort of as an afterthought, and in a peripheral — although important — way. Everything else was considered to have already been settled. The crypto scheme that addresses the problem, and I'll talk about that in a moment, was all resolved – NSA had done that jointly with TRW and was fully satisfied with the scheme and the protocol. The transducers that would sense the presence of a missile either existed or else it was clear that they could be developed. It was essential to have a believable secure store for these transducers and sensors that would prevent the package from being undetectably moved or tampered with which is why Sandia was approached by TRW.

The essential notion that NSA had endorsed — and for a long time I gave them a bad time for what I'm about to show you, without realizing there was a logical explanation of how that happened — was that they were going to use concatenated encryption as the essential element in solving the problem. The Soviet Union and the US would each have a crypto algorithm (figure 3). At that time it was fashionable to talk about the key as keying variable, and so Vi merely represents the keying variable for the one party or the other. The purpose of the concatenation was to cause a cipher to be generated that couldn't have been generated by either party acting alone after the container was sealed. These Vi are secret; and are used in a sequence as shown in the block diagram. The resulting cipher could only have been generated by virtue of the source text having been operated on by the encryption systems with the keying variables of each party. Consequently, neither party alone could generate a fraudulent cipher. I don't even remember all the acronyms shown in the vugraphs. OCC is the Control Center but I don't remember what O stands for, perhaps Operational.

The essential notion that was supposed to protect the integrity of this information, was that the cipher that contained the information to be reported back to the Soviet Union could not have been forged by the US because we couldn't create the Russian ciphers, nor could it be forged by the Russians to be falsely attributed to the US since they couldn't create the US cipher. The most important notion of all in this scheme was that both the clear text (and I'll come back to what that consisted of) along with the encrypted information would be output by the transducer package.

The final test was to compare the plaintext that had been sent out in clear with the result obtained by undoing the two encryptions. The US would make this comparison as a test to decide whether to forward the message to the Russians or not; the Russians would make it to determine the authenticity of what they received. To repeat, you generate a cipher that can only be produced by encrypting with crypto variables that belong to the two nations, so that neither party can forge it, and you also pass out the plaintext that has been superencrypted to produce the cipher. As shown in the figure, both parties then decide whether the data is legitimate or not by decrypting it first with the one and then the other crypto scheme, in the appropriate order, and comparing the result with the plaintext.

Now comes the part wherein the problem lies. The bottom line in the figure indicating NSA's approval of the scheme is the item that is really inexplicable (figure 5). By the way, I should point out that ciphers from different silos had to be distinct, otherwise the US could just interrogate an empty silo a thousand times. So each silo had to produce a silo unique signal, but the Russians couldn't know anything that would associate the unique portion of the plaintext with the silo it came from. The silo unique information consisted of a randomly generated identifier to be entered by the US after the transducer packages were emplaced, and the Russians (and presumably the UN observers) had verified their correct operation. Obviously, the storage had to be write only, so that once a number was entered, it couldn't be modified without opening the secure data store. The Russians would have had to be satisfied that this was true before they would have accepted the scheme.

The point was that each silo would have a unique — but fixed — identifier associated with the output from its transducer package, but the Russians should not be able to associate the numbers with silo identities. It's just that they expected to see those serial numbers every time they received a response to a challenge they issued. The outputs also had to be in response to a query made by the Russians that could only be decrypted by their equipment — otherwise the US could cause the transducers to spit out ciphers when the Russians hadn't asked for them.

But this bottom line in the figure is the crucial thing. This is the fatally flawed notion the NSA had endorsed. If when a cipher was decrypted, the decryption matched the plain text — and I emphasize, every bit of the plaintext was known in advance to the US — the assumption was that the message (the complete text that was going to be passed along to the Russians) couldn't have even a single bit that was in equivocation to the US. The US knew the serial number of the unit; they knew the time; they certainly knew whether the silo was occupied or unoccupied. There was one bit of information there that was unknown in advance to the Russians. That was whether the silo was occupied or unoccupied. NSA's belief, that they acted on and accepted, was that if when you decrypted the cipher and the information was bit for bit identical to what it was supposed to be, then there could be nothing concealed in the cipher. We (Sandia) weren't invited to consider any of this. We were only brought in to make the tamper sensitive container for the transducers.

From the presentations you've heard today, you already know that NSA's assumption was not only wrong, it was fatally flawed in this case. I remind you that we're talking about 1976/77 — the notion of public key cryptography had only appeared the previous year. We only had a couple examples of asymmetric cryptoschemes at the time, so it's hard for us now to think back to the cryptographic framework we were working in at that time. The NSA participants mentioned in the TRW vugraphs, Bill Marks and Tim White, both figured heavily here. Rick Proto, who shows up in my narrative in a moment, is currently head of the R (Research) Division of the NSA. These were heavyweights at NSA that were involved in both the evaluation of this scheme and in its approval.

As I've already pointed out, this was a time before we knew a great deal about public key cryptography. The people at the Agency, Tim White in particular as shown in the vugraph, were anxious that the Russians propose their own crypto scheme. As he said, it would reveal something about their crypto technology (figure 5). So it was proposed that the Russians be left to provide their own crypto system. The United States would put forward a crypto algorithm that we felt was acceptably secure, but not too revealing. We were going to ask the Russians to provide their own algorithm hoping it would give us a window into their technology. This is an important point to my narrative, since it left open the possibility that the Russians could have devised a crypto scheme of the sort I will describe in a moment. There were some general requirements, such as the output of the one algorithm had to be compatible as an input to the other etc., but in principle the algorithms could be totally different from each other.

Now why would the NSA, with their expertise in this area, make such an assumption? Well it's explainable in several respects. The first one is that you would expect this if you were conditioned to think in terms of classical (read symmetric) cryptography where you do not normally have two ciphers that decrypt to the same text with the same key. In other words, what you expect in symmetric cryptography is that if you take a text and encrypt it with two different keys, you get two different ciphers and these ciphers — if it's a good system — are going to be essentially two random bit streams with respect to each other. You don't expect to find any — well if it's a good system you'd better not find any — structure surviving from input to output. If you take the two ciphers and decrypt them with the two keys, you will get back the text.

I immediately spotted that it was possible (in fact I had an example in hand at this point) to devise a crypto system that has the following property. I'm going to do the one bit example, but the concept is the same for any number of bits of covert communication. A crypto system that has the property that for every text and key pair, there are a pair of distinguishable ciphers that decrypt to that text with that key. When I say distinguishable, I don't care precisely what that means, say one cipher is odd and one is even, or one cipher is red and one is black — it doesn't matter. It's just that the ciphers in each of these pairs are distinguishable to me (with inside information), i.e. are different, and most importantly, that I can recognize the difference. Even though the ciphers are different, when they are decrypted with the common key one gets the same text.

Now if I — speaking as the Soviet Union — can get the US to accept a scheme like that, then I can sneak through one bit of subliminal communication. In the TRW scheme, the United States first decrypts the cipher and compares the text with the text they know is supposed to be there. If it is bit for bit precisely what it is supposed to be (in the protocol that was approved by the NSA) the US says that's fine, there's nothing concealed, and forwards the plaintext/ciphertext pair to the Soviet Union as a response to their challenge. But consider what the Soviet Union does when they receive the cipher. Before they decrypt it, they look to see if it's the odd or even cipher — or whether it's the red or the black cipher, i.e. they look to see which cipher they've received. That gives them the subliminal bit of information. They then they go ahead and decrypt the cipher to recover the plaintext.

To complete this simple example, I'll reduce the Minuteman problem to where there are only two silos and a single missile in one of them. One silo's crypto equipment sends only the odd cipher while the other sends only the even. As a member of the emplacement team I know which equipment is where. What I don't know (initially) is the unique identifier number assigned to the transducer package by the US after it was emplaced and turned on. This simple example would probably be too obvious to sneak by a vigilant host, but let's assume for the moment that the Russians were able to do this. The plaintext you get once you decrypt the message will tell you whether a silo is occupied or unoccupied, while the subliminal bit will identify which silo the response came from. So the one bit that came through subliminally would have completely defeated the purpose of shuffling the one missile around between the two silos. Obviously, after the first response, we would also have unambiguously identified the silos with their unique identifiers as well. Ten subliminal bits would have done the same thing for 1024 silos, i.e. for the Minuteman scheme that was being proposed by the Carter administration.

I thought this discovery so important, that I called for a meeting in 1978 at the NSA to tell them about the problem with the TRW scheme, and to describe subliminal channels as I then understood them. The meeting was held at the NSA facility at the Baltimore Friendship Airport, and was well attended. Bill Marks, Tim White, Rick Proto and Brian Snow, all figures that we know, were present. Dick Leibler, was there too, and much to his credit, was the only NSA person — then or later — to recognize the significance of what I was reporting. I made a thorough presentation on the topic, including a way to realize a one bit subliminal channel.

The NSA response was "Well, that was interesting, but there aren't any ciphers like that". Well there were: even at that point in time. There was a convincing (to me at least) example that could be constructed using a result that had just appeared in public key cryptography. Since it hasn't been used, some of you may not have encountered the Rabin variant to the RSA scheme. Rabin's scheme was an early implementation of RSA: its advantage being that on the one hand, you're essentially squaring to encrypt, and on the other hand you only have a $\log(n)$ difficult computation to extract a modular square root to decrypt. The encryption consists of taking the message m and forming $c = m*m+b$ (mod n), (b being a binary vector). Decrypting can't be done as it is in RSA though (by raising the cipher c to an exponent that is the multiplicative inverse to the encryption exponent with respect to the Euler ϕ function of the modulus), since 2 is not relatively prime to the Euler ϕ function of n, and hence has no multiplicative inverse. It is easy (order $\log(n)$ computational difficulty) to calculate the four values of m that would encrypt to c though.

It was this non-uniqueness of the inverse operation that was the weakness of Rabin's scheme for crypto purposes. A cipher formed by computing $m * m + b$ and reducing it with respect to the modulus n could be decrypted by essentially taking a square root, as you can easily see by completing the square on the righthand side of the encryption expression. This is only $\log(n)$ difficult if you know the factorization of n, but provably just as difficult as factoring n if you don't. If m wasn't divisible by either p or q the completed square would have four square roots — which will be the case with probability $(1 - 1/p - 1/q)$, i.e. with virtual certainty.

What that means is, for a given cipher, there are four choices for the message. Later, Hugh Williams came up with a scheme that got rid of this ambiguity by requiring p and q to come from specified residue classes with respect to 8 which allowed him to specify a canonical message out of the set of four square roots. This isn't important to my narrative though, since I saw how to adapt the ambiguous Rabin scheme to provide a one bit subliminal channel. This was the example that was sitting there, waiting to be applied.

What we were concerned with was not secrecy, since the plaintext was sent in the open, but authentication or signatures. The important thing in the scheme that I've described, was that the US and the Soviet Union would each sign the cipher, by carrying out an operation that each of them was uniquely able to do, but which the other could verify. Both parties were to be able to decrypt the ciphers unilaterally, but it took both of them — or to be precise, their proxy crypto systems inside the tamper sensing container — to generate a cipher. The crucial thing was that the message was to be authenticated or signed. This could be done by using the inverse of the Rabin scheme. In other words, instead of encrypting by using $m * m + b$ (mod n) when we had a message, we extract a square root of the completed square of the encryption expression (of which there are four in general) and one of those is the "cipher" that is sent. Verification of a signature required only that the cipher be squared mod n and the result compared to the plaintext.

Now we have a crypto scheme that has the property that for every message there are four ciphers, all four of which decrypt to the same message with the same key. Furthermore the four ciphers belong to four classes that are easy to recognize. How do I recognize them? Well the Russians knew the factorization of their modulus so it was an easy task for them ($\log(p)$ plus $\log(q)$ difficult) to calculate the Legendre symbol of the message with respect to each of the primes. That is to say, they looked to see if the root they received was a quadratic residue with respect to each of the two primes. So it was trivial for them, when they received a cipher, to put the cipher into one of four classes, which should be good for two bits of subliminal communication.

As I think Rick Proto said after my presentation, "We'd never accept a system like that" and it's true that the US could limit the Russians in this example to one subliminal bit. This is because the US could calculate the Jacobi symbol of the cipher without knowing the factorization of n and could insist that the only ciphers they would forward would have a specific Jacobi symbol of either +1 or −1. Within one of these classes, however, it is impossible to distinguish the two members without knowing the factorization of the modulus n. If the Jacobi symbol was a −1 the US would know that the cipher was not a quadratic residue with respect to one of the primes, but they would not be able to say which one. Similarly, if the Jacobi symbol was +1, they would know that the cipher was either a quadratic residue with respect to both p and q, or else both were quadratic nonresidues, but they couldn't distinguish between the two cases. The result is that it is not possible to close the one bit subliminal channel in this example. This remains one of the staple items in all sorts of protocols for us today.

Again, NSA's response was, "That's silly, we wouldn't accept a system like that". Furthermore, a one bit existence proof wasn't regarded as a real threat. Ten bits were needed to identify the silos in the Minuteman concealment scheme, and this was only a one bit channel. A one bit existence proof wasn't enough to convince them. As a matter of fact, it was a more serious threat, even at that point, than I realized.

Remember, the elliptic curve factoring technique was a long way in the future. The best factoring method we had in those days, was either CFRAC (the continued fraction algorithm), or the quadratic sieve. We didn't even have the present powerful versions of the quadratic sieve. It was to be some time yet before Davis and I and subsequently Peter Montgomery would develop the techniques that made the quadratic sieve so powerful. But the point I wanted to make about those factoring techniques is that they could not distinguish between numbers of special form and numbers of general form. So at that time if I had a number whose factorization I desired, say a number that was 200 decimal digits in size, and it was made up of five roughly 40 digit components, the fact that there were 40 digit factors didn't aid me in factoring at all. The only choice was to run one of the general purpose factoring routines.

Now I need to remind you what the state of the art of factoring was at that time. 1978 is the year that the Sandia Labs fielded the first implementation ever made of RSA. This was for controlling access to the zero power plutonium reactor at Idaho Falls. Very few things were more sensitive. Only a nuclear weapon perhaps is more sensitive, because the very character of a plutonium pulse reactor is that you have a supercritical mass of plutonium. It's bare and you bring it together; in other words you bring the assembly right to the point of nuclear explosion, and study the onset of the nuclear reaction. It isn't even in pieces, nor is it concealed. It is a mechanism that has more plutonium than you need to make a bomb.If you brought the two pieces to close together you'd have, not a bomb, but a disastrous reaction. An accident of this sort happened with fatal consequence at Los Alamos several years ago.

So you want to have carefully controlled access to a zero power plutonium reactor. We implemented an RSA controlled portal into the place where there was access to this plutonium. The point of my story is this: we gave a lot of consideration at Sandia as to how large a modulus was needed. Note that we are not talking about cryptographic keys, which may have critical value even if they are stale — witness the Walker spy case — but rather access control, whose only value is contemporary. We wanted the modulus to be large enough, so that the difficulty of factoring it would define a suitable level of security for the reactor, but we also wanted to not make it larger than necessary so as to not make the computational burden greater than necessary.

We were caught between a rock and a hard place. In 1978, 334 bits, roughly 100 decimal digits, was orders of magnitude beyond anyone's ability to factor. We implemented the access control for the plutonium reactor using RSA and a 334 bit modulus. This was done using discrete components. It wasn't just that we didn't have special purpose circuits available — TRW had special purpose 16x16 bit multipliers in a single chip implementation (that ran red hot) but it was easier to design with general purpose logic chips, than to make a Rube Goldberg design around a few special purpose chips. VLSI wasn't that far along yet, and so you were compelled to do no more computation than you had to. By that I mean only the amount that you had to do to be secure, so no one would have suggested using a 200, 300 or 400 digit modulus. Moduli of this size, and the need for the security they provide, was to come much much later.

But let's go back now to the scenario that I was describing a moment ago using the Rabin's variation on RSA in the number theoretic setting just described. Since we couldn't take advantage of a comparatively small factor in the modulus to peel it off, had we gone to 160 digit modulus, we could have easily made it up of four 40 digit primes which would have been far beyond anyone's ability to factor in those days. A number of this size — 160 digits — with no small factors is still moderately difficult to factor, but using the elliptic curve factorization technique, it is now easy to peel off the 40 digit factors. As I said though, the elliptic curve technique that exploits smaller factors was still a long time in the future, and so we could have concealed a number of bits in a Rabin type signature using such a modulus because the number of square roots grows as a power of 2 — 2 to the power of the number of factors.

Consequently, the existence proof one-bit subliminal channel I presented in 1978 was already a threat that wasn't taken seriously. In other words, using what I have just described — in a subliminal channel which to the best of my knowledge the NSA could not have detected at the time — the uncertainty to the Russians in the Minuteman concealment scheme could have been cut by a factor of 16, which probably was already enough to defeat the purpose of the missile shell game. Fortunately that wasn't what the decision to abandon the missile shell game hinged on. It was the silliness (and cost) of it all — shuffling these hundred missiles round amongst a thousand holes in the ground — that ultimately killed it. But this was the origin of the subliminal channel.

Since I'm covering history, I want to talk about the problem of constructing two or more ciphers that decrypt to the same meaningful text with a single key. I said earlier that it is hard to find ciphers of this sort. If it's a good cipher, you expect that going the other way round, i.e. that given a plaintext encrypting it with two different keys should give two uncorrelated, i.e. apparently random, numbers.

The next two examples are more for David's (Kahn) pleasure than anyone else's. This is just fun and games – but it does illustrate a serious point. This is a cipher I constructed specifically for this example which we are going to decrypt by simple (schoolboy) substitution. The setting is that this cipher has been intercepted on a Persian courier in the time of the Greek and Persian wars.

```
EQDGZW MWLMH NWPQVFMWN
```

```
Ciphertext: ABCDEFGHIJKLMNOPQRSTUVWXYZ
Plaintext:  FGJBMAIHKPQNTDSCOUVWRXEYZL (KEY)
```

```
MOBILE TENTH DECORATED
```

If we use the substitution key shown first, this is the text that pops out. It is a meaningful text. I don't know that they had that many foot armies in the field in Greece, but when we decrypt the cipher, it says "mobile tenth decorated". However, the same cipher, when decrypted with a different key gives a totally different text — with a much different meaning:

```
EQDGZW MWLMH NWPQVFMWN
```

```
Ciphertext: ABCDEFGHIJKLMNOPQRSTUVWXYZ
Plaintext:  MWFGAPISKBZXTDHCRNOLJYEQUV (KEY)
```

```
ARGIVE TEXTS DECRYPTED
```

Well I made a couple of such ciphers. By the way, these aren't easy to make because even substitution ciphers are kind of random and unicity distance catches up with you at around 25 to 30 letters. It isn't that easy to make up a cipher that decrypts into two meaningful texts, but it becomes especially difficult if you place constrains on the text you are willing to accept – as I have done in these two examples. With the "mobile tenth decorated", you will observe that the word breaks and word sizes have been preserved between the ciphertext and the plaintext.

In the second example I've taken greater liberties with the construction — that was because I was having trouble making another example that had a sort of cryptographic content to one of the plaintexts and still had the desired property. I'll ask you, since we're only playing, to give me the freedom to put the wordbreaks where I want them.

```
QWNMF OSRWH WRPGF OWQWN
```

```
Ciphertext: ABCDEFGHIJKLMNOPQRSTUVWXYZ
Plaintext:  BDFGHPXSJKMOYTLECNARUVIWQZ (KEY)
```

```
CITY PLAN IS INEXPLICIT
```

This is the ciphertext, no particular setting for it, which when decrypted with the first substitution key, says; "City plan is inexplicit". I have no idea what the setting might be for that text, but it is arguably a meaningful plaintext. However, with the other substitution key it decrypts to "(the) red t(ele)phones (are) enciphered":

```
QWNMF OSRWH WRPGF OWQWN
```

```
Ciphertext: ABCDEFGHIJKLMNOPQRSTUVWXYZ
Plaintext:  MWFGAPISKBZXTDHCRNOLJYEQUV (KEY)
```

```
RED TPHONES ENCIPHERED
```

One of my reasons for showing you these examples was to illustrate one of the reasons NSA was so confident that if the plain text matched the decryption of the cipher text bit for bit, there couldn't be anything concealed. It is precisely because of the difficulty of doing what I've just shown you. These were toy examples and even so they are still difficult to construct. But the NSA had an even better reason to believe as they did, and I didn't tumble on this until much later. At the time I'd been working at Sandia — that sounds a little too pretentious so let me change that to say — Sandia had been working with the Department of Defense and the Arms Control and Disarmament Agency with assistance from the NSA for 10 years, developing unattended seismic observatories to monitor compliance with a contemplated comprehensive nuclear weapons test ban treaty. We'd had treaties dating back to 1962 limited testing of nuclear weapons in the atmosphere, in the oceans and in near space, but both sides continued until recently testing nuclear weapons underground, and one of the reasons that loophole was left was the because of the difficulty of verifying compliance.

Each party could verify by national means — in this case by seismic nets (of which we have one stretching up through Scandinavia still) whether the other side had tested nuclear weapons down to a threshold on the order of 100 kilotons at these distances. Now what was desired was to negotiate a treaty in which the detectable threshold (so that you could tell if people were cheating) dropped down to the order of one kiloton, because it was believed that no meaningful weapons development, and hence advancement of the state of art in nuclear weaponry to gain an advantage over the other side, was possible if you couldn't actually field test devices of greater than one kiloton.

What we (the US) had done was to develop families of seismic sensors and the algorithms and technology to analyze that data, which would allow us, if we could get in a little closer with unmanned sensors, to tell if the other side was testing, and hence cheating. This technology had been under active development for some time and those of you that have a copy of the IEEE book on Contemporary Cryptology, the last chapter in there is devoted to how to ensure that data taken to verify compliance with such a treaty is trustworthy [2]. Now I've made a lot of fun of NSA thus far, so now I'll make a little fun of myself. Over a period of roughly a decade, I kept thinking I had completely solved this problem, only to find a new facet to the problem that I had completely overlooked before.

At first it was crucial that the data be authenticated; obviously if you can't trust the data, there's no point in putting the sensors out there. Then it was essential that the data be verifiable to third parties because we realized we if we caught the Russians cheating, or vice versa, and that the aggrieved party would almost certainly going to go to some third party — the United Nations, NATO or the world community and say, "The other side is violating the treaty and here's the proof". And so little by little, we saw success in steps. At the end of the chapter I conclude by saying a number of things. No part of the message can be concealed, in particular from the host (that means the host nation who is allowing the other side to put sensors in their territory). I've already indicated at that time we didn't know about subliminal channels and so that statement isn't quite true.

But the relevance of this to NSA's assumption (that if the decryption of the ciphertext matched the plain text, nothing was concealed) was that ten years of intensive work had been devoted essentially to achieving this long list of functional abilities that were needed for treaty verification by concatenating encryption. For ten years we'd been developing a progressively more complicated scheme in which we had ensured that the interests of all the parties were protected by using concatenated encryption, so that you ended up with ciphers that no party or anticipated cabal of parties could have forged. So long as you didn't reveal your key, no-one would ever be able to falsely attribute a message to you etc.

In a sense, we (Sandia) set NSA up — there was no malicious intent in this, but they were conditioned to believe in concatenated encryption where you compared the plain text to the decryption of the ciphertext as a means of insuring the authenticity of data. So it isn't totally inexplicable that they would have made the assumption they did.

I will close my narrative rather quickly now. That's the history of how the subliminal channel came to be. We quickly began devising practical subliminal channels. By practical, I mean ones that were edging up to getting enough information through to be of real use; not just one bit, or two bits, or a few bits as we'd done initially, but a meaningful amount of information. And now I am going to repeat myself, and Ross and Yvo.

Ross spoke this morning about subliminal channels in El Gamal signatures and waved his hands a little about similar channels in signatures generated using the US digital signature algorithm (DSA). I only want to repeat a couple of things; the digital signature algorithm, now the part of the digital signature standard, is as Ross described it [3]. You have a modulus whose size is between 512 and 1,024 bits in 64 bit increments depending on the security you want. You choose a prime q of 160 bits and that's where most of your signature security is going to reside. The exact steps or details I think are known to everyone here.

By the way, this would have been a fully acceptable scheme at the time the pair of treaties were being negotiated. NSA was planning to ask the Russians to put forward their scheme. So had this been put forward, we would have assuredly accepted it. The user chooses a secret key, the knowledge of which is equated with his identity, so he'd better protect that. If he lets that get away, he's letting his identity get away. That's x in the vugraph. He then does a modular exponentiation of the publicly known element g to produce a public version of his key.

Ross showed you this morning the system for generating the signature, so I won't repeat that since it isn't essential to the point I wish to make. When a message is to be signed, it is first hashed down to a standard size. The hashing generates an element in $GF(q)$. The crucial point is that the signer next chooses a session key k, a "random" element in the field. If he's executing the protocol faithfully, he flips a 2^{160} sided coin and gets a random element. He then calculates these two quantities r and s, and the important thing is not how that's done, but rather that the signature to a message consists of two 160 bit extensions. The final signed message is the concatenation of the original message and those two 160 bit quantities. The security of the signature against forgery is just the probability given m and s say, of choosing an r that is a companion to them under the operations Ross described in detail this morning, that is to say one in 2^{160}.

So we have 320 bits of equivocation in the signature, 160 of which are used for security, and the other 160 of which are potentially available for subliminal communication. There is no necessity that there be 320 bits of redundant information to get 160 bits worth of security, but in all cases you have some superfluous bits hanging out there which may be convertible to subliminal communication. The history of subliminal channels has been the recognition and exploitation of this fact.

At this point, something important with respect to subliminal signatures or communications needs to be said. There are two types of subliminal channels distinguished by whether the subliminal transmitter unconditionally trusts the subliminal receiver or not. In a scheme of the type just described which typifies many digital signature schemes — not all but many — if I wish to communicate subliminally, and I'm willing to unconditionally trust the intended subliminal receiver, meaning I'm willing to give him the ability to utter undetectable forgeries of my signature then, as Ross pointed out this morning, we can use the full equivocation of the remaining 160 bits. As a matter of fact, it is in principle possible to use all the equivocation in a signature that isn't used for security to buy subliminal communication. Whether you can actually do this or not will depend on the particular signature scheme. In this case it is possible, but at the expense of having to unconditionally trust the subliminal receiver.

Well now in the scheme I was describing for resolving the dilemma between the two treaties, naturally the Soviet Union unconditionally trusted the receiver — since they were the receiver. Hence, the equipment in the transducer box could have transmitted, had they proposed the DSA for their signature algorithm, the full 160 bits, while they only needed 10 to completely defeat the Minuteman concealment. But the point is, in that setting, the subliminal transmitter and the subliminal receiver are one and the same in the sense that they work with common purpose. Now there are many other instances or applications in which the subliminal transmitter isn't willing to unconditionally trust the receiver, and that leads to the second class of problems concerning subliminal channels. How much information can you get through when the subliminal transmitter considers the receiver suspect, i.e. he's either only willing to partially trust him or not at all.

My object is not to repeat what Ross said, but to illustrate another concept. Go back to the example I used at the time I tried to persuade the NSA that subliminal channels were a bona fide threat, in the setting in which I devised them. I want to use the same number theoretic principle to describe to you now a subliminal communication that appears very strong. Why was subliminal communication possible in signatures generated using either the El Gamal or the DSA? It was possible because the subliminal transmitter did not have to behave faithfully. The protocol assumed he was going to draw the session key k randomly, but he didn't have to do that. Furthermore, there was no way that an observer could tell from what range he chose the key or with what probability distribution. So the signer could deliberately choose the key to convey the information he wanted to send. That communication was totally dependent on the fact that the subliminal transmitter was free to pick the key k. If you want to deny him that ability you must take away from him the freedom to choose k.

Although it isn't obvious, no one else can choose, or even know, the session key either, since that information would make it possible for them to utter undetectable forgeries of the signers signature. Hence in order to close subliminal channels and maintain the integrity of digital signatures, no one individual can choose the session key. I have devised and reported an interactive protocol between two parties – the signer and a trusted key generation bureau (the KGB) that achieves this end.

But what I wanted to close by showing you, was a neat result harking back to the example where we were looking at quadratic residuosity with respect to the prime factors of a composite modulus. We will do something quite different here. The subliminal transmitter and its receiver choose a large prime known only to them. Their convention is going to be that when a signature is seen they will calculate the Legendre symbol of the signature with respect to this prime which only they know. They will get a binary bit (+1 or –1). That is a fair procedure in the following sense: if we exclude the collection of numbers whose square is less than a given prime, the remaining collection of numbers less than the prime will have quadratic residues distributed 50/50.

So from the standpoint of an observer looking at the signature that's sent, the subliminal transmitter must be able to manipulate the signature by the randomness that he puts in, but all he's doing is causing the signature that he's willing to transmit forward, be in the appropriate quadratic residue class with respect to a particular prime, i.e. to have the right Legendre symbol with respect to this prime that only he and the receiver know. So this is completely fair and unbiased, and hence undetectable.

Now what if he wishes to send ten bits as was needed to defeat the Minuteman concealment scheme. Here number theory isn't quite up to our needs. There is every reason to believe that if we chose ten large primes at random, and chose residues less than these modulii, that the number of occurrences of each of the possible ten bit binary numbers as labels of the residue classes with respect to the primes would be uniform. We don't know of any instance in which the quadratic residue/non-residue sequence for two primes are related, but we have no proof of that either. So all that I can prove is that this is a secure and sound channel for sending one bit. Whether it is an equally secure and sound channel for sending ten bits would depend on whether ten randomly chosen primes and randomly chosen residues, would uniformly map out all possible 2^{10} residue/non-residue classes between them. It is almost certainly true but I have no idea of how to go about proving it.

I will close by returning to approximately where I started, and pointing out that the quadratic residue technique that provided the existence proof that demolished the assumption NSA had made — that if the decryption of the ciphertext matched the plaintext nothing could be hidden — also provides a technique that appears to offer the possibility of communicating subliminally so long as the transmitter has the freedom to accept or reject signatures, even if he can't force the choice of the session key.

Thank you for your patience and attention.

Question: How can the Soviets be sure that you didn't just put some noise source in that will generate a biased probability or some other hardware hack like that?

Simmons: The plan was that the Russians would build their own crypto-hardware and the US would build theirs and the sensors would have been evaluated and accepted by both parties. A point I'll make here is that when they issued a challenge and asked for the status of the Minuteman field, the response to that query had to be a response from all thousand sensor packages. If they failed to get a sensible response from any sensor package, then ipso facto the US was violating the treaty. They could then go to the United Nations and say, "It looks like the Americans are playing fun and games with us".

Question: So if they did this with random messages, you would get approximately the right number of missiles and could get fluctuations.

Simmons: That would have been easy to detect. There is a long list of conditions the system had to satisfy — and there are surprisingly many — which I couldn't describe in the time available today, most of which had no bearing on the discovery of subliminal channels. It turns out that they can all be satisfied except that the subliminal channel which I've described to you is left open. If you are interested in a more complete description of the system, I would refer you to the paper that appeared in the European Transactions on Telecommunications. Are there any other questions? Then I would like to thank you again for your attention.

References

1. G.J. Simmons, "Subliminal Channels: Past and Present", in *European Transactions on Telecommunications* v 5 no 4 (July–August 1994) pp 459–473
2. G.J. Simmons, "How to Insure That Data Acquired to Verify Treaty Compliance Are Trustworthy", in *Contemporary Cryptology — The Science of Information Integrity*, IEEE Press 1992, ISBN 0-87942-277-7
3. R.J. Anderson, S. Vaudenay, B. Preneel, K. Nyberg, "The Newton Channel", *this volume*

SYSTEM CONCEPT

- EACH AIMPOINT CONTAINS A TRANSDUCER WHICH WILL DETECT PRESENCE/ABSENCE OF A MISSILE

- OUTPUT OF TRANSDUCER WILL BE TRANSMITTED TO OCC UPON DEMAND

- COLLECTED DATA WILL BE FORWARDED BY OCC TO HIGHER AUTHORITY

- DATA WILL BE IN TWO FORMS
    - CLEAR TEXT
    - ENCRYPTED

- CLEAR TEXT AND ENCRYPTED DATA WILL BE FORWARDED BY HIGHER AUTHORITY FOR VERIFICATION

- VERIFICATION WILL BE ACCOMPLISHED BY DECRYPTING AND COMPARING ENCRYPTED AND CLEAR TEXT DATA.

figure 1

TRANSDUCER BLOCK DIAGRAM

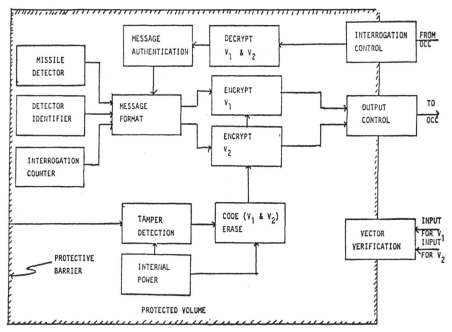

figure 2

OBSERVATION SEQUENCE

- OBSERVER PREPARES INTERROGATION USING V_1 AND FORWARDS TO HIGHER AUTHORITY

- HIGHER AUTHORITY CONCURS AND FORWARDS INTERROGATION TO OCC ENCRYPTED WITH V_2

- OCC INSERTS INTERROGATION AND RECEIVES REPLIES ENCRYPTED WITH V_1 AND V_2

- OCC FORWARDS REPLIES TO HIGHER AUTHORITY

- HIGHER AUTHORITY DECRYPTS V_2 DATA AND OBSERVES RESULT

- HIGHER AUTHORITY FORWARDS CLEAR TEXT RESULTS AND V_1 ENCRYPTED DATA

- OBSERVER DECRYPTS DATA WITH V_1 AND COMPARES WITH CLEAR TEXT

- RESOLVE ANY DIFFERENCES IN TWO DATA SETS (EQUIPMENT MALFUNCTION)

figure 3

256

TRANSDUCER INSTALLATION FLOW

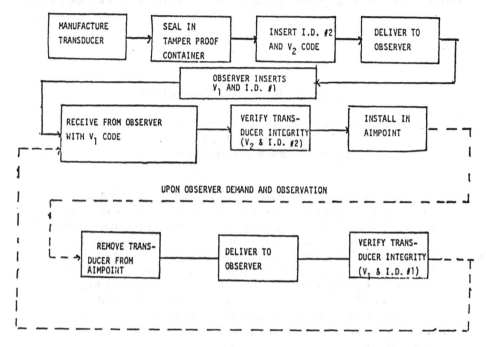

figure 4

SUBSEQUENT ACTIVITY

A COPY OF THE BRIEFING WAS SENT TO NSA (S83). BILL MARKS ASKED ME TO DISCUSS THE BRIEFING

ON 31 AUGUST. THE RESULTS WERE:

NSA DOES NOT SEE ANY DIFFICULTY IN THE CRYPTO PROCESSING TO ACHIEVE GOALS

THERE IS NO PROBLEM IN TECHNOLOGY DISCLOSURE SINCE THE U.S. HAS TRANSDUCERS
IN THE S.U. ALREADY USING THE SAME TECHNOLOGY

NSA (TIM WHITE) WOULD PREFER TO HAVE THE TRANSDUCER DEVELOPED BY THE S.U. SO
THAT THEY COULD LEARN MORE ABOUT SOVIET CRYPTOGRAPHY.

NSA REQUESTED THAT WE PROVIDE MORE DETAILS ON THE CONCEPT IN THE AREAS OF
MISSILE DETECTION, CRYPTO PROCESSING, AND CODE CONTROL.

IT WAS SUGGESTED THAT SANDIA BE ASKED TO LOOK AT THE TRANSDUCER AS AN EXTENSION
OF THEIR CODE STORAGE STUDY.

figure 5

Blind Decoding, Blind Undeniable Signatures, and Their Applications to Privacy Protection

Kouichi SAKURAI   *Yoshinori YAMANE*

Dept. of Computer Science and Communication Engineering,
Kyushu University, 812-81 Japan.
e-mail: sakurai@csce.kyushu-u.ac.jp

Abstract. A cryptographic concept, *blind decoding* is discussed: a client has a message encrypted with a server's public key and the client asks the server to decode the message without revealing what is the decoded plaintext nor learning the server's secret key. Blind decoding is a useful tool for protecting user's privacy in on-line shopping over the Internet. The RSA-based blind decoding is easily converted from the similar protocol as the Chaum's blind signature scheme, and a blind decoding protocol for the ElGamal encryption scheme is newly proposed. Moreover, the practical gap between the known RSA-based blind decoding and our ElGamal-based scheme is discussed in the application to protecting copyright matter of electronic documents.

In blind decoding scheme, undetectability of the decrypted message has both negative and positive aspects: a negative aspect is considered as the problem of spotting the oracle and a positive aspect is applicable to making undeniable signatures blind against the signer.

Key words: Blind decoding, undeniable signatures, ElGamal encryption, privacy protection, online shopping, digital money

1 Introduction

A blind decoding scheme is a protocol between Alice and Bob, in which Alice has a message encrypted with Bob's public key and Alice asks Bob to decode the message without revealing the decoded original text nor learning Bob's secret key.

A similar concept for signature schemes was introduced by Chaum [Cha82] as a blind signature scheme, in which Alice receives a valid signature for a message from a signer Bob without his seeing the message nor her obtained signature. The first blind signature presented by Chaum is based on RSA scheme [RSA78]. In the case of the RSA cryptosystem [RSA78], decoding a encrypted message has the similar operation as signing a message, then we easily convert the blind signature protocol into a blind decoding protocol. In fact, Micali [Mic92] applied the blind decoding protocol based on RSA scheme into fair cryptosystems for making trustees oblivious.

Recently, Carmenisch, Piveteau, and Stadler [CPS94] developed a sophisticated technique on a blind signature protocol based on ElGamal public-key cryptosystems. However, ElGamal encryption scheme is a different operation from the signature scheme, then, unlike RSA scheme, the blind signature by Carmenisch et al. [CPS94] cannot be directly applied into blind decoding.

A general model on blind computation is theoretically investigated by Abadi, Feigenbaum, and Kilian [AFK89]. In the paper [AFK89], they described a method of computing blindly a discrete logarithm. However, the computing power of the oracle assumes to be unlimited, so their method does not answer to our practical problem on decoding ElGamal ciphers.

In this article, we presents a blind decoding protocol for ElGamal encryption scheme [ElG85]. The proposed protocol uses a similar mechanism of the discrete logarithm as used in the mental poker protocol proposed by Shamir, Rivest, and Adleman [SRA79]. A problem of the blind decoding protocol for ElGamal encryption scheme is that Alice cannot verify the correctness of decrypted message by herself, whereas in the case of RSA scheme the correctness the decrypted message is checked by anybody with the encrypted message and the public key (self-verification property). Therefor, in the case of ElGamal encryption scheme, Alice needs the Bob's help for the verification of the decrypted message. We overcome this problem by applying the undeniable signature scheme developed by Chaum and van Antwerpen [CvA89].

We can apply blind decoding into electronic on-line shopping for protecting customer's privacy: hiding information which material a customer buys from the seller. We further discuss the practical gap between the RSA-based blind decoding and our Elgamal-based blind decoding. The RSA-based blind decoding gives a transitive self-certificate on the decoding message, which is regarded as a digital signature, whereas the Elgamal-based blind decoding releases no self-certificate matter. This gap indicates the different application in electronic commerce systems.

The proposed blind decoding protocol achieve perfect undetectability of the decrypted message against the decrypter, which has both negative and positive aspects. A negative aspect is remarked as the spotting problem of the oracle, which is generally discussed in [AN95]. We also consider a positive aspect of this problem, and apply to a method of making undeniable signatures blind against the signer. Though no paper [CBDP91] have investigated the blind-version of undeniable signatures, we suggest that blind undeniable signatures would be useful for ON-line electronic money systems, whereas (RSA-based) blind signatures are known as a fundamental tool for off-line digital-cash [Cha82].

2 The notion of blind decoding

2.1 Chaum's blind signature scheme based on RSA

Chaum [Cha82] proposed the following blind signature scheme the based on RSA-scheme.

Let N be the public RSA modulus of the signer Bob and e be his secret exponent, i.e., the signature on a message m is $t = m^e$ (mod N). Also let d be the public verification exponent: Alice checks if the signature t on a message m satisfies $t^d = m$ (mod N).

Alice: Alice randomly selects $r \in_R Z_N^*$ and sends $X = r^d M$ (mod N) to Bob.

Bob: Bob computes $Y = X^e$ (mod N) and sends Y to Alice.

Alice: Alice computes $Z = Y/r$ (mod N) and uses Z as Bob's signature on the message M.

The blind signature scheme allows to realize electronic payment systems protecting customer's privacy as well as other cryptographic protocols protecting the participants' anonymity like as electronic voting schemes.

2.2 The blind decoding

The blind signature scheme is defined for public-key signature scheme, whereas the blind decoding scheme is defined for a (public-key) encryption scheme. It is a protocol between Alice and Bob, in which Alice has a message encrypted with Bob's public key and Alice asks Bob to decode the message without revealing what is the decoded original text nor learning Bob's secret key.

An application of blind decoding protocols is a pay magazine system over the Internet with protecting user's privacy. A publisher distributes the users several electronic documents, each of which is encrypted with the publisher's secret keys. (Note that only abstracts are sent as the plaintext form and the users can freely read them.) After receiving these encrypted documents, if a user want to read a complete document, the user ask the publisher to decode the encrypted document. However, this simple request releases which document the user asks.

Blind decoding protocol is useful to protect such user's privacy. First the publisher distributes encrypted documents with the publisher's same secret keys to each user. Next the user asks the publisher to decode the encrypted document that the user want to read via a blind decoding protocol. This reveals nothing on information which document the user requests. Furthermore, the user cannot read other documents than the user asks because the user does not obtain the the publisher's secret keys.

2.3 The RSA-based implementation

A blind decoding can be implemented using the RSA encryption scheme via the similar protocol as the RSA-based blind signature scheme developed by Chaum [Cha82].

Let N be the public RSA modulus of Bob's key, e be the public exponent for encrypting, and d be his secret exponent for decoding. (i.e., encryption of

a message m is $t = m^e$ (mod N), and the decryption is $m = t^d$ (mod N).)
Suppose that Alice has a message C, which is encrypted with Bob's public-key
e.

Alice: Alice randomly selects $r \in_R Z_N^*$ and sends $X = r^e C$
(mod N) to Bob.

Bob: Bob computes $Y = X^d$ (mod N) and sends Y to Alice.

Alice: Alice computes $Z = Y/r$ (mod N) and checks if $Z^e = C$
(mod N). If so, Alice convinces that Z is a plaintext of C.

In fact, Micali [Mic92] applied the blind decoding protocol based on RSA scheme
into fair cryptosystems for making trustees oblivious. However, Micali's fair cryptosystem is based on the Diffie-Hellam key exchange scheme [DH76], which uses
the discrete-logarithm problem. Thus, if we would have an Elgamal-based blind
decoding protocol, then we could construct a fair cryptosystems with making
trustees oblivious by using the sole cryptographic assumption of hardness of the
discrete logarithm problem. We give a positive answer to this problem.

3 Our proposed blind decoding

3.1 ElGamal's Public-Key Cryptosystem

Now we consider the ElGamal's public-Key cryptosystem [ElG85]. Bob sets $g \in$
Z_p^* as the base, picks $x \in Z_{p-1}^*$ at random, and computes $y = g^x$ (mod p). Bob
publishes y, g, p as his public key whereas he keeps x as his secret key. Suppose
Alice wants to send a string m to Bob. Alice picks $r \in Z_{p-1}^*$ at random, computes
$C_1 = g^r$ (mod p), $C_2 = my^r$ (mod p) and sends (C_1, C_2) to Bob. On receiving
(C_1, C_2), Bob uses his secret key to compute $m = C_2/(C_1)^x$ (mod p).

3.2 Shamir's 3-Pass Message Transmission Scheme

This is also called the Massey-Omura's cryptosystem (see, e.g. [Kob87b]), and
originally proposed as a tool for mental poker by Shamir et al. [SRA79, Riv90].
Alice and Bob agree on p before their communication. Suppose Alice wants to
send a string (message) s to Bob. Alice picks $a \in Z_{p-1}^*$ at random, computes
$A = s^a$, and sends A to Bob. On receiving A, Bob picks $b \in Z_{p-1}^*$ at random,
computes $C = A^b$, and sends C to Alice. On receiving C, Alice uses her secret a
to compute $B = C^{a^{-1}}$ (mod p) and sends B to Bob. On receiving B, Bob uses
his secret b to compute $s = B^{b^{-1}}$ (mod p).

3.3 The proposed protocol

Suppose that Bob's public key is (P_B, g, p) and his secret key is S_B. Also assume that Alice has a cipher text C, which is encrypted by Bob. Namely,

$$C = (C_1, C_2) = (g^r \bmod p, P_B^r \cdot M \bmod p)$$

for a text M and a Bob's randomly selected r.

Step 1: Alice picks $a \in Z_{p-1}^*$ at random, computes $X = C_1{}^a$, and sends X to Bob.

Step 2: On receiving X, Bob computes $Y = X^{S_B}$, and sends Y to Alice.

Step 3: On receiving Y, Alice uses her secret a to compute $Z = Y^{a^{-1}}$, which is

$$Y^{a^{-1}} \equiv (X^{S_B})^{a^{-1}} \equiv X^{S_B \cdot a^{-1}} \equiv C_1^{a \cdot S_B \cdot a^{-1}} \equiv C_1^{S_B} \pmod{p}.$$

Then, Alice obtain the original message M by computing $C_2/Z = C_2/C_1^{S_B} \pmod{p}$.

Remark. A similar technique for making a discrete-log based cryptosystem blind is used in [CP92].

3.4 Perfect undetectability against Bob

Even though we take a base g as primitive element of Z_p^*, the set

$$S(r) = \{(g^r)^a \bmod p : a \in Z_{p-1}\}$$

could be a very small set than Z_p^* for a randomly selected r. This could release certain information on Alice's secret.

A simple method to avoid this problem is to choose the prime modulus p with the form $2q + 1$, where q is also prime, and further take the base g as the prime order q. Another way is to take the discrete logarithm defined over elliptic curves [Mil85, Kob87a], of which number of points is prime.

3.5 Avoiding decoder's cheating

In the RSA-based blind decoding scheme, the correctness the decrypted message is checked by anybody with the encrypted message and the public key, namely it has a self-verification property. However, in the case of the ElGamal encryption scheme, Alice cannot verify the correctness of decrypted message by herself, because the encrypted message is randomized then is not unique in the ElGamal encryption scheme. Therefore, in the proposed protocol, Bob has a chance to cheat Alice by sending $\tilde{Y} = X^T$, where $T \neq S_B$. To avoid such a cheating by Bob, we consider an additional subprotocol, in which Bob shows indeed that he correctly computes Y from X. The confirmation protocol of undeniable signature scheme [CvA89] achieves the requirement, in which the prover shows that $Y :=$ $X^S \bmod p$ by using public information $(g, X, P = g^S \bmod p)$. Here we assume that the modulus p has the form $2q + 1$, where q is also prime, and the base g has the prime order q.

> *Step 1:* Alice picks $e_1, e_2 \in \mathbf{Z}_q^*$ at random, and computes $c :=$ $Y^{e_1} P_B^{e_2} \bmod p$, then sends c to Bob.
>
> *Step 2:* Bob computes $d := c^{S_B^{-1} \bmod q} \bmod p$, and sends d to Alice.
>
> *Step 3:* Alice accepts Y as a correctly computed result if and only if the equation $d \equiv X^{e_1} g^{e_2} \pmod{p}$ holds.

The correctness of this protocol is shown in [CvA89].

3.6 RSA versus Elgamal in blind decoding for on-line market

We discuss the gap between the RSA-based blind decoding and our ElGamal-based one in practical settings. As we mentioned at subsection 3.5, in the case of RSA-based scheme the correctness the decrypted message is checked by anybody with the encrypted message and the public key (self-verification property), whereas in our Elgamal-based blind decoding, Alice cannot verify the correctness of decrypted message by herself.

Then, in the case of RSA-based scheme, Bob can transfer Alice's certification, which is the encrypted message, on the decoded message to any third party as the ordinary digital signature schemes. On the other hand, our Elgamal-based scheme has no such property: even Alice publishes a pair of (encrypted message, decoded message), nobody can check the validity without Bob's help via interaction. The latter of our Elgamal-based scheme has a positive application to restrict illegal distribution of copyright on electronic documents. Note that the Chaum's undeniable signature [CvA89] has the same property as this non-transitivity.

4 Spotting the oracle

In the blind decoding, Bob applies his secret key to an arbitrary quantity X that is supplied to him without any authentication. If Alice is honest, the quantity X must be transformed from a decrypted message with Bob's secret key. However, a cheating Alice has a chance to get the Bob's secret-key operation on any message. Such a problem is generally discussed as an abuse of an oracle against himself [AN95].

A method of overcoming this abuse would be that Bob requests some authentication on Alice's supplied message, though this solution sacrifices perfect undetectability against Bob in the blind decoding. We should note that perfect untraceability of blind signatures could allow perfect crime [vSN92].

Unfortunately, until now, the authors has no idea to solve the problem, "the abuse of an oracle against Bob versus undetectability against Bob," and finding an elegant solutuon is left as an open problem. Instead, the next section considers a positive aspect of this problem.

5 Blind undeniable signatures

The developed technique for blind decoding of the Elgamal encryption is also applicable to making Chaum's undeniable signatures [CvA89, CBDP91] blind agaist the signer.

Blind Signatures is originally introduced for publicly-verifiable signatures (e.g. RSA-based scheme) [Cha82], and is applied for untraceable payments. However, the previous works [CBDP91] mention nothing on blind-version of undeniable signatures, which is non-transitive.

The RSA-based blind signature is used to achive untraceability in an *off*-line ditigal-cash system, while the Elgamal-based blind undeniable signature is applicable in an ON-line electoronic money system, where the verification of the signature is executed in an interactive matter. A concrete e-money system based on the blind undeniable signature is described in the final version of this paper.

6 Concluding remarks

This paper considered a cryptographic concept, blind decoding, which is the encryption-version of the widely-known blind signature scheme Especially, this paper newly proposed a blind decoding protocol for ElGamal encryption scheme. Thus, we construct a fair cryptosystems with making trustees oblivious [Mic92] by using the sole cryptographic assumption of hardness of the discrete logarithm problem.

Moreover, we clarified that the ElGamal-based blind decoding has an advantage over the RSA-based blind decoding in the application to protecting copyright matter of electronic documents. We also remarked that our technique of the ElGamal-based blind decoding is applicable to making a undeniable sinature scheme blind.

A future topic is to develop several applications of blind decoding and blind undeniable signatures into digital money, electronic voting, etc. for protecting privacy.

Acknowledgment

The authors would like to thank Ross Anderson for his comment on the spotting problem of the oracle in blind decoding, which leads the authors to attention the blind-version of the undeniable signature.

References

[AFK89] M.Abadi, J.Feigenbaum, and J.Kilian, "On hiding information from an oracle," JCSS 39, pp.21-50 (1989).

[AN95] R.Anderson and R.Needham, "Robustness principles for public key protocols," Advances in Cryptology-CRYPTO '95, LNCS 963, pp.236-247 (1995).

[CBDP91] D. Chaum, J Boyar, I.Damgaard, and T.Pedersen, "Undeniable signatures: applications and theory," Technical Report (1991).

[Cha82] D. Chaum, "Blind Signatures for untraceable payments," Advances in Cryptology Proceedings of Crypto '82, pp. 199-203 (1983).

[CP92] D. Chaum and T. Pedersen, "Wallet Databeses with Observers," Advances in Cryptology, CRYPTO'92, pp. 89-105 (1993).

[CvA89] D. Chaum, H. van Antwerpen, "Undeniable Signatures," Advances in Cryptology-CRYPTO '89, pp.212-216 (1990)

[CPS94] J. L. Carmenisch, J. -M. Piveteau, M. A. Stadler, "Blind signature schemes based on the discrete logarithm problem", Proc. of Eurocrypt '94, pp.428-432 (1995).

[DH76] Diffie, W. and M. E. Hellman, "New directions in cryptography," IEEE Trans. Inform. Theory, IT-22, No.6, pp.644-654, (Nov. 1976).

[ElG85] T.ElGamal, "A public key cryptsystem and a signature scheme based on discrete logarithms" IEEE Trans. on IT, **31**, pp.469-472 (1985).

[Kob87a] Neal Koblitz, "Elliptic curve cryptosystems," Math. Comp., vol.48, No.177, pp.203-209 (1987).

[Kob87b] Neal Koblitz, "A Course in Number Theory and Cryptography," GTM114, Springer-Verlag, New York (1987).

[Mil85] Victor S. Miller, "Use of elliptic curves in cryptography," CRYPTO'85, pp.417-426.

[Mic92] Silvio Micali, "Fair public key cryptosystems," Proc. Crypto '92, pp.113-138 (1993).

[Riv90] Rivest, R. L., "Cryptography," Chapter 13 of Handbook of Theoretical Computer Science, Vol.A, Algorithms and Complexity, edited by Jan van Leeuwen, *The MIT*, pp.717-755 (1990).

[RSA78] R.L.Rivest, A.Shamir, and L.Adleman, "A method for obtaining digital signatures and public key cryptosystems," *Comm. ACM*, **21**, pp.120-126 (1978).

[SRA79] A.Shamir, L.Rivest, and L.Adleman, "Mental Poker," MIT/LCS, TM-125 (1979)

[vSN92] S. von Solms and D. Naccache, "On blind signatures and perfect crimes," Computers and Security. Vol.11, No.6.

Practical Invisibility in Digital Communication[*]

Tuomas Aura

Helsinki University of Technology
Digital Systems Laboratory
FIN-02150 Espoo, Finland
Email: Tuomas.Aura@hut.fi

Abstract. This paper gives an overview of cryptographically strong mass application invisibility in digital communication. It summarizes principles and methodology, clarifies terminology, and defines some new concepts. A new algorithm for hiding bit selection in digital images is proposed and an experimental implementation of the algorithm is described. Finally, the paper closes with a discussion of the implications of the availability of invisible communication.

Keywords. Information hiding, invisibility, hiding bit selection in random access covers, pseudorandom permutation.

1 Introduction

The aim of encryption is to conceal the contents of secret messages. *Invisibility* goes yet further, it attempts to hide the fact that any messages even exist. The secret messages are hidden in ostensibly harmless data (*cover*) that can be casually stored and communicated without raising suspicion. While the designers of encryption algorithms assume that a resourceful enemy will do anything to decrypt the messages, the designer of an invisibility algorithm takes it granted that an enemy will try to reveal the existence of the secret message. Invisibility algorithms should be based on principles not unlike those of the encryption algorithms:

- Messages are hidden using a public algorithm and a secret key.

- Only a holder of the correct key can detect, extract or prove to a third party the existence of the hidden messages. Nobody else should be able to find any statistically significant evidence of their existence.

- Even if the enemy knows or is able to select the contents of the hidden messages, this should be no advantage in detecting other hidden messages.

---

[*] An early version of this paper was presented at the HUT Seminar on Network Security in November 1995 [1].

– The algorithm must be cryptographically strong. That is, it is theoretically impossible or computationally infeasible to detect hidden messages.

There are several well-known methods for hiding secret messages in digital signatures and other well defined but scarce components of digital communication. In this paper, we look at similar techniques for bulk data, photographs and audio and video signals that are routinely transfered in large quantities. There are few references to such algorithms in literature, but a body of knowledge exists in the cryptographic community. Our goal is to survey the methods that are best suited for mass application, and to present a new algorithm.

In Section 2 we will overview hiding techniques and related terminology. Sec. 3 will go deeper into the the kinds of data that can have secrets hidden into it and the hiding algorithms. In Sec. 4 we present a practical algorithm for hiding data in digitized images. This is the main contribution of the paper. Sec. 5 briefly describes an implementation of the algorithm. We conclude with a brief discussion of the implications of the technology on organizations and society in Sec. 6.

2   Hiding data in digital communication

Practical invisibility algorithms are based on replacing a noise component of a digital message with a pseudorandom (usually encrypted) secret message. We call the noisy message *cover* and the bits carrying the noise *cover bits*. The bits of the pseudorandom secret message are *secret bits*. The cover bits actually substituted with the secret bits will be called *hiding bits*. We call this kind of a system *substitution method* of invisibility.

The cover data must be sufficiently noisy in order for a slight increase in its randomness not to be noticeable. The cover bits are typically the least significant bits (LSBs) of some inexact values. These can be results of a series of measurements. A digitized image or a sound track is, in fact, a huge array of measurement results, all with a significant random error component. The hiding bits can also be coded in the cover in more complicated ways than simply by replacing the LSBs. For instance, [3] describes how to find the least significant differences between data values in a palette colored image.

The least significant bits can, although they are noise from a measurement accuracy viewpoint, have some special statistical characteristics. Fig. 1 shows how the run lengths of LSBs in a signal from a low quality digital video camera differ from those in purely random noise. It has been often suggested that the encoding of the secret message should mimic the characteristics of the cover bits, a goal not easily achieved. One possibility is to generate a large number of alternative cover messages all in the same way and to choose one that happens to have the secret code in it. This is called *selection method* of invisibility. For example, we can digitize the same photograph again and again, every time producing a slightly different digital image. These images are then reduced with a message digest algorithm to, say, 8 bit numbers. If we want to hide an eight bit number, we pick the first scanner file that incidentally produces the particular number as a digest. This image has exactly the statistical properties that any other digitized image has. Selection invisibility can be viewed as the ultimately secure method, tantamount to one-time pad in encryption. The only problem with this approach is that, even if optimally organized, it can hide only small quantities of data with lots of work.

Another approach is to model the characteristics of the cover bit noise. A mimic function should be built that not only encodes the secret message, but also respects the model of the original noise. In the extreme case, the entire message is constructed according to the model. We call this *constructive* invisibility. The strategy has inherent dangers. Modelling the noise or an error component in data is not easy. Building the model requires significant effort, creative work to be done again for every communication channel or cover data source. It is likely that someone with greater resources and more time will be able to develop a better model of the noise and still differentiate between the original signal and the replacement. Furthermore, the patterns created by the model may reveal the secret message instead of increasing security. If the adversary knows the model, he can with little investment find flaws in it. The model of the noise is a part of the hiding algorithm and keeping the algorithm secret is in violation of good cryptographic practices as it is likely to leak to the hands of the unfriendly in any case.

Since attempts at mimicking the original noise either result in questionable security or far too low bandwidth for most applications, it is best to go back to the basic substitution procedure. Select a class of sufficiently noisy messages, cover messages, and identify the bits that carry the noise, cover bits. Then, approximate how large portion of the cover bits can be replaced with pseudorandom data without significantly changing the characteristics of the cover.

For instance, if the cover message is a digitized photograph, the cover bits are naturally the least significant bits of the grayscale or RGB values, or the Fourier coefficients in a JPEG compressed image. One might want

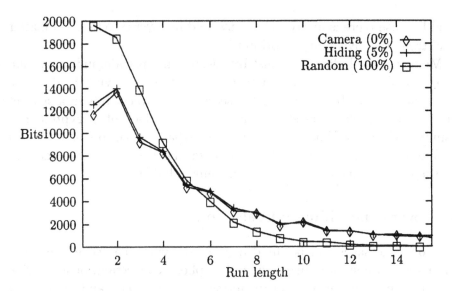

Fig. 1. Deviation of bits to runs of consecutive 0s or 1s.

to play safe and alter only every 100th pixel of the image. In that case, a one megabyte uncompressed image can hide about one kilobyte of secret data. In Fig. 1 we see that replacing as much as 5 % of the LSBs with pseudorandom bits does not significantly change the run length distribution. On the other hand, it is obvious that the popular practice of simply replacing all LSBs with secret bits is no option for serious cryptographers. As a consequence, secure invisibility inevitably depends on covers being at disposal in quantities.

The secret message should be encrypted with a strong cryptographic algorithm in order for it to look like random data. Substituting pseudorandom bits for a few of the noisiest bits of the cover will only slightly increase its noise level. On the other hand, inserting bits of a plaintext could drastically change the character of the cover. In theory, encryption is not essential to security if the invisibility algorithm is reliable. The pseudorandomness of the secret message could be achieved in other ways such as effective compression. The random permutation method presented in Sec. 4 does not even require pseudorandom secret bits, only ones with equal frequency of zeros and ones. In any case, we suggest that it is a good idea to both compress and encrypt the secret message before hiding. Compression decreases the number of secret bits thus improving security, and strong encryption will protect the contents of the secret message even if the much less mature invisibility techniques fail. This should be kept in mind because there is always a risk involved in cover selection, no matter how strong the invisibility algorithm is.

Moreover, the hiding bits must be selected in a pseudorandom fashion as a function of a secret key. Otherwise, an enemy having hold of the algorithm will be able to extract the secret bits. If these bits in a suspect message are completely random looking, as the products of encryption, but a similar selection of bits in another message has a some sort of statistical deviation different from purely random data, the enemy can conclude that the suspected image most probably contains a hidden data.

3 Covers and hiding bit selection

The cover messages can be divided into two types. The cover can be a continuous data stream, like a digital telephone connection, or a file, like a single bitmap image. We call the former a *stream cover* and the latter a *random access cover*.

In a stream cover, it may not be possible to tell in advance when the cover message begins, when it ends, or how long it will be. The cover may be continuous or very long, so that several secret messages need to be hidden in the same cover message. Furthermore, one may not know in advance what the next bits of the cover will be, but the secret message has to be inserted into the stream as it is transmitted, before the next bits of the stream have even been produced. The hiding bits have to be selected with a keystream generator that gives the distance between consecutive bits in the stream [6]. We call this *random interval method* of hiding bit selection.

In a continuous data stream, it is difficult for the receiver to tell when a hidden message begins. There can be no visible (or audible) synchronization sequence. Still, the receiver has to synchronize its keystream generator with the hidden message in order to pick the correct hiding bits from the stream. If the data stream has some inherent synchronization signals or packet boundaries, the hidden message should start right after one of them. The receiver will then try to synchronize its random number generator to the hidden message after those points. Usually, only garbage is found, but at times, an encrypted secret message is revealed. In the easiest case, if the data stream is of a finite length and reopened often, like telephone conversations, the secret message may always start at the opening of the session. For the sender, it may be a problem if he cannot trust the cover stream to be long enough for the entire secret message. With stream covers, it is also difficult to evenly spread the hiding bits all over the cover.

Invisibility in stream covers has a close relation to spread spectrum techniques, where the message is spread pseudorandomly over a large bandwidth. Spread spectrum communication is used mostly because of its resistance to interference and jamming but the same techniques can be used to hide that there is any communication at all [2].

Fixed length files as cover messages do not have the same disadvantages as stream covers. The sender knows in advance the size of the file and its contents. The hiding bits can be evenly selected with a suitable pseudorandom selection function from all parts of the message. Random access to the cover bits can be utilized to achieve this. Because of the random access, it is not necessary to insert the secret bits into the hiding bits in any particular order. For example, header info can be written after the secret message, whereas in a stream cover, the header has to be sent first. The main drawback of random access covers is that the cover size is often much shorter than a data stream, and it cannot easily be adjusted to fit the needs.

Despite us not giving much value to statistical models of cover noise above, they may still be helpful in detecting abnormally bad covers. Since random access covers are known in full before they are chosen for data hiding, good covers can be selected. For instance, in a series of digitized images well fit for hiding, there might be some that are completely black, not so noisy etc. These should be recognized and discarded. If covers are produced automatically in large quantities, statistical tests or visual inspection should be applied to ensure their quality before sending.

It should be noted that the the random interval method is not especially well suited for a hiding bit selection in random access covers. First of all, even distribution of hiding bits is only achieved probabilistically. That is, one cannot know in advance if all the secret bits will fit in the cover. Therefore, one has to play safe and make the average interval between bits so short that they will be all written before the file ends. Normally, the secret message will end far before the end of the message. It is then necessary to pad the secret message with random bits in order to cause an equal change in randomness in the beginning and end of the cover. Another disadvantage is that the distances between hiding bits are uniformly distributed between the shortest and longest allowed distances, while true random noise would have exponential distribution of interval lengths. It is, of course, possible to generate pseudorandom exponentially distributed numbers but this is usually too laborious. It is debatable whether the difference between exponential and uniform distribution of interval lengths will make any difference in the statistical characteristics of a noisy cover message. We tested the effect on run lengths in digital image data. When the hiding bit density is low enough compared to the run lengths, so that at most one bit in any run is likely to be altered, there is no difference in the resulting run length distribution. There are, however, other selection functions for random access covers that both escape the question of secret message padding and produce a random distribution of hiding bits: pseudorandom permutation functions. These will be discussed in detail in Sec. 4.

An interesting alternative to simple replacement of pseudorandomly selected cover bits with secret bits is to alter the parity of bit sequences. In a stream cover, the length of the next bit sequence is determined with a keystream generator, and in random access cover, a set of bits is picked with a selection function. If the parity of the selected bits is not the same as the next secret bit, the parity is changed by flipping any bit in the set. The bit to be altered can be chosen to cause minimum deviation from the original statistical characteristics of the cover. This approach has the same disadvantage as the constructive invisibility systems. Namely, the model according to which the choice of the altered bit is made may not be good enough, and the enemy might detect the secret message by looking at the places where a bit is most likely to be altered. Still, we believe that the parity method can be as strong as any of the pseudorandom substitution strategies if the model-based choice of the altered bit is made only to avoid the worst cases of random selection.

4 A secret key algorithm for hiding bit selection in random access covers

In this section, we describe a secret key method for pseudorandom selection of the hiding bits. The basic idea is to use a *pseudorandom permutation* of the cover bits. We have no knowledge of any previous invisibility algorithm or program where the choice of hiding bits is based on pseudorandom permutations. Let N be the number of cover bits available and let P_0^N be a permutation of the numbers $\{0, \ldots, N-1\}$. Then, if we have a secret n-bit message to hide, we can simply insert the secret bits into the cover bits $P_0^N(0), P_0^N(1), \ldots, P_0^N(n-1)$. The permutation function must be pseudorandom, i.e. it has to select bits in an apparently random order. Consequently, the hiding bits will be evenly spread all over the cover bits. No padding of the secret message with random data or other trickery is needed to assure even spreading.

For our purposes, the permutation function also has to depend on a secret key K. Therefore, we need a *pseudorandom permutation generator* P^N, a function which for every parameter K (secret key) produces a different pseudorandom permutation of $\{0, \dots, N-1\}$. We denote by P_K^N the permutation generator instantiated with key K. If the permutation P_K^N is computationally secure, that is, nobody can guess or reason the permutation without having access to the secret key K, it is impossible for anyone to guess which cover bits were chosen for hiding bits.

A secure pseudorandom permutation generator can be efficiently built from a *pseudorandom function generator* [5]. A pseudorandom function generator is like a pseudorandom permutation generator in that it produces a different unpredictable function for each secret key value, but the range of the function does not need to equal the domain. A pseudorandom function generator is easily constructed from any secure hash function H, such as SHS, by concatenating the argument i with a secret key K and feeding the resulting bit string to H.

$$f_K(i) = H(K \circ i),$$

where $K \circ i$ is the concatenation of the bit strings K and i. The result $f_K(i)$ is a pseudorandom function of i that depends on the parameter K.

The pseudorandom permutation generator of Luby and Rackoff [5] is constructed as follows. $a \oplus b$ denotes the bit-by-bit exclusive or of a and b and the result has the same length as a. Let i be a binary string of length $2l$. Divide i in two parts, Y and X, of length l and the key K into four parts K_1, K_2, K_3 and K_4. Compute

$$Y = Y \oplus f_{K_1}(X);$$
$$X = X \oplus f_{K_2}(Y);$$
$$Y = Y \oplus f_{K_3}(X);$$
$$X = X \oplus f_{K_4}(Y);$$
$$\text{return } Y \circ X;$$

For every key value K, the algorithm gives a pseudorandom permutation of $\{0, \dots, 2^{2l}-1\}$. Luby and Rackoff show that the permutation is as secure as the pseudorandom function generator. They also give a similar algorithm for permutation of $\{0, \dots, 2^{2l+1} - 1\}$. If the values of the function f_K are long enough bit strings, the same effect could be achieved simply by letting Y be the l first bits of i and X be the last $l+1$ bits.

The above construction produces a permutation $P_K^{2^k}$ of $\{0, \dots, 2^k - 1\}$ for an arbitrary k. However, when the number of cover bits is N, we need a permutation P_K^N of $\{0, \ldots, N-1\}$. Our advantage here is that we can restrict ourselves to feeding arguments to P_K^N in the order $0, 1, 2, \ldots$. Let $k = \lceil log(N) \rceil$. Then, $2^{k-1} < N \leq 2^k$. Simply compute the values $P_K^{2^k}(0), P_K^{2^k}(1), P_K^{2^k}(2), \ldots$, discarding from the sequence any numbers above $N-1$, and take the remaining values for $P_K^N(0), P_K^N(1), P_K^N(2), \ldots$. This is feasible when the permutation function is evaluated for increasing argument values starting from 0, as in our case. Thus, a permutation generator P^N for arbitrary N can be constructed from the Luby-Rackoff algorithm.

However, when N is known to be composite, there is a more convenient way to construct the pseudorandom permutation generator. The following algorithm is based on a block cipher with arbitrary block size [4]. The number of cover bits has to be a composite number with two factors of almost equal size, that is, $N = x * y$ for some x and y. When data is being hidden in the least significant bits of a digitized photograph, the factors x and y are, naturally, the dimensions of the image. To get the index of the ith ($i \in \{0, \ldots, N-1\}$) hiding bit, compute

$$Y = i \text{ div } x;$$
$$X = i \bmod x;$$
$$Y = (Y + f_{K_1}(X)) \bmod y;$$
$$X = (X + f_{K_2}(Y)) \bmod x;$$
$$Y = (Y + f_{K_3}(X)) \bmod y;$$
$$\text{return } Y * x + X;$$

The two first rounds of the algorithm are needed for even spreading of hiding bits amongst the cover bits. Figure 2 illustrates how the first round randomizes the Y-coordinates of the hiding pixels and the second round randomizes the X-coordinates. The third round is necessary because of a chosen plaintext attack. With only two rounds, let $i = B * x + A$ and let $P_K^N(i)$ be the permuted value. If the cryptanalyst can guess A and can obtain a plaintext–ciphertext pair $(i' = C * x + A, P_K^N(i'))$ for some C, he is able to deduce B. Even though we believe the algorithm to be secure with three rounds, it may well be that adding a fourth round would still significantly increase strength of the algorithm, at least when employed as a cipher.

Example. Assume that we have a grayscale image of size 800×600, an encrypted secret message of 1 kilobytes and a key $123, 456, 789$. We want to hide the secret message to the least significant bits of the image. $x = 800$,

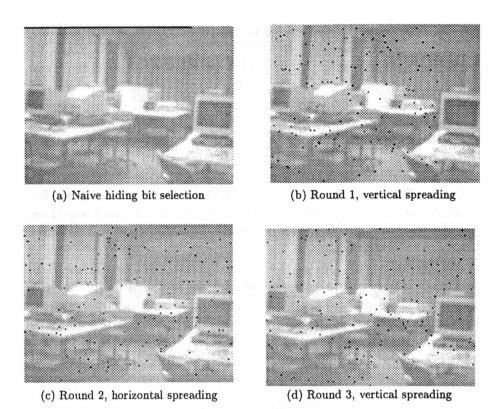

(a) Naive hiding bit selection

(b) Round 1, vertical spreading

(c) Round 2, horizontal spreading

(d) Round 3, vertical spreading

Fig. 2. Spreading the hiding bits evenly all over the image

$y = 600$, and the number of cover bits equals the number of pixels in the image, $N = 800 \cdot 600 = 480000$. There are $1024 \cdot 8 = 8096$ secret bits. Less than 1 % of the pixels will be altered. The hiding pixels are selected with the above algorithm, starting from secret bit number 0. We now show how to compute the hiding pixel for the 1001st secret bit. (The values of the secure hash function H have been arbitrarily chosen.)

$$Y = 1001 \text{ div } 800 = 1,$$
$$X = 1001 \bmod 800 = 201,$$
$$Y = (1 + H(123 \circ 201)) \bmod 600 = (1 + 7377) \bmod 600 = 178,$$
$$X = (201 + H(456 \circ 178)) \bmod 800 = (201 + 3854) \bmod 800 = 55,$$
$$Y = (178 + H(789 \circ 55)) \bmod 600 = (178 + 1124) \bmod 600 = 102.$$

The result is $102 * 800 + 55$, meaning that the 1001th secret bit is inserted into the least significant bit of the cover pixel whose x-coordinate is 102 and y-coordinate 55.

This procedure for selecting the hiding bits is best in accord with digitized photographs as covers. In other file types, such as audio files, the number of cover bits may not always have a suitable factorization. Then, one is forced to go back to the previously described system of discarding some of the permutation function values.

In addition to a reasonable noise level, the algorithm makes some assumptions about the covers. *The same cover message must never be used again. The original cover file must be completely destroyed.* With two differing copies of the file, it is easy to see which bits are the hiding bits. This makes it plain and clear to the enemy that messages are being hidden. It would be best if the original cover message is never saved anywhere, but the secret message is inserted immediately after the cover has been produced.

Another question arises when the algorithm is applied in practice. If the secret key and cover size remain unchanged, the hiding bits will always be the same. Obviously, the same key should never be used for more than very few images. Fortunately, one can get around this problem by making the key dependent on the cover message. Let K_u be the secret key of the user and H' a random function on the user keys and cover messages that does not change when the hiding bits are altered. Then, take the key K to be

$$K = H'(K_u \circ cover).$$

The function H' has to depend so heavily on the cover that two different covers will not produce the same value, but it has to be independent of the choice and contents of the hiding bits. For example, in a bitmap image where the cover bits are the least significant bits, the function H' can be a message digest of the user key and the image after all LSBs are set to zero. It is extremely unlikely that there will ever be two digitized images only differing in the LSBs. By making the key K a function of the cover, the same user key K_u can be used for as many covers as needed. The same key cannot, of course, used again for the same cover, since the covers must never be reused.

One more practical concern is that the secret message length must be short compared to the cover size. What is the maximum ratio of secret message size to the cover size, remains to be determined separately for each cover source and application. We do advice to choose covers that are so abundant that there is not reason to exploit more than a few percent of the cover bits for hiding.

The strength of an invisibility algorithm will always depend heavily on the properties of the cover. If we select cover bits with a random error component and keep the hiding bits to cover bits ratio low, the security of the presented algorithm depends on the random function f_K being computationally secure. We are rather safe here since the pseudorandom nature of the secret message makes a brute force attack infeasible: The enemy would be trying to identify a pseudorandom bit sequence, but almost any choice of a key will give one. What the attacker can do is to erase the hidden message by adding his own noise to the cover. It is not even necessary to erase all random bits but only alter some of them, and the encrypted secret message cannot be recovered.

5 An experimental implementation

The algorithm of Sec. 4 was implemented to hide files in PGM grayscale bitmap images. The reasons for the choice are that the PGM is a widely accepted standard format that is easily converted to other non-lossy compression image formats. Masses of grayscale images are at hand, for instance, from surveillance cameras. Nonetheless, there is no reason why the algorithm could not be implemented on other file formats or color images.

The least significant bits were chosen as the cover bits. The secret message is encrypted with the IDEA cipher to make it pseudorandom. f_K is constructed from the secure hash function SHS. An SHS message digest is computed on the user key and the 7 most significant bits of the image. The digest is used as the encryption and hiding key K.

A magic number, and the name and length of the secret file are hidden along the secret message. It is important to note that they all are encrypted and hidden into the cover bits the same way as the secret message itself. The secret key is needed for extraction and decryption. If the secret message is short in comparison to the image size, it is impossible to detect or prove the existence of the secret message without the key.

An advantage of our algorithm in comparison to the random interval method is that it is very easy to implement. A disadvantage is the speed. The algorithm requires three evaluations of a random function per hidden bit, while the random interval method manages with one. SHS with its 160 bit range is not an optimal choice for the random function since only around 10 bits are needed. Computational costs of the algorithm are hidden in the random function, it being thus the most promising part for further optimization. Nevertheless, the implementation of the algorithm proved to be efficient enough for interactive hiding of data into persistent image files. It is questionable whether the speed is sufficient for on-the-fly hiding in a stream of images. As expected, the hiding does not change the visual appearance of digital photographs at all. When only a few percent of the image pixels were utilized for hiding, the run length distribution of the LSBs did not change significantly in comparison to the natural variation between images. The assumption that more advanced statistical methods cannot spot the hidden data remains to be tested.

6 Conclusions and discussion of the implications of invisibility

We have given an overview of mass application invisibility and proposed a new method for pseudorandom hiding bit selection in random access covers. An experimental implementation of the algorithm on grayscale images was described. All along, we have stressed cryptographic strength of the invisibility techniques. Apart from optimization of the algorithms, future research should concentrate on statistical methods for detecting the increased noise in real covers. A concrete measure would be needed for how much data it is safe to hide in a given cover. We still need to make some conclusions on how the described technology can be applied and what kind of effect it has on the society.

The availability to effective data hiding has serious practical implications. Any type of information can be saved and transfered invisibly where there is a sufficient storage or flow of noisy digital data. The most common types of data transfered in volumes, digital audio and video signals and digital image files, are exactly the ones most apt for hiding secret messages.

The establishments that are perhaps most dramatically affected by the danger of uncontrollable information flows are military organizations. Military security is traditionally based on keeping secret or confidential data in physically controlled locations, so that even the trusted personnel cannot move anything more than they can memorize over the physical boundaries. Special rules have been established for reviewing and formally downgrading data before it can be moved to a lower security area. The possibility of automatically hiding confidential documents in unclassified data flows presents a new challenge to the military information infrastructure. These organizations must, nevertheless, take full advantage of new information technology. On the bright side, information hiding can be utilized to frustrate traffic flow analysis attacks.

The inability to control the types of data transfered also has a profound influence on the commercial communications service providers. It would be in the interest of telecom operators to charge an optimum price for all different types of data. Bulk rates would apply when data is transfered in large quantities, as in video conferencing. Low bandwidth communication, such as electronic mail, would be more expensive per bit. It is, however, impossible to differentiate between the forms of communication. Where digital video is regularly transmitted, any amounts of mail can be hidden into the signal. This implies that the pricing of communication resources has to be based on bandwidth, and availability and reliability of the service, not the types of data transfered.

Probably the most controversial issue about widely available secure communications is that the same technology can be employed for legally and morally questionable purposes. It has been claimed, for example, that free application of cryptography enables drug traffickers and terrorists to communicate in secret, without the law enforcement officials being able to intercept their messages. In some countries, strong encryption has been banned or the keys have to be escrowed for government officials. With invisibility readily available to anyone with moderate programming skills, it is obvious that any such measures are ineffective. Restrictions on encryption cannot stop criminals from using it, but only hurt the law-abiding businesses and individuals who would greatly benefit from mass application of cryptographic techniques.

References

1. Tuomas Aura. Invisible communication. In *Proceedings of the HUT Seminar on Network Security '95*, Espoo, Finland, November 1995. Telecommunications Software and Multimedia laboratory, Helsinki University of Technology.
2. Hannes Federrath and Jürgen Thees. Schutz der Vertraulichkeit des Aufenhaltsorts von Mobilfunkteilnehmern. *Datenschutz und Datensicherung*, (6):338–348, June 1995.
3. Maxwell T. Sandford II, Jonathan N. Bradley, and Theodore G. Handel. The data embedding method. In *Proceedings of the SPIE Photonics East Conference*, Philadelphia, September 1995.
4. Paul C. Kocher. Personal communication, October 1995.
5. Michael Luby and Charles Rackoff. How to construct pseudorandom permutations from pseudorandom functions. *SIAM Journal on Computing*, 17(2):373–386, April 1988.
6. Steffen Möller, Andreas Pfitzmann, and Ingo Stierand. Rechnergstützte Steganographie: Wie sie funktioniert und warum folglich jede Reglementierung von Verschlüsselung unsinnig ist. *Dateschutz und Datensicherung*, (6):318–326, June 1994.

Other sources are the steganography mailing list archive at http://www.thur.de/ulf/stegano/ and documentation and source files of several invisibility programs. Kaisa Nyberg made some helpful comments on the session key generation.

Fractal Based Image Steganography

Paul Davern
Dept of Computer Science,
Carlow Regional Techical College,
Carlow,
Ireland.
davern@rtc-carlow.ie

Dr. Michael Scott,
Department of Computer Applications,
Dublin City University,
Glasnevin,
Dublin.
75001969@vax1.dcu.ie

Abstract

This paper describes a new and novel steganographic method for inserting secret information into image files. The method uses fractal image compression techniques in the production of these steganographic image files. The method allows a user to specify a visual key when hiding the secret information. The visual key must then be used when retrieving the hidden data. The paper describes enhancements to the method which may enable the steganographic data to survive through normal processing which reduces image quality. The method may therefore be used to insert copyright labels into image files.

1. Introduction

Steganography[1] is an old science, but its application in computer based methods is new. Computer based steganography is usually based on randomness. There are many occurrences of randomness in computer based information. Steganographic data can be hidden into this random information. The merits of a steganographic method are judged on whether the addition of the steganographic data changes the randomness.

Images files are good examples of random data for the following reasons:-

- The data in images files represents a set of pixels which when displayed on a computer system give an approximation to a particular image.
- Image files are made up of portions that are visually constant. For example, in a scanned picture of a person, parts of the person's face may look visually constant. But the pixel values representing these parts are not normally constant.
- An image file usually contains a random spread of noise.

Most of the image based steganographic methods[2] we investigated exploit the random spread of noise over an image as a means to data hiding. The method described in this paper exploits the visually constant parts of an image as a means to data hiding[3].

Multimedia documents are very easy to copy and distribute in an illicit manner[4]. So publishers of such documents are reluctant to provide electronic distribution of much useful information on media such as CD-ROMs. Copyright labelling[5] [6]is a process which may help to reduce the illicit copying of multimedia documents. Labelled multimedia documents[7] [8]contain a code which identifies the owner of the document. If a labelled multimedia document is illicitly copied the copy will also contain the label. The method described in this paper can be used as one such method of image copyright labelling. Ideally the label should be robust enough to withstand normal image processing activities which do not significantly alter the images appearance or affect its value. For example image compression, transforming to a different format etc.

2. Introduction to the Method

- The method takes as input an image file and the steganographic data and produces a new image file that contains the steganographic data. The output image file is called the steganographic image file and it is similar to the input image file.
- Fractal image compression[9] techniques were chosen as a basis for the method.
- Fractal image compression techniques naturally identify parts of the image that are most suited for data hiding.
- The Fractal image compression process splits the image into blocks. Blocks that are visually similar are identified.
- One bit of steganographic data is hidden by
  1. Transforming one similar block into an approximation for another.
  2. Storing the approximation in position of the original block in the steganographic image file.
- The transforming block is random and so the transformed block is also random. The pixels themselves have not changed in randomness. The relationship between pixels in the steganographic image file have changed.
- The idea of a visual key naturally evolved from the method. The image is split into two regions. Blocks in one region are modified as described above. Blocks from the other region are used in the comparison process. The user selects the position of each region in the image by moving bounding boxes over the image. When retrieving the steganographic label the user would have to specify the correct two regions.
- Multiple steganographic labels may be hidden in the same image. Giving the ability to store bogus messages.
- The steganographic label can be encrypted before being hidden. The encryption key could be stored in another part of the image.

- The steganographic data can survive image processing by including error detection and correcting into the retrieval process. This idea needs to be further investigated.
- As far as we are aware this is the first time an attempt has been made to apply steganography to fractal image compression.
- Because fractal image compression techniques have been applied to moving pictures our steganographic method can also exploit this medium.
- Section 3 describes an implementation of the algorithm. The implementation is not complete and was intended as a proof of concept.

The objective in fractal image compression is to find parts of an image that match one another. The matching process involves finding a transformation which maps a portion of the image to a smaller portion. The output of the fractal image compression process is a set of these transformations. Fractal image decompression takes as input a set of transformations, any start image and yields an image which is an approximation to the original. A Fractal[10] is a set of transformations which when applied to any image always yield the same output image. The output image is known as an *attractor*[11].

3. The Steganographic Algorithm

In this section we discuss our algorithm which is specific to the the B-Tree fractal image compression method. However almost any of fractal image compression methods[12] could have been used.

3.1 The hiding steganographic data algorithm

- The image file is copied to produce a new image file which we refer to as the steganographic image file.
- The user graphically selects two non-overlapping areas of the image. One is known as the range region the other is known as the domain region. These areas of the image form the visual key. We refer to sub-images within the range region as range blocks. We refer to sub-images within the domain region as domain blocks.
- Blocks in the range region are modified. Blocks in the domain region are used in modifying the range blocks.
- We refer to the set of domain blocks as the domain library.
- A domain library[13] is build from a set of blocks in the domain region. The domain library is split into two halves.
- Fractal image compression theory is used to identify a random series of range blocks and a corresponding series of matching domain blocks[14]. The matching process produces for each range block the best matching domain block and a

corresponding fractal transform. We may be unable to find a good match for some domain blocks.

- The algorithm selects the domain block if any that produces a new range block which is most visually like the original range block.
- If the current bit of steganographic data is a 0. We search for a match in the first half of the domain library. Otherwise we search the second half.
- The algorithm selects a random range block and then for each domain block in the selected half of the domain library determines a fractal transform.
- The fractal transform basically involves multiplying a pixel in the selected domain block by an average scaling factor and adding an offset factor to the result. This calculation produces a corresponding pixel in the range block. The pixel value stored is an integer approximation.
- The fractal transform is applied to the domain block to produce a new range block that is visually like the original range block. This new block is written to the steganographic image in place of the old range block.
- Hiding the steganographic data involves producing a new range block in the manner described for each bit of steganographic data.

3.2 The retrieving steganographic data algorithm

- The retrieving steganographic data algorithm is the reverse of the hiding.
- In retrieving the user specifies the position of the range and the domain regions. These form the visual key.
- The domain library is build from a set of blocks in the domain region. The domain library is split into two halves.
- To find a bit of steganographic data in the steganographic image file we select a range block from the range region in the same order as in the hiding algorithm and find a corresponding domain block that matches it by a linear relationship.
- The linear relationship is that each pixel in the range block is formed by multiplying the corresponding pixel in the domain block by a scale factor and adding an offset factor.
- We cannot used fractal image compression techniques for the match as the relationship between the two blocks is a linear one. If we used fractal image compression techniques they would yield some blocks that are similar but have not been used in data hiding.
- The match is successful if we can find this linear relationship between the two blocks.
- Error factors have to be included to allow for the fact that an integer approximation is stored for each pixel in the range block.
- Error factors also have to be included for any introduced noise in the steganographic image file.

- The criterion of a match between a range block and a domain block is so simple that even in a very noisy environment it should be possible to determine if a match exists between two such blocks.

3.3 Implementation

The algorithm has been implemented based on the following assumptions and the results are presented in the next section.

- We have a square grey scale image of size 256x256.
- That each byte in the image data represents a pixel whose level of grey is from 0 to 255.
- The hiding algorithm builds a new range block from the domain block. When applying scaling and offset factors to pixels of the domain block to build a new range block:-
  - We calculate new scaling and offset factors which are based on producing an integer result in one of the first p pixels in the range block.
  - We apply these new scaling and offset factors to the rest of the pixels in the domain block and produce corresponding pixels in the range block.
- When retrieving steganographic data we need to determining if a range and domain block match:-
  - We calculate potential scaling and offset factors from the first p pixels in the range and domain blocks.
  - We apply these scaling and offset factors to the rest of the pixels in the domain block and determine if a corresponding pixel exists in the range block.
- We have relaxed the error detection on retrieval. The implementation assumes an unmodified steganographic image file.

The hiding algorithm takes as input and image I and a set of steganographic data *steg*. The hiding algorithm outputs a visually identically image I_{new} that has the steganographic data hidden in it.

The unhiding algorithm takes as input an image I and outputs the steganographic data *steg*.

We select two square parts of the image. These parts can be at any location in the image. One part is used as a domain region the other is used as the range region. Let the range region be I_1 and the domain region be I_2.

Let R be the collection of useable range blocks represented by $\{r_0, r_1, ..., r_u\}$. The range blocks are non-overlapping. Each range block is a square sub-image. We determine R by partitioning I_l recursively using a quadtree partition until each range block is of a minimum size, for example 16x16. We now continue to partition I_l until all range blocks are of a maximum size, for example 4x4. During this process we add all range blocks of size 16x16 to size 4x4 to R.

A domain library[15] is build from a set of blocks in the domain region. These blocks are bigger than the range blocks. For example choose for the collection D of permissible domains all the sub-squares in I_2 of size 8x8, 16x16, 32x32, and 64x64. These domains are overlapping.

Let the domain library D be represented by the blocks $\{d_0, d_1, ..., d_t\}$. Where t is the number of blocks in the domain library. The domain library D is split into two halves $\{d_0, d_1, ..., d_{t/2}\}$ and $\{d_{(t/2)+1}, d_{(t/2)+2}, ..., d_t\}$. Let us call the first half of D D_0 and the second half of D D_1.

Let $\{x_0, x_1, ..., x_n\}$ represent the pixels in a range block. Let $\{y_0, y_1, ..., y_n\}$ represent the averaged pixel values in the corresponding domain block. The length of any side in a domain block is twice that of a range block therefore there are 4 times as many pixels in a domain block than there are in a range block. Therefore in matching we will take an average of 4 pixels in a domain block for each range block. We do the averaging so that in the domain block y_n is the last pixel value. Therefore the domain block and the range block have been made the same size. This is also a generalisation of the algorithm as is shown in section 6.3.

3.3.1 The add steganographic data algorithm

When hiding we use the Root Mean Square metric (RMS) to determine if the range matches a domain[16]. Using the RMS metric we seek to find a d_i whose pixel gray scale values most match the r_i. While calculating the RMS metric we also calculate an average scaling s and offset o factors. When these factors are applied to the pixels of the domain block they yield a new block r_{new} which looks like the original range block. We replace the original range block with r_{new}. See Appendix 1 for a definition of the RMS metric.

Each replacing of a range block by its equivalent new block allows us to hide 1 bit of the steganographic data. To allow the retrieving process determine that a particular range block has been changed, we modify s and o before applying them to the domain block. This modification allows the retrieving process recalculate s and o and so determine if a particular block has been modified.

Let the steganographic data *steg* be represented as a binary bit stream $\{b_0, b_1, ..., b_n\}$. Let n be the number of bits in the bit stream. We append a 0 byte to the end of the stream to indicate to the retrieving algorithm that the end of the steganographic data has been reached. This 0 byte is included in the calculation of n. Let *CurrentBit* be the current bit in the stream. We realise that the use of the 0 byte only allows us store ASCII data. We would have to use two size bytes at the start of the steganographic data to enable the hiding of encrypted data.

Let the predetermined tolerance RMS value be E.

We use a set of selected range blocks represented by *SelectedRanges* which is initially the empty set { }. The hiding algorithm then randomly selects a range block r_i from R where r_i and any of its sub-blocks do not belong to *SelectedRanges*. We then add r_i and all its sub-blocks to *SelectedRanges*. For example if r_i is of size 8x8 it will be made up of 4 sub-blocks of size 4x4.

We now search for a match in one of the domain Libraries D_0 or D_1. If *CurrentBit* is 0 we search D_0 otherwise we search D_1. This search involves finding a corresponding domain block if any that has Root Mean Squared(RMS) value of the selected range block less than E. To make a successful match the range block is rotated so that its quadrants are placed into a predefined order. This order is associated with the brightness of the quadrants. There are eight rotations that can take place. These rotations increase the likelihood of a match between the range block and a domain block. Let us call the associated transformation matrix v_i .

If this search is successful then:- Let d_{RMSmin} represent the domain block that matches the range block r_i. We will be able to determine v_i, s_i, o_i for transforming d_{RMSmin} to r_i. We build a new block r_{new} by applying the transformations to the domain block d_{RMSmin} . Let $\{x_0 , x_1 ,...., x_n\}$ represent the pixels of r_{new}.

When we apply s_i and o_i to a pixel d_{RMSmin} they produce a real result. But we have to store an integer approximation to this real number in r_{new}. To allow the retrieving process determine that a particular range block has been changed, we modify s_i and o_i and we apply these new scaling and offset factors to the pixels in d_{RMSmin} which produces corresponding pixels in r_{new}. The calculation of these new scaling and offset factors s_{new} and o_{new} are based on producing an integer result in one of the first p pixels in the range block. (See Appendix 1 for the scaling and offset modification algorithm.)

We place r_{new} in the appropriate position in I_{new}. The produced block will not be visually effected by using the modified scaling and offset factors.

3.3.2   The Retrieve Steganographic Data Algorithm

Let the steganographic data *steg* be represented as a binary bit stream which is initially set to { }.

We use a set of selected range blocks represented by *SelectedRanges* which is initially the empty set { }. The retrieving algorithm then randomly selects a range block r_i from R where r_i and any of its sub-blocks do not belong to *SelectedRanges*. We then add r_i and all its sub-blocks to *SelectedRanges*. For example if r_i is of size 8x8 it will be made up of 4 sub-blocks of size 4x4.

We need to determine if the selected range block r_i has been replaced by a new block as described in the hiding algorithm. We search for a match in the domain library D. If a match occurs in D_0 we set *CurrentBit* to 0 otherwise if a match occurs in D_1 we set *CurrentBit* to 1.

We search through D and calculate possible scaling s and offset o factors for each domain block d_i. We apply these factors to each d_i and compare the results with the pixels of r_i. If the calculated pixels match the pixels of r_i then this range block has been modified by the hiding algorithm. We determine if d_i belongs to D_0 or D_1. We call this domain block d_{Found}. See Appendix 2 for details of the retrieval algorithm matching process.

The addition of error correction into the retrieval process is currently at an early stage. The matching of a domain block with a range block to a predefined error margin has been investigated. However the error correction methods used do not work in a highly noisy environment.

4. Results

Figure 1 shows an original bitmap girl.bmp and a new bitmap test.bmp. With the steganographic data *This is a test* hidden in test.bmp.

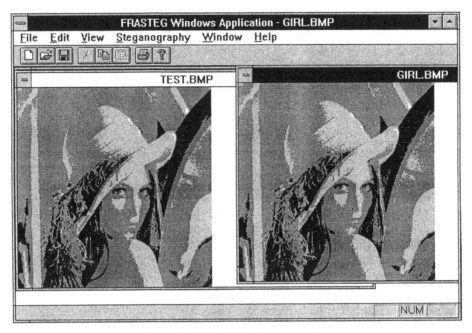

Figure 1. Girl with hidden data 1

The steganographic data has been hidden in the bottom left corner of the test.bmp. But as you can see the two bitmaps are virtually identical.

Figure 2 shows the pixel values in a portion of the original bitmap file (a) and the corresponding portion of the resulting bitmap file (b).

5e	49	79	39	**4a**	**50**	**51**	**5e**
82	7f	31	36	**36**	**48**	**4f**	**52**
76	2f	27	25	**2a**	**37**	**3e**	**4d**
2a	25	1e	24	**2a**	**32**	**3c**	**47**
31	**2c**	**2b**	**24**	**30**	**32**	**30**	**38**
27	**33**	**28**	**26**	**33**	**2d**	**31**	**31**
27	**25**	**25**	**2e**	**28**	**2e**	**3b**	**2e**
2d	**2b**	**2d**	**29**	**28**	**20**	**25**	**2c**

5e	49	79	39	**4f**	**56**	**5c**	**60**
82	7f	31	36	**3e**	**47**	**53**	**58**
76	2f	27	25	**2c**	**32**	**3d**	**4b**
2a	25	1e	24	**36**	**36**	**39**	**44**
2b	**29**	**29**	**29**	**31**	**31**	**34**	**33**
2a	**2c**	**2a**	**29**	**30**	**31**	**31**	**30**
2a	**2b**	**27**	**28**	**2e**	**30**	**30**	**2c**
2b	**2a**	**2a**	**29**	**26**	**22**	**23**	**25**

(a)   (b)

Figure2. Portion of image with steganographic data.

5. Conclusions

The conclusions that we have drawn as a result of testing the implementation of our algorithm are as follows:-

- The amount of data one can store is small. It is only possible to store one bit per range block. This can be increased if the tolerance level is relaxed. Some ranges cannot be covered when the tolerance is low. Increasing the tolerance level would allow us to use all range blocks in the range region given an increase in the amount of steganographic data that can be stored. However we would normally require the tolerance to be low in order to give an image that is visually close to the original and therefore does not have visual discrepancies.

  The range region cannot overlap the domain region. This restricts the amount of steganographic data that can be stored. However the bigger the range region is the more data that can be stored. But there has to be a compromise as to the size of the domain region. The smaller the domain region is the worse the quality of the produced image will be.

- The process of data hiding is slow. It depends on the amount of steganographic data and how high the tolerance is set. The time taken also depends very much on the size of the domain region. But the bigger the domain region the better the quality of the produced image. The data retrieving is even slower. This is because the comparison processes is more intensive. In data hiding we can determine the best orientation of the range block and then try for a match with this. However when retrieving the calculation of the orientation of a block can yield a differing position than was calculated in hiding. So all orientations have to be tried.
- The method as it stands is not robust against image processing that affects the visual quality of the image. For example lossy image compression applied to the steganographic bitmap would cause the steganaographic data to get corrupted. However section 6.6 discusses how to apply the method to image files and have the steganographic data survive image processing.

- The method is very successful in hiding steganographic data. The fractal image compression techniques used have identified the most suitable parts of the image for data hiding. The hidden data is totally innocuous in that the resulting changed parts of the image looks the same as any other part. A cryptanalyst would have to know that the method has been applied to a particular image to have any hope of retrieving the steganographic data. The next section describes enhancements to the method which make it more secure to attack. These enhancements provide more security even if a cryptanalyst knows the method has been applied to a particular image.

- Computer based steganography is becoming increasingly important in this era of world-wide communications. One of the major advantages of steganography is that it can easily be combined with traditional cryptographic methods. For example one could hide a DES encoded message into an image file. This would give two levels of security.

6. Further Developments.

In this section we list possible further developments to the data hiding method. The emphasis on these further developments make the data hiding more secure and robust. Some of these enhancements are already catered for in our algorithm but have not yet been implemented.

6.1 Other Range and Domain block Partitioning methods

This section describes a simple update to the algorithm in chapter 4. The data hiding algorithm would work in exactly the same way. It is only the underlying fractal method that changes. The use of a more sophisticated algorithm than quadtree could be used as the basis for the method. For example the H-V partitioning[17] of the image. In this algorithm rectangles are used as the basis for the range and domain blocks. A range block is recursively partitioned either horizontally or vertically to form two new rectangles. The decision to split horizontally or vertically is based on the context. The use of this algorithm as a basis for the data hiding method would make it even more difficult for a cryptanalyst to find the hidden data.

The triangular partition[18] scheme would yield even better results if used as the basis for the data hiding method. In this method the ranges are built by splitting the image into two triangles. Each of these triangles is recursively subdivided into four triangles. This process continues until a range can be covered by a domain. The domain blocks in the domain library are also triangular.

6.2 Selecting Domain and Range Regions

The method allows part of an image to be chosen as a range region and part to be chosen as the domain region. A user could then implement further protection on the steganographic data by selecting known parts of the image for range and domain regions. These regions would form a kind of key. This key is visual in that the user can select regions by moving bounding boxes over a displayed image.

For example it would be relatively easy to implement a system where by a user marks a square part of the image as the range region I_1 and another square part of the image as the domain region I_2 . The data hiding algorithm would then proceed as described in section 3. When retrieving the steganographic data one would have to specify the correct initial squares for the range and domain regions. There are many possible combinations here. For example in a 256×256 image with the range region being 32×32 and the domain region being 32×32. There are 225*225 = 50625 possible range regions of this size. The domain regions cannot overlap the range regions. Therefore in this case there are 193*193 = 37249 possible domain regions for each of the 50625 range regions. This yields a potential total of 1,885,730,625 possibilities.

However the domain region does not have to be the same size as the range region. Also the regions themselves don't have to be square. For example we could have a range region of size 21×43 and a domain region of 31×46. Therefore a cryptanalyst would have to try all domain and range regions of size say 32,33,34, and so on. In fact for a 256×256 size image there are 4,232,771,690,642 possible range and domain regions beginning at size 32.

6.3 Range and Domain block sizes

Within a range region of say size 64 we can choose to use ranges of size 4,8,16,32 or any combination of those sizes. The quadtree algorithm has domain blocks of twice the size as the domain region. The hiding algorithm would work for domain blocks smaller or bigger by various factors. For example domain blocks that are 1.5 times as big as the range blocks. All that is required is a consistent averaging function which brings the domain block size to that of the range region. It is even possible to have domain blocks that are say 0.5, 0.75,1.0,1.25,1.5 etc. times the size of the range blocks.

6.4 Distributed Blocks

It is possible to distribute a block throughout a region. This means that a block is made up a pseudo random set of pixels taken from different parts of the region. The only limitation required is that a pixel only belongs to one block. A range and domain block may be distributed.

If this scheme of things was implemented then it would yield an almost impossible amount of searches. The pseudo random pixel selector would have to choose pixels for a block that are reasonably close together in terms of pixel value.

6.5 Multiple messages in the same steganographic image file

It is possible to store multiple steganographic messages into the same image file. The only restriction is that the user would need to store the messages into different range regions. This facility could be used to hide bogus messages and so hide the real message from a cryptanalyst.

6.6 Robustness in Multimedia environments

The steganographic method can be used as a multimedia document label. However the algorithm would need to be modified to handle normal image processing which does not seriously reduce the quality of the image. The algorithm as described relies on the fact that bitmap with the steganographic data inside remains constant.

The retrieval algorithm is based on being able to determine the scaling and offset factors for a modified range block. The determination of close approximation to these factors is vital to the success of the current algorithm. However if for each comparison of a domain block to a range block:-

- We check corresponding pixels in each block and determine scaling and offset factors to an error margin.
- We then match the produced scaling and offset factors for each pixel to an error margin. If this comparison is within an error level then the match is deemed to be successful.

This whole area is currently being researched. The criterion for a match between a range block and a domain block is so simple that even in a very noisy environment it should be possible to determine if a match exists between two such blocks.

Appendix A   Hiding algorithm

A.1 Modification of scaling and offset factors.

- Applying v_i, s_i and o_i to $y_0 \in d_{RMSmin}$ and storing the result in $x_0 \in r_{new}$. Apply v_i, s_i and o_i to $y_i \in \{y_1, y_2,..,y_p\}$ producing $x_i \in \{x_1, x_2,..,x_p\}$ until $x_i \neq x_0$. If $x_i \in \{0,255\}$ we skip this pixel. Because in this case the real result has been rounded from a value that is greater than 255 or less than 0.

- If we cannot get a result different from x_0, d_{RMSmin} is unusable and we have to try another domain block.

- We now calculate s_{new} and o_{new} as follows:-

$$s_{new} = \frac{y_i - y_0}{x_i - x_0},$$

$$o_{new} = y_i - s_{new} x_i$$

where $y_i, y_0 \in d_{RMS\,min}$

and where $x_i, x_0 \in r_{new}$

- Apply v_i, s_{new} and o_{new} to $y_j \in \{y_i, y_{i+1}, .., y_n\}$ producing $x_j \in \{x_j, x_{j+1}, .., x_n\}$

- We now apply v_i, s_{new} and o_{new} to y_0 producing a new x_0.

- We now have to modify any $x_j \in \{x_1, x_2, ..., x_{i-1}\}$ such that $x_j \neq x_0$ and $x_j \notin \{0, 255\}$. This modification makes the $x_j = x_0$.

- We place r_{new} in the position of r_i in I_{new}.

A.2 The RMS metric.

Given two squares containing n pixel intensities $a_1, ..., a_n$ from d_i and $b_1, ..., b_n$ from r_i

$$d_{rms} = \sqrt{\frac{1}{n}\left[\sum_{i=1}^{n} b_i^2 + s\left(s \sum_{i=1}^{n} a_i^2 - 2 \sum_{i=1}^{n} a_i b_i + 2o \sum_{i=1}^{n} a_i\right) + o\left(no - 2 \sum_{i=1}^{n} b_i\right)\right]}$$

Where

$$s = \frac{\left[n \sum_{i=1}^{n} a_i b_i - \sum_{i=1}^{n} a_i \sum_{i=1}^{n} b_i\right]}{\left[n \sum_{i=1}^{n} a_i^2 - \left(\sum_{i=1}^{n} a_i\right)^2\right]}$$

and

$$o = \frac{1}{n}\left[\sum_{i=1}^{n} b_i - s \sum_{i=1}^{n} a_i\right]$$

Appendix B Retrieval algorithm.

B.1 The retrieval algorithm matching process.

$$\{x_0, x_1, x_2, ..., x_p, ..., x_n\} \in r_i$$

$$x_j \in \{x_1, x_2, ..., x_p\} \text{ and } x_0 \neq x_j$$

Then

$$s = \frac{y_i - y_0}{x_i - x_0}, \text{ where } y_i, y_0 \in d_{Found}$$

$$o = y_i - sx_i$$

Then

$$\forall x_i, x_j \in \{x_p, x_{p+1}, ..., x_n\}$$

$$\frac{y_i - y_j}{x_i - x_j}, y_i - sx_i$$

are constant

where $y_i, y_j \in d_{Found}$

The constant terms in the above equations are the scaling and offset factors that are used to transform a domain to a range in the hiding algorithm above. Each of the eight possible range block positions have to be tried in the above process.

References

[1] David Kahn, *The Codebreakers*, Macmillan Publishing, 1967

[2] netcom.com , /pub/qwerty, FTP site for reviewed image based steganographic software

[3] E. Koch, J. Zhao, *Embedding Robust Labels into Images for Copyright Protection*, Proc. of the International Congress on Intellectual Property Rights for Specialized Information, Vienna, Austria, Aug 1995

[4] J. Brassil, S.Low, N. Maxemchuk, *Electronic Marking and Identification Techniques to Discourage Document Copying*, AT&T Bell Labs, Murray Hill, NJ

[5] E. Koch, J. Rindfrey, J. Zhao, *Copyright Protection for Multimedia Data*, Proceedings of the International Conference on Digital Media and Electronic Publishing, Dec 1994, Leeds UK

[6] A. Choudhury, N. Maxemchuk, S. Paul, *Copyright Protection for Electronic Publishing over Computer Networks*, AT&T Bell Labs, June 1994

[7] E. Koch , J. Zhao, *Towards Robust and Hidden Image Copyright Labelling*, Proc. of 1995 Workshop on Nonlinear Signal and Image Processing,Neos Marmaras, Greece, June, 1995

[8] K. Matusi, K. Tanaka, *Video Steganography: How to secretly embed a signature in a picture*, IMA intellectual Property Project Proceedings, vol. 1, no. 1,1994

[9] M. Barnsley, *Fractal Image Compression*, AK Peters,1-56881-000-8

[10] M. Barnsley, *Fractals Everywhere*, Academic Press,0-12-079061-0

[11] H. Peitgen, D.Saupe, H. Jurgens, Springer Verlag, *Fractals for the Class Room*,New York,1991

[12] Y. Fisher, *Fractal Image Compression Theory and Application*, Springer-Verlag,0-387942114

[13] Y. Fisher, E.W. Jacobs, *Fractal Image Compression Using Iterated Transforms*, NOSC Technical Report, Naval Ocean Systems Center, San Diego CA 92152-5000

[14] Y. Fisher, *Fractal Image Compression Theory and Application*, Chapter1, Springer-Verlag,0-387942114

[15] Y. Fisher, E.W. Jacobs, *Fractal Image Compression Using Iterated Transforms*, NOSC Technical Report, Naval Ocean Systems Center, San Diego CA 92152-5000

[16] Y. Fisher, *Fractal Image Compression*, SIGGRAPH'92 Course Notes

[17] Y. Fisher, *Fractal Image Compression Theory and Application*, Chapter1, Springer-Verlag,0-387942114

[18] Y. Fisher, *Fractal Image Compression Theory and Application*, Chapter1, Springer-Verlag,0-387942114

Echo Hiding

Daniel Gruhl, Anthony Lu, and Walter Bender

Massachusetts Institute of Technology Media Laboratory

Abstract. Homomorphic signal-processing techniques are used to place information imperceivably into audio data streams by the introduction of synthetic resonances in the form of closely-spaced echoes. These echoes can be used to place digital identification tags directly into an audio signal with minimal objectionable degradation of the original signal.

1 Introduction

Echo hiding, a form of data hiding, is a method for embedding information into an audio signal. It seeks to do so in a robust fashion, while not perceivably degrading the host signal (cover audio).[1] Echo hiding has applications in providing proof of the ownership, annotation, and assurance of content integrity. Therefore, the data (embedded text) should not be sensitive to removal by common transforms to the stego audio (encoded audio signal), such as filtering, re-sampling, block editing, or lossy data compression.

Hiding data in audio signals presents a variety of challenges, due in part to the wider dynamic and differential range of the human auditory system (HAS) as compared to the other senses. The HAS perceives over a range of power greater than one billion to one and a range of frequencies greater than one thousand to one. Sensitivity to additive random noise is also acute. Perturbations in a sound file can be detected as low as one part in ten million (80dB below ambient level). However, there are some "holes" available in this perceptive range where data may be hidden. While the HAS has a large dynamic range, it often has a fairly small differential range. As a result, loud sounds tend to mask out quiet sounds. Additionally, while the HAS is sensitive to amplitude and relative phase, it is unable to perceive absolute phase. Finally, there are some environmental distortions so common as to be ignored by the listener in most cases.

A common approach to data hiding in audio (as well as in other media) is to introduce the data as noise. A drawback to this approach is that lossy data compression algorithms tend to remove most imperceivable artifacts, including

---

[1] At the Information Hiding Workshop held in Cambridge, England, the adjectives *cover*, *embedded*, and *stego* were choosen to describe the various signals used in data hiding. The term *"cover"* *signal* is used to describe the original signal in which the data is to be hidden. The information to be hidden in the *cover signal* is called the *"embedded"* *signal.* The *"stego"* *signal* contains both the *"cover"* *signal* and the *"embedded"* *signal* and is the final encoded signal. The word "signal" can be replaced by more descriptive terms such as audio, text, stills, video, etc.

typical low dB noise. Echo hiding introduces changes to the cover audio that are characteristic of environmental conditions rather than random noise, thus it is robust in light of many lossy data compression algorithms.

Like all good stegonagraphic methods, echo hiding seeks to embed the data into a media stream with minimal degradation of the original media stream. By minimal degradation, we mean that the change in the cover audio is either imperceivable or simply dismissed by the listener as a common non-objectionable environmental distortion.

The particular distortion we are introducing is similar to resonances found in a room due to walls, furniture, etc. The difference between the stego audio and the cover audio is similar to the difference between listening to a compact disc on headphones and listening to it from speakers. With the headphones, we hear the sound as it was recorded. With the speakers, we hear the sound plus echoes caused by room acoustics. By correctly choosing the distortion we are introducing for echo hiding, we can make such distortions indistinguishable from those a room might introduce in the above speaker case.

Care must be taken when adding these resonances however. There is a point at which additional resonances severely distort the cover audio. We are able to adjust several parameters of the echoes giving us control over both the degree and type of resonance being introduced. With carefully-selected parameter choices, the added resonances can be made imperceivable to the average human listener. Thus, we can exploit the limits of the HAS's discriminatory ability to hide data in an audio data stream.

2　Applications

Protection of intellectual property rights is one obvious application of any form of data hiding. Echo hiding can place a digital signature redundantly throughout an audio data steam. As a result, a reasonable level of hidden information is maintained even after operations such as extracting or editing. This information can be, but is not limited to, copyright information. With redundantly placed copyright information, unauthorized use of protected music becomes easy to demonstrate. Any clipped portion of the stego audio will contain a few copies of the digital signature (i.e. copyright information). Even "sound bites" distributed over the internet can be thus protected. Before placing an original sound bite on a web site, the creator can quickly run the Echo Hiding encoder. The creator can then periodically send out a web crawler that decodes all sound bites found, and reports if the given signature is in them. For such applications, detection and modification of the embedded text must be limited to only a select few. The embedded text is only for the benefit of the encoder and is of little use to the end user. We would like it to be immune to removal by unauthorized parties. With the correct parameters, echo hiding can place the data with a very low probability of unauthorized interception or removal.

Another application of audio data hiding is the inclusion of augmentation data. In most cases, this type of data is placed for the benefit of the end user. As such, detection rules are more lenient. Since the data is there for the benefit of all, malicious tampering of the data is less likely. Echo hiding can be used to non-objectionably hide data in these scenarios also. We can place the augmentation data directly into the cover audio in a binary format. One benefit of our technique is that annotations normally require additional channels for both transmission and storage. By hiding the annotations as echoes in the cover audio, the number of required channels can be reduced.

While the inclusion of augmentation data does not require strict control over detection by third parties, echo hiding provides a low interception rate as an option. The uses of augmentation data include closed-captioning (of radio signals and CD's, etc.) and caller-id type applications for telecommunications systems. With echo hiding, the sound signal could contain both the audio information and the closed-captioning. A decoder can then take that signal and output the audio or display the captioning.

More interesting examples are caller-id and secure phone lines. We can use echo-hiding techniques to place caller information during a phone call. A decoder on the receiving end can detect this information revealing who the caller is and displaying other supplemental data (i.e., client information, client history, location of caller, etc.). The information is attached to the caller's voice and is independent of the phone or phone service used. In contrast, current caller-id schemes only reveal the number of the device used to place the call. With echo hiding, it is possible to attach the information directly to the voice. As such, we have a form of voice identification and voice authentication. This can be useful in large conference calls when many people may try to talk, and identification of the current speaker is difficult due to low bandwidth. Phone calls that require a high degree of assurance of the identity of either party (e.g. oral contracts between an agent and employer) can also benefit from this application of echo hiding.

Echo hiding can also be useful to companies dealing with assuring that audio is played. For instance, when a radio station contracts to play a commercial, it can be difficult to know with certainty that the commercial is indeed being played as frequently as contractually agreed upon. Short of hiring someone to listen to the stations 24 hour a day, there is little they can do. Using echo hiding, we can place a "serial number" in the commercial. A computer can be set up to "listen" to the radio station, check for the identification number, and keep a tally of the number of times the commercial was played and how much of it was played (played in its entirety, cut off half way through, etc.). Echo hiding can also be useful when a radio station is multi-affiliated. Given similar commercials by two different companies, the radio station is by law required to play the tape given by each company in order to count for advertising by each company. This holds true even if the commercials are identical. By encoding each commercial using echo hiding techniques, the companies can keep track of which commercial is played. We can encode identical commercials with a different signature for each company.

Finally, tamper-proofing (prevention of unauthorized modification) can also be accomplished using echo hiding. A known string of digital identification tags can be placed throughout the entirety of the cover audio. The stego audio can easily be checked periodically for modified and/or missing tags revealing the authenticity of the signal in question.

3   Signal Representation

In order to maintain a high quality digital audio signal and to minimize degradation due to quantization of the cover audio, we use the 16-bit linearly quantized Audio Interchange File Format (AIFF). Sixteen-bit linear quantization introduces a negligible amount of signal distortion for our purposes, and AIFF files contain a superset of the information found in most currently popular sound file formats. Various temporal sampling rates have been used and tested, including 8 kHz, 10 kHz, 16 kHz, 22.05 kHz, and 44.1 kHz. Our methods are known to yield an acceptable embedded text recovery accuracy at these sampling rates.

Embedded text is placed into the cover audio using a binary representation. This allows the greatest flexibility with regards to the type of data the process can hide. Almost anything can be represented as a string of zeroes and ones. Therefore, we limit the encoding process to hiding only binary information.

4   Parameters

Echo Data Hiding places embedded text in the cover audio by introducing an "echo." Digital tags are defined using four major parameters of the echo: initial amplitude, decay rate, "zero" offset, and "one" offset (offset + delta) (Figure 1). As the offset (delay) between the original and the echo decreases, the two signals blend. At a certain point the human ear hears not an original signal and an echo, but rather a single distorted signal. [2]

The coder uses two delay times, one to represent a binary one ("one" offset) and another to represent a binary zero ("zero" offset). Both delay times are below the threshold that the human ear can resolve the echo and the cover audio as different sources. In addition to decreasing the delay time, we can also ensure that the distortion is not perceivable by setting the echo amplitude and the decay rate below the audible threshold of the human ear.

5   Encoding

The encoding process can be represented as a system that has one of two possible system functions. In the time domain, the system functions we use are discrete

---

[2] This point is hard to determine exactly. It depends on the quality of the original recording, the type of sound being echoed, and the listener. In general, we find that this fusion occurs around one thousandth of a second for most sounds and most listeners.

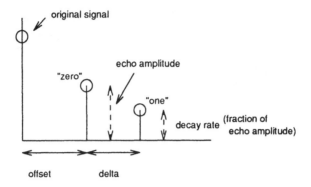

Fig. 1. Adjustable parameters

time exponentials (as depicted in Figure 2) differing only in the delay between impulses.

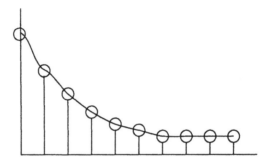

Fig. 2. Discrete time exponential

In this example, we chose system functions with only two impulses (one to copy the cover audio and one to create an echo) for simplicity.

We let the kernel shown in Figure 3(a) represent the system function for encoding a binary one, and we use the system function defined in Figure 3(b) to encode a zero. Processing a signal with either system function will result in an encoded signal (see example in Figure 11).

The delay between the cover audio and the echo is dependent on which kernel or system function we use in Figure 4. The "one" kernel (Figure 3(a)) is created with a delay of δ_1 seconds while the "zero" kernel (Figure 3(b)) has a δ_0 second delay. In order to encode more than one bit, the cover audio is "divided" into smaller portions. Each individual portion can then be echoed with the desired bit by considering each as an independent signal. The stego audio (containing several bits) is the recombination of all independently encoded signal portions.

In Figure 5, the example signal has been divided into seven equal portions labeled a, b, c, d, e, f, and g. We want portions a, c, d, and g to contain a

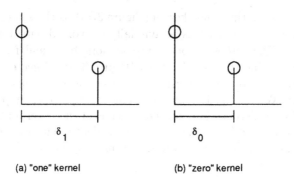

(a) "one" kernel (b) "zero" kernel

Fig. 3. Echo kernels

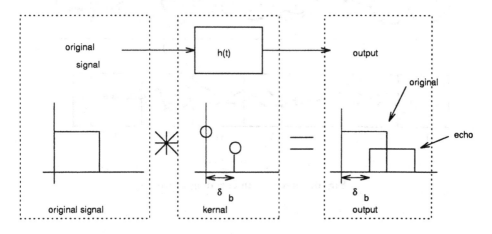

Fig. 4. Echoing example

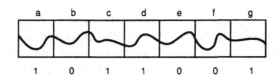

Fig. 5. Divide the cover audio into smaller portions to encode information

one. Therefore, we use the "one" kernel (Figure 3(a)) as the system function for each of these portions i.e. each is individually convolved with the appropriate system function. The zeroes encoded into sections b, e, and f are encoded in a similar manner using the "zero" kernel (Figure 3(b)). Once each section has been individually convolved with the appropriate system function, the results are recombined. While this is what happens conceptually, in practice we do something slightly different. Two echoed versions of the cover audio are created using each of the system functions. This is equivalent to encoding either all ones or all zeroes. The resulting signals are shown in Figure 6.

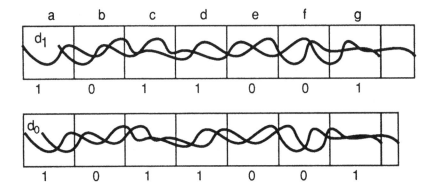

Fig. 6. First step in encoding process

In order to combine the two signals, two mixer signals (Figure 7) are created. The mixer signals are either one or zero (depending on the bit we would like to hide in that portion) or in a transition stage in-between sections containing different bits.

The "one" mixer signal is multiplied by the "one" echo signal while the "zero" mixer signal is multiplied by the "zero" echo signal. In other words, the echo signals are scaled by either 1 (encode the bit) or 0 (do not encode bit) or a number in-between 0 and 1 (transition region). Then the two results are added. Note that the "zero" mixer signal is the binary inverse of the "one" mixer signal and that the transitions within each signal are ramps. Therefore, the resulting sum of the two mixer signals is always unity. This gives us a smooth transition between portions encoded with different bits and prevents abrupt changes in the resonance of the stego audio, which would be noticeable. A block diagram representing the entire encoding process is illustrated in Figure 8.

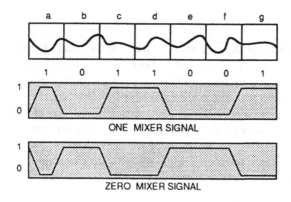

Fig. 7. Mixer Signals

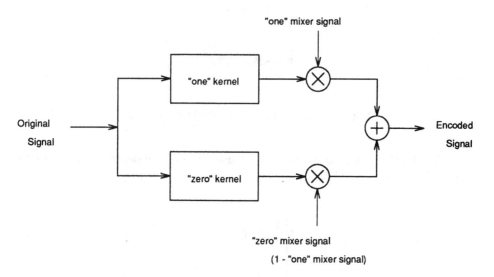

Fig. 8. Encoding process

6 Decoding

Information is embedded into an audio stream by echoing the cover audio with one of two delay kernels as discussed in Section 5. A binary one is represented by an echo kernel with a δ_1 second delay. A binary zero is represented with a δ_0 second delay. Extraction of the embedded text involves the detection of spacing between the echoes. In order to do this, we examine the magnitude (at two locations) of the autocorrelation of the encoded signal's cepstrum (Appendix B). The following procedure is an example of the decoding process. We begin with a sample signal that is a series of impulses such that the impulses are separated by a set interval and have exponentially decaying amplitudes. The signal is zero elsewhere (Figure 9).

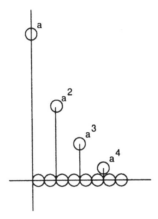

Fig. 9. Example signal: $x[n] = a^n u[n]$; $0 < a > 1$

We echo the signal once with delay δ using the kernel depicted in Figure 10. The result is illustrated in Figure 11.

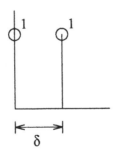

Fig. 10. Echo kernel used in example

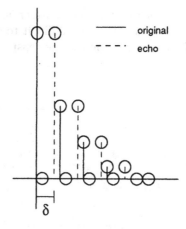

Fig. 11. Echoed version of the example signal

The next step is to find the cepstrum (Appendix A) of the echoed version. Taking the cepstrum "separates" the echoes from the original signal. The echoes are located in a periodic fashion dictated by the offset of the given bit. As a result, we know that the echoes are in one of two possible locations (with a little periodicity).

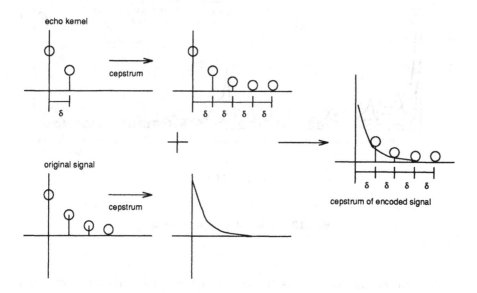

Fig. 12. Cepstrum of the echo-encoded signal

Unfortunately, the result of the cepstrum also "duplicates" the echo every δ seconds. In Figure 12, this is illustrated by the impulse train in the output.

Furthermore, the magnitude of the impulses representing the echoes are small relative to the cover audio. As such, they are difficult to detect. The solution to this problem is to take the autocorrelation of the cepstrum.

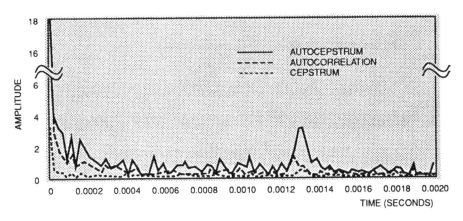

(A) ZERO (FIRST BIT)

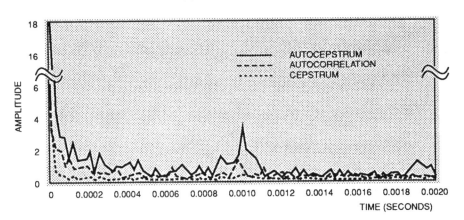

(B) ONE (FIRST BIT)

Fig. 13. Result of autocorrelation

The autocorrelation gives us the power of the signal found at each delay. With the echoes spaced periodically every δ_1 or δ_0, we will get a "power spike" at either δ_1 or δ_0 in the cepstrum. This spike is just the power (energy squared) at echo spacings of δ_1 or δ_0. The decision rule for each bit is to examine the power at δ_0 and δ_1 in the cepstrum and choose whichever bit corresponds to a higher power level (see Figure 13).

7 Results

Using the methods described, we can encode and decode information in the form of binary digits in an audio stream with minimal degradation at a data rate of about 16 bps[3] By minimal degradation, we mean that the output of the encoding process is changed in such a way that the average human cannot hear any objectionable distortion in the stego audio. In most cases the addition of resonance gives the signal a slightly richer sound.

Using a series of sound clips provided by ABC Radio, we have obtained encouraging results. The sound clips cover a wide range of sound types including music, speech, a combination of both, and sporadic sound (music or speech separated by empty space or noise). We created a tool to test these clips over a wide range of parameter settings in order to characterize the echo hiding process. Running the characterizations on 20 sound clips of varying content and length, we discovered that the relative volume of the echo (decay rate) was the most important parameter with regards to the embedded text recovery rate. With 85% chosen as a minimally acceptable recovery rate (defined in Equation 1) all stego signals showed acceptable accuracy with a decay rate (relative volume of the echo compared to the original signal) between 0.3 and 0.85.

$$recovery\ rate = \frac{(number\ of\ bits\ correctly\ decoded) * 100}{number\ of\ bits\ placed} \qquad (1)$$

At 0.5 and 0.6, few can resolve the echoes. While these results are encouraging, we would like to push the relative volume down even more. Between 0.3 and 0.4 even those with exceptional hearing have difficulty noticing a difference. We observed that in general the recovery rate was linearly related to the relative volume. However in certain cases, we observed deviations from this general rule, caused by the particular structure of the specific sound signal. Figures 14 through 17 illustrate the correlation (for three select files) between relative volume and embedded text recovery rate. The sound files chosen are representative of the entire set of sound clips. For the plots provided in this paper, the sample most amenable to encoding by Echo Hiding (a6, a segment of popular music), the sample least amenable to encoding (a1, a spoken news broadcast), and one mid-range sample (a14, spoken advertising copy) were used. In general, the more difficult samples are typically the ones with large "gaps" of silence (similar to a1, the example of unproduced spoken word) while those easiest to encode are those without such "gaps" (similar to example a6, the popular music clip).

Initially, we tested the process in a closed-loop environment (encoding and decoding from a sound file). The results are illustrated in Figure 14. All the files reached the 85% mark with relative volumes less than or equal to 0.8. a6 required a relative volume of only 0.3 to recover an acceptable number of bits. By 0.4, we were able to recover 100% of the hidden bits. a1 and a14 required a higher relative volume of 0.5 in order to achieve the 85% mark.

---

[3] This is dependent on sampling rate and the type of sound being encoded. 16bps is a typical value, but the number can range from 2bps-64bps.

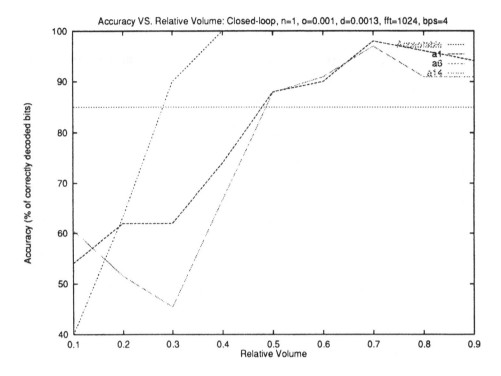

Fig. 14. Accuracy vs. relative volume: closed-loop

We also tried encoding on one machine, transmitting the sound file over an analog wire (with appropriate D/A and A/D conversions), and decoding on another machine (Figure 15). The required relative volume of **a14** increased to 0.8. Both **a1** and **a14** experienced a noticeable decrease in accuracy at higher relative volumes, but an acceptable recovery rate could still be reached. **a6** was approximately the same except that the 100% mark was not reached until 0.5.

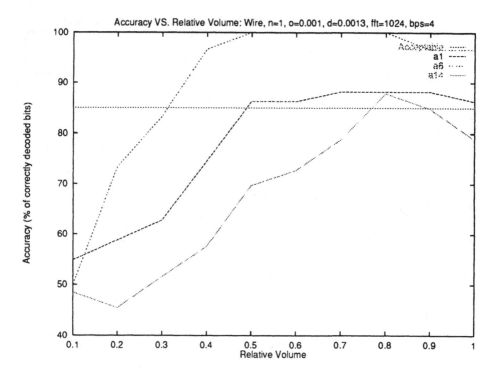

Fig. 15. Accuracy vs. relative volume: Analog wire

After testing an analog connection between two machines, we experimented with compression and decompression before decoding. We used two compression methods: MPEG (Figure 16) and SEDAT (Figure 17). The SEDAT compression was done with a test fixture provided by ABC Radio. In both cases, the recovery rate of **a1** and **a14** significantly decreased. **a6** was only slightly effected by the compression and decompression.

The other parameters (number of echoes, offset, and delta), seemed to produce acceptable results regardless of their value. This does not, by any means, indicate that these parameters are useless. Instead, these parameters play a significant role in the perceivability of the synthetic resonances. These interactions are in some cases highly non-linear, and better models of them are an area of continuing research. As discussed earlier (Section 4), a smaller offset and delta result in an increased "blending" of the resonances with the cover audio mak-

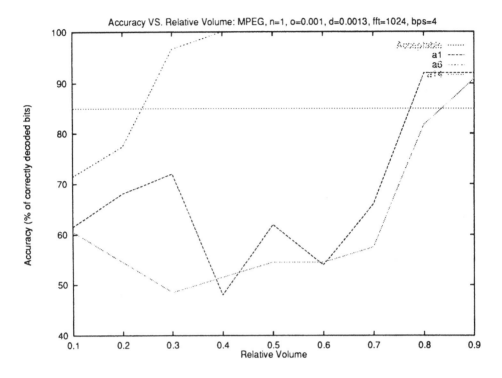

Fig. 16. Accuracy vs. relative volume: analog wire and MPEG

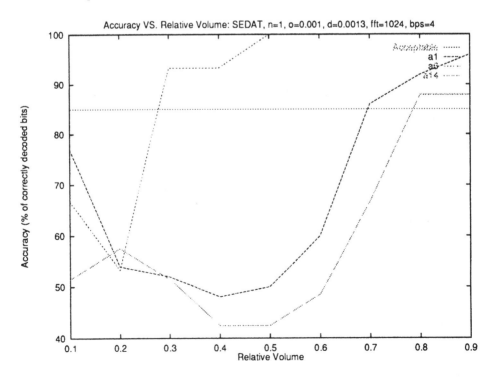

Fig. 17. Accuracy vs. Relative volume: analog wire and SEDAT

ing it increasingly difficult for the human observer to resolve the echo and the cover audio as two distinct signals. Offsets greater than 0.5 milliseconds produced acceptable recovery rates. The average listener cannot resolve the echoes with an offset of 0.001 seconds. Below a 0.5 millisecond offset, even the decoder had difficulty distinguishing the echo from the cover audio.

Extensive testing reveals that the two most important echo parameters are relative volume (decay rate) and offset. The relative volume controls the recovery rate. While the offset is the major factor in the perceptibility of the modifications.

The results illustrated in Figures 14 through 17 were obtained at sampling rates of 44.1 kHz (closed-loop) and 10 kHz (wire, MPEG, and SEDAT). Other sampling rates tested include 8 kHz, 16 kHz, and 22.05 kHz all yielding similar (but appropriately scaled) results.

As can be seen, echo hiding performs very well in situations where there is no additional degradation (such as that produced by D/A conversion, line noise or lossy encoding). In this respect, its performance is similar to many existing techniques. It's strength lies in its reasonable performance even in the much more challenging cases where such degradation is present.

At the present time, echo hiding works best on sound files without gaps of silence. This is unsurprising as it is difficult to analyze and recover echoes in regions of silence (such as inter-word pauses in speech). We are working on various thresholding techniques to try to avoid these difficulties by encoding only those areas where there is sound, and skipping areas of silence completely.

8 Future Work

Echo hiding can effectively place imperceivable information into an audio stream. Nevertheless, there is still room for improvement. We have been examining the use of different echoing kernels and their effect on recovery accuracy and echo perceivability. In particular, we are actively researching both multi-echo kernels (adding another level of redundancy) and pre-echo kernels (echoing in negative time). With the old kernels, we are modifying the encoding process to be self-adaptive. Completion of these modifications will allow the encoding program to decide which parameters yield the highest recovery rate given the user's constraints on perceptibility and sound degradation. In addition, we will use echo hiding as a method for placing caller identification type information in real time over 8-bit, 8 kHz, analog phone lines.

9 References and Notes

1. W. Bender, D. Gruhl, N. Morimoto, "Techniques for Data Hiding," Proc. of the SPIE, 2420:40, San Jose, CA., 1995.

2. W. Bender, D. Gruhl, N. Morimoto, A. Lu, "Techniques for Data Hiding," To appear in IBM Systems Journal, Vol. 35, No. 3&4, 1996.

3. S. Baron, W. Wilson, "MPEG Overview," SMPTE Journal, pp 391-394, June 1994.

311

4. R. C. Dixon, Spread Spectrum Systems, John Wiley & Sons, Inc., 1976.

5. L. R. Rabiner and R. W. Schaffer, Digital Processing of Speech Signal, Prentice-Hall, Inc., NJ, 1975.

6. A. V. Oppenheim and R. W. Schaffer, Discrete-Time Signal Processing, Prentice Hall, Inc., NJ, 1989.

7. Conversations with Scientific Atlanta regarding SEDAT Evaluation Test Fixture.

Appendix

Much of the following short tutorial was derived from Oppenheim and Schaffer's Discrete-Time Signal Processing. Please refer to the original text for a more complete discussion.

A Cepstrums

Cepstral analysis utilizes a form of a homomorphic system that converts the convolution operation to an addition operation. As with most homomorphic systems, the cepstrum can be decomposed into a canonical representation consisting of a cascade of three individual systems. These systems are the fourier transform ($\mathcal{F}$), the complex logarithm (see Section C), and the inverse fourier transform ($\mathcal{F}^{-1}$) as depicted in Figure 18.

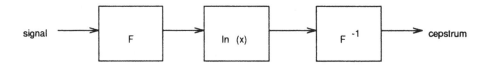

Fig. 18. Canonical representation of a cepstrum

The operational conversion is the result of a basic mathematical property: The log of a product is the sum of the individual logs and multiplication in the frequency domain is identical to convolution in the time domain. To exploit this fact, we use the first system in the canonical representation of the cepstrum to place us in the frequency domain by taking the fourier transform. In the frequency domain, the desired modifications are linear. The next system is a linear, time-invariant (LTI) system that takes the complex logarithm of the product of two functions. This simply becomes the sum of the logarithms. It is analogous to using a slide rule. In fact, the principle is the same. Multiplication becomes simple addition by first taking the logarithm. The final system puts us back in the original (time) domain. In order to express the "conversion" mathematically, let's convolve two finite signals $x_1[n]$ and $x_2[n]$.

$$y[n] = x_1[n] * x_2[n] \tag{2}$$

After taking the fourier transform of y[n], we get:

$$Y(e^{j\Omega}) = X_1(e^{j\Omega})X_2(e^{j\Omega}) \tag{3}$$

Now, we take the complex log of $Y(e^{j\Omega})$:

$$\log Y(e^{j\Omega}) = \log(X_1(e^{j\Omega})X_2(e^{j\Omega})) = \log X_1(e^{j\Omega}) + \log X_2(e^{j\Omega}) \tag{4}$$

Finally, we take the inverse fourier transform.

$$\mathcal{F}^{-1}(\log Y(e^{j\Omega})) = \mathcal{F}^{-1}(\log X_1(e^{j\Omega})) + \mathcal{F}^{-1}(\log X_2(e^{j\Omega})) \tag{5}$$

By the definition of the cepstrum, this becomes (where $\tilde{x}[n]$ is the cepstrum of x[n]):

$$\hat{y}[n] = \tilde{x}_1[n] + \tilde{x}_2[n] \tag{6}$$

Figure 19 illustrates the entire conversion process.

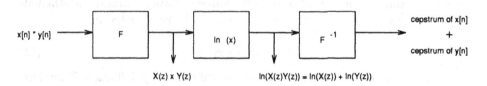

Fig. 19. Conversion of convolution in the time domain to the equivalent cepstral addition while still in the time domain

The inverse cepstrum is the reverse of the process described above and is depicted in Figure 20.

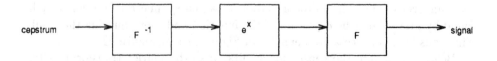

Fig. 20. Inverse cepstrum (canonical representation)

B Autocorrelation using cepstrums

Autocorrelation can be done while taking the cepstrum. Recall that the auto-correlation of any function x[n] is defined as:

$$R_{xx}[n] = \sum_{m=-\infty}^{+\infty} x[n+m]x[m] \tag{7}$$

With a change of variable (letting k=n+m and substituting m=k-n), the equation for the autocorrelation of a given function x[n] becomes:

$$R_{xx} = \sum x[k]x[k-n] \tag{8}$$

Now let's rearrange the second term in the summation (the x[k-n] term) so that:

$$R_{xx} = \sum x[k]x[-(n-k)] \tag{9}$$

Recall that convolution is defined as:

$$x[n] * h[n] = \sum_{k=-\infty}^{+\infty} x[k]h[n-k] \tag{10}$$

There is a similarity between the convolution equation (Equation 10) and the "modified" autocorrelation equation (Equation 9). The only difference is the negation of time in the second term of the autocorrelation equation. Mathematically speaking, the autocorrelation equation can be represented as:

$$R_{xx} = x[n] * x[-n] \tag{11}$$

If a signal is self-symmetric, x[-n] is identical to x[n] by definition. Therefore, the autocorrelation of a self-symmetric signal becomes:

$$R_{xx} = x[n] * x[n] \tag{12}$$

In the frequency domain (i.e. after taking the fourier transform of the inputs), this becomes:

$$S_{xx}(e^{j\Omega}) = (X(e^{j\Omega}))^2 \tag{13}$$

Using cepstrums, the autocorrelation of a self-symmetric function can be found by first taking the cepstrum of the function and then squaring the result. The steps in this process are depicted in Figure 21 and Figure 22.

Before we square the cepstrum, we first take the fourier transform. After-wards, we take the inverse fourier transform. The reason is the same as when we were finding the cepstrum (Appendix A). The fourier transform places us in the frequency domain where modifications are linear. A linear system (x^2) actually performs the operation. Finally, the inverse fourier places us back in the time

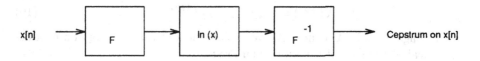

Fig. 21. The first step in finding the Cepstral Autocorrelation is to find the cepstrum of x[n]

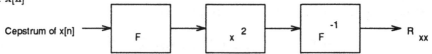

Fig. 22. Once we have the cepstrum, we square it

domain. The inverse fourier transform from step one (Figure 21) and the fourier transform from step two (Figure 22) will cancel each other when combined. In the end, we are left with the system shown in Figure 23.

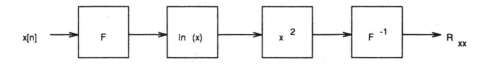

Fig. 23. Systems representation of Cepstral Autocorrelation

Autocorrelation is an order n^2 operation. Using the system in Figure 23, the operation is reduced to a $n \log(n)$ operation. Thus for large n, finding the autocorrelation while taking the cepstrum is much more efficient.

C Complex Logarithm

The fourier transform is a complex function of ω. It can be decomposed into magnitude and phase/angle terms. Thus, if we have some finite signal x[n], the Fourier transform can be represented as a magnitude and an angle:

$$X(e^{j\Omega}) = |X(e^{j\Omega})|e^{jARGX(e^{j\Omega})} \tag{14}$$

ARG (angle modulus 2π) is used instead of arg (angle) since adding 2π (where n is any arbitrary integer) to an angle has no effect:

$$e^{j(x+2n\pi)} = e^{jx}e^{j2n\pi} = e^{jx}(\cos 2n\pi + j \sin 2n\pi) = e^{jx} \tag{15}$$

In most cases, the phase will be a non-zero value. Therefore, we can not use the natural logarithm when taking the cepstrum (Figure 18). Instead, we must use the complex logarithm which is defined as:

$$\log X(e^{j\Omega}) = \log(|X(e^{j\Omega})|e^{jARGX(e^{j\Omega})}) \tag{16}$$

Once again (as in Appendix A) we exploit the fact that the log of a product is identical to the sum of the individual logs:

$$\log X(e^{j\Omega}) = \log(|X(e^{j\Omega})|) + \log(e^{jARGX(e^{j\Omega})}) \tag{17}$$

Exploiting that log and e^x are inverses, we get:

$$\log X(e^{j\Omega}) = \log|X(e^{j\Omega})| + jARGX(e^{j\Omega}) \tag{18}$$

In order to further motivate the idea of converting from convolution to addition, let's mathematically re-examine Appendix A in light of the complex logarithm. We begin by first convolving two finite signals $x_1[n]$ and $x_2[n]$:

$$y[n] = x_1[n] * x_2[n] \tag{19}$$

Convolution becomes multiplication in the frequency domain:

$$Y(e^{j\Omega}) = X_1(e^{j\Omega})X_2(e^{j\Omega})) \tag{20}$$

Taking the complex log:

$$\log Y(e^{j\Omega}) = \log(X_1(e^{j\Omega})X_2(e^{j\Omega}) \tag{21}$$

Finding the mathematical equivalent:

$$\log Y(e^{j\Omega}) = \log(X_1(e^{j\Omega})) + \log(X_2(e^{j\Omega})) \tag{22}$$

Now, we can substitute the result from Equation 17 and rearrange to get:

$$\log Y(e^{j\Omega}) = (\log|X_1(e^{j\Omega})|+\log|X_2(e^{j\Omega})|)+(jARG(X_1(e^{j\Omega}))+jARG(X_2(e^{j\Omega}))) \tag{23}$$

The use of the complex logarithm in cepstral analysis allows the addition of signal components instead of the convolution of the signals.

Tamper Resistant Software:
An Implementation

David Aucsmith, IAL

Abstract

This paper describes a technology for the construction of tamper resistant software. It presents a threat model and design principles for countering a defined subset of the threat. The paper then presents an architecture and implementation of tamper resistant software based on the principles described.

The architecture consists of segment of code, called an Integrity Verification Kernel, which is self-modifying, self-decrypting, and installation unique. This code segment communicates with other such code segments to create an Interlocking Trust model.

The paper concludes with speculation of additional uses of the developed technology and an evaluation of the technology's effectiveness.

Introduction

One of the principal characteristics of the PC is that it is an open, accessible architecture. Both hardware and software can be accessed for observation and modification. Arguably, this openness has lead to the PC's market success. This same openness means that the PC is a fundamentally insecure platform. Observation or modification can be performed by either a malevolent user or a malicious program. Yet there are classes of operations that must be performed securely on the fundamentally insecure PC platform. These are applications where the basic integrity of the operation must be assumed, or at least verified, to be reliable such as financial transactions, unattended authorization and content management. What is required is a method which will allow the fundamentally insecure, open PC to execute software which cannot be observed or modified.

This paper presents the notion of *tamper resistant software*. Tamper resistant software is software which is resistant to observation and modification. It can be trusted, within certain bounds, to operate as intended even in the presence of a malicious attack.

Our approach has been to classify attacks into three categories and then to develop a series of software design principles that allow a scaled response to those threats. This approach has been implemented as a set of tools that produce tamper resistant

Integrity Verification Kernels (IVKs) which can be inserted into software to verify the integrity of critical operations.

This paper describes the threat model, design principles, architecture and implementation of the IVK technology.

Threat Model

Malicious observation and manipulation of the PC can be classified into three categories, based on the origin of the threat. The origin of the threat is expressed in terms of the security perimeter that has been breached in order to effect the malicious act. This translates generally to who the perpetrator is, outsider or insider.

- *Category I* – In this category, the malicious threat originates outside of the PC. The perpetrator must breach communications access controls but must still operate under the constraints of the communications protocols. This is the standard "hacker attack." The perpetrator is an outsider trying to get in.

- *Category II* – The Category II malicious attack originates as software running on the platform. The perpetrator has been able to introduce malicious code into the platform and the operating system has executed it. The attack has moved inside the communications perimeter but is still bounded by the operating system and BIOS. That is, it must still utilize the operating system and BIOS interfaces. This is the common virus or Trojan horse attack. The perpetrator is an outsider who had access at one time to a system.

- *Category III* – In Category III attacks, the perpetrator has complete control of the platform and may substitute hardware or system software and may observe any communications channel (such as using a bus analyzer) that they wish. This attack faces no security perimeter and is limited only by technical expertise and financial resources. The owner of the system is the perpetrator.

Category I attacks do not require the use of tamper resistant software, rather, require correctly designed and implemented protocols and proper administration. As, by definition, the perpetrator has no direct access to the platform's hardware or software, Category I attacks are better defended by robust access control mechanisms. Frequently, the goal of a Category I attack is to mount a Category II attack.

Category II attacks are caused by the introduction of malicious software into the platform. The malicious software may have been introduced with or without the user's consent and may be explicitly or implicitly malicious. Examples of such software include viruses and Trojan horses as well as software used to discover secrets stored in other software on behalf of other parties (such as another user's access control information).

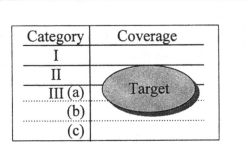

Category	Coverage
I	
II	
III (a)	Target
(b)	
(c)	

Figure 1: *Threat Model and Tamper Resistance*

An important characterization of Category II attacks is that they tend to attack classes of software. Viruses are a good example of a *class attack*. Viruses must assume certain coding characteristics to be constant among its target population such as the format of the execution image. Other examples would include a Trojan horse program that searches a particular financial application in order to purloin credit card numbers because it knows where within that application such numbers are stored. It is the consistency of software across platforms that enables Category II attacks.

In an absolute sense, Category III attacks are impossible to prevent on the PC. Any defense against a Category III attack must, at best, merely raise a technological bar to a height sufficient to deter a perpetrator by providing a poor return on their investment. That investment might be measured in terms of the tools necessary, and skills required, to observe and subsequently modify the software's behavior. The technological bar, from low to high, would be:

a) *No special analysis tools required.* These include standard debuggers and system diagnostic tools.

b) *Specialized software analysis tools.* Tools here include specialized debuggers such as SoftIce and software breakpoint-based analysis tools

c) *Specialized hardware analysis tools.* These tools include processor emulators and bus logic analyzers.

Our goal for tamper resistant software is to defend against Category II attacks and Category III attacks up to the level of specialized hardware analysis tools. We believe that this provides a reasonable compromise. It is axiomatic that threat follows value, thus this level of tamper resistance is adequate for low to medium value applications, and for high value applications where the user is unlikely to be a willing perpetrator (such as applications involving the user's personal property).

Principles

It is our premise that for software to be tamper resistant it must be immune from observation and modification (within the bounds stated earlier). This requirement implies that the software contains a secret component. Preventing operation on the secret component is the basis for the trust that the application has not been tampered with. Were it not for the secret component, a perpetrator could substitute any software of their choosing for the correct software.

It is the existence of this secret component that compels the user to use that specific software for that specific function rather that some other software. For example, the secret may be a cryptographic key used to encrypt a random challenge in an authentication protocol. Possession of the cryptographic key creates the trust that the software is legitimate.

As another example, consider the need to guarantee that the software has completed a predetermined set of steps. If each step contributed some information to the formation of a shared secret then the presentation of that secret would provide proof that the steps have been executed correctly.

The design principles that we have developed are based on the need to hide a secret in software and ensure that the recovery or alteration of that secret is difficult. Four principles were developed:

- *Disperse secrets in both time and space* The secret should never exist in a single memory structure, where it could be retrieved by scanning active memory. Additionally, the secret should never be processed in any single operation, where anyone monitoring code execution could easily deduce it.

- *Obfuscation of interleaved operations* The complete task to be performed by the software should be interleaved so that a little bit of each part of a task is performed in successive iterations or rounds of the executing code. The goal is to achieve software atomicity, i.e., an "all or none" execution of the software. Such interleaving could be done in a multi-processing environment with cooperating threads. Additionally, the actual execution should be obfuscated to prevent easy discovery of the interleaved component results. Such obfuscation could be accomplished by self-decrypting and self-modifying code.

- *Installation unique code* In order to prevent class attacks, each instance of the software should contain unique elements. This uniqueness could be added at program installation in the form of different code sequences or encryption keys.

- *Interlocking trust* The correct performance of a code sequence should be mutually dependent on the correct performance of many other code sequences.

None of these principles alone will guarantee tamper resistance. Tamper resistance is built from many applications of these ideas aggregated into a single software entity. We have applied these principles in the construction of *Integrity Verification Kernels*

(*IVKs*) which are small, tamper resistant sections of code that perform critical functions.

Architecture

The tamper resistant software architecture consists of two parts:

1. *Integrity Verification Kernels* These kernels are small code segments that have been "armored" using the previously mentioned principles so that they are not easily tampered with. They can be used alone, to ensure that their tasks are executed correctly, or they can be used in conjunction with other software, where they provide the assurance that the other software has executed correctly. That is, they can be used as verification engines.

2. *Interlocking Trust Mechanism* This mechanism uses the inherent strength of the IVK in a robust protocol so that IVKs may check other IVKs. This mutual checking greatly increases the tamper resistance of the system as a whole.

Both of these parts are described in more detail in the following sections.

Integrity Verification Kernel

The IVK is a small, armored segment of code which is designed to be included in a larger program and performs the following two functions:

- Verifies the integrity of code segments or programs

- Communicates with other IVKs To accomplish these functions securely, an IVK utilizes five defenses:

  1. *Interleaved tasks* An IVK may also perform other functions as required but all functions will be interleaved so that no function is complete until they are all complete. Thus, for tasks *A*, *B*, and *C* where *a*, *b*, and *c* are small parts of tasks *A*, *B*, and *C* respectively, the IVK executes *abcabcabcabc* rather than *aaaabbbbcccc*. This is done to prevent a perpetrator from having the IVK complete one of its functions, such as performing the integrity verification of the program, without performing another function, such as verifying the correct functioning of another IVK.

  2. *Distributed secrets* The IVK must contain at least one secret (or the IVK could be bypassed by any code written to respond in a pre-determined way). In general, one of these secrets will be a private key used to generate digital signatures.[1] The public key would be used to verify the integrity of the program and to verify the responses to challenges in the *Integrity Verification Protocol*. In accordance with one of the previously mentioned

principles, secrets are broken into smaller pieces and the pieces distributed throughout the IVK.

3. *Obfuscated code*   The IVK is encrypted and is self-modifying so that it decrypts in place as it is executed. The cipher used ensures that, as sections of the code become decrypted, other sections become encrypted and memory locations are reused for different op-codes at different times.

4. *Installation unique modifications*   Each IVK is constructed at installation time in such a way that even for a given program, each instance of the program contains different IVKs. This way, a perpetrator may analyze any given program but will not be able to predict what the IVK on a particular target platform will look like, making class attacks very unlikely. The uniqueness is a property of installation specific code segments and cryptographic keys.

5. *Non-deterministic behavior*   Where possible, the IVK utilizes the multi-threading capability of the platform to generate confusion (for an attacker) as to the correct thread to follow.

The structure of an IVK is illustrated in figure 2. The IVK is divided into 2^N equal size cells (or code segments) where $N > 2$. Each cell contains blocks of execution code and, with the exception of the first cell, are encrypted. Cells are not executed linearly but in a pseudo-random order determined by a key. The cell is thus the smallest level of granularity which is ever exposed unencrypted. Cells are exposed by decryption one at a time.

The first cell contains the IVKs entry point. The entry point accepts parameters and begins execution of the IVK. Once control has been transferred to the IVK, one of the parameters is passed to the *generator function*. The generator function uses one of the parameters as the key seed vector, *KV*, to a pseudo-random number function and XORs the generated pseudo-random number string, *KG*, with all of the IVK's remaining cells in a pseudo-one-time-pad manner. So that for an IVK, *M*, which is composed of m bytes

$$m_0 \leq m_i \leq m_B$$

where there are a total of *B* bytes in *M* and KG is composed of bytes kg_i, then

```
For i = cell_size to B
   m[i] = m[i] XOR KG[i]
```

This sets up the initial state of the IVK. All further states of the IVK are a function of all of the preceding states. Thus, the initial state defines the possible values of future states.

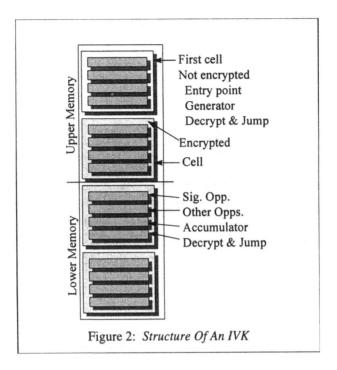

Figure 2: *Structure Of An IVK*

Once the initial state is set up, the *decrypt and jump function* is executed. The decrypt and jump function XORs every cell in upper memory with a partner cell in lower memory and with a substitution key value. An upper memory cell's lower memory partner is chosen according to the value of a transposition key. Thus the value of each lower memory cell is a function of a keyed substitution-transposition derived from cells in upper memory.

The results of the decrypt component of the decrypt and jump function is that at least one cell in lower memory consists of valid op-codes (non-encrypted), referred to as *plaintext*. The jump component then jumps to that one plaintext cell. Once the plaintext cell has been executed, its decrypt and jump function XORs every cell in lower memory with a partner cell in upper memory and with a substitution key value. Thus, obliterating previous plaintext cells in upper memory and exposing at least one new plaintext cell in upper memory and jumping to it.

The decrypt component is as follows: Given C cells in the IVK where m_i denotes a cell in C such that

$$m_0 \le m_i \le m_C$$

and

$$m_i \in C \quad \text{and} \quad C = 2^N$$

There are two encryption keys, *KP*, the permutation key, and, *KS*, the substitution key. Where *KP*[*i*] is the *i*th element of *q* total elements and *KS*[*i*] is the *i*th element of *t* total elements respectively. Both keys, *KP* and *KS*, are random bit strings.

Next, we define the *partner function*, *P*, as

$$P(i,j) = (KP[j \bmod q] \lor 2^{N-1}) \oplus i$$

where *i* is an index of cells such that

$$0 \le i \le 2^{N-1} - 1$$

and *j* is monotonically increasing for

$$0 \le j \le \infty$$

Then the **decrypt function** is

```
For i = 0 to 2^N-1-1
  m[P(i,j)] = m[P(i,j)] XOR m[i]
    XOR KS[j mod t]
  j = j+ 1
```

for odd rounds, and

```
For i = 0 to 2^N-1-1
  m[i] = m[i] XOR m[P(I,j)]
    XOR KS[j mod t]
  j = j + 1
```

for even rounds. One round being one execution of a decrypt and jump function such that even rounds are executed by plaintext cells in upper memory and odd rounds are executed by plaintext cells in lower memory.

Note that *KS* and *KP* do not explicitly exist, rather; the values *KS*[*i*] and *KP*[*i*] are derived at IVK creation and are hard-coded.

The decryption function has many interesting properties. By controlling specific values in *KP* and *KS*, arbitrary cycles can be introduced. These cycles can be used to process function calls or loop structures in the original code. This property is an artifact of XOR exchange. To exchange two values *a* and *b* with out using temporary storage the following sequence can be exercised:

$$a = a \oplus b$$

$$b = a \oplus b$$

$$a = a \oplus b$$

Performing the sequence again will return the original values of a and b thus creating a cycle.

The other property of interest is that any arbitrary end state can be produced such that a different *KG* could be needed for the IVK to run again.

Returning back to figure 2, once a decrypt and jump function has jumped to a new cell, the new cell begins executing the interleaved tasks in that cell. The cell first process some part of a digital signature, then one part of some additional function such as checking to see if the process is being debugged. Any task can be performed as long as it can be interleaved among many cells.

Next the cell executes the accumulator function. This function computes one round of a hash function where the current cell's value is added into the accumulating product. This accumulating product can be checked by any cell to insure that all previous cells were executed correctly and in the correct order. Given cell m, hash function H, and the value of H at i as h_i then

$$h_i = H(h_{i-1}, m_i)$$

After the accumulator function has run, the cell executes its decrypt and jump function; and a new cell is uncovered and begins execution.

Integrity Verification Kernel Creation

IVKs are constructed using two specialized tools. Tool 1, which is run by the creator of the program in which the IVK is to be embedded and tool 2, which is run at installation time by the install script. Figure 3 illustrates the steps in creating an IVK. In step 1, public keys are feed into Tool 1. Tool 1 computes the components of the private keys and generates "C" source code for performing digital signatures using those components.

In step 2, the generated "C" code is interleaved with other, pre-written "C" code, including standard preambles and footers to produce the source code for the IVK. The source code for the IVK is then compiled in step 3 to generate object code for the IVK.

The object code for the IVK is processed in step 4, along with other parameters, at installation time, to generate a vector of encrypted bytes. The encrypted bytes have a defined entry point which is not encrypted. The encrypted bytes are the IVK. They are then inserted into the target program in step 5 into a location left "empty" when the original program was created.

We will now look at each of these steps in more detail.

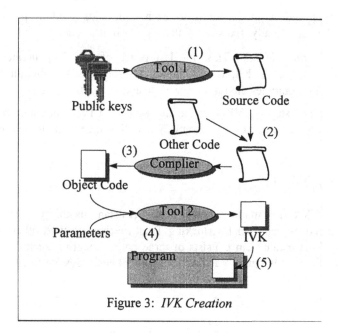

Figure 3: *IVK Creation*

Step 1 In step 1, one or more public/private keypairs are fed into tool 1 to generate "C" code that produces digital signatures. The source code which is output contains the "unrolled", optimized code for computing a cryptographic hash followed by the modular exponentiation. The public keys are hard coded into the source code as part of the mathematical operations.

Step 2 In step 2, the source code generated by tool 1 is combined with standard pre-written source code. The pre-written code includes the IVK's entry code, generator code, accumulator code and other code for tamper detection. This step is a primarily manual step. The code for the decrypt and jump function is not added during this step. It is added by tool 2 in step 4.

Step 3 The combined source code is compiled by a standard compiler in step 3 to produce relocatable object code.

Step 4 Step 4 is performed at installation time. The relocatable object code is processed by tool 2. Tool 2 has the following four phases:

   I. *Peephole Randomization* In this phase, a peephole randomizer passes over the object code and replaces code patterns with random equivalent patterns chosen from a dictionary of such patterns.

  II. *Branch Flow Analysis* In this phase, a branch flow analyzer passes over the object code and rearranges and groups the code into small linear code segments.

 III. *Cell Creation* In this phase, tool 2 determines the number of cells to be used, allocates code segments to the cells, adds the accumulator and the decrypt and jump functions to each cell, adds random padding where needed, and finally, fixes-up all the address in the code.

IV. *Obfuscation Engine* This, the last phase of tool 2, generates the three random keys, KP, KS, and KG, computes the visibility schedule for each of the cells, computes the initial start state and encrypts the IVK.

Step 5 In the last step of IVK creation the encrypted IVK generated by tool 2 is copied into a reserved area of the program. The IVK is then ready to be invoked.

Interlocking Trust

Although the IVK can be made generally tamper resistant, its ability to defend itself is greatly enhanced by using an Interlocking Trust mechanism with other IVKs. The Interlocking Trust mechanism consists of three parts: Integrity Verification Kernels (described earlier), an Integrity Verification Protocol and a System Integrity Program.

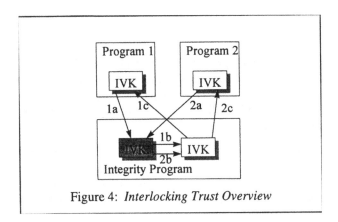

Figure 4: *Interlocking Trust Overview*

These three components work together to create an Interlocking Trust mechanism.

As illustrated in figure 4, the objective of the mechanism is to protect programs 1 and 2 from manipulation. As with any non-trivial program, programs 1 and 2 are too complex to be adequately protected. In our implementation we create a small, verifiable, defensible Integrity Verification Kernel. An IVK is included as a part of both programs 1 and 2 as well as part of a system Integrity Program which is accessible to all programs.

Each IVK is responsible for the integrity of the program in which it is embedded. Integrity is verified by calculating the digital signature of the program in which they are contained and comparing the calculated signature value with the correct, hard-coded value, stored in an IVK itself. If desired, the IVK could verify the integrity of any other software component, in addition to the program in which it is contained.

A program may have more than one IVK and may execute them at any time. As long as the IVK is actually executed and is executed correctly, the program cannot be modified without detection. Thus, the vulnerability rests on IVK's correct execution.

Each IVK is constructed according to the previously enumerated principles to make them tamper resistant. They are self decrypting and installation unique. All of their functions are interleaved and self-verifying. These mechanisms are described in detail in the next section of this paper. But, to eliminate a single point of attack, IVKs are interlocked so that a failure or by-pass of any one IVK will be detected by another.

The architecture assumes that there is a System Integrity Program running on the PC that is available to all programs. This System Integrity Program contains a special IVK called the Entry Integrity Verification Kernel (eIVK), shown with a "hatched" background in figure 4, and one or more other IVKs. IVKs within the System Integrity Program verify the integrity of the System Integrity Program and any IVKs embedded in the System Integrity Program.

Upon installation of the System Integrity Program, one or more IVKs are created that are installation unique. The eIVK has a published, external interface that can be called by any other IVK using the Integrity Verification Protocol.

Using figure 4 to illustrate, program 1 executes an embedded IVK. The IVK verifies the integrity of program 1 and then calls (label *1a* in figure 4) the eIVK. The eIVK then verifies the integrity of the System Integrity Program and all contained IVKs and calls another IVK in the System Integrity Program (label *1b* in figure 4). The additional IVK then verifies the integrity of the System Integrity Program and all contained IVKs and calls the original IVK in program 1 (label *1c* in figure 4).

To tamper with program 1, the perpetrator would need to tamper with both program 1 and the System Integrity Program. However, as can be seen in figure 4, any other program (program 2 in figure 4) will also be using the IVKs in the System Integrity Program. Thus, to tamper with any program all programs would have to be compromised.

Integrity Verification Protocol

The integrity verification protocol is used to establish a distributed trust environment. It is the protocol by which IVKs request mutual verification as described in figure 4.

As is shown in figure 4, the protocol is a three party communication between:

1. An IVK embedded in an application (which could be the System Integrity Program)

2. the eIVK, and

3. an IVK embedded in the System Integrity Program.

The protocol provides a challenge/response authentication between the IVK elements and information (such as the success or failure of the verification action) passed in such a way as to be bound to the authentication.

Table 1 gives the definitions of the objects used in the protocol. In the table, subscripts refer to the software module where the value originates. The subscript values may be either A, E, or S for the application module, the eIVK module or the Software Integrity Program respectively.

Object	Definition
K_X^{-1}	Private key of IVK embedded in module X.
K_X^1	Public key of IVK embedded in module X.
A_X	Address of the entry point of the IVK embedded in module X.
H_X	Hash value computed over the code of module X.
R_X	Random value derived by module X.
F_X	Flag value (success or failure) of operation originating from X. The flag is 9 bits where each bit is the result of an operation and where a 0-bit is a success and a 1-bit is a failure.

Table 1: Protocol Components
The protocol is a simple signed message protocol with random values added to provide protection against replay.

Table 2 lists the information known by, and present in each of the parties *a priori*. Table 2 uses the following notation:

- M encrypted with public key of X. $\qquad K_X^1[M]$
- M concatenated with N. $\qquad M|N$
- X sends M to Y $\qquad X \rightarrow Y{:}\,M$
- Bit 0 of F is equal to the result of a test of $M = N$. $\qquad F_0 = (M = N)$

Party	Information
Application (A)	K_A^1 public key of A
	K_E^1 public key of E
	$K_A^{-1}[H_A]$ signature of A under A
	$K_E^1[H_A]$ signature of A under E
	A_E address of E
	A_A address of A
eIVK (E)	K_E^{-1} private key of E
	$K_E^1[H_E]$ signature of E under E
	A_S address of S
System Integrity Program (S)	K_S^1 public key of S
	K_E^1 public key of E
	$K_S^{-1}[H_S]$ signature of S under S
	$K_S^{-1}[H_E]$ signature of E under S
	$K_E^1[H_S]$ signature of S under E
	A_E address of E

Table 2: Initial state knowledge of participates

The protocol can be described in the following steps:

1. *A* verifies signature of *A* and reports any failure
$$F_0 = (H_A = K_A^1[K_A^{-1}[H_A]])$$

2. *A* sends signature, flag, and random number to *E*
$$A \rightarrow E: K_E^1[K_E^1[H_A]\| F| A_A| R_A]$$

3. *E* verifies signature of *E* and reports any failure
$$F_1 = (H_E = K_E^{-1}[K_E^1[H_E]])$$

4. E verifies signature of A and reports any failure

$$F_2 = (H_A = K_E^{-1}[K_E^1[H_A]])$$

5. E sends signature and address of A, flag and random number to S

$$E \rightarrow S: K_E^{-1}[H_A | A_A | F | R_E]$$

6. S verifies signature of S and reports any failure

$$F_3 = (H_S = K_S^1[K_S^{-1}[H_S]])$$

7. S verifies signature of E and reports any failure

$$F_4 = (H_E = K_S^1[K_S^{-1}[H_E]])$$

8. S verifies signature of A and reports any failure

$$F_5 = (H_A = K_E^1[H_A])$$

9. S sends E signature, flag and random number

$$S \rightarrow E: K_E^1[K_E^1[H_S] | F | R_E]$$

10. E verifies that received random number is the same

$$F_6 = (R_E = K_E^{-1}[K_E^1[R_E]])$$

11. E verifies signature of S and reports any failure

$$F_7 = (H_S = K_E^{-1}[K_E^1[H_S]])$$

12. E sends flag and random number to A

$$E \rightarrow A: K_E^{-1}[F | R_A]$$

13. A verifies that received random number is the same

$$F_8 = (R_A = K_E^1[R_A])$$

14. A verifies that flag equal 0 and reports any failure $(F = 0)$

The above protocol is not particularly efficient but is reasonably robust. It requires no prior knowledge of the application from the other parties is the case given the installation specific uniqueness.

System Integrity Program

The System Integrity Program is a program module that constantly monitors the integrity of the security components of the computer system. While the System Integrity Program monitors the integrity of the security components, it depends on the eIVK to monitor its own integrity.

The System Integrity Program is created at installation time so that both the eIVK and the embedded IVK can be made unique. The System Integrity Program insures that the eIVK has a known entry point an a known public key.

Technology Extensions

The current design of the IVK could be expanded in numerous ways to make it more effective. These technology extensions fall into two broad categories: *active defense* and *hardware assisted protection.*

Active defense is code, added to the IVK, that detects attempts to observe or modify the execution of the IVK and then fights back. Detection possibilities include scanning running code for "signatures," much the way viruses are detected. Signatures of debuggers or emulators can be scanned. Additionally, one may look for specific interrupt vectors which are used by particular programs. Once detected, the IVK may disconnect interrupts used by the debugger or modify the target's code so that it fails.

Hardware assisted protection uses some characteristic of the hardware to assist the software tamper resistance. Several techniques are currently under investigation. The first utilizes the processor's execution counter to measure the time used by the process. Once this is done then the secret, a private key, is not actually stored in the IVK using tool 1, as described earlier, but, rather, the statistical timing characteristics of operating on the secret are stored instead. The IVK then guesses at the correct key and utilizes the timing characteristics in an auto-correlation process to derive the secret. Any attempt to manipulate the code while the auto-correlation is executing would keep the IVK from deriving the correct secret. This method is a use of Kocher's cryptanalysis of fixed exponent systems.[2]

Additional hardware assistance can be derived by locking the execution of the IVK in the processors on-chip cache.

Conclusion

This paper presented an implementation of tamper resistant software, the true resistance of which can only be judged empirically. As such, only time will confirm whether the principles described herein are valid and the implementation sufficient.

Acknowledgment

The author would like to thank the many people whose comments, criticism, and abuse have keep me refining my approach.

References

[1] Rivest, R., Shamir, A., and Adleman, L. A Method for Obtaining Digital Signatures and Public-Key Crypotsystems. *Communications of the ACM*, vol. 21, issue 2, Feb. 1978, pp. 120-126.

[2] Kocher, P. Cryptanalysis of Diffie-Hellman, RSA, DSS, and Other Systems Using Timing Attacks. *Private Extended Abstract*, 7 December 1995.

Oblivious Key Escrow

Matt Blaze

AT&T Laboratories, Murray Hill, NJ 07974
mab@research.att.com

Abstract. We propose a simple scheme, based on secret-sharing over large-scale networks, for assuring recoverability of sensitive archived data (*e.g.*, cryptographic keys). In our model anyone can request a copy of the archived data but it is very difficult to keep the existence of a request secret or to subvert the access policy of the data "owner." We sketch an architecture for a distributed key escrow system that might be suitable for deployment over very large-scale networks such as the Internet. We also introduce a new cryptographic primitive, *oblivious multicast*, that can serve as the basis for such a system.

1 Introduction

In any system in which sensitive information must be stored for future use there is a fundamental tension between ensuring the *secrecy* of data against those who are not authorized for access to it and ensuring its continued *availability* to those who are. Secrecy is often best served by making only a small number of carefully-guarded copies of the data, while availability favors a policy of the widest possible dissemination in the hope that at least one copy will be intact at the time it is required. In general, a balance has to be struck between these two goals based on the requirements of and resources available to the particular application, but in any case copies of the sensitive data must be controlled in some careful manner (*e.g.*, through the use of an off-site, trusted backup facility employing guards and other effective, if expensive, security practices).

Another approach is "key escrow," in which sensitive data are encrypted so that the ciphertext can be widely copied and backed-up via conventional methods, but the decryption keys are controlled in some careful manner by trusted third parties who assume responsibility for revealing the keys to authorized entities in the event of an emergency. One advantage of escrowing keys instead of the raw data is the flexibility to perform the escrow at any time, even prior to the actual creation of the data, and the ability for one escrowed key to represent arbitrarily much encrypted information. A number of key escrow schemes have been proposed for a variety of applications, most with the aim of facilitating law enforcement access to encrypted data, but also for commercial data recovery [NIST94, WLEB96, Denn96].

Third party backup, whether of data or keys, has a number of disadvantages, however. The "escrow agents" must be highly trusted and carefully protected, since compromise of a single escrow site (or small set of sites, in the case of split data) can result in an irrevocable loss of security. Since protecting such data is likely to be expensive, one escrow site can be expected to serve many different sets of data, making each site an attractive "fat target" for attack. Finally, legal, liability, and conflict-of-interest issues sometimes make it difficult to ensure that an escrow agent will act only in the best interests of the data owner, especially when served with a legal demand to turn over keys or tempted with some inducement to misbehave. One of the frequently-raised objections to government-run key escrow systems (*e.g.*, the "Clipper" chip) is the fear that the escrow centers will, perhaps secretly, assist a rogue government in violating its citizens' privacy.

In this abstract, we propose a different model for assuring both recoverability and protection of sensitive data based on two concepts: secret-sharing and the decentralized nature of large, heterogeneous networks such as the Internet. In our model, anyone can request a copy of anyone's data but it is not possible to keep the existence of such a request secret or to subvert the access policy of the data "owner" without subverting a significant fraction of participants in the network. There are no explicit "escrow agents"; instead, key shares are distributed widely to ordinary networked computers spread across a wide variety of administrative and geographic boundaries.

2 "The Net" as an Escrow Agent

The goal of our scheme is to make it difficult to recover escrowed data without the knowledge and consent of its owner, while still assuring high availability in an emergency. Its security rests on the premise that highly distributed systems spread over many administrative, political, and geographic domains (such as the Internet), are more robust than any single site or small set of sites, no matter how well protected. Other systems, such as Eternity [Ande96], have recognized and exploited this property of global networks for maintaining information availability; we simply expand this notion to include secrecy as well.

We assume that each node (or a large fraction of nodes) in the network runs an "escrow server" that performs most of the steps of the protocol, and that there is some broadcast mechanism for reaching them (which could be based on existing mechanisms such as Usenet news). The first step in using "the net" as an escrow agent is to split the key to be escrowed using some secret-sharing scheme [Simm92] with a very large number of shares (*e.g.*, a k-out-of-n threshold scheme where $k = 500$ and $n = 5000$, but we leave the details of determining an appropriate access structure to the reader). Next, we package each share along with a key identifier, a digital signature of the share, and a policy describing the circumstances under which the share should be disclosed (discussed below). Finally, we select, at random (or according to some other policy) as many sites as we have shares and send one share to each site, over a secure channel. We then destroy the shares and the list of sites to which they were sent.

To recover escrowed data, we broadcast a request for shares for the key identifier we want to recover, using some mechanism that is likely to be received by the shareholders' escrow servers. Upon receipt of a request for shares, each escrow server logs the request and, if it holds a share for the key in question, checks the policy contained in the share package. If the request conforms to the policy we send the share to the requester. The requester (who can verify the authenticity of each share by checking the signature) can recover the key once enough shares have been received.

Whether such a scheme is robust, secure, or otherwise adequate depends primarily on three factors: the reliability (with respect to continued availability, security against compromise, and ability to follow instructions) of the nodes that handle the key shares, the access structure of the secret-sharing scheme, and the nature of the policy that each node is supposed to follow.

If the nature of today's Internet is any indication, we must assume that the individual nodes are not very reliable, especially over time. Some nodes will simply disappear. Others will maliciously fail to follow instructions. Still others will fail to safeguard their shares, sometimes due to malice but more often as a result of mistake, incompetence, or failure of some underlying security mechanism. It is likely that as the net grows these issues will become even more pronounced. Therefore, the security of the scheme depends on a choice of access structures and policies that assumes that a large fraction of shareholders will not follow the correct protocol.

The secret-sharing access structure must be chosen to require enough shares to prevent key recovery by collusion among a few nodes, yet with enough redundancy to allow recovery in the likely event that most nodes are not available or did not retain their shares at the time key recovery is required. Unlike almost all other problems in distributed computing, scale appears to actually help here; consider, for example, a 500-out-of-5000 threshold scheme, which permits key recovery even when 90% of nodes have failed and yet retains its security until at least 500 nodes have been compromised. The distribution of nodes could also play a part here, particularly when the key is split with a more sophisticated access structure. For example, key shares could be distributed to nodes selected across a variety of administrative, legal, political and geographic domains, with the access structure selected to require that shares be collected from nodes in several different categories.

Each shareholder is asked to enforce the access policy included with the share. The policy must be designed to facilitate emergency access without also permitting undetected disclosure. Because shares can only be recovered by broadcasting, we can take advantage of the inherently public nature of requests in formulating the access policies. For example, the policy might specify a public signature key (to which the real key owner knows the corresponding secret) and instructions to delay revealing key shares for some period of time, say one week. If an unauthorized request for a key is broadcast, the legitimate key owner would have one week to notice the request and broadcast another message, signed with the signature key, requesting that the shareholders ignore the original request and turn over information that might aid in tracking down the source of the unauthorized request. Policies might also include instructions on the minimum identification that share requests must include and instructions on how share requests should be logged (*e.g.*, by posting to a news group or even advertisements in newspapers). They might also include an expiration date beyond which the share is to be deleted. We defer the question of how policies should be specified, but it may be sufficient for the server, upon receipt of a share request, to send a message to its (human) operator containing instructions (written in English) that were included in the share package.

It may also be desirable to obscure the nature of the data held by each shareholder from the shareholders themselves. Key identifiers might best be chosen so that an outside attacker cannot derive the purpose or owner of the key from its identifier and so that shareholders do not know exactly what their shares are for. (One approach is to use a randomly generated key ID, long enough to be collision free, that is stored with the ciphertext. A more sophisticated approach involves using multiple key IDs for each key, generated from a random seed stored with the ciphertext, so that shareholders cannot determine whether they hold shares for the same keys as one another. Still another approach is to base the key ID on the signature key used to sign the shares.)

Some infrastructure is required. Key owners would need a directory or other mechanism for identifying and communicating with escrow servers at the time the shares are created. A broadcast mechanism for key recovery is also required. It is possible that existing mechanisms could suffice for both these purposes (*e.g.*, DNS for server identification and Usenet news for broadcasting) but more specialized systems would be required if this scheme were to be fielded on a large scale. Finally, of course, the escrow servers would need to be deployed widely, perhaps included as a standard feature in networked operating systems.

Share distribution must be secure against both eavesdropping and traffic analysis. The need for security against eavesdropping is obvious, since observing all the shares allows recovery of keys without the assistance of the shareholders. Resistance to traffic analysis is required to ensure that shares can only be recovered by broadcasting. If the identities of the shareholders are known, an attacker could "target" the sites believed to be weakest, and, if successful, recover shares without broadcasting the request and without following the share access policy. Ideally, shares would be distributed via a completely anonymous communication protocol in which neither sender nor receiver learn one another's identity, nor can an eavesdropper. Share distribution should be deniable as well; it should be infeasible for a third party to determine that a given node has sent or received a key share.

More formally, shares should be distributed via a cryptographic primitive we call *oblivious multicast*. In a k-out-of-n oblivious multicast, the sender sends a message to a list of n potential receivers from which he is guaranteed that at most k will actually receive it. Each potential receiver should not be able to "cheat" the protocol to increase its probability of receiving a given message to beyond k/n, and the sender's influence should be limited to selecting the list of potential receivers. Under this model, if the key is split into 5000 shares to be distributed throughout a network of 10^6 nodes, each share would be sent using a 1-out-of-10^6 oblivious multicast. We give a simple oblivious multicast protocol in the Appendix.

Even in the absence of a true oblivious multicast protocol, it may be sufficient in some applications simply for the sender to select, at random, each shareholder from among the nodes on the network and send each share via an anonymous communication scheme such as a "Mix" [Chau81]. Of course, the list of shareholders or potential shareholders need not, and indeed should not, be retained by the key owner once the shares have been distributed.

3   Emergency Access – "Angry Mob Cryptanalysis"

Under ordinary circumstances when key recovery is required, the original key owner will initiate the request. The owner extracts the key ID and broadcasts the request to the network, performing whatever (presumably public) logging is required by the policy that was sent to the shareholders. Upon receipt of the broadcast, each server checks whether it is a shareholder for the requested key. If it is, it checks whether request satisfies the access policy (perhaps by transmitting a copy of the English-specified policy to the server operator, perhaps by automated means if the policy is more formally specified). If the access policy is satisfied (e.g., a message announcing the request appeared in some established place, a certificate of the identity of the requester was included in the request, or whatever) and after expiration of a policy-specified waiting period to allow for repudiation of the request by the legitimate key owner, the share is transmitted back to the requester over a secure channel. The requester can then combine these shares to recover the key; corrupted shares will not affect the protocol since legitimate shares were digitally signed by the original key owner at the time they were distributed.

Sometimes, however, an extreme emergency might make it necessary to recover keys in a manner contrary to the policy specified in the original shares. For example, it may be necessary to recover keys before the policy-imposed delay has elapsed, or to obtain access in spite of the objections of the original key owner. Such a situation is most likely to arise from some kind of law enforcement or public safety emergency in which the requester makes the case that public policy should supersede the access policy of the key owner. Of course, such a situation is fraught with difficult issues of judgement and policy, and fears of abuse, fraud, or coercion are among the primary objections raised against key escrow in general. Our scheme places the burden of determining whether exceptional access requests should be granted on the shareholders.

Indeed, the dependence on the collective judgement of the widely distributed shareholder operators may be the scheme's most important property. Under normal circumstances, the shareholders can be expected to behave approximately as specified in the share policies (with occasional pathological exceptions, limited in their effect by the nature of the secret-sharing access structure). In exceptional situations, however, a public appeal can be made in an attempt to convince the shareholders to reveal their shares in a manner not permitted by the stated policy (e.g., the police could broadcast an appeal for key shares on television news, stating the facts of the case under investigation). In particular, because the identities of the shareholders are not known, such an appeal must be done publicly and in a manner designed to attract considerable attention. It is not possible to secretly induce, through legal means or otherwise, shareholders to reveal their shares. For some applications (*e.g.*, personal information associated with an individual), such a scheme could be acceptable even when key escrow is not. (We propose the rather lighthearted phrase "angry mob cryptanalysis" to refer to the threat of enough shareholders being convinced to violate the share access policy to permit key recovery. It is distinguished from "rubber hose cryptanalysis," in which keys are derived by means of legal or extra-legal coercion[1].)

4 Conclusions

Key escrow is a confusing subject, especially so because there is little general agreement as to even its basic goals and requirements. We have proposed a scheme that has a number of interesting properties that may make it appropriate for protecting secrecy and availability in certain kinds of applications. A number of open problems remain, of course, before such a scheme could be made completely practical. Areas for further study include the effects of different access structures, specification of policy, economic, performance and reliability analysis, and efficient protocols for large-scale oblivious multicast. The most challenging problems arise from the practical difficulty of introducing a standardized escrow service and deploying it on a large scale.

Of course, we do not in complete seriousness propose this scheme as a general solution to the key recovery problem, but hope primarily to open a new avenue of discussion. Although not designed specifically for law enforcement, the scheme appears to address many of the concerns voiced by critics of "government" key escrow as well as many of the (stated) concerns of law enforcement.

5 Acknowledgements

Much of the inspiration for this scheme arose from Ross Anderson's description of the motivation and principles behind the Eternity service, in conversations at Cambridge and AT&T Bell Labs. We also thank Joan Feigenbaum, Yvo Desmedt and Raph Levien for their helpful comments, and the Isaac Newton Institute for Mathematical Sciences, Cambridge, for hosting the author while most of this work was done.

References

[Ande96]   Ross Anderson. "The Eternity Service." Invited paper to appear at *Pragocrypt 96*. 30 September – 3 October 1996, Prague.

---

[1] The phrase "rubber hose cryptanalysis" appears to be due to Phil Karn.

[Chau81]   David Chaum. "Untraceable Electronic Mail, Return Addresses, and Digital Pseudonyms." *CACM*. February 1981.

[Chau82]   David Chaum. "Blind Signatures for Untraceable Payments." *Proc. CRYPTO82*. August 1982.

[Denn96]   Dorothy Denning. "A Taxonomy for Key Escrow Encryption Systems." *CACM*. March 1996.

[NIST94]   National Institute for Standards and Technology. Escrowed Encryption Standard, *FIPS 185*. U.S. Dept. of Commerce, 1994.

[Rabi81]   M. Rabin. "How to Exchange Secrets by Oblivious Transfer." *TR-81*. Harvard Aiken Computation Laboratory, 1981.

[Simm92]   G.J. Simmons. "An Introduction to Shared Secret and/or Shared Control Schemes and their Applications." In *Contemporary Cryptology*, Simmons, ed. IEEE, 1992.

[WLEB96]   Stephen T. Walker, Stephen B. Lipner, Carl M. Ellison, and David M. Balenson. "Commercial Key Recovery." *CACM*. March 1996.

Appendix: Oblivious Multicast

It is possible to build an approximation of k-out-of-n oblivious multicast out of conventional oblivious transfer primitives [Rabi81], *e.g.*, by performing, with each of n potential recipients, an oblivious transfer in which the message has probability k/n of being delivered correctly. The overall outcome of such a protocol is only probabilistically specified, however, since the outcome of each transfer is determined independently from the others.

We give here a non-probabilistic k-out-of-n oblivious multicast protocol, based on blind signatures [Chau82], in which the sender controls exactly the number of successful transfers but cannot learn who the successful recipients are from among the set of potential receivers. We illustrate the scheme with RSA, but it can be adapted trivially to any other blind signature scheme. We assume that there is an authenticated, secret channel between each pair of nodes in the network (*e.g.*, each node publishes trusted public signature and encryption keys), an anonymous communication mechanism that hides the identity of a message's sender, and a broadcast mechanism that allows one-way communication between one node and all other nodes.

The players include a sender, S, and a set of n potential receivers R. S generates (either once or, optionally, once for each multicast, if S wishes her identity to remain secret) an RSA key (S_{pub}, S_{priv}, m), where m is the modulus.

To begin the protocol, S publishes its public key and broadcasts to the members of R a request that they begin the protocol. Each node $R_i \in R$ selects, at random, a *key token* t_i and a *blinding factor* b_i (with inverse b_i^{-1}). R_i calculates and sends the blinded key token

$$\overline{t_i} = t_i(b_i^{S_{pub}}) \bmod m$$

to S, keeping both b_i and t_i secret. (R_i signs this message to establish its origin to S.) For each such message received, S first verifies that it has not previously received a message from R_i, calculates the blind signature

$$\overline{\alpha_i} = \overline{t_i}^{S_{priv}} \bmod m$$

and returns $\overline{\alpha_i}$ to R_i.

Upon receipt of $\overline{\alpha_i}$, R_i can compute the unblind signature of t_i by calculating:

$$\alpha_i = b_i^{-1}\overline{\alpha_i} \bmod m$$

When S has transmitted $\overline{\alpha}$ values to all members of R, each $R_i \in R$ sends the signed key tuple (t_i, α_i) to S, encrypted with S's public encryption key and using a communication mechanism that hides R_i's identity.

Note that once each member of R has completed this phase of the protocol, S has received n unique (t, α) signed key tuples (one from each $R_i \in R$). S can verify that each message came from a different member of R (by checking the uniqueness of the message and by verifying the unblinded signature α) but cannot determine the mapping of key tuples to individual nodes (because the signature was blinded). Thus each t serves as a secret key known only to S and a single, unknown, member of R.

Finally, to oblivious multicast to k members of R, S encrypts k copies of the message (using a symmetric-key cryptosystem), with a different t key selected at random from among the valid received key tuples for each. Each of these encrypted messages is broadcast to all members of R. The successful recipients are those who generated (and therefore know) the keys that S selected. An implementation can allow nodes to determine whether they ware successful in several ways. The simplest is to require each member of R to attempt to decrypt every message with its t. If the message follows a pre-determined format (*e.g.*, it includes a fixed value field of sufficient length that it is unlikely to have the correct value at random), the decrypted message can be compared against the expected form. Another, perhaps more efficient, option is to prefix to each message a one-way hash of the t with which it was encrypted.

The most obvious application of this protocol to key share distribution uses a separate 1-out-of-n oblivious multicast to distribute each share. Since each multicast requires two exchanges with every node, if there are m shares and n potential shareholders in the network a complete share distribution requires at least $2nm$ exchanges over the network. It is possible to eliminate the factor of m, however. Observe that it is not necessary in the last stage of the protocol that the same message be encrypted with each t. All shares could be distributed with a single pass of the protocol, with a different share distributed with each selected t. This optimization, which reduces communication to only $O(n)$ message exchanges plus $O(m)$ broadcasts, has the added virtue of making it possible to guarantee that each node receives at most one share.

Clearly, to be of practical utility for share distribution, the protocol must be efficient even when n is very large. The blind signature-based protocol above is of dubious efficacy if n represents, *e.g.*, every node on the Internet, but it could, depending on the processing and network cost model, provide adequate performance when used with a subset of nodes large enough to make it difficult to target the entire set of potential receivers.

We suspect that there are applications besides key share distribution that could make efficient use of an oblivious multicast primitive (*e.g.,* distribution of papers to reviewers, blind surveys, etc.).

HMOS: Her Majesty's Orthography Service

Sir Norman Bentbyte

Ministry of Truth

(AKA Tom Berson, Anagram Laboratories)

As multimedia computing becomes pervasive throughout the land we are faced with an ever-darkening national tragedy. Our precious pristine bandwidth is being sullied by examples of poor spelling, abysmal layout, muddy images, and noisy music. So battered are our bytes that, without prompt and effective remedial action by the Government, our nation risks becoming a laughingstock amongst the cyberati.

Moreover, our precious national resources are being wasted. In the timeless search for correct spelling alone consider that there are at least 10^7 personal computers in the UK, that each of these personal computers has at least one English dictionary, and that each English dictionary occupies perhaps 2×10^5 bytes of rotating storage. So in aggregate at least 2×10^12 bytes of dictionary are spinning around in the UK at any one time. These dictionaries are redundant, incomplete, and obsolete. They also contribute to the nation's angular momentum and therefore to global warming.

To address these problems, and others, we are pleased to announce the formation of HMOS: Her Majesty's Orthography Service. HMOS is connected via high-capacity routers to the national backbone internet. HMOS offers data filtering and correction services to all comers, and often entirely free of charge.

Here is how HMOS works. Users send Raw Data Objects to HMOS, either by default routing (in which case HMOS services are free) or manually (in which case there is a small charge). HMOS's modern operations center in Router-on-Thames is staffed 24 hours a day, every day of the year, by teams of lexicographers, editors, fact checkers, linguists, graphics artists, imagery experts, recording engineers and analysts. These trained experts inspect and massage the Raw Data Objects, removing spelling errors, spacing anomalies, errors of fact, background noise, unwanted echoes, and so forth. By the time they are done, and they work very quickly, the Raw Data Object has been transformed into a Thing Of Beauty. This Thing Of Beauty is digitally signed with HMOS's private key and returned to the user for inspection.

The user may then send the signed Thing Of Beauty to its intended recipient. HMOS's signature on the Thing Of Beauty acts as a seal of approval. It ensures preferential routing through the national information infrastructure. As an added benefit we guarantee that messages carrying HMOS's digital signature will forever be exempt from any key escrow requirement.

So clean up your act. Avoid embarrassing gaffes. Get better networking service. Try HMOS, where our motto is, "New bytes for old." To sign up complete the application in triplicate at http://www.hmos.gov.uk.

Information Hiding Terminology

— Results of an informal plenary meeting and additional proposals —

Collected by Birgit Pfitzmann

The common opinion among the participants of this workshop was that all the topics that Ross Anderson had chosen, such as steganography and fingerprinting, had indeed much in common, and that we all profited by learning about the treatment of these topics in usually quite different communities and from different points of view. To facilitate this, we decided to agree on some common terminology in the final session of the workshop. I have tried to collect the results of this session, and added a few additional proposals.

The Terms Agreed Upon

We decided that most of the applications have the following common core:

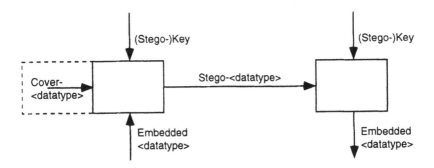

We decided upon the terms for the in- and outputs in the left-hand side of this diagram. We only fixed adjectives or qualifiers; everyone can prefix them to their favorite word for the datatype they use, i.e., <datatype> stands for "text", "message", "image", or whatever seems appropriate. In the explanations, I use "message".

1. Embedded <datatype>. Something to be hidden in something else.

2. Stego-<datatype>. The output of the hiding process; something that has the embedded message hidden in it.

3. Cover-<datatype>. An input with an "original" form of the stegomessage. In some applications, such a covermessage is given from the outside, in others, it can be chosen during the hiding process. The latter is represented by the dashed extension to the inner hiding process.

4. Stegokey or simply key. Additional secret data that may be needed in the hiding process. In particular, the same key (or a related one) is usually needed to extract the embedded message again.

There was no time to decide on names for further objects, but individual authors are strongly encouraged to introduce additional or deviating terminology by extending or modifying the figure above.

A Few Additional Proposals

I will venture to make a few more proposals, at least as a reference for other proposals:

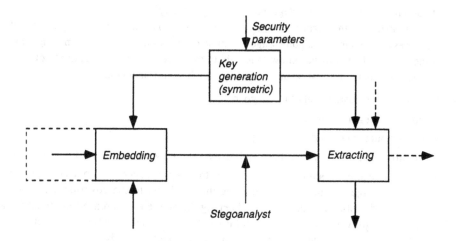

A. The process of hiding the embedded message is called embedding.

B. Getting the embedded message out of the stegomessage again is called extracting.

C. The party from whom the embedded message is hidden is called the stegoanalyst.

D. The key has to be generated, often depending on one or more security parameters (e.g., one for the cryptographic security of a pseudorandom sequence and another for the collusion size). The standard case where the same key is used in embedding and extracting is called symmetric.

E. An entity or person that embeds and extracts is called an embeddor or an extractor, respectively.

Differences Between the Models

Noticing differences between models is often equally important as noticing similarities. Hence I also sketch some points where the various applications differ once we consider more than the core components. These differences are not all independent.

- Is there a given covermessage, and if yes, does it have to be used several times?

    For instance, in fingerprinting there is typically the original image or music to be sold. In contrast, in steganography, the covermessage can often be designed specifically for hiding the embedded message, or the stegomessage may be constructed immediately.

    If the same covermessage is used several times with different embedded messages, collusion attacks have to be considered. This is typical for fingerprinting.

- Does the covermessage play any role in extracting, too? In the second figure, two dashed arrows represent the cases where it is an input or an output, respectively.

  For instance, in fingerprinting, the covermessage can be an input in extracting, because the merchant is both the embeddor and the extractor. In steganography, the covermessage is usually neither an input nor an output, but some situations may be so restricted (e.g., war letters home) that the embeddor cannot afford to lose the legitimate bandwidth offered, and thus the covermessage must be extracted.

- What information should the stegoanalyst get legitimately?

  For instance, in fingerprinting, the stegoanalyst is the buyer and pays for the stegomessage. Thus the stegomessage has to be quite similar to the covermessage, even if the stegoanalyst does not know much about the covermessage and cannot notice the difference. Treaty verification and steganography have no such goal.

- What is the adversarial goal of the stegoanalyst:
  - to detect stegomessages;
  - to find out the embedded message;
  - to prove that a message has been embedded, or even what message, to third parties;
  - to remove the embedded message from the stegomessage without changing the stegomessage too much, e.g., retaining the similarity to the covermessage (as an illegal redistributor might) or even keeping the active interference unnoticed (as a censor might who wants to conceal his existence, or a telecommunication provider who claims to guarantee a transparent channel of a certain bandwidth);
  - or to jam, i.e., to remove all possible embedded messages without much care about the covermessage?

  The first three goals will usually be achieved by passive observation, the last two by active interference.

- What does the stegoanalyst know about the covermessage a priori? He might know it entirely, or a probability space that it is chosen from, or a family of probability spaces indexed by external events (e.g., that a letter "it is raining" is less likely in good weather), or some predicate about it. This knowledge will often be quite fuzzy.

More Examples

So far, the examples were mainly for fingerprinting and steganography. Here are a few more:

- Covert channels are similar to steganography, but the coverdata are the whole behaviour of a system. This fact also gives the stegoanalyst more freedom in being active, in particular in designing the probability space of the coverdata in the first place.

- Subliminal channels in authentication protocols are interesting in cases where the message to be authenticated is completely known to the stegoanalyst and the stegoanalyst may jam wrong messages. In these cases, the only available coverdata are the authentication data. Here the stegoanalyst has a precise criterion, valid authentication, and may change the stegodata as long as valid authentications remain valid.

- Traitor tracing for broadcast encryption is a kind of fingerprinting of a cryptographic key, i.e., the coverdata are a key needed to decrypt the ciphertexts that are broadcast. The stegodata must retain this property, and so must the data the stegoanalyst produces, i.e., the keys for pirate decoders.

- Avoiding traffic analysis means hiding locations or addresses. This is somewhat different from the other examples in that "location" is not a message. Some schemes do work by hiding messages in continuous dummy traffic, but even those are often multi-party protocols, i.e., many embeddors must send their "stegomessages" in a coordinated way. I propose not to use the terminology in this application.

One simple conclusion can also be drawn: If the covermessage can be chosen by the embeddor, and the stegoanalyst does not know it completely and is not allowed to jam, the embeddor and extractor can always defeat the stegoanalyst by encoding the embedded message within their legitimate choice among covermessages. Of course, this is not quite so clear if, in practice, none of the parties has a formal probabilistic model of the source. But it still shows that some steganography is possible whenever any normal communication is possible. More complicated statements are treated in the individual papers.

Index

Springer
and the
environment

At Springer we firmly believe that an
international science publisher has a
special obligation to the environment,
and our corporate policies consistently
reflect this conviction.
We also expect our business partners –
paper mills, printers, packaging
manufacturers, etc. – to commit
themselves to using materials and
production processes that do not harm
the environment. The paper in this
book is made from low- or no-chlorine
pulp and is acid free, in conformance
with international standards for paper
permanency.

 Springer

Lecture Notes in Computer Science

For information about Vols. 1–1099

please contact your bookseller or Springer-Verlag